Literature, Cinema and Politics 1930–1945

Literature, Cinema and Politics 1930–1945

Reading Between the Frames

Lara Feigel

Edinburgh University Press

For my parents, Ilse and Marcel Feigel

© Lara Feigel, 2010

Edinburgh University Press Ltd
22 George Square, Edinburgh

www.euppublishing.com

Typeset in Minion
by Servis Filmsetting Ltd, Stockport, Cheshire, and
printed and bound in Great Britain by
CPI Antony Rowe, Chippenham and Eastbourne

A CIP record for this book is available from the British Library

ISBN 978 0 7486 3950 2 (hardback)

Contents

Acknowledgements

This book has emerged from my doctoral thesis, undertaken at the University of Sussex. Here, foremost thanks must go to my supervisor, Laura Marcus, who guided my work with tremendous wisdom and generosity. After Laura's move to Edinburgh, Peter Boxall stepped in, bringing a formidable mind and much laughter to the final stages of the project. The thesis was made possible by a research grant from the AHRC and was enhanced by the meticulous proofreading of Seb Perry.

In the progression from thesis to book, I have been lucky to have the support of my external examiner, Rod Mengham. Rod's insightful comments have guided the shape of the final monograph, and his sustained belief in the book has been a great help to me. I have also been very fortunate in the faith and encouragement of my editor at Edinburgh University Press, Jackie Jones.

I have written the book itself at King's College London, and I am very grateful to my colleagues and students for making my life here so pleasant. My understanding of modernist literature has benefited hugely from discussion with Richard Kirkland, Max Saunders and Anna Snaith. Anna has also cast a generous eye over sections of the typescript. My time at King's has been enlivened by the friendship of Neil Vickers and of Clare Brant who, together with Max Saunders, has welcomed me very warmly into the Centre for Life-Writing Research. Students of my MA courses and my BA Cinematic Modernism course have continually challenged my ideas, making this a very stimulating period. I am also indebted to the School of Humanities for a grant enabling the illustrations.

This book would not be what it is without the enthusiasm, advice and friendship of Alex Harris. Alex's integrity and passion as a critic are always exemplary, and her reading of this typescript has been generous and exacting. She has also reminded me that the 1930s was in part a glamorous and frivolous decade, and brought much glamour and frivolity to our collaborations. Matt Taunton has read the typescript attentively, making incisive comments that were much appreciated. My thinking about the 1930s has gained from lively discussion with Richard Overy and John Sutherland.

The book is dedicated to my parents, whose support has meant a great deal. My mother's unstinting warmth has always been a source of reassurance, while it is to my father that I owe my love of literature and my desire for crisp prose. Finally, my husband, John, has been the mainstay throughout, and it is thanks to him that this has been a very happy time.

List of Figures

Introduction

'The influence of the films'

The 1930s was a decade as black and white as it was red. When left-wing writers were not observing the working classes in the north of England or fighting on their behalf in Spain, they were side by side with them in the picture palaces, glorying in the black-and-white shadows projected onto the flickering screen. Often, as with Christopher Isherwood, who took a turn as a camera while frequenting the Berlin slums, the two went together. Isherwood, W. H. Auden and Stephen Spender brought home from Berlin a commitment to socialism and a love of avant-garde German and Russian film. Both passions fitted comfortably into late 1930s London, home of May Day demonstrations, vehement anti-fascism and one of the most enthusiastic cinema-going publics in Europe.

It was also a decade of movement. While George Orwell rushed from Paris to London to Wigan to Spain, Auden was dashing round Berlin, Iceland and China, furiously snapping his Leica camera along the way. J. B. Priestley covered the whole of England, and crew from the people-watching group Mass-Observation followed the Bolton workers to the seaside to dizzy themselves on the rollercoaster. Wherever they were, 1930s writers were accompanied by the rhythm of the cinema, which defined and was defined by the rhythm of the modern metropolis. For the intellectual Left, the movement of this popular art form came to seem symbolic of its power to shock. Its fast contrasts were ideally suited for mimicking the painfully abrupt contrasts of the capitalist city; its flickering sensual overload brought the potential for a radical appropriation of distracted spectatorship.[1]

This book reads between the frames of 1930s literature and cinema, exploring the politics of the engagement (or entanglement) of the two media. The 1930s and 1940s saw the birth and death of a tradition of politically committed filmic British writing which overtly aligned the socialist and the cinematic. The self-styled working-class novel-ist Walter Allen looked back on the decade as a period when 'a lot of people were experimenting with novels written from several points of view':

> the influence of cinema was tremendous, I think, on the 'montage' novel . . . what I usually used to do was to try and get on the page the image as a film-director might present it. That was what I was after, and what I think everybody was after.[2]

Allen himself is a representative figure of the 1930s. Taught by Louis MacNeice at Birmingham University, he quickly found a welcoming home in a literary London reaching out for contact with the more palatable specimens of the British working class. At the same time, he remained at the centre of what MacNeice saw as a flourishing group of working-class Birmingham writers, which included Walter Greenwood, author of the bestselling *Love on the Dole* (1933). Allen's 'everybody' invokes an entire generation of would-be cinematic writers who were experimenting with montage.

In her 'Leaning Tower' essay, delivered to the Brighton Workers' Educational Association at the end of the decade, Virginia Woolf put in his place the young writer of the 1930s, whom she saw as both unduly political and unduly cinematic. She compared the Bloomsbury intellectual Desmond MacCarthy's account of his pre-war student days, when he was 'not very much interested in politics' and more concerned with 'aesthetic emotions', with the university experiences of Auden and his friends, for whom 'in 1930 it was impossible – if you were young, sensitive, imaginative – not to be interested in politics'.[3] Woolf saw this avowed political commitment as resulting in the 'peda-gogic, the didactic, the loud speaker strain' dominating 1930s poetry, and saw 'the lack of transitions' and the 'violently opposed contrasts' in their work as explained by the 'influence of the films'.[4]

Woolf here firmly separates herself, together with her (working-class) audience, from the younger generation of male writers. But I shall argue later that Woolf's essay is more slippery than it at first appears and that she herself displays a marked engagement with poli-tics and with cinema in her 1930s fiction. At the end of the essay, she aligns herself with her audience in hoping that 'the world after the war will be a world without classes or towers'. Here it becomes clear that 'we' (the writer and her audience) and 'he' (the 1930s poet) have more in common than it at first appeared.[5]

This book brings together a wide cross-section of the 1930s Left, allowing Allen, Auden and Woolf to brush shoulders, politically and aesthetically. Eric Hobsbawm has seen the Second World War as a civil war between pro- and anti-fascist forces, with broadly left-wing intellectuals uniting in fighting a common enemy.[6] For Orwell, this coming together resulted in a new brand of Communism, with the slogans 'suddenly [fading] from red to pink' as 'World revolution' gave way to 'Defence of democracy'.[7] Spender wrote in a 1994 Afterword to his autobiography *World Within World*:

> Fascism created a new political class – the anti-Fascists. It did so because Fascists or Nazis rejected certain people on account of their race – Jews or Gypsies – or their vocation – artists, writers, teachers – seen as either allies or as enemies of the regime. This defined anti-Fascism in the lives of those who were its real or potential victims.[8]

For these anti-fascist writers, literature was inevitably political. The poet Michael Roberts, a champion of the Auden cohort, stated in 1935 that his generation could 'no more forget the world of politics than the soldier-poets could forget the wounded and the dead'.[9]

Most left-wing writers in the period saw the cinema as ideally suited for socialism, and consequently sought to make their own writing filmic. The appeal of the cinema was threefold. First, its popularity as a mass medium meant that it attracted audiences the novelist could only dream of. In 1934, there were about 963 million cinema admissions in Britain, with the majority of seats selling for no more than a shilling.[10] Cecil Day Lewis spoke for many of his contemporaries when he announced in 1936 that for poetry to survive it must be popular.[11] What better chance of popularity, or of a genuinely democratic audience, than to appeal to filmgoers? In 1937, the film director Alexander Korda celebrated the fact that nineteen million people a week visited the cinema, stating that no better example of 'effective democracy' had ever existed than the popular taste that dictated the subject-matter of the films.[12]

Secondly, film's nature as a recording medium meant that it was capable of representing the working classes. The German cultural theorist Walter Benjamin famously linked film's popularity with its power to represent the masses in his 1936 'The Work of Art in the Age of Mechanical Reproduction'. For Benjamin, the popularity and accessibility of cinema meant that 'everybody who witnesses its accomplishments' could be 'somewhat of an expert', while 'the newsreel offer[ed] everyone the opportunity to rise from passer-by to movie extra'.[13] The same was often said of photography, which Auden described in 1937 as '*the* democratic art', extolling 'amateur snapshots' as 'the only decent photographs'.[14] Since the Danish-American photographer and muckraker Jacob Riis had turned his camera on the squalid everyday life of the New York slums in 1888, photographers had come to see 'ordinary' (working-class) life as their natural province. In the 1930s, British filmmakers followed suit.

Although working-class characters had always appeared periodically in mainstream British cinema – notably in films by Charlie Chaplin and Gracie Fields – it was with the formation of John Grierson's documentary film unit in 1930 that there was a sustained attempt to capture everyday working-class life on film. A Scottish Presbyterian and a committed socialist, Grierson saw the documentary film as a specifically socialist medium. He was determined to represent the working class accurately, wanting to portray the men who 'work brutally and starve ignobly' in the industrial world.[15] Accordingly, writers sought both to emulate and to be involved in documentary film. The politically campaigning novelist Storm Jameson encapsulated the feelings of many of her contemporaries when she asserted in the left-wing magazine *Fact* in 1937 that the 'nearest equivalent' of what was wanted in the novel existed already 'in another form in the documentary film'.[16] Valentine Cunningham states that, from the start, Mass-Observation saw their work in documenting the masses as 'the best sort of cinema', aligning themselves with Grierson's tradition.[17]

Thirdly, specific filmic techniques seemed ideally suited to propound a radical message. Left-wing writers were attracted by cinema's capacity to create a democracy between objects and humans and by its power for long-shots, enabling it to represent crowds. Perhaps most crucially, they were excited by cinematic montage. It is significant that Walter Allen labels the 1930s cinematic text the '"montage" novel'; during the late 1920s, montage as practised by Russian directors such as Sergei Eisenstein and Dziga Vertov had gained popularity among the intelligentsia in Britain.[18] For the Russians, the chief function of montage was to shock and rouse the audience by bombarding it with a succession of rapid images and to expose social inequality by juxtaposing working-class and upper-class lives. As I shall show in Chapter 1, Eisenstein privileged montage partly because it was well placed to represent the Marxist dialectic and partly because it enabled the artist to be a quasi-manual labourer. Most of the British 1930s intelligentsia was familiar with Eisenstein's techniques. By this point, various film societies had found ways to get round the censors and screen Russian films.[19] At the same time, writers who were more interested in popular than avant-garde cinema could get their montage second-hand from directors such as Alfred Hitchcock and Anthony Asquith. One of the attractions of the montage film was its fast pace. In a decade of movement, writers sought to emulate film partly because, fusing left-wing politics with high modernist aesthetics, speed was seen as inherently radical. In 1923 Vertov had lauded the cinema for liberating man from the constraints of 'human immobility'. The kino-eye, unlike the human eye, is in 'constant motion': 'I move apace with the muzzle of a galloping horse, I plunge full speed into a crowd.'[20]

The politically and cinematically engaged literature that emerged in the 1930s was far from uniform. Different groups of writers tended to privilege cinema for different reasons, and cinematic technique does not always entail cinematic subject matter. Filmic books need not necessarily be left wing, any more than the films themselves. The nature of the cinematic text also changed over the course of the decade. We can sketch the broad rise and fall of the 1930s cinematic text by looking at the career of the experimental British novelist Henry Green, whose work will appear throughout this book. Green was an enthusiastic cinema fan, though, like several 'highbrow' writers, he tended to be more captivated by the popular than the avant-garde, seeking pleasure rather than left-wing enlightenment. As an Oxford undergraduate in the 1920s, he visited the cinema on a daily basis and found it the perfect place 'in which to work out the sense of guilt, to conquer that nausea of lunch after the night before's drinking'.[21]

Green's second novel, *Living*, published in 1929, can be seen as the first major example of the tradition examined in this book. It is as startling in its overt cinematic montage as in its sympathy for its working-class protagonists. In 1927, disappointed by Oxford and suffering from a burgeoning sense of class guilt, the young Henry Yorke went to work at his father's factory in Birmingham. Two years later, Harold Heslop lauded Yorke, in his new guise as Henry Green, as a writer of 'proletarian stock' at the Second International Conference of Proletarian Revolutionary Writers in Kharkov.[22] Later, Allen praised Green for relating his story 'in very short episodes rather in the manner of a film' and for capturing 'as never before or since what can only be called the poetry of working-class life'.[23]

Living can be seen to define the tradition that would emerge over the next ten years in the hands of writers as diverse as Allen, James Barke,

Isherwood, Storm Jameson, MacNeice and John Sommerfield. Green himself would write one more left-wing cinematic novel in 1939, though the focus of *Party Going* is more with its upper-class than its working-class characters. This sparkling cinematic romp seems more the product of a Bright Young Thing than a writer of proletarian stock. In 1943, Green would repudiate just the kind of cinematic writing he had helped to spawn. With the outbreak of war, Green's relationship with both cinema and politics had become more complex. His own wartime experiences spent in the fire service gave him a sense that wartime life itself was inherently cinematic. In one wartime story, he presents firemen viewing London by the 'cinema light' of their electric torches, and in his 1943 *Caught,* the fire and searchlights of the Blitz are the cause of cinematic chiaroscuro.[24]

At the same time, war complicated Green's understanding of class. It made him see that there were 'not two or three social classes but hundreds well defined throughout Britain'.[25] It also made the possibility of upper-class identification with the working classes at best ambivalent and at worst patronising and unwanted. The result was a new kind of political cinematic text; a novel which interrogates both left-wing notions of class and the cinematic itself, demonstrating a stubborn literariness just where it foregrounds the cinematic. It suggests that ultimately the imagination is 'literary', even in the most cinematic of circumstances.[26] In Second World War writing by Elizabeth Bowen, William Sansom and Spender as well as by Green, the relationship between literature and cinema and between cinema and politics became more problematic.

'The moral universe of the 1930s being no longer ours'

Green is at once typical and anomalous among the writers whose work I have used him to frame. As an upper-class writer who made a somewhat naïve commitment to the working classes, he is typical of Auden and his 'Gang'. With his enthusiasm for cross-cutting the experiences of characters from different classes, Green resembles documentary novelists from Storm Jameson to the working-class, card-carrying Communist writer John Sommerfield. Green's interest in politics, though, was wayward at most. In this respect he has less in common with Auden or Sommerfield than with Woolf or Elizabeth Bowen, whose 1930s work was only loosely cinematic or political. In the pages that follow it will often be the more anomalous works that help to define and complicate cinematic literature. Green himself is a key figure in this book because he succeeds single-handedly in both creating and undermining the broad tenets of the tradition I describe.

Green, like Auden, Isherwood, Spender and Jameson, would later pour scorn on his political engagement in the 1930s, even suggesting that it never occurred: 'I don't think I'm a political person', he said in an interview in 1975, where he declared that he usually voted Conservative. 'Damn all politicians.'[27] These writers are not alone in questioning the artistic merit of the red decade. The cultural critic Susan Sontag, looking back at the American documentary photography of the 1930s, expressed incredulity at Walker Evans' desire for his photographs to be 'literate, authoritative, transcendent'. According to her, in 1977,

> The moral universe of the 1930s being no longer ours, these adjectives are barely credible today. Nobody demands that photography be literate. Nobody can imagine how it could be authoritative. Nobody understands how anything, least of all a photograph, could be transcendent.[28]

Sontag questions both the poetry and the reality of 1930s 'poetic realism'.

'The moral universe of the 1930s being no longer ours.' Sontag is confident in separating herself from an age that she sees as naïve in its politics and its faith in representation. It seems telling that the historian Richard Overy is less certain that we have escaped the moral sensibility of the 1930s. In his recent cultural history of the inter-war period, Overy defines the 1930s as a 'morbid age', much like our own: 'For some years now there has existed a popular belief that the Western world faces a profound crisis.'[29] Our twenty-first-century 'morbid fears' have a legacy in that earlier 'age of anxiety, doubt or fear'.[30] So, reading Sontag and Overy together, it seems that we have inherited the doubt, but lost the hope. We, who have seen the consequences of that both red and black-and-white decade, are too cynical, too worldly-wise, to embrace the promise of socialism or the mass media.

Here I am not contesting Sontag's repudiation of that earlier moral universe, but I do think it is worth devoting an entire book to the 'barely credible'. The story of socialist engagement with the mass media in Britain is a story of excitement and hope, even if it is the daredevil hope of the man condemned to death. Overy's morbid age is Orwell's decade of 'the teapot, endlessly stewing', with civilisation signalling 'decay'.[31] But there is also the 1930s whose hope in the face of horror was expressed rousingly by Michael Roberts:

> The writers in this book have learned to accept the fact that progress is illusory, and yet to believe that the game is worth playing; to believe that the alleviation of suffering is good . . . to believe that their own standards are no more absolute than those of other people, and yet to be prepared to defend and to suffer for their own standards.[32]

According to MacNeice, poets of his generation such as Spender turned to Communism because it 'asserted purpose in the world'; 'because the world was *ours*'.[33] Looking back on the 1930s, Spender saw his optimism as specifically cinematic. In his 1951 autobiography, he recounts visits to films by Eisenstein and Pudovkin which 'conveyed a message of hope like an answer to *The Waste Land*'.[34] These writers were censured by Orwell for their 'Boy Scout atmosphere of bare knees and community singing', evident in Roberts' sense of the game worth playing.[35] Nonetheless, Roberts' hope that suffering can be alleviated given the right principles is matched by commentators throughout the decade, whether they are card-carrying Communists, working-class writers, documentary filmmakers or Mass-Observers. This book, then, is partly an attempt to restore the excitement and hope to the 'morbid' inter-war decade. It is also an attempt to disentangle the complex politics and aesthetics of an era that can too easily be dismissed as merely a naïve aberration, not only by subsequent commentators but by the key figures of the decade themselves.

It seems pertinent here to consider Raymond Williams' strange, late engagement with the 1930s in his 1985 essay on 'Cinema and Socialism'. Here Williams charts the hopes and failures of the 1930s Left, who saw film 'as an inherently popular and in that sense democratic art' and saw cinema, like socialism itself, as 'a harbinger of a new kind of world'.[36] Williams, like Sontag, sees the movement as failing. What the Left failed to notice, he suggests, is that 'there are others than radicals and democrats interested in being popular'; commercial entrepreneurs were as excited as left-wing idealists about the possibilities of the new technologies and new audiences.[37] As a result, the medium was hijacked by the Right, and even its potentially radical techniques (Williams is convinced by the radicalism of speed and montage) could be appropriated for right-wing messages.

But Williams is more sympathetic than Sontag to the moral universe of the earlier era, largely because he himself remained committed to socialism until his death in 1988. He asks what it would mean 'to celebrate the socialist films that we have and to find ways of making new ones'.[38] It is here that his essay becomes strange, because his plans, which come through obliquely, bear a remarkable similarity to the 1930s project he has described as failing. He asks, in rhetoric heavily reminiscent of the 1930s, for films that portray 'the lives of the great majority of people' who 'have been and still are almost wholly disregarded by most arts'. He engages with cynics who suggest that merely reproducing the existing reality represents 'a passivity, even an acceptance of the fixed and the immobile'.[39] These cynics might be Sontag, stating that to take a picture 'is to have an interest in things as they are, in the status quo remaining unchanged'.[40] They could also be Spender in 1939, suggesting that until society has changed, 'working-class literature will remain a rather grim form of travel book'.[41] Williams insists, in answer to these qualms, that art can lead life, and that artistic techniques and genres exist to tell truths about a dislocated culture which conceals the truth about itself.[42]

I quote Williams not to belittle him or to imply that the moral universe of 1985 was also less cynical (or informed) than our own. Instead, I would like, by way of Williams, to suggest that the moral universe of the 1930s was more complex than it might first appear, not least because Walter Benjamin was not alone among his peers in being fully aware that the cinema and the mass media in general could be a vehicle for the Right as well as the Left. For Benjamin, cinema was both the 'home of illusions' and the potential 'home of experiences'.[43] Williams asks how we can put our hopes in the popular media, even if we know they are corrupt and corruptible. This was also the question asked in the 1930s, not just by Benjamin, but by British artists and sociologists such as the 1937 founders of Mass-Observation.

In their initial letter to the *New Statesman*, the poet Charles Madge, the sociologist Tom Harrisson and the surrealist-*cum*-documentary filmmaker Humphrey Jennings proclaimed that their organisation

> does not set out in quest of truth or facts for their own sake, or for the sake of an intellectual minority, but aims at exposing them in simple terms to all observers, so that their environment may be understood and thus constantly transformed.

They went on to say that the 'foisting on the mass of ideals or ideas developed by men apart from it' was causing 'mass misery' and 'international shambles'.[44] It becomes clear in Mass-Observation's 1939 book *Britain* that Harrisson blamed the mass media for mass ignorance, seeing the newspaper conglomerates and Hollywood studios as abusing their power over the gullible masses. 'The newspapers', he complained, 'not only state *their* version of the facts – they also state *their* version of the public opinion of the moment.'[45] This anger with the right-wing monopolies is one we find throughout the left-wing engagement with the mass media in this period, whether it is Woolf announcing that an educated woman must take six newspapers if she has any hope of learning the truth, the critic Iris Barry complaining that the 'spoon-fed' public should ask for 'slightly better dreams', or Sommerfield announcing that 'millions' of innocent viewers are 'ruled, exploited, cheated, and swindled' at the picture palace.[46] I shall consider the literary portrayal of mass cinema audiences in Chapter 3. Here I would like to return to the significance of Mass-Observation's hope that the environment can be understood and thus 'constantly transformed'.

The notion of perpetual transformation through a new kind of self-analysis or observation resonates with the ideas of German theorists in the same period. The founders of Mass-Observation seem to advance the idea of a perpetual becoming that evokes Benjamin's 'Now of recognisability' in his late 1930s *Arcades Project*.[47] For Benjamin, whom Leo Charney has described as the 'poet laureate of the modern as the momentary', in the moment of awakening the 'Then' flashes its images into the 'Now'. [48] In the next moment, the revelation is 'always irretrievably lost' and, implicitly, the process must begin again, inevitably and immediately. Here Benjamin describes the 'Now of recognisability' as a 'dialectical image'; elsewhere he describes the entire process of the *Arcades Projects* as a sort of (cinematic) dialectical montage.[49] For Benjamin, the cinema provides both model and metaphor for the redemptive transformation of individual and society just as, in the 'Work of Art' essay, it provides the solution to the current fascist crisis. Here, Benjamin suggests that the way to counteract the aestheticisation of politics and to save the mass media from the fascists is to respond 'by politicising art'.[50] Similarly, for Mass-Observation, the mobilisation of the public as individual artistic producers seems to be one way to save them from the stupefying efforts of the authorities. If, as Barry suggests, people are currently being fed the wrong dreams, it is up to them to take hold of their own dreams and transform them. And, indeed, Mass-Observation provided its subjects with dream diaries for that very purpose.

Cultural critics and historians, including Michel Foucault, Guy Debord and Jonathan Crary, have seen the late nineteenth and early twentieth centuries as an era in which the British subject became a passive, credulous viewer. For Foucault, the key factor in effecting this change was the increase in public surveillance, leading the subject to internalise the gaze of the authorities and regulate his own actions.[51] Crary suggests that Foucault's surveillance is compatible with Debord's sense of the modern subject as the trapped audience of a series of isolating spectacles, predicated on an increasing inseparability between the subject and object of the gaze.[52] According to Crary, the capitalist authorities used spectacle to push their subjects into inattentiveness, only to attempt to solve the problems of attention by regulating perception through surveillance.

We can see Crary's theories as elucidating the preconceptions behind Mass-Observation. In their initial letter, Harrisson, Madge and Jennings suggest that the 'masses' have become inattentive to their surroundings. With their emphasis on self-observation (and an analytic process of documentation) they attempt to counteract passive viewing. And their subjects frequently refer to a new kind of attentive excitement that is produced by the knowledge that they are subsequently to record their experiences.[53] This is the same impulse that motivated many of the documentary filmmakers and novelists. Grierson and his colleagues hoped to galvanise the working classes into a Benjaminian awakening through presenting them with their own lives or, ideally, to turn them into proletarian writers or filmmakers themselves.

All three of the founders of Mass-Observation were particularly interested in the effects of mass spectacle in public life, with one of their first major projects involving the documentation of the reactions of hundreds of ordinary citizens to the public pageantry surrounding the coronation of George VI. In his documentary films of the late 1930s and early 1940s, Humphrey Jennings displays a fascination with the effects of local spectacle or pageantry, which he portrays as creating shared community experiences. There is communal singing, acting and dancing in *Listen to Britain* (1942) and a form of public pageant in *Words for Battle* (1941). Implicitly, for Jennings, these small participatory spectacles (and his own pageant-like films) can be set against the larger, subjugating work of the large-scale (potentially fascist) spectacle. Similarly, Harrisson and Madge made much of the joys of the Lambeth Walk, explicitly contrasting its joyful individuality with the swagger of the fascist goosestep, suggesting that small folkish rituals can counteract the bombastic roar of fascism.[54] In his account of the newfound insularity of late modernism, Jed Esty has read the more general revival of pageants in this period in similar terms, and I shall return to the pageant form in 1930s and 1940s literature and cinema in Chapter 5.

According to Karen Jacobs, in her complex study of the relationship between modernist aesthetics and perception, the high modernist texts of the 1920s reflected and engaged in early twentieth-century anxiety about the impossibility of Cartesian spectatorship. Jacobs, like Sontag, chastises 1930s writers for turning their back on the discoveries made by their 1920s predecessors, suggesting that their love of photography blinded them to its 'constructive and discursive power'.[55] I would suggest, though, that we can see just such an awareness of the power behind any form of representational media operating not just in the work of Mass-Observation but in the majority of political cinematic texts.

While the manifestos behind these texts may sometimes be naïve, the literary texts themselves often demonstrate scepticism about the nature of the visual itself. In much of the literature examined in this book, the writing of a visual text becomes not merely an attempt at straightforward representation (as Jameson's manifesto for the documentary novel might suggest), but a defiance of the visual, through the visual. Writers as diverse as Sommerfield, Isherwood and Woolf sought to undermine the subjugating power of the mass spectacle by exploring what it is like to live in a passive visual culture or, more specifically, to experience the world as a camera. Viewing the world as a film or a photograph, these writers experienced cinema as a form of powerlessness, which aided the aestheticisation of politics that Benjamin had attributed to the fascists. In Chapter 4, I investigate the anxiety implicit in camera consciousness, which works against the confidence of the documentarists. It is difficult to turn the masses into active spectators when camera consciousness is always in danger of inducing passivity. And the aestheticisation of experience became more marked in the Blitz, when the flash of the bombs rendered the world more cinematic than ever and the cinematic text imploded on itself.

The 'ultracinematographic'

The texts I analyse in this book tend to be most revealing (and politically potent) when read, in detail, on their own terms. What follows is therefore structured around a series of close readings of the texts themselves and of the films I see them as engaging with. In Chapter 1, I set out some of the cinematic techniques or aspects of the filmic medium itself that I see as crucial to the 1930s cinematic text. Here I refer to a number of films from early cinema to the Second World War, combining the popular with the avant-garde. As I have said, many of the writers who feature in this book were more enthusiastic fans of Hitchcock or Gracie Fields than of Pabst or Vertov. I agree with David Trotter that the current focus of literature-cinema studies on the avant-garde ignores the mixed make-up of the cultural climate in interwar Britain.[56] From 1927 onwards, cinemas were forced to show a significant percentage of British films each month, which meant that even the most highbrow of cineastes was likely to be exposed to home-grown fare when visiting the local cinema.[57]

It is of course difficult to know who would have seen which films, except when writers mention specific titles in diaries or essays. Even then, it is easy to become obsessed with the two or three films a writer such as Woolf refers to, when we know from her diary that she was making regular visits to the 'picture palace' to see films so popular she did not consider their titles worthy of recording. Ultimately, this is a conceptual as well as an historical study; or at least it is a histori-cal study of a conceptual question. In considering the engagement of writers with cinema, I am interested in the nature of the two media as much as the individual works – and this was certainly true of the writers themselves. Woolf, in her important 1926 essay on 'The Cinema', records sensations and thoughts evoked by a screening of *The Cabinet of Dr Caligari* without mentioning a single scene in the film. Indeed, her interest is aroused not by the German Expressionist sets or montage, but by a shadow that accidentally is cast on the screen. Her manifesto, when it comes, is for a new kind of cinema, a 'new art' that will unroll the past, annihilate distance and release 'some unknown and unexpected beauty'.[58] Similarly, in her 1937 cinema essay, Bowen admits her laziness as a film fan and her lack of interest in film as art, only to suggest that she is waiting for the cinema of the future when she hopes that films will catch up 'with the possibilities of the cinema', changing its audience 'as art can change one'.[59]

Both Woolf and Bowen seem more captivated by the potential of the medium than by the actual films they have seen. Many writers who engaged with cinema approached it in this abstract way, extrapolat-ing from individual films the special properties of the cinema itself. According to the postwar film critic André Bazin, the modernist novel in general was not influenced by film but by a filmic vision of the world:

> If we maintain that the cinema influences the novel then we must suppose that it is a question of a potential image, existing exclusively behind the magnifying glass of the critic and seen only from where he sits. We would

then be talking about the influence of a nonexistent cinema, an ideal cinema, a cinema that the novelist would produce if he were a filmmaker; of an imaginary art that we are still awaiting.

In fact, he suggests, the cinema has always been fifty years behind the novel, and the film has much to learn from the so-called cinematic text:

> we do not know if *Manhattan Transfer* or *La Condition humaine* would have been very different without the cinema, but we are certain on the other hand that *Thomas Garner* and *Citizen Kane* would never have existed if it had not been for James Joyce and Dos Passos. We are witnessing, at the point at which the avant-garde has now arrived, the making of films that dare to take their inspiration from a novel-like style one might describe as ultracinematographic.[60]

It is precisely the 'ultracinematographic' that I am interested in defining in Chapter 1.

In thinking about the engagement between literature and cinema, rather than always the direct influence of one on the other, I am indebted to Bazin and to more recent work by David Trotter and Laura Marcus. In his study of *Cinema and Modernism*, Trotter echoes Bazin in focusing on 'film as medium before film as art', suggesting that it was 'not cinema which made literary modernism, but cinema's example'.[61] Trotter suggests that we must study the 'parallel histories' of the two media and does this by analysing the interplay of filmic absence and presence in Joyce, Woolf and Eliot. In *The Tenth Muse*, Marcus places film criticism by writers alongside filmic literature and literary films, producing a very full overview of the interaction between the two worlds from the birth of cinema until the 1930s.[62]

Adopting a similar model of parallel histories, I am concerned to explore the mutual engagement of film and literature in 1930s and wartime Britain. I do this through a series of investigations into grouped texts, each of which redefines the relationship between literature, politics and cinema. Chapters 2 and 3 look at the documentary novel and film in 1930s Britain, combining documentary reportage by Orwell with 'montage novels' by a range of writers, including Green and Sommerfield. Chapter 2 explores the complicated question of the documentary gaze, investigating the documentarists' dual desire for distanced observation and subjective, intimate understanding. I pay particular attention to the notion of the 'masses', which developed in the 1930s, and which is also crucial to Chapter 3. Here I focus on the representation of mass, working-class leisure activities. Leisure appealed to the documentarists as a time when the working classes could be individuals while also forming a united community. This chapter ends in wartime, when, whatever the limitations of the so-called 'people's war', what I term cross-class montage was abandoned in favour of a form of across-class montage, and leisure was celebrated as a factor in Britain's superiority to Germany.

In Chapter 4, I look at 1930s experiments with camera consciousness. Taking Isherwood's 'I am a camera' to mean 'I feel like a camera', I examine a group of texts that seem to explore the act of writing cinematically in an age in which it has become impossible to conceive of reality unmediated by the camera eye. Alongside Isherwood, I look at his comrades Auden, MacNeice and Upward, together with Walter Allen and Patrick Hamilton. I also consider the Spanish Civil War as the first war to take place in Jean Baudrillard's 'hyperreal' or Slavoj Žižek's 'desert of the real'.[63] The texts in this chapter work against the texts in the documentary chapters, anxiously subverting the hopes for clear-sighted witnessing and political change. For Woolf, as for Benjamin, one way to counteract this passivity was with the flash of history, which could be brought into the present moment through the spatial visualisation of cinema. The focus of Chapter 5 is the framing of history in Woolf's final two novels, *The Years* and *Between the Acts*. Here I read *Between the Acts* alongside the pageant films of Humphrey Jennings. In 1940, the flash of history was interrupted by the flash of bombs. Chapter 6 explores British literature responding to the cinematic and photographic qualities of the Blitz. Here I suggest that the bombs brought an intensification of the 1930s sense of camera consciousness as helplessly passive.

This book is necessarily limited in its scope, but in a sense it need merely contribute a chapter to the large body of exciting literature emerging in the field of literature–cinema studies. It is best read alongside not just Marcus and Trotter, but also Sara Danius, Michael North and Keith Williams. Danius's work on the role of embodied perception in high modernism provides invaluable background to my book, as does Michael North's work on the relationship of (largely American) high modernism with cinema and photography and Keith Williams' exhaustive study of the interaction between 1930s literature and media.[64] David Seed's recent *Cinematic Fictions* also provides a helpful parallel history of American literature in the period.[65] It is thanks to these critics that I can take as read the 1880–1930 cinematic, literary, epistemological and social contexts, focusing my own attention on the specific tradition of the politically engaged (or disengaged) cinematic British 1930s and 1940s text. Although Chapter 1 spans a larger period in its attempts to elucidate the 'ultracinematographic', the focus of the other chapters is exclusively on the fifteen-year period 1930–45. In returning to this moral universe so distant from our own, I hope to advance our understanding of an era in which a whole generation seem to have believed, against all odds, in both politics and vision. This book is about the contradictions inherent in this belief. It is about the way these writers figured the cinema as at once political and apolitical; as simultaneously enabling and disabling political engagement.

CHAPTER 1

Radical Cinema

The writers who found cinema a source of revolutionary hope focused on its techniques as well as its popularity. Cinema could expose social inequalities by cutting between upper-class and working-class lives. Through the close-up, it could decentre the human, creating a democracy between people and objects. By implicating the viewer physically in the picture, filmmakers could counter apathy with an embodied alertness. At the same time, cinema could confront the spectator with an unsettling form of absent presence, rendering the world ghostly and unreal.

This chapter investigates a series of photographic or cinematic techniques or properties, as part of a more general attempt to pinpoint what it meant to be simultaneously cinematic and politically engaged in the 1930s. The radical properties of cinema were located in subject matter as well as style. Left-wing filmmakers could portray working-class life and leisure or they could use techniques such as montage in the service of a left-wing political message. Here I focus more on filmic technique, with filmic subject matter forming one of the main strands of discussion in Chapters 2 and 3. I also explore the appeal of the inherent characteristics of the filmic medium. Cinema's status as an indexical medium and its power to promote a new kind of embodied spectatorship were seen as radical because they gave it the force to transform the relationship between subject and world.

Reflecting the mixed film culture of the period, I move freely between silent and sound cinema, ranging from the 1920s to the 1940s. Trotter has suggested that 1920s modernist literature was more engaged with the 'cinema of attractions' of the first decade of the twentieth century than with 1920s cinema.[1] A similar time-lag applies in the 1930s, when writers tended to centre their discussions of film on the golden age of silent narrative cinema, as it developed in Russia, Germany, France, America and Britain in the 1920s. Most attempts to define the cinematic medium in this period still focused on the properties of the silent cinema. The French filmmaker René Clair was typical in complaining in 1950 that the introduction of speech and sound had prevented the cinema from dreaming.[2] Film's story-telling tendency, enhanced by sound, was seen to induce an inferior drugged slumber in the mass cinema audiences, turning them into passive spectators. At the same time, though, writers visiting their local cinemas were more likely to see 1930s popular sound films than 1920s avant-garde masterpieces. Over the course of the 1930s, even the most intellectual cinemagoers tended to become gradually acclimatised to sound. Already in 1929, Kenneth MacPherson admitted in *Close Up* that he had learnt to 'miss the sound now in a silent film'.[3]

Most of the European films I refer to were screened in London in the 1920s or 1930s. From 1925, the London Film Society exhibited a regular programme of international avant-garde cinema, and audiences could see films by Fritz Lang, Walter Ruttmann, Sergei Eisenstein, Vsevolod Pudovkin, Dziga Vertov, Fernand Léger and Man Ray. The majority of avant-garde films discussed here were screened by the Film Society in the late 1920s. The London Film Society screenings were attended chiefly by the intelligentsia. Filmmakers, writers and artists came together to appreciate the avant-garde.[4] But soon several workers' film societies sprang up to show Russian films, exploiting loopholes in the censorship regulations which allowed for the screening of any 16 mm film. In 1929 the London Workers' Film Society was launched by the *Sunday Worker* and included the Communist journalists Henry Dobbs and Ralph Bond among its founder members. Bond later enthused about the Workers' Film Movement, detailing the 'passionate interest' with which workers followed the showing of Pudovkin's *The End of St Petersburg* (1927) and describing the cinema as 'a weapon of the class struggle', stating that workers could fight capitalism by 'exhibiting the films of the only country where the workers are the ruling class'.[5] In November 1929 Dobbs announced that 600 workers had turned up in Tooting to see the first programme, which included a Chaplin comedy and Stabavov's *Two Days*, a 'vital study of the old and the new in the days of the Russian White rebellion'. According to Dobbs, 'the roof rang' at the end of the film and all were disappointed when the London County Council banned the showing of *Snapshots of Soviet Russia* at the last minute.[6]

Where appropriate, I look at photography alongside cinema. When considered in abstract terms, the two media are often hard to separate.

In 1930 the French screenwriter Carlo Rim used photography to define the modern age:

> the advent of modern times dates from the moment the first daguerreotype appeared on the scene . . . Thanks to the photograph, yesterday is no more than an endless today.[7]

Rim was more a filmmaker than a photographer and was writing in 1930, long after the novelty of photography had worn off. Yet he privileged photography over film for its capacity to defy death and transform the world. This is just the view of photography refuted by Benjamin's colleague Siegfried Kracauer in his 1927 'Photography' essay. Here he suggested that the attempt to defy death through photography had failed because the photograph inevitably draws attention to its pastness.[8] Nonetheless, both Rim and Kracauer were clear in seeing photography as radically new because of its indexical power to record reality. Both saw film as an extended, mobile version of what is essentially a photographic phenomenon.

For Rim and Kracauer, the 'ultracineamtographic' is unthinkable without the 'ultraphotographic'. And several of the elements of film that figured as radical in the 1930s appear in early discussions of its predecessor. Photography, even more than cinema, was seen from the start as a democratic art. In 1857, Lady Elizabeth Eastlake announced that photography united men 'of the most diverse lives, habits, and stations, so that whoever enters its ranks finds himself in a kind of republic'.[9] With the arrival of the Kodak 'Brownie' in 1901, the photographer's subjects could very easily become photographers themselves. In the 1920s, the New Left in Russia had pursued a dream of a collective workers photography, attempting to transform representation into construction.[10] By the 1930s, it was extremely common to own a camera in Britain and Jennings, like Auden, celebrated photography as '*the* system with which the people can be pictured by the people for the people'.[11] Though Grierson's documentary film movement had dreams of involving the workers in film production, film was inevitably a more expensive and cumbersome art form. It would be a good fifty years before the video camera became part of the daily life of the ordinary individual.

Montage

In 1925, Eisenstein stated that what the filmmaker needed was not a 'cine-eye' but a 'cine-fist', making clear the explicitly political purpose of his cinematic practices.[12] The cine-eye he dismissed was Vertov's, although Vertov himself still saw his credo of recording life '*as it is*' as explicitly revolutionary.[13] For Eisenstein, cinema's radicalism came chiefly from its capacity to create contrast through fast-cutting montage. He linked montage itself to Marx's notion of the dialectic, departing from the parallel montage advocated by contemporary Russian filmmakers Kuleshov and Pudovkin, and insisting instead on its capacity for dialectical juxtaposition. In his 1929 essay on the 'Dramaturgy of Film Form', Eisenstein stated that the dialectical system, projected into the brain, produces philosophy and art and that 'in the realm of art this dialectical principle of the dynamic is embodied in CONFLICT'.[14] Eisenstein also saw montage as radical because of its capacity to turn the artist into a manual constructor. The Russian word for montage, 'montazh', retains several of its original meanings, including 'machine assembly'. For Eisenstein, as for the Russian constructivist artist Gustav Klutsis, whose photomontages can be seen as providing the origins of dialectical montage, part of what made montage radical was its affinity with the machine age. In Klutsis's 1920 paean to Lenin, *Electrification of the Entire Country*, Lenin is set beside an architectural cross-section of a building which dwarfs the other figures in the picture, and is himself carrying metal scaffolding. A year earlier, Eisenstein had written in his diary:

> one does not create a work, one constructs it with finished parts, like a machine. Montage is a beautiful word: it describes the process of constructing with prepared fragments.[15]

It would not be long before Eisenstein himself became just such a machine constructor.

Eisenstein's ideas made their way into England partly through his films, partly through his articles, which were published in the British film magazine *Close Up* in the late 1920s and early 1930s, and partly through a series of lectures he gave in London in November 1929, under the auspices of the Film Society. These focused on his theories of montage. The documentary filmmaker Basil Wright later looked back on these lectures as crucial to his cinematic education: 'here was someone laying down (and we must remember laying down for the first time), the laws and principles of the youngest of the arts'.[16] Where Eisenstein enthusiasts in the 1920s tended to downplay the political radicalism of his work (presumably partly to placate the resolutely obdurate censors), by the 1930s left-wing writers lauded the Russians

1.1 *'You press down hard and you get – juice'*
Sergei Eisenstein, *Strike* (1924)

precisely for their revolutionary message.[17] In 1932 the socialist surrealist poet Herbert Read lauded montage as 'mechanised imagination', echoing Eisenstein and describing it as 'the most important stage in the whole process of film-production'.[18] For many British writers, the chief attraction of Russian cinema now lay in its revolutionary message and its frequent use of cross-class montage.

In his three classic 1920s films, *Strike* (1924), *Battleship Potemkin* (1925) and *October* (1928), Eisenstein used montage to illustrate the disparity between the wealth and privileges of Russia's rulers and the poverty of ordinary men. In *Strike* the capitalist factory owner, using an expensive and unnecessary gadget to mix his drink, is juxtaposed with the workers, who are brutally crushed by the police at his decree. The caption 'you press down hard and you get – juice' is used simultaneously to describe the crunch of the drinks machine and that of the police horses, trampling out the blood of the workers (see Figure 1.1). Similarly, a close-up showing the mutilated face of a dead man, trapped as the bridges shut, cutting off the workers from the city, is cross-cut in *October* with a close-up of the face of an upper-class woman, laughing grotesquely as she triumphs at the workers' defeat (see Figure 1.2). Perhaps Eisenstein's most famous use of dialectical shock montage is in the Odessa Steps sequence in *Potemkin*. Here he cuts between the boots and guns of the soldiers as they advance and fire on the crowd, and the scene of desecration on the steps (see Figure 1.3).

This contrasting of rich and poor through montage came to dominate both Russian and German cinema in the late 1920s and was used explicitly in Lang's *Metropolis* (1927). Here the intertitle states that 'as deep as lay the workers' city below the earth, so high above it towered the complex named the "club of the sons"'. The beleaguered,

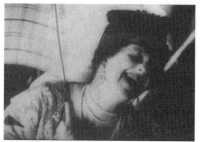

1.2 *The bridges shut*
Sergei Eisenstein, *October* (1927)

1.3 *The Odessa Steps*
Sergei Eisenstein, *Battleship Potemkin* (1925)

dehumanised mass of dark-clothed workers is juxtaposed with the upper classes, dressed in white and frolicking in the sun (see Figure 1.4). More specific contrasts between the rich and poor occur in two late 1920s city symphonies, Walter Ruttmann's *Berlin: Symphony of a Great City* (1927) and Dziga Vertov's *The Man with a Movie Camera* (1929), both of which had a profound impact on the intellectual consciousness in Britain.

1.4 *The lower and upper cities*
Fritz Lang, *Metropolis* (1927)

The key cross-class montage in *Berlin* occurs in the middle of the day when Ruttmann cuts between working-class labourers eating lunch, wealthy businessmen in an expensive restaurant and hungry children and animals eating their midday meal in the street and zoo respectively (see Figure 1.5). Siegfried Kracauer famously condemned both the cross-section itself and the inclusion of animals:

> a sleeping man on a bench is associated with a sleeping elephant. In those cases in which Ruttmann furthers the pictorial development through specific content, he inclines to feature social contrasts. One picture . . . juxtaposes hungry children in the street and opulent dishes in some restaurant. Yet these contrasts are not so much social protests as formal expedients. Like visual analogies, they serve to build up the cross section, and their structural function overshadows whatever significance they may convey.[19]

David Macrae has successfully illustrated the flaws in Kracauer's view in so far as Kracauer incorrectly regards Ruttmann as a would-be 'documentarist, socio-economic analyst or political pressure figure' rather than as a 'pioneering and progressive visual artist'.[20] However, while

1.5 *Class contrasts*
Walter Ruttmann, *Berlin: Symphony of a Great City* (1927)

I agree with Macrae that Kracauer is mistaken in judging Ruttmann according to a pre-configured set of standards, I would argue that *Berlin* stands up well to being judged as the work of a documentarist and socio-economic analyst.

The contrast between the hungry children and the opulent dishes is indeed a social protest. Although Ruttmann was later to go on to make films for Adolf Hitler, at this point in his career he was a committed Communist, and this is evident in *Berlin*. It is difficult to watch the lunch sequence without thinking about the comparative luxury of the food and wealth of the diners. The hearty lunch eaten by the workers from the building site (filmed slightly faster than the other shots so that their chewing appears extremely vigorous) is far removed from the dainty lunch eaten by the fat men or from the gourmet food in the restaurant. Significantly, the restaurant scene begins with the food being prepared. Ruttmann offers consecutive glimpses of the various roles of staff in the kitchen and shows the finished dishes before he focuses on the diners themselves. When he does move to the dining room, it is filmed from above. The viewer is prevented from identifying with the diners but remains on the side of the kitchen staff. These diners,

1.6 *Behind the scenes*
Walter Ruttmann, *Berlin: Symphony of a Great City* (1927)

who have had nothing to do with the process of production, are seen as less worthy of their food than the workers who open the sequence (see Figure 1.6).

Half-way through *The Man with a Movie Camera*, Vertov cuts between members of the bourgeoisie in the process of being beauti-fied and workers in the act of difficult or strenuous labour. A woman smiling indulgently as she is carefully made up in a beauty salon is juxtaposed with a poor woman slapping mortar on a wall. The contrast is reinforced by the focus on their separate gazes. A shot of the rich woman's eye having make-up applied to it is immediately followed by the working woman turning and looking calmly at the camera, before returning to her work (see Figure 1.7). In the sequence that follows, the contrast between the two modes of life is played out in other spe-cific visual contrasts. The foam produced by the hairdresser washing a woman's hair in the beauty salon becomes the foam of a working-class woman washing clothes. A razor being sharpened for the purpose of beautification becomes an axe being sharpened for the purpose of hard work (see Figure 1.8). This is a whimsical film. Vertov is having too much fun experimenting with cinema to be pedalling a message didactically. Nonetheless, this sequence does seem to glorify work and denigrate self-indulgent play.[21]

Cross-class montage also migrated into British popular cinema, partly through the screenplays of Eliot Stannard. Perhaps influenced, like Eisenstein, by the groundbreaking parallel montage of D. W. Griffith in America, Stannard had been writing fast montage sequences into his scripts from 1917 onwards. Christine Gledhill suggests that Stannard, working with the director Maurice Elvey, was a pioneer in developing 'a constructional system antagonistic to the norm estab-lished by Hollywood'.[22] Stannard described his method for their 1917

1.7 *Work and play*
Dziga Vertov, *The Man with a Movie Camera* (1929)

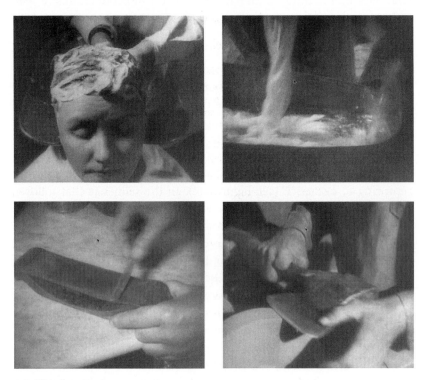

1.8 *Visual contrasts*
Dziga Vertov, *The Man with a Movie Camera* (1929)

adaptation of John Galsworthy's *Justice* in terms that resonate with Eisenstein's: 'the mental agony of the guilty is contrasted by the mental innocence of children playing in the sunshine'. The *Bioscope* critic complained that the 'sudden flashing from one subject to another has too much the effect of a mechanical trick', levelling a complaint that was frequently made against Eisenstein.[23]

For Eisenstein, the chief function of dialectical montage was to shock the audience members out of their complacency and force them to re-examine their world. Eisenstein disapproved of Griffith for using parallel montage merely to describe a situation without disrupting it: 'the structure that is reflected in the concept of Griffith montage is the structure of bourgeois society.' Rather than reproducing the status quo, Eisenstein wanted to create a new social reality in his films.[24] Arthur McCullough links Eisenstein with Brecht and Benjamin in their view that the artist should play an active role in challenging the audience, stating that for all three:

> the more intense aesthetic was needed to break down a stimulus shield that people developed to anaesthetise themselves against the barrage of perceptual assaults of the modern city.[25]

Benjamin connects theatre and film in his description of epic theatre in 1939:

> like the pictures in a film, epic theatre moves in spurts. Its basic form is that of the shock with which the single, well-defined situations of the play collide. The songs, the captions, the lifeless conventions set off one situation from another. This brings about intervals which, if anything, impair the illusion of the audience and paralyse its readiness for empathy.[26]

In an earlier essay he explicitly referred to Brecht's use of filmic montage, stating that Brecht, in his 'selection and treatment of gestures', uses montage in 'such a way that it ceases to be a modish technique and becomes a human event', interrupting 'the context into which it is inserted' and therefore '[working] against creating an illusion among the audience'.[27]

There are numerous parallels to be drawn between Brecht's work and Eisenstein's, and it is significant that Eisenstein's own theories of filmic montage originated in his work with the theatre. He saw the theatre as comprising a succession of 'aggressive moment[s] . . . mathematically calculated to produce specific emotional shocks in the spectator in their proper order within the whole'.[28] Brecht used the term 'montage' to describe his own work in his seminal essay 'The Modern Theatre Is the Epic Theatre', in 1930. In a chart outlining the differences between dramatic and epic theatre, he opposes the 'montage' found in the epic theatre with the traditional 'growth' of the dramatic theatre.[29] His montage technique is evident in *The Threepenny Opera* (1928), where he cross-cuts between the apparently middle-class and respectable Mr Peacham's hypocritical and exploitative treatment of the beggars and MacHeath's ultimately more honest criminality, revealing the contradictions and hypocrisies of the corrupt world of Victorian London (and implicitly 1920s Berlin). Even the Chief of Police is secretly in league with the beggars. The short scenes, which are often interrupted by song, prevent the audience from identifying with the characters. In his notes on the play Brecht insisted that the actors should show a self-conscious awareness that they were now singing:

> nothing is more revolting than when the actor pretends not to notice that he has left the level of plain speech and started to sing.[30]

During the songs, audience and characters alike pause to survey and consider the action so that the constable quietly watches MacHeath sing the 'Ballad of Immoral Earnings' before arresting him.[31] This song, in which Jenny and MacHeath refer casually to his criminality and her whoring and abortion – 'in the end we flushed it down the sewer' – shocks the viewer into an awareness of the sordid state of the world, without inviting straightforward sympathy for Jenny's plight.

Brecht's *Verfremdungseffekt* is characteristic of 1920s radical cinematic montage. The Odessa Steps scene in *Potemkin* creates the shock of collision that Benjamin finds in epic theatre, disturbing the audience at the same time as it prevents it from dwelling on any point of view for long enough to empathise in a straightforward, escapist manner. Lang creates a similar effect near the climax of *Metropolis*, when the viewer is made to think about the irresponsibility of the revolutionary workers and the corruption of Frederson and the other bigwigs through a powerful montage sequence. The film cuts between a stream of children desperately fleeing the flood, Maria banging the gong, the power house and the rancorous machine, crazily destroying the world it controls (see Figure 1.9). At the end of the sequence the upper city, formerly seen glittering in its lavish ostentation, goes dark. As in *Potemkin*, the montage sequence here prevents easy identification with any point of view. At this point, the film is on the side of Maria and her lover, Frederson's son Freder, but through the montage sequence the audience knows far more than them about what is going on throughout the city. The images of desperate children indict the foolish workers who unleashed the flood, while at the same time the images of Frederson in

1.9 *Cross-cutting*
Fritz Lang, *Metropolis* (1927)

his vast office are a reminder that he incurred the workers' hatred in the first place. The montage places individual characters and anxieties within the wider political and social framework.

Brecht's tendency to interrupt the original (diegetic) context of the story found a parallel in the montage film. In Brecht's case, this is done through the songs and titles that punctuate the story, and in film it can be achieved through non-diegetic images montaged with the story, which give the audience another lens through which to view the events of the film. An obvious example is the waking lion in *Battleship Potemkin*. Here Eisenstein juxtaposes three shots of stone lions in progressive states of alertness to shock the viewer from beyond the diegetic world of the film (see Figure 1.10). Critics such as V. F. Perkins condemn the lions for serving 'no purpose in the movie beyond that of becoming components of a montage effect'.[32] It is difficult to contextualise them if we attempt, as Perkins does, to work out their exact role in the massacre, and it seems easier to accept Eisenstein's broad explanation that the lion 'leaps up . . . in protest against the bloodshed on the Odessa Steps'.[33] Eisenstein describes the lions as an example of alogical (essentially non-diegetic) montage, comparable to the Baroque Christ

1.10 *The waking lion*
Sergei Eisenstein, *Battleship Potemkin* (1925)

with beams exploding from its halo used to reveal General Kornilov's
militarist tendency in *October*.[34] The success of the lions as shock effect
is affirmed by Pudovkin's description of the contemporary audience's
reaction: the lions 'matched so perfectly the shots of the explosion that
. . . the audience applauded not because it was pleased but because it
was shaken'.[35] The lions can be seen as precipitating and echoing the
audience reaction to the Odessa Steps, forcing an active reaction to the
scene. The viewer is placed in a position of having to think over and
beyond the characters, responding to the wider political message of the
director.[36]

A comparable use of non-diegetic montage occurs in G. W. Pabst's
Kameradschaft (1931), which was widely hailed throughout Europe
as an important humanitarian film. 'You must see *Kameradschaft*',
announced Grierson in a review. 'It will bring tears to your eyes and
honour to your bosom.'[37] Its central message is to uphold Marxist
solidarity between workers and condemn the bourgeois industrialists,
who incite divisions between nations and encourage war. Like Lang
in *Metropolis*, Pabst uses montage to follow the escapades of several
characters at once, making the audience aware of the overall politics

of the film. Pabst reinforces this with the use of Eisensteinian non-diegetic montage, which acts as a Brechtian alienation tool, taking the viewer out of the frame of the story. The film begins with a scene portraying a French boy and a German boy playing marbles. The boys' game is interrupted when the French boy becomes angry and accuses the German boy of stealing his marbles and the German boy dares the French boy to come across the border and get them. This results in a fight, which necessitates the involvement of adults, questioning the possibility of harmony between nations. Russell Berman writes:

> the point of the gaming commencement is not simply that adults are behaving like children but, more importantly, the suggestion that the wrong game is being played since the aleatory moment of free play, the rolling marble, has been displaced by an appropriate game of agonistic embattlement.[38]

The marbles scene introduces a recurrent theme of conflict. Significantly, the first shot of the game is an ambiguous close-up of the ground where it is being played, which seems like a battlefield with a trench-like hole in the middle.

The marbles scene is followed by a comparable fight between adults, when a German man is offended because a French woman refuses to dance with him. Unlike the marbles scene, this scene is part of the diegesis of the film: Pabst later shows how both characters are affected by this event. However, it functions as part of the montage, jolting the viewer out of easily following a story. It raises questions about the possibility of harmony between nations that then frame the body of the film, which is essentially the chronological portrayal of a fire and the rescue by the German miners. The narrative thrust is interrupted once, when the delirious French miner tries to fight his German rescuer. Seeing the German wearing his mask and hearing a German voice, the Frenchman has a flashback to the First World War, which Pabst juxtaposes with the present scene. This reminds the audience of the seriousness of divisions between nations and introduces a realistic note into the otherwise optimistic scenario, preventing enjoyment of the film as a fantasy account of comradely love triumphing over international hatred. This is reinforced by the scene at the end of the film where the German and French officials reinstate the border inside the mine. Berman sees this scene as undermining and weakening the rest of the film, but it seems to be merely another example of the shock effect and as such forces the viewer to rethink the happy ending. Like the lions in *Potemkin*, these scenes in *Kameradschaft* operate as a Marxist awakening, precipitating the 'awakening of the world', or rather of the audience, 'from its dream about itself'.[39]

Bodies

For Benjamin, such an awakening, if it was to be found in film, would occur through the practice of embodied viewing. According to Miriam Hansen, the cinema emerges as the foremost battleground of contemporary art and aesthetics in Benjamin's project, not because of a futurist or constructivist enthusiasm for technology, but because film is the only medium that might yet counter the catastrophic effects of humanity's (already) 'miscarried reception of technology' which had come to a head in the First World War.[40] Benjamin anticipates Debord in what Susan Buck-Morss sees as a dialectic, or vortex, of 'anaesthetisation' and 'phantasmagoria'. The fascist spectacles have anaesthetised the masses, and technology can be redeemed only when 'in technology body and image space so interpenetrate that all revolutionary tension becomes bodily collective innervation'.[41]

Benjamin was not alone in seeing the rehabilitation of the body as crucial to the appropriation of technology by the Left.[42] For Marx, vision had the innate tendency to reify the world, and Marxist film theorists therefore sought to fight reification through a haptic mode of vision.[43] Eisenstein often saw cinema as producing an actual vibration in the spectator. In his 1929 essay on 'The Filmic Fourth Dimension' he argued that 'I feel' should enter the cinematic vocabulary alongside 'I hear' and 'I see', claiming that cinema at its best can evoke in the spectator *'a totally physiological sensation'*.[44] Later, writing about 'Dickens, Griffith and the Film Today', Eisenstein credited the Soviet cinema with the 'esthetic growth from the *cinematographic eye* to the *image of an embodied viewpoint on phenomena*'.[45] The embodied viewer is vividly conjured by *Potemkin*, which as David Bordwell has pointed out engages in a mode of cinematic assault:

> Cossacks slash at the viewer, the mother carrying her child shouts in anger at the camera, a woman with an exploded eye howls in close-up, and cannons lift to aim directly at the audience. In the last shot, the Potemkin's keel splits the frame, overcoming the audience. Heroic realism, on Eisenstein's understanding, drives its kinaesthetic and emotional energy into the very fibres of the spectator.[46]

In this reading, the viewer of *Potemkin* is unable to remain passive; the assaulted body must rise in protest with the workers.

In his *Theory of Film*, Kracauer quoted Pudovkin insisting that film teaches through 'the whole body' and Grierson stating that 'in documentary you do not shoot with your head only but also with your stomach muscles'.[47] For Kracauer, too, embodiment was one way to counteract the drug-like nature of the film, one way to rescue the cinemagoer from hypnosis.[48] Tim Armstrong, in his study of the relationship between body and technology in the period, argues that film functioned for the modernists as 'a visual illusion which exploits the limits of perception, but which also offers the cinematic body as recompense for the fragmented body of technology'.[49] In this model, cinema functions as a a prosthesis and the human body on the screen becomes an appendage to our own.

This provides a model for one kind of bodily identification on behalf of the audience. In Chaplin's films from the 1920s and 1930s, it is the constant movements of Chaplin's body that animate the film. Whether he is dancing, rollerskating or falling over, Charlie is insistently embodied, and the viewer cannot help but identify with the bizarrely malleable, often hapless body on the screen. The contest in Chaplin's films, as Bazin has pointed out, is always between a human mode of embodiment and a mechanised dehumanisation of the body. According to Bazin, 'mechanisation of movement is in a sense Charlie's original sin, the ceaseless temptation'. His use of the mechanical is 'the price he is forced to pay for his nonadherence to the normal sequence of events and to the function of things'.[50] This is evident in *Modern Times* (1936), a quintessential Chaplin film where, in an extreme parodic version of the technological ideal, Charlie becomes one with the machine. The film opens with Charlie employed in a *Metropolis*-like gleaming factory, engaged in clipping what seem like the buttons of an unspecified product. As the Frederson figure urges his second-in-command to make the machines go faster and faster, Charlie becomes so demented in his attempt to keep pace that he continues his mechanical action even when the machine is switched off (see Figure 1.11). In Bazin's reading, Charlie's helpless mechanical repetition of the gesture results from his inability to understand why he is doing it in the first place. He fails to understand the situation in which he is placed. Charlie also displays mechanical qualities, though, in situations where he is very much in control. In *The Gold Rush* (1925) he allows himself to collapse limply in the snow outside the house of the philanthropic Hank, who takes him into his hut for food and resuscitation. As Hank manipulates

1.11 *Charlie's mechanisation*
Charles Chaplin, *Modern Times* (1936)

Charlie, Chaplin allows his body to become a malleable object, pulled into a sequence of decidedly mechanical postures.

Where is the viewer left in the interplay between the living and the mechanical in Chaplin's films? The moments when his body becomes mechanical seem to interrupt our haptic identification with that body, reminding us that it is merely the product of a mechanical projection of stills on a screen. The play here is between absence and presence. Trotter has suggested that, on the one hand, 'the Tramp has generally been regarded as the very embodiment of the illusion of presence cinema alone can generate', and, on the other, presence dissolves into absence when it is revealed that 'the stylisation that went into the Tramp created a mechanism rather than a persona'.[51]

The mechanisation of Charlie's body reminds us that the present, living body is absent. But, conversely, it serves to highlight the living-ness of that living body. The experience of watching a Chaplin film remains an insistently embodied one. Gilles Deleuze has critiqued Henri Bergson's sense that the experience of watching cinema (or thinking cinematographically) is disjointed and mechanical, suggesting instead that while we may know that the film is made up of a series of mechanically projected stills, we experience it intuitively as a smooth succession of movements: 'cinema does not give us an image to which movement is added, it immediately gives us a movement-image.'[52] Similarly, the delight of watching a Chaplin film seems to stem from the illusion of embodiment, made all the more pleasurable through the mechanisation that reveals that illusion to be precarious. Chaplin reveals that it is possible to experience mechanisation haptically, thereby going some way to fulfilling Benjamin's hope for an imbrication between the body and technology.

Film theorists and practitioners in the 1920s and 1930s also advanced another kind of embodied viewing, less dependent on our identification with the body on the screen. Here, in a mode of cinema that developed from what Tom Gunning has termed the 'cinema of attractions', the viewer is forced to identify haptically with the camera itself, undergoing a virtual experience of motion. Lynda Neade has shown that this kind of embodied viewing began prior to cinema, with the experience of train travel and then fairground attractions such as the Ferris wheel; as the audience and activity were 'merged in a variety of kinaesthetic amusements', 'the spectator had been redefined as participant'.[53] With the cinema came a more complex version of this experience. Most famously, viewers of the early train films were reputed to flee the screen as the train pulled into the auditorium.[54] For Gunning, the early viewers were more thrilled than fearful; this was an exhibitionist cinema which openly solicited the attention of the spectator by 'supplying pleasure through an exciting spectacle'.[55]

The excitement of these early films remained with film enthusiasts into the 1930s. The then film reviewer Alistair Cooke extolled the embodiment induced by the cinema in an essay in Charles Davy's 1938 *Footnotes to the Film*. According to Cooke:

> Whether we like it or not, we are *in* a movie all the time, we're not seeing, as we do in the theatre, a level picture grouped at a given distance. We are on trains and falling down cliffs, we are watching with a quick turn of the head a whip hurtling towards a man's ankle, we are staring face downward in a pool, we are at one second watching from the gallery, at the next we are in the stalls, the wings, or the flies.[56]

Cooke seems more excited by silent cinema than by the sound films that had come to dominate the industry. The trains and cliffs are the province of the very early cinema of attractions, while the rapid movements between scenes suggest the more technically sophisticated silent

1.12 *Joe assaults the viewer*
Anthony Asquith, *A Cottage on Dartmoor* (1929)

cinema of the 1920s, which exploited the potential of the moving body on the screen. The viewer of Anthony Asquith's experimental *Cottage on Dartmoor* (1929) is assaulted by Joe's body at the beginning of the film. Watching the escaped prisoner run across the moors, we are not given the chance to identify with him physically because he jumps out at us, making us flinch, just as the early viewers flinched at the oncoming train (see Figure 1.12). As the capacities of film became more complex, 1920s and 1930s filmmakers advanced the early techniques of the 'cinema of attractions' into a complex and dizzying spectacle. Maurice Elvey's 1927 *Hindle Wakes*, scripted by Eliot Stannard, provides a prime example.

Hindle Wakes is a joyous celebration of the freedom possible at the mass seaside resort. Elvey follows two working girls from the cotton mills to Blackpool for the annual 'Wakes week' holiday and uses the techniques of avant-garde cinema to capture the delights of the seaside on screen. He offers the viewer something akin to the experience of actually being in Blackpool, so that the audience often takes the place of the characters, rather than merely observing them. This is most evident in the extended sequence on the rollercoaster. For most of the time the camera is positioned with the heroine, Fanny, and her lover, Allan, so that the audience rises and plummets with them. We are faced at one minute with the ground rising towards us and at the next with the sky. At strategic points, Elvey reverses the camera so that we see the couple,

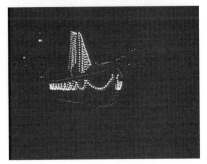

1.13 *Seaside spectacle*
Maurice Elvey, *Hindle Wakes* (1927)

giggling or leaning towards each other, and seem to have our own reactions mirrored or elicited by theirs. When the couple go to look at the Blackpool Illuminations, the audience is given its own spectacle. The black screen is illuminated by lights and the camera pans the display, so that a brightly dotted boat seems to move across the screen (see Figure 1.13).

These techniques are taken even further in *Sing as We Go* (1934), a Gracie Fields film scripted by J. B. Priestley, which seems to reference *Hindle Wakes*. Here again there is a long journey from the cotton mills to Blackpool, though in this film Fields is driven by unemployment rather than leisure time. Again, the director Basil Dean uses Blackpool as an excuse for an exuberant display of the powers of the cinema, inscribing the viewer's body onto the screen. The showpiece sequence comes when Gracie is running away from a policeman and has the whole resort at her disposal. Blackpool is more frightening now; its more outlandish spectacles are in danger of crossing from fantasy into reality. The viewer feels the danger of the void as Gracie falls down the hatch in one ride, and then becomes disoriented when the ghosts and monsters of the ghost train jump out at us from the screen. Gracie and

1.14 *Gracie escapes the policeman*
Basil Dean, *Sing as We Go* (1934)

the policeman continue their chase in the fun house, where both spin on the spinning disk. The camera speeds up when she runs around a fountain, and we are in danger of feeling nausea as she continually runs towards the receding camera (see Figure 1.14).

Andrew Higson writes that, in *Sing as We Go*, the 'attractions are the point of the film, not its flaws'.[57] He sees Dean as toying with the radicalism of Bakhtinian carnival, reproducing the performative spontaneity and variety of music-hall.[58] Where Higson sees the audience as observing the crowd quietly, 'from the safety and security of the cinema seat', I would suggest that the attractions prevent this distance, coercing us into a more active, embodied mode of viewing.[59] Higson argues that the cinema of attractions in *Sing as We Go* works against the more radical montage, but I see the two as conjoined. Like Eisenstein's fast montage, these moments of embodied spectatorship disrupt the more passive experience of viewing a narrative film. It is notable that this is a sound film, but that it jettisons speech for its most spectacular sequence, abandoning the narrative to create a visual display.

If cinema-viewing at its most radical is a haptic activity, the writer who engages with cinema does not necessarily merely privilege the visual. Jonathan Crary, Tim Armstrong and Sara Danius have all advanced a study of modernism that restores the body to 'visual' studies. For Crary, it is important to understand 'perception' not just in terms of the 'single-sense modality of sight', but also of 'irreducibly *mixed* modalities', incorporating the entire human sensorium.[60] If, in Benjamin's terms, the radicalism of cinema could lie partly in a return to the body, then a radical literary text might inscribe the reader in a haptic mode of reading.

Close-ups and objects

The cinema's capacity to intensify bodily experience has often been located in the close-up. In 1921, Jean Epstein extolled the beauty of the American close-up:

> A head suddenly appears on screen and drama, now face to face, seems to address me personally and swells with an extraordinary intensity . . . Now the tragedy is anatomical . . . Waiting for the moment when 1,000 metres of intrigue converge in a muscular denouement satisfies me more than the rest of the film. Muscular preambles ripple beneath the skin.[61]

For Epstein, a type of embodied, rapt spectatorship is induced not by bodies but by their magnified parts: 'If I stretch out my arm I touch you, and that is intimacy.'[62] As in the accounts by Crary and Danius, the acute perception induced by the close-up is at once visual, haptic and even olfactory. Epstein sees the process of looking at close-up after close-up as mimicking the embodied experience of living: 'I look, I sniff at things, I touch. Close-up, close-up, close-up.'

Kracauer echoed Epstein in seeing the clasped hands in the trial scene in Griffith's *Intolerance* (1916) as tactilely expressive:

> It almost looks as if her huge hands with the convulsively moving fingers were inserted for the sole purpose of illustrating eloquently her anguish at the most crucial moment of the trial; as if, generally speaking, the function of any such detail exhausted itself in intensifying our participation in the total situation.[63]

In Kracauer's account, this bodily detail serves to involve the viewer in an active mode of participation. Indeed, the hands themselves become embodied organisms, 'quivering with a life of their own'.[64] But where Epstein saw the close-up as enhancing our embodied participation in the film, for Kracauer it serves also to draw attention to the film's inherent materiality, borne out in the film medium's characteristic capacity to make objects interesting. The cinema synecdochically cuts off body parts, turning them into objects, which it then animates.

It seems significant that Kracauer and Epstein focus on the hand, which was the favoured body part of the 1920s radical director. Perhaps inspired by the fame of Griffith's hand in *Intolerance,* director after director exploited the potential of fingers to animate the hand into a quasi-living organism. The artist and experimental filmmaker Fernand Léger described the hand in 1925 as 'an object with multiple, changing meanings', adding that 'before I saw it in the cinema, I did not know what a hand was!'[65] Brecht, in taking his montage from the theatre to the film, made much of the hand in his screenplay for Slatan Dudow's *Kuhle Wampe* (1932). Here, a close-up of Mrs Bönike's hand, writing a careful list of household expenses, is juxtaposed with Mr Bönike's account of Mata Hari's trial. The hunger of the unemployed is illustrated by close-ups of hands grabbing food from quickly emptying plates. Hands pervade Pudovkin's *The Mother* (1926) and *Storm over Asia* (1928), where the bloody hand of the white man, juxtaposed with the intertitle 'avenge the white man's blood', becomes a metonym for the self-righteousness and supremacy of the white capitalists.[66] The bloody hand resonates with a close-up of fists gesticulating, speeded up in the air, as the capitalists wage war on the Asian workers, and with a later close-up of the hand of the chief commander's wife pampered with a lavish beauty routine.

Fists also dominate *Potemkin*, with the men of Odessa clenching their fists by their sides in rage as they incite themselves to violence, then brandishing them in the air with revolutionary enthusiasm as they decide to act. Once these people have been cowed and destroyed by the soldiers, their hands become symbols of grief, wiping away tears and covering eyes. In *Strike*, the capitalist factory owner's hand is memorably used as a symbol of his power. The workers' meeting discussing the next step in the strike is montaged with the factory owner preparing their arrest. Eisenstein shows him reading through the document he will use to apprehend them and then reveals his hand, superimposed on a shot of the workers, crossing the screen and then signing the document in close-up in the next shot (see Figure 1.15). In England, Hitchcock used hands in the wedding scene in *The Manxman* (1929). Here the marriage of Kate to a man she does not love is figured by a close-up of a ring being placed on her finger, superimposed onto her apprehensive, veiled face. The hand becomes a metonym for ownership when Pete gestures she should put her arm in his. This sequence ends

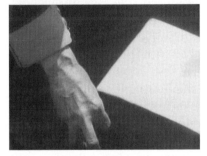

1.15 *The hand of authority*
Sergei Eisenstein, *Strike* (1924)

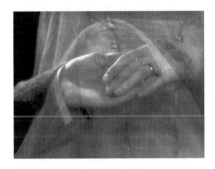
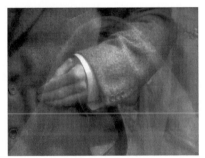

1.16 *Wedding vows*
Alfred Hitchcock, *The Manxman* (1929)

with a close-up of her entrapped arm; her body has become an object, denied the possibility of autonomy or desire (see Figure 1.16).

Once body parts are dehumanised and estranged by becoming objects, it is easy for objects to be elevated, to assume an importance comparable to humans. According to the filmmaker Robert Bresson, it was the task of the filmmaker to 'make the objects look as if they want to be there'.[67] In an unpublished article titled 'Acting with Objects and Acting through Objects', written while editing *Potemkin*, Eisenstein highlighted the importance of objects in his films, stating that whereas in theatre you have acting *with* an object, in cinema you have acting *through* an object.[68] Graham Greene showed his appreciation of Eisenstein's objects in a 1936 review of *October*, stating that the 'most vivid impression of revolution' in the film came from its objects: 'the committee-room door swinging continually open, the people pushing in and out, the telephone bells ringing'.[69] Certainly, the film is dominated by close-ups of objects that form their own narrative; most obvious are the barrels of machine-guns, menacing even when they are divorced from the main body of the gun, and the flags. Throughout the film, Eisenstein uses close-ups of flags as metonyms for revolution, carried high in moments of hope and trampled underfoot in defeat. In *Potemkin*, Eisenstein creates narratives with the priest's cross and a pair of pince-nez with similar effect. He first shows the crucifix when the priest appears at the back of the ship during the initial rebellion, and taps it across one hand and then the other. It then reappears in close-up as a symbol for the priest, heralding his arrival during the fight scene. The final view of it is a repeated close-up after the priest has been captured, signalling the victory of the workers against religion as well as capitalism (see Figure 1.17).

The pince-nez are a more complex symbol in *Potemkin* because more than one character wears them. The first person is the ship's doctor, Smirnov, and Eisenstein reveals his spectacles in close-up when he is inspecting some meat. Here the shot of the maggots that have contaminated the meat is viewed through his lenses, revealing Smirnov's complicity in perpetuating the squalor. The final shot of this particular pair of spectacles is after Smirnov's death, when the dangling pince-nez become a metonym for the defeat of the middle classes (see Figure 1.18). The function of the pince-nez mutates when middle-class characters pledge their support for the revolution in Odessa. A man removes his pince-nez to weep in sympathy with the revolutionaries and a schoolmistress wearing pince-nez pledges her support for the revolution. Her defeat, like Smirnov's, is symbolised by a close-up of her smashed glasses, but now this is a moment of sorrow rather than triumph, as the middle classes too have become the victims of capitalist oppression (see Figure 1.19). It is her exploded eye that Bordwell sees as howling in close-up; the dehumanised body part and animated object come together in the associated images of pince-nez and eye.

Several commentators have seen cinema's capacity to elevate objects as creating a democracy between objects and humans. In the same year that he eulogised the cinematic hand, Léger suggested that the essence

1.17 *The cross*
Sergei Eisenstein, *Battleship Potemkin* (1925)

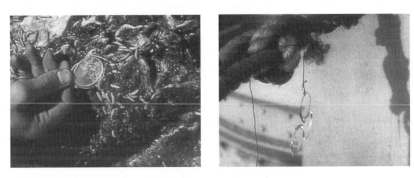

1.18 *Smirnov's pince-nez*
Sergei Eisenstein, *Battleship Potemkin* (1925)

of cinema was found in 'A pipe – a chair – a hand – an eye – a typewriter – a hat – a foot, etc. etc.'. 'In this enumeration', he explained,

> I have purposely included parts of the human body in order to emphasise the fact that in the new realism the human being, the personality, is very interesting only in these fragments and that these fragments should not be considered of any more importance than any of the other objects listed.[70]

1.19 *Defeat*
Sergei Eisenstein, *Battleship Potemkin* (1925)

Léger's point is more about formalist art than about politics, but for much of the 1920s and 1930s Left it was film's capacity to elevate objects that made it an inherently materialist, Marxist medium. 'Film mixes the *whole world* into play', said Kracauer, in 1940, 'be that world real or imagined'. He would elaborate this in his *Theory of Film*, where he writes that films are 'true to the medium to the extent that they penetrate the world before our eyes':

> film clings to the surface of things. They seem to be the more cinematic the less they focus directly on inward life, ideology, and spiritual concerns.[71]

Here 'more cinematic' comes to mean 'less personal'. The film succeeds when it decentres human consciousness, granting the material world a democratic centre stage.

Benjamin, unpacking his library, communed with his books, enjoying the intimacy ownership created between the collector and his objects. 'Not that they come alive in him', he added; 'it is he who lives in them.'[72] The human becomes more alive by being surrounded by objects. Benjamin here suggests that the ideal relationship between the human and object worlds is reciprocal. His pleasure in surrealism came from the surrealists' appreciation of objects; the surrealists were, according to him, 'less on the trail of the psyche than on the track of things'.[73] This would become clear in the 1933 surrealism exhibition held in Paris, which included fabricated objects, mathematical objects, irrational objects, mobile objects and dreamt objects. The Dadaist poet Tristan Tzara, considering the exhibition, suggested that one might see Man Ray's photograms or 'rayographs' as the dreams of objects themselves. These adventures in camera-less photography were, Tzara suggested, 'the projections, caught in transparency, by the light of tenderness, of objects that dream and that talk in their sleep'.[74]

For the Russian Constructivists, a socialist relationship between humans and objects would be less ethereal and more practical. Christina Kiaer has shown that where Marx had suggested that humans were alienated from things, the Constructivists redeemed things as comrades.[75] 'Our things in our hands must be equals, comrades', the artist Alexander Rodchenko announced in a letter in 1925, 'and not these black and mournful slaves, as they are here'. According to the designer Boris Aratov, where the commodity form rendered the object passive, fixed and dead, the socialist object would be transparent and mobile. Aratov lauded modernist design, which displayed its mode of construction and function. He was also attracted by the Americans' attitude towards their things, which they valued for their convenience and flexibility rather than for their mere exchange value. In America:

> the thing was dynamised. Collapsible furniture, moving sidewalks, revolving doors, escalators, automat restaurants, reversible outfits, and so on constituted a new stage in the evolution of material culture. The Thing became something functional and active, connected like a co-worker with human practice.[76]

The thing as co-worker, or comrade, engages its owner in a democratic relationship.

In Aratov's account, a crucial attribute of the socialist object is its mobility. This is also a quality ascribed by commentators to objects on film. 'To things and beings in their most frigid semblance', said Epstein, 'the cinema thus grants the greatest gift unto death: life'.[77] According to Leo Charney,

> For Epstein, the defamiliarising moment occurs at the intersection of mechanical reproduction and the external world. By becoming part of the photogenic, the object on screen differs from what it was before; the new context makes it a new object, even if it can be traced referentially to the concrete object that existed in front of the camera.[78]

Or, in Martin Heidegger's terms, once animated on the screen, the mere object acquires the substance and profundity of the Thing. Heidegger himself might refute this distinction. For him, the jug represented on television is a mere object, where the jug used as a jug is a Thing: 'the thingly character of the thing does not consist in its being a represented object'; instead 'the jug's thingness resides in its being *qua* vessel'.[79]

Nonetheless, movement is crucial to Heidegger's conception of the Thing; it is at the moment of pouring that 'the thing things. Thinging gathers.'[80] In granting objects life and movement, cinema could be seen to turn the object into a Heideggerian Thing.

Like Heidegger's jug, filmic objects have a potential to take on a metaphysical significance. Epstein's filmic object is linked to his more general concept of *photogénie*, which can broadly be seen as an attempt to pinpoint the ineffable in film. The lives of things on film, he said:

> are like the life in charms and amulets, the ominous, tabooed object of certain primitive religions. If we wish to understand how an animal, a plant, or a stone can inspire respect, fear, or horror, those three most sacred sentiments, I think we must watch them on the screen, living their mysterious, silent lives, alien to the human sensibility.[81]

According to Lesley Stern, in her study of things on film, certain objects are cinematically destined. These include telephones, typewriters, banknotes, guns, dark glasses, coffee cups, raindrops and teardrops, leaves blowing in the wind, kettles and cigarettes. In materialising these objects,

> the cinema invests them with pathos, renders them as moving. Cinematic apprehension simultaneously fills the objects with movement and contrives to move the viewer, to trigger a mode of knowing that is somatic, experienced through the duration of touch. This is often actualised mimetically via a gestural framing. But sometimes the cinematic thing has a capacity to touch us in more mysterious and circuitous ways, as is the case with raindrops and teardrops, and with leaves in the wind, with kettles and with cigarettes.[82]

Stern here seems bravely to theorise Epstein's rather vague sense of the sacredness of cinematic objects. Her list of inherently cinematic objects is helpful for considering both film and filmic literature, and I shall come back to the leaves blowing in the wind in particular in the discussion of Elizabeth Bowen in Chapter 6.

According to Stern, Kracauer and Epstein, the film has the capacity to unhinge the solidity of the things that it animates. By setting them in motion and offering them centre stage, it endows them with life and also reveals the ephemerality of that life. It is in this fragility that their Thingness is revealed. This is particularly clear in scenes where we see objects being broken, as is the case in the classic 1931 Gracie Fields film *Sally in Our Alley*, directed by Maurice Elvey. As a sound film, this is unusual in the weight it gives objects. Once people could actually speak, the prosopopeia granted to objects in films generally became less potent, or less noticeable. But Sally's life and personality are still to a large extent defined by the objects that surround her in her cramped flat.

The centrepiece scene occurs when the unrelentingly benevolent Sally forces her malevolent-*cum*-deranged friend Florrie to break each of her own treasured possessions, one by one. Florrie has just wrecked Sally's only chance of happiness with her fiancé, George, who has miraculously returned after she has given him up for dead. Sally hopes to make Florrie aware of the reality of her actions by forcing her into empathy. Though she abhors herself as she does it, Florrie's fascination with Sally, or her things, or both, is such that she breaks Sally's wash basin and then all her china cups and plates, spellbound by her own capacity for destruction. It is only when presented with Sally's watch, a gift from George, that Florrie's spirit breaks; she dissolves in tears and falls into the forgiving arms of her friend (see Figure 1.20). Apparently cured by this bizarre version of object therapy, she rushes off to try to repair Sally's relationship. The objects here function as obvious metonyms for the wider themes of the film. But what makes them remarkable is not their symbolic status, but their cinematic presence. At the moment of breaking – of changing states – the objects reveal themselves in all their Thingness. According to Heidegger in *Being and Time*, the breaking of an object highlights its conspicuousness, its obtrusiveness and its obstinacy.[83] The scene's power derives from the fact that the objects, at the moment of breaking, are overcharged. Nonetheless, we briefly accept the full-on tragedy of this wilful act of destruction. The objects take centre stage to the extent that they destabilise the normal course of emotional response.

The object caught at the moment of changing states, or function, is crucial in Chaplin's films. According to Bazin, where in our world 'things are tools', they 'do not serve Charlie as they serve us':

> every time that Charlie wants to use something for the purpose for which it was made, that is to say, within the framework of our society, either he goes about it in an extremely awkward fashion (especially at table) or the things themselves refuse to be used, almost it would seem deliberately.[84]

Thus in *East Street* (1917), Charlie's truncheon merely bounces off the Bully, ineffectual in his hands, but the street lamp is converted to save the day as an anaesthetist's mask. Later, in *The Gold Rush* (1925),

1.20 *Broken objects*
Maurice Elvey, *Sally in Our Alley* (1931)

Charlie in all seriousness carves his cooked shoe as though it is a chicken and, in one of the most absurd yet lyrically beautiful moments in the film, he does a miniature dance with the aid of cutlery and bread rolls. These objects draw attention to themselves in their strangeness. Unlike Heidegger's jug, they do not fulfil their function. Nonetheless, in changing function, they expose their Thingness. Animated at the point of transition, they reveal the film's potential to transform and revivify objects.

The objects in Chaplin's films are always on the verge of becoming animated. Most obviously, his hat functions both as metonym and synecdoche, representing its owner at the same time as it forms an extension of his body. The hat is frequently the subject of gags and frequently exhibits a will of its own. In *The Immigrant* (1917), the waiter removes Charlie's hat again and again, while Charlie places it back on his head, apparently perplexed, as though the hat could easily have migrated on its own accord (see Figure 1.21). The majority of Chaplin's objects function as just such an extension of his body, echoing his own restless movements. In the process, they dehumanise his body, turning him into an automaton. This is literally the case in *Modern Times*, where Charlie becomes a machine, dominated by the objects he is processing. Trotter has seen this as taking advantage of the cinema's characteristic capacity to turn its actors into automata.[85] For Trotter, as for Bazin, the actor in (at least early) cinema is always on the verge of being mechanical; the audience do not forget for long that the person seen moving on the screen is an illusion created by a machine. This is a phenomenon exploited in both *Berlin* and *The Man with a Movie Camera*, where Ruttmann and Vertov include mechanical dummies alongside the human characters. Ruttmann's film includes a surreal group of barely clad, rotating mannequins and Vertov's an animated bicycle-riding dummy.

Vertov exploits cinema's inherent mechanisation by making his automata engage with the story. At the beginning of the film, when the city still seems to be sleeping, he uses the Kuleshov effect to make it seem like the mannequins are looking at, and implicitly controlling, the city. A mannequin staring blankly into the camera is immediately juxtaposed with an eye-line match to a cityscape, suggesting that this is her city and she is surveying it before the humans awake (see Figure 1.22). Vertov first shows the bicycle-riding dummy in a still shot amidst the montage of the sleeping city. Ten minutes later, as the city wakes, the dummy learns to ride the bicycle through the aid of human legs that are juxtaposed onto the frame (see Figure 1.23). Like Chaplin,

1.21 *Charlie's hat*
Charles Chaplin, *The Immigrant* (1917)

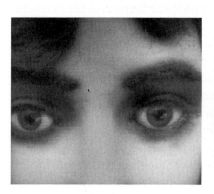

1.22 *Surveying the city*
Dziga Vertov, *The Man with a Movie Camera* (1929)

Vertov uses the mechanisation of cinema to emphasise the mechanisation of the modern city. But unlike Chaplin, Vertov approves of this mechanisation. In Soviet Russia, Stalin had just embarked on a series of five-year plans aimed to transform Russia into a major international player.[86] For Russian Marxists, the commodification of society could be fought through technology. The machine was the way forward, and

1.23 *The bicycle-riding dummy*
Dziga Vertov, *The Man with a Movie Camera* (1929)

cinema, as a machine itself, was well placed to celebrate the mechanisation of the human.

In Britain and Germany, socialists tended to follow a more romantically Marxist line in condemning the dehumanising aspects of industrialised society. Lang sets the forces of good against the machine in *Metropolis*, where the saintly figure of the real Maria finally wins the battle against the false Maria, who is an automaton created to wreak havoc on the world. *Modern Times* is in part a slapstick response to *Metropolis*, and Chaplin follows Lang's line in vilifying machines. In his lunch break, Charlie the automaton is subjected to the humiliation of being the first to try out the new automated eating machine foisted on him by the greedy factory owner. At first he is impressed by the complicated contraption, looking on with pleasure as soup is tipped into his mouth, the automatic wiper homes in on his lips and a bite of pre-chopped food is thrust towards him. However, inevitably, the machine quickly runs away with itself, much like Charlie himself, dementedly foisting soup onto his lap and attacking his face with the wiper (see Figure 1.24). Although this is a humorous scene, Chaplin indicts the greediness of the factory owner for attempting to turn even eating into a controlled, mechanical action.

Baudrillard has suggested that humans anthropomorphise automatic objects in a different way from traditional mechanical objects:

> it is no longer his gestures, his energy, his needs and the image of his body that man projects into automated objects, but instead the autonomy of his consciousness, his power of control, his own individual nature, his personhood.[87]

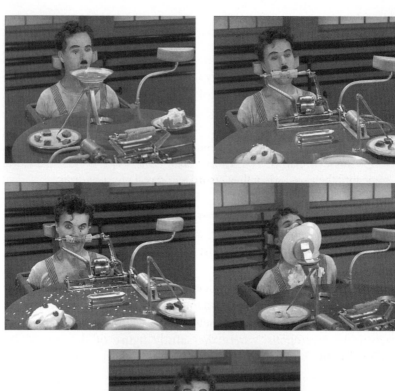

1.24 *The eating machine*
Charles Chaplin, *Modern Times* (1936)

With the eating contraption, Chaplin encourages this anthropomorphism by making Charlie into a machine at the same time as he renders the object a psychopathic version of a human. This is a democracy of people and objects taken to an extreme. In a sense, the eating machine is Aratov's ideal object. It moves in any number of ways and directions and engages precisely, and apparently intuitively, with the needs of its user. But in the cinema, where the mechanism of the medium itself has the power to turn the human into an automaton, there is always the danger that things will not merely overshadow but overwhelm their users, as their Thingness exceeds both object and human.

Indexicality

In emphasising the materiality of the cinema, Kracauer was referring specifically to the indexicality of the film medium. In this sense, Kracauer saw film as an extension of photography, writing in the original preface to his *Theory of Film*:

> film is essentially an extension of photography and therefore shares with this medium a marked affinity with the visible world around us. Films come into their own when they record and reveal physical reality.[88]

By 'marked affinity', Kracamer he meant 'physical trace'. Here he built on a theory of photography first elaborated by Charles Sanders Peirce in his work on signs. In 1895 Peirce remarked that photographs are 'instructive' because:

> we know that they are in certain respects exactly like the objects they represent. But this resemblance is due to the photographs having been produced under such circumstances that they were physically forced to correspond point by point to nature.[89]

Bazin would take this further, stating that the photograph and the object photographed share a common being, after the fashion of a fingerprint.[90] The fingerprint analogy is powerful in capturing the having-been-there of the finger or photographic object. The photograph-as-trace contains a deathly reminder of a former presence.

The cinema's indexicality appealed to filmmakers and writers in the 1930s for two, partly contradictory reasons. For the 1930s documentarists, the indexicality enabled photographers and filmmakers to go beyond mere witnessing, incorporating a trace of the world they were documenting in their art. In this sense, it went hand in hand with the cinema's capacity to use montage to make social protests and its tendency to foreground objects. At the same time, there is a competing tendency within cinema (and cinematic writing) to alienate the filmmaker and the viewer from the world on the screen. By indicating the absence of what appears to be present, the photograph-as-trace calls into question the solidity of reality itself. This ghostly aspect of photography and film had special appeal for filmmakers and writers working in the Blitz, with Bowen in particular making the most of the parallels between the ghostliness of cinema and the ghostliness of a war that was itself visually cinematic.

1.25 *The student and his double*
Henrik Galeen, *The Student of Prague* (1926)

In their capacity to retain the trace of the now absent subjects, photography and film were well suited for the portrayal of spirits. From early on, photographers did a thriving trade in the new medium of 'spirit photography'. Superimposed images were advertised as containing indexical traces of ghosts.[91] The 1913, 1926 and 1935 films of *The Student of Prague* experimented with the possibility of portraying a ghost on film. Loosely based on stories by Edgar Allan Poe and E. T. A. Hoffmann, these films recount a Faust-like pact made by a poor student, Balduin, with a Mephistophelian tempter, Scapinelli. In exchange for enough money to win the affection of a charming heiress, Balduin supplies Scapinelli with all of his possessions. Unwittingly, Scapinelli thus relinquishes his reflection, the cinematic equivalent of his soul. In the popular 1926 German Expressionist version, directed by Henrik Galeen, the snatching of the soul provides the vehicle for a virtuoso scene in which Balduin (played by Conrad Veidt) walks fearfully towards the mirror at the same time as his reflection glides towards him, breaking through the glass in an assertion of triumphant independence from the original (see Figure 1.25).

From this point, Balduin is haunted by his ghost-like double. Fighting a dual to win his beloved, in which he has promised only to scratch his opponent, he is waylaid by a broken carriage and replaced by the more malevolently inclined reflection. Despite the difference in dress (the reflection retains the poorer garb of Balduin the student, whereas the real man is now decked out in finery), it becomes increasingly hard to tell the two men apart, largely because the real Balduin falls into evil ways as he is repeatedly thwarted in his worthier projects by his alter ego. Eventually, he murders his reflection, enjoying a brief moment of triumph before he realises that the wound to his double's heart has also punctured his own (see Figure 1.26).

1.26 *Murder*
Henrik Galeen, *The Student of Prague* (1926)

The brilliance of Galeen's film lies in its equivalence of form and content. This story about an uncanny reflection is in a sense cinema's own story. There is always the danger that the actor who endows the film with a trace of his body will be eclipsed by that film, so losing his original identity. Every actor, surveying his image on screen, is faced with the uncanny doubling exploited by *The Student of Prague*. Every actor who dies on screen reappears, ghostlike, to star in subsequent films. According to a contemporary review by Noël Simsolo, this was

> perhaps the first film which speaks of cinema. A person's picture, framed like a cinema-image, is stolen . . . the actor is responsible for the deeds that this image performs in accordance with another's wishes – director or wizard.[92]

The similarity between the doubling of the mirror and the doubling of cinema is made explicit by Benjamin in his 'Work of Art' essay. Here Benjamin quotes the Italian playwright Luigi Pirandello's description of the inevitable estrangement felt by the film actor, who

> feels as if in exile – exiled not only from the stage but also from himself. With a vague sense of discomfort he feels inexplicable emptiness: his body

> loses its corporeality, it evaporates, it is deprived of reality, life, voice, and
> the noises caused by his moving about, in order to be changed into a mute
> image, flickering an instant on the screen, then vanishing into silence . . ..
> The projector will play with his shadow before the public, and he himself
> must be content to play before the camera.[93]

For Benjamin, this strangeness 'is basically of the same kind as the estrangement felt before one's own image in the mirror'.[94] *The Student of Prague* draws attention to the projector's manipulative play with the actor's shadow by exploiting the natural estrangement induced by the mirror. By illustrating the theft of the reflection, the film reminds us that cinema always steals something of its subjects, imprinting them in negative onto the film reel. This is a film that exhibits the ghostliness of cinema by drawing attention to its indexicality.

The indexical image becomes similarly uncanny in Powell and Pressburger's 1943 *The Life and Death of Colonel Blimp.* Exiled in a German hospital before the First World War, Clive Candy falls in (requited) love with the spirited governess, Edith, played by Deborah Kerr, only to misguidedly sacrifice her to his new German friend, Theo. He is unable to love again until he finds a young woman, Barbara, who bears a startling resemblance to his lost love. This is rendered all the more uncanny for the audience by the fact that Barbara, too, is played by an unaged Deborah Kerr. After his wife's death, Candy retains a shrine to his dead love(s), presided over by a painting of Kerr, in which she comes to stand for both the women he has lost. With the arrival of Theo, Candy's former friend and rival, now also widowed, the painting comes to act as a macabre bond between the two men, enabling Candy to admit that he loved Edith at the same time as he describes his yearning for his own wife.

The arrival of the third Deborah Kerr character complicates things still further, especially as Theo fails to recognise Johnny as Edith. Theo, unlike Candy, is not trapped in the past, and remembers Edith as an old woman rather than as a frozen young girl. In the guise of Johnny, Candy's feisty wartime driver, Kerr exudes bubbling presence, making Candy himself seem like a worn, absent figure. The Kerr reappearances, intersecting as they do with the filmed painting, serve to draw attention to the indexicality of the film itself. We become aware of the ease with which the same woman can appear and disappear on the celluloid. By the time that Johnny appears, we fail to suspend our disbelief, knowing that her presence is a mere trick and that she is as dead as her other two incarnations. It becomes clear that Kerr herself is as ghostly as the women she plays; she remains as impossibly absent for us as she is for Candy himself.

The tangible and the ghostly attributes of film as an indexical medium came together in the surrealist enthusiasm for photography. André Breton and Salvador Dali both appreciated the physical connection between the indexical image and the world. The surrealist use of photographs has often been seen as antithetical to the documentary impulse towards fact. Henri Lefebvre dismissed the surrealists for their tendency to 'belittle the real in favour of the magical and the marvellous'.[95] But surrealism as proposed by Breton was explicitly engaged with the political realities of its day.[96] Breton did not separate himself from reality itself but from the more conventional forms of realist art. In his surrealist manifesto, Breton described the surrealist desire

> to deepen the foundations of the real, to bring about an ever clearer and at the same time ever more passionate consciousness of the world perceived by the senses.[97]

Crucially, the results of surrealist investigations should 'be capable of facing the breath of the street'.

It was perhaps for this reason that Breton interspersed photographs throughout his 1928 novel *Nadja*, which, although ostensibly a romance, is as much a montage of Paris as a portrait of Nadja. Nadja's shabby grandeur, 'poorly dressed' and reflecting 'some obscure distress and at the same time some luminous pride', is the shabby grandeur of Paris, as it 'slides . . . burns . . . sinks into the shudder of weeds along its barricades'.[98] Nadja is defined by the places where Breton meets her: the Rue Lafayette and the Rue du Faubourg-Poissonière; the 'Nouvelle France', which is pictured in all its faded dignity in Boiffard's photograph. Breton's emphasis on the external world is aided by the indexicality of the photographic image, which imports a trace of that world into the picture.

Similarly, Dali saw the surrealist practice of incorporating actual objects within their art as an attempt to narrow the line between the image and the real. In 1931 Dali described the surrealist quest for experimental 'novelties' that would unify 'thought with the object' through some '*direct* contact with the object'.[99] In this context, Tzara's enthusiasm for Ray's 'rayographs' becomes more obvious. These photograms contained indexical traces of the world, unmediated even by the camera. For Tzara, the object's trace transmogrifies into the object's dream.

At the same time, the surrealists exploited the inherent nostalgia in the photograph's quality of having-been-there. According to Benjamin, they were the first to appreciate the 'revolutionary energies that appear in the "outmoded"'.[100] Benjamin was intrigued by Breton's relationship with the photographed objects and street scenes in *Nadja*, suggesting that Breton is 'closer to the things that Nadja is close to than to her'.[101] These scenes have a ghostly emptiness which contributes to their 'outmoded' quality. The captions of the photographs jar with the absence of people in the scenes, emphasising their strangeness. Under plate 20, a typical picture of a Paris façade framed by a lamppost and tree, the caption reads: 'we have our dinner served outside by the wine seller'. However, neither Breton and Nadja, nor the wineseller, nor even the seating for the café is visible in the picture. And it is the indexicality of the images that in part accounts for the ghostliness of the street scenes. Witnessing the traces of light thrown on the negative by these objects, we are reminded that the objects once had a physical existence.

Arguably, the film medium emphasises its own indexicality most overtly when it engages specifically with photography. This is achieved in two ways. Either photographs can be included as objects on film, or the film still or photogram can be suspended on the screen, reminding us that the movement of the cinema is the illusionary product of a series of still frames. Photographs-as-objects are particularly prevalent in war films of the period, where they are often used to stand for an absent loved one. This happens in *Sally in Our Alley* where George, seemingly crippled by war, bids a sad farewell to his photograph of his fiancée, treating it as the indexical *memento mori* Kracauer, Barthes and Sontag saw it as.[102] Sally, left alone, relies on George's photograph to stand as a proxy lover and is annoyed when Florrie carelessly covers it up with her movie-star pinups (see Figure 1.27). Left alone with George, Florrie denies Sally's love for him by hiding his photograph in her drawer. It is with the discovery of the photograph that Sally becomes aware of her friend's treachery. Meanwhile, George has been led back to Sally partly by the photograph of her he still carries in his wallet – a possession which Florrie stealthily purloins, depriving him of his metonymic lover at the same time as she steers him away from the real woman. It is significant that these photographs are by now several years old. Although Sally and George do manage to repair their relationship, the ageing of the photographs makes it clear that the original loved one is effectively dead to the world. The war has acted like the camera itself in freezing their memories of each other at a lost moment in time that can never be recovered.

1.27 *Photographs*
Maurice Elvey, *Sally in Our Alley* (1931)

Three avant-garde city symphonies in this period are often cited as exploiting the frozen photogram. In America, Paul Strand made the first city symphony, *Manhatta* (1921), out of a series of stills; in Russia, Vertov engaged in an Eadweard Muybridge-like experiment with stilled motion in *The Man with a Movie Camera*; and in Germany, Curt and Robert Siodmak stilled time in their city symphony-*cum-actualité*, *People on Sundays* (1929).[103] Rudolf Arnheim discussed the phenomenon in his 1933 *Film*, suggesting that:

> A still photograph inserted in the middle of a moving film gives a very curious sensation; chiefly because the time character of the moving shots is carried over to the still picture, which therefore looks uncannily petrified.[104]

Arnheim mentions *People on Sundays*, a film in which the use of photograms draws attention to the physical absence of the characters from the spectator. The absence is more poignant because they are actual Berliners, rather than actors, caught on camera during what appears to be an ordinary Sunday. Our knowledge that these are ordinary people makes their presence stronger and more surprising. While watching the film, it is easy to believe that Wolf, Brigitte and Annie have been energetically present, arguing in this room, swimming on this lake, kissing on those dunes. By inserting the freeze-frames, the directors acknowledge the presence of the reel of film, making the characters at once more tangibly present (in the traces they have left on the celluloid) and irretrievably absent. These frozen moments when Christl smiled or Wolfgang waved his arms in the air can never return.

Initially, the directors freeze the film with no explanation, a split second at a time. It is not clear if there is merely an error in the projection or if it is an artistic decision. The freezes then become longer, so that the film seems to be played in a bizarre slow-motion. Finally, they are given a diegetic context when a photographer arrives on the beach to take people's photographs. As in *The Man with a Movie Camera*, the photographer's presence makes the film meta-cinematic, drawing attention to the artificiality of the medium. His appearance also makes the connotations of the frozen frames thematically explicit. These people have their photograph taken because they want to remember the happiness of their day by the lake. There is nostalgia already present within the moment, which the film medium makes it its business to capture.

The inserted photogram is not always specifically photographic. Garrett Stewart suggests that Arnheim was mistaken in seeing the stills in *People on Sundays* as resulting from a 'photographic' interpolation into the film, 'rather than a reprinting of its own cellular constituents'.[105] The presence of the photographer in *People on Sundays* seems to refute this, but I think Stewart's analysis of the photogram applies better than Arnheim's to *The Man with a Movie Camera*. For Stewart, the photogram is what has 'always and already' become of the image of celluloid strip when 'the single print cell is stirred forward from the photographic into the filmic on the way toward the cinematic'.[106] The frozen still marks the convergence of two time schemes, those of the presentation (the diegetic story) and the narration, subordinating the former to the latter so that the cinema is revealed through meta-cinema.[107]

Vertov uses the photogram to explore the mechanics of movement, splitting the movements and gestures of people and even, in an overt allusion to Muybridge, horses, into their component parts (see Figure 1.28). Aided by the presence of the energetically moving cameraman and editor, the viewer is never allowed to forget that this is a film being

1.28 *The anatomy of motion*
Dziga Vertov, *The Man with a Movie Camera* (1929)

edited rather than a display of photographs, as in *Manhatta*. Deleuze
suggests that this is no longer the moment when motion stops, but the
instant when motion changes. For him, the photogram 'does not "ter-
minate" the movement without also being the principle of its accelera-
tion, its deceleration and its variation'.[108] Where in *People on Sundays*
time does seem to be suspended, in *The Man with a Movie Camera* it is
not time but motion that is suspended, and there is always the promise
that the motion will continue. In drawing attention to the indexicality
of his film, Vertov draws our attention also to its filmicness. This is
cinema at its most triumphantly meta-cinematic, defying time through
artifice.

In some ways, the indexicality of the film separates cinema irrevocably from literature. Literature can engage in its own meta-textual
version of meta-cinema, but the differences between the two practices
merely illustrate the differences between the two media. However,
the text has the power to exploit the deathly nostalgia evoked by the
indexicality of the film when it includes either photographs or freeze-
frames within its narrative or diegesis. Thus, we find Proust famously
exploring mortality by envisaging his living grandmother as a photograph; a photographic moment that forms the basis for Kracauer's
own meditations on photography and death in his 'Photography'
essay.[109]

My discussion in this chapter has hovered around the terms 'absence'
and 'presence', which film theorists from Kracauer, to Bazin, to Cavell,
to Trotter have seen as fundamental to both photography and film.
Woolf, in her essay on 'The Cinema', sees cinematic beauty as created
by the cinema's gift of absence. We behold 'the King, the boat, the
horse'

as they are when we are not there. We see life as it is when we have no part
in it . . . From this point of vantage, as we watch the antics of our kind, we
have time to feel pity and amusement . . . we have time to open our minds
wide to beauty and register on top of it the queer sensation – this beauty
will continue, and this beauty will flourish whether we behold it or not.[110]

According to Cavell, photography 'maintains the presentness of the
world by accepting our absence from it'. Films do not so much present
us with the world as permit 'us to view it unseen'.[111] Here he echoes
both Woolf and the 1920s film critic Alexander Bakshy who, as Laura
Marcus has pointed out, figured 'absence' as 'invisible presence'. In a
1927 review, Bakshy describes the spectator as acquiring the ability to
be 'invisibly present in the very midst of the events he observes, and of
following them from place to place'.[112] It is in these terms that Stern
reads what she sees as the quintessentially cinematic trope of leaves
blown by the wind. According to Stern, leaves rustling in the breeze
can be read 'as an acute example of cinema's capacity to register a
world as if caught "off-guard"'.[113] This off-guardness fascinates the
cinematic viewer, luring us into what Kracauer might see as a suicidal
urge to contemplate simultaneously the world as it would be without
us and the world as it once has been.

For Cavell, the unseen quality of the cinematic world necessitates
a political question. According to Marcus, central to Cavell's thesis
in *The World Viewed* is the question 'what do we wish to view in this
way?'[114] This question resonates strongly with the 1930s engagement
with cinema. For the documentarists or the Mass-Observers, the
answer would be not the leaves drifting to the ground but the working
classes – the London slum-dwellers, the Blackpool crowds, the northern coalminers. In this case, cloaked in invisible presentness, the
viewer would be able to learn about the lives of the less fortunate with a
new objectivity. But the majority of the observers and documentarists
were aware that this illusion of objectivity was false. The films that bore
the index of their subjects also bore the traces of the cameraman. The
next chapter will investigate the will-to-invisible presence of the 1930s
documentary movement.

CHAPTER 2

Mass Observing: The 1930s Documentary Gaze

In seeking to be at once invisible and present, the documentarists were destined to fail. They could not be simultaneously present and absent, any more than they could be objective witnesses of subjective scenes. The contradictions inherent in the documentary movement as a whole were encapsulated by Mass-Observation, which was unable to succeed on its own terms. Its aims were at once surrealist and anthropological, poetic and scientific. Jennings, Harrisson and Madge wanted to survey the masses empirically at the same time as they wanted to get to know them as individuals, creating a democracy of witnessing in which everyone could be an observer. They intended to analyse mass behaviour, using it to explain or even decode society, and to allow the voices of their subjects to speak for themselves.

The documentary writers and filmmakers, though generally less all-encompassing in their demands, were equally unsure about their relationship with their subjects and about the desirability of analysis within their work. The middle-class documentarists were unclear about whether they wanted to mingle with the workers or to observe them unseen. Part of the hope of the decade lay in thinking that it might be possible to join the working class. But even before Orwell chastised them for their boy scout idealism, Auden, Isherwood and Spender were ruefully aware of their privileged vantage point. And although Spender wanted to get to know the workers, he also hoped to analyse them from afar, developing an English version of Soviet social realism. He insisted that the socialist artist was obliged to '[realise] in his work the ideas of a classless society', 'applying those ideas to the life around him, and giving them their reality'.[1]

The notion of 'reality', and with it 'realism', which was used very widely in the 1930s, was itself a source of contradictions. According to Grierson's colleague Paul Rotha, 'realism' developed in documentary film at the point when the filmmakers themselves 'got down to the themes and materials under its nose' with a 'closer observation of work and workers than the Russians'.[2] Andrew Higson sees this realism as resting on separate, but not irreconcilable, claims to authenticity of setting (a 'surface realism') and moral realism (a commitment to a left-wing set of social problems and a desire to solve them).[3] Grierson states in his article on 'Documentary Film' that the 'basic force' behind the creation of the documentary film units was 'social not aesthetic'; 'We were, I confess, sociologists, a little worried about the way the world was going.'[4] At the same time, Grierson was open to what Higson describes as 'poetic realism', which is evident in Grierson's own catch-phrase, 'the creative treatment of actuality'.[5]

The documentarists were aware of the paradox that the Marxist theorist Fredric Jameson has pointed out in the phrase 'representation of the real'. According to Jameson, 'the emphasis on this or that type of truth content will clearly be undermined by any intensified awareness of the technical means or representational artifice of the work itself'. It is impossible to believe what you are representing is real if you are aware of the process of representation. Instead, it is likely that in attempting 'to shore up the epistemological vocation of the work', the artist is suppressing its 'formal properties' and denying its nature as representation. But for Jameson, 'no viable conception of realism is possible unless both of these demands or claims are honoured simultaneously, prolonging and preserving – rather than "resolving" – this constitutive tension and incommensurability'.[6] The British documentarists attempted to resolve this paradox by emphasising the process of representation through a poetic approach and by simultaneously understating that process of representation by downplaying aesthetics.

This chapter disentangles the hopes and achievements of the 1930s observers, investigating the multiple and complex viewpoints that were combined in the documentary gaze. It also explores the way that filmic technique, and in particular cross-class montage, enabled documentary writers to present their material on its own (subjective) terms, at the same time as subjecting it to analysis. By using cross-class montage, they made their own role in the process of representation explicit, at the same time as they tried to eliminate themselves from the individual scenes in a quest for both invisibility and realism.

The helmeted airman versus the figure in the crowd

Mass-Observation, GPO films, W. H. Auden, George Orwell

A generation of filmmakers and writers were, like Spender, committed to bringing Soviet social realism to England. As a Communist doctrine, social realism was first brought to international public attention at the All Union Congress of Soviet Writers held in Moscow in August 1934.[7] In the proceedings of the conference, published in Britain later that year, the Communist Party functionary Andrei Zhdanov stated that the heroes of the new Soviet literature were 'the active builders of a new life – working men and women'.[8] The Soviet manifestos appealed to the British intelligentsia clustered around the *Left Review*, partly because they offered a more forceful version of their own rhetoric. Julian Bell, Woolf's nephew, who would die fighting for the Republicans in the Spanish Civil War, stated that 'being socialist for us means being rationalist, commonsense, empirical; means a very firm extrovert, practical, commonplace sense of exterior reality'.[9] Left-wing writers in Britain agreed that such a commonplace exterior reality would be attained through representing working-class life.

1930s writers wanting to attract and represent the working classes turned to films for subject matter as well as technique. One of the chief attractions of cinema was that it allowed the working classes to speak for themselves, whether in Gracie Fields films or GPO documentaries. Edgar Anstey's *Housing Problems* (1935) contrasts the condition in the slums with the new social housing, aided by a series of working-class talking heads. Films like *Housing Problems* provide a visual counterpoint for a series of literary exercises happening in the same period under the auspices of *Fact,* the *Left Review* and the Left Book Club. In 1934 *Left Review* ran a competition for workers to describe a morning on an ordinary day. They published the nine winning extracts alongside an enthusiastic commentary by *Left Review* editor Amabel Williams-Ellis, suggesting that more established literary figures might find much to emulate in the efforts of the workers: 'there is not a novelist writing today who has not got something to learn here. We claim that LEFT REVIEW puts fresh material before them.'[10]

Already in the late 1920s, socialist novelists had made a concerted effort to tackle working-class subject matter. In 1926 H. H. Barbor published *Against the Red Sky*, in which a middle-class hero helps the workers to take power in England. 1929 saw the publication of both Henry Green's *Living* and the translation of the German writer Leonhard Frank's 1927 *Carl and Anna*, which the *Sunday Worker* rather extravagantly described as the 'revolutionary' 'first love story ever written in which the lovers are working people'.[11]

The attempt to represent the working classes brought with it a series of ethical questions and challenges. Most crucial was the dilemma of positioning. There was the danger that the observer would end up patronising his (or occasionally her) subjects, either by looking down on them or by being too chummy. The hazards of surveying the working classes from too great a height had been revealed in the late nineteenth century by writers who were part of the Into Unknown England movement. This was a genre of writing documenting intrepid trips into the slums, factories or workhouses made by upper- and middle-class well-wishers. Kathryn and Philip Dodd have suggested that 'the titles and subjects of some of the writings could serve for the much later projects of the documentary film-makers'. Certainly, titles like Lady Bell's *At the Works* (1907), Stephen Reynolds' *A Poor Man's House* (1909) and George R. Sims' *How the Poor Live* (1883) sit comfortably with both Griersonian documentary film and Orwellian documentary literature.[12]

In 1866 James Greenwood published *A Night in a Workhouse*, which can be seen as a direct precursor to Orwell's *The Road to Wigan Pier*. Greenwood documents the trials of a night spent among the homeless, an experiment that the editor of the *Morning Post* described as 'An act of bravery . . . which ought to entitle him to the VC'.[13] Greenwood makes no attempt to become intimate with the other inmates. Indeed, he is so far from seeing them as fellow men that he views them as a collection of corpses:

> Some were stretched out at full length; some lay nose and knees together; some with an arm or a leg showing crooked through the coverlet. It was like the result of a railway accident: these ghastly figures were awaiting the coroner.[14]

He distances himself from them morally as well as physically, describing their jokes as 'so obscene as to be absolutely appalling'. The reader is expected to sympathise with his disgust at the bread he is supposed to eat and to admire his ingenious attempt to give it away: 'You may have half of it, old pal, if you're hungry.'[15]

Perhaps the most disturbing similarities between the Into Unknown England writing and the 1930s documentary comes from the specifically anthropological gaze. The Dodds have pointed out the parallels between Sims' sense of the need to travel 'into a dark continent that is within easy walking distance of the General Post Office' and Grierson's desire to 'travel dangerously into the jungles of Middlesborough and the Clyde'.[16] The whole project of Mass-Observation, with its anthropological outlook, is in danger of taking on this perspective. Harrisson, who was the primary mover behind Mass-Observation's development after 1938, notoriously stated that his

> experience living among the cannibals in the New Hebrides . . . taught me the many points in common between these wild looking, fuzzy haired, black smelly people and our own, so when I came home from that expedition I determined to apply the same methods here in Britain.[17]

Of course, Harrisson did see Harrow students as well as East End slum-dwellers as cannibalistic subjects worthy of the anthropologist's scrutiny.[18] Nonetheless, Harrisson's and Grierson's statements reveal anthropologically-minded documentarists who were happy to survey their subjects from a considerable distance. 'From the beginning', Grierson would say, the documentary film was 'an adventure in public observation'.[19]

The solution to the more patronising aspect of these attempts at objective witnessing was proposed by Storm Jameson in her 1937 'Documents' essay. Jameson begins this with a social-realist-inspired demand for 'writing concerned with the lives of men and women in a world which is changing and being changed' (p. 9). She sees this commitment to change as specifically 'revolutionary' but suggests, unlike Spender in his 1935 article, that socialist literature need not 'concern itself only or mainly with working-class life':

> The process of change, of decay, of growth, is taking place everywhere all the time: it does not matter where you open up the social body if you know what you are looking for. (p. 10)

For Jameson, the middle-class novelist generally fails in his attempt to write a proletarian novel because 'too much of his energy runs away in an intense interest in and curiosity about his feelings'. The socialist writer must learn that there is 'no value in the emotions'. In order to move his readers, he must keep his own emotions in the background; if he goes on a journey to the slums, he must react objectively (p. 11).

Jameson recommends a mode of observation akin to the 'participant observation' advocated by 1930s social anthropologists such as Bronislaw Malinowski, a champion and critic of Mass-Observation. In

Malinowski's doctrine, the ethnographer has to attune himself to his host culture, immersing himself and following the cultural practices of the native. However, at the same time as going native, he has to maintain an objective distance which he would express through the metalanguage of the ethnographer. He must strive for 'self-elimination', for independence from 'the idiosyncrasies of the individual mind'.[20] Jameson sees Orwell as approaching the ideal participant observer in the first half of *The Road to Wigan Pier* (1937), where she lauds him for living among his subjects but still observing them clearly. Jameson's suggestion that the writer should give 'an objective report' may seem naïve, but her 'objective' seems to imply a lack of subjectivity more than an actual scientific empiricism. She is fully aware that the process of presentation itself will be more subjective. It is here that she brings in the documentary film:

> Perhaps the nearest equivalent of what is wanted exists already in another form in the documentary film. As the photographer does, so must the writer keep himself out of the picture while working ceaselessly to present the *fact* from a striking (poignant, ironic, penetrating, significant) angle . . . His job is not to tell us what he felt, but to be coldly and industriously presenting, arranging, selecting, discarding from the mass of his material to get the significant detail, which leaves no more to be said, and implies everything. (pp. 15–16)

Presumably Jameson might incur the scorn of Karen Jacobs or Susan Sontag for implying that the camera can have unmediated access to reality.[21] In fact, in recommending that the cameraman keeps himself out of the picture, she seems to suggest no more than a literal separation of observer from observed. The cameraman is physically unable simultaneously to film and be filmed, and Jameson proposes that the writer should likewise keep the spotlight away from himself. But she is fully aware of the creative role of choice and interpretation and, like Isherwood in his 'I am a camera' passage, conscious of the crucial role played by the subjective process of editing.[22] The documentary book, like the film, will be poignant and ironic; there is still room for aesthetics in this version of socialist art.[23]

This distanced, public observation is evident in the majority of documentary films produced by Grierson's film unit, including the experimental *Coal Face* (1935), which contains poetry by Auden and music by Benjamin Britten. Like Grierson's epoch-building *Drifters*, *Coal Face* has a Marxist focus on the process of production, charting the journey of coal from mine to domestic hearth. It is a classic documentary, informing the viewer through a detailed commentary, spoken in deep, authoritarian tones and including statistics and maps. Sections are devoted to explanations of devices such as the 'Davy safety lamp', and the film explains not only the production but also the distribution of coal. The gaze remains distanced and public; we rarely see any miner as an individual. This is the documentary gaze described by Andrew Higson, who writes that the 1930s documentary shifted the camera angle from the Hollywood point-of-view shot to a more 'public gaze' which '[enacts] the moral and physical separation of the documentarist from his or her object of investigation'.[24] We tend to see the miners in groups that are too large and too dimly lit for any character to be singled out.

The more innovative aspects of the film serve to reinforce the abstraction. The director Alberto Cavalcanti uses artistic camerawork, often shooting the men from a skewed angle or strangely cropping the frame, which thwarts our identification with them through a Brechtian *Verfremdungseffekt* (see Figure 2.1). Similarly, the dissonant score composed by Britten refuses to be merely harmonious and ignorable background music. Consequently, it reminds us that we are watching

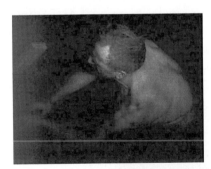
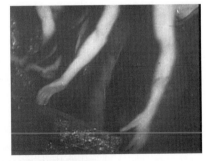

2.1 *Artistic camerawork*
Alberto Cavalcanti, *Coal Face* (1935)

2.2 *A miner eating*
Alberto Cavalcanti, *Coal Face* (1935)

a film, rendering the miners a spectacle to be viewed from without. The music continues even into the shot where the film comes closest to portraying an individual, which shows a single miner hurriedly eating (see Figure 2.2).

Lacking individuating detail, the film presents the everyday life of the workers symbolically. *Coal Face* emphasises both the heroism and the plight of the workers. Elizabeth Cowie writes that it portrays the miners as 'muscular rather than brutish', and the frequent shots of semi-naked miners do present them as heroically strong.[25] At the same time, we are not allowed to forget the appalling conditions in which they work. As the music builds to a climax, the commentary informs us that one in five miners is injured. We then see a fragile hand hammering a nail into a track and are reminded of the frailty of the human body.

In Malinowski's or Jameson's terms, Mass-Observation failed, at least in its early years, to maintain the objectivity found in films like *Coal Face*. Malinowski himself took Mass-Observation to task for the extent to which they left their material to speak for itself. He was particularly disappointed by *May the Twelfth* (1937), the first book published by Mass-Observation, which was intended to be the literary equivalent of the disconnected montage film.[26] In planning the book, Humphrey Jennings and Charles Madge commissioned hundreds of accounts of the coronation of George VI, hoping for some revealing class contrasts. The results are self-consciously cinematic. The editors describe themselves as obtaining 'three kinds of focus': 'close-up and long shot, detail and ensemble were all provided'.[27] They also affiliate themselves with the documentary tradition, claiming that the material is 'arranged in a simple documentary way' (p. 347). In line with the documentary, the authors do provide lengthy explanations of the day at the beginning of the book, interpreting the ceremony through Freudian analysis and sociology. They also use the editing process to comment on the class system. Stuart Laing has compared *May the Twelfth* to Sommerfield's *May Day* given their mutual focus on a single ceremonial day and the use of montage in both.[28] Like Sommerfield, who would go on to work for Mass-Observation in Bolton, Jennings and Madge interrogate the usual class distinctions with a version of cinematic cross-class montage. Ben Highmore writes:

> the collaging of day-surveys could bring an account of a day in the life of a wealthy suburban woman (entirely 'ordinary' in itself), into collision with the same day as experienced by a working woman in Glasgow to produce a shocking contrast, which not only vivifies both accounts, but allows them both to be defamiliarised, made strange.[29]

It is ironic that a self-styled 'Platonist' who opposes the coronation on Marxist grounds, spending the morning defiantly reading Communist manifestos, is immediately followed by an apparently genuinely working-class woman who is uninterested in Marxism or the coronation, complaining 'Sod the Pope and everything – if there's one thing that maddens me, it's electric fuses' (p. 319). The fact that neither the Platonist nor the working-class woman care about the coronation itself unites the two classes. At the same time, there is a surreal humour in the way that the enjoyably practical working-class irritation with the coronation thwarts the more ponderous Marxist concern of the upper-class Platonist. A similar effect occurs when a bank clerk reading *The Road to Wigan Pier* is juxtaposed with a housewife near Birmingham, who is unaware of herself as part of a subjugated proletariat.

Nonetheless, Malinowski is right to suggest that the analysis in the book is implicit. *May the Twelfth* was compiled by two surrealist poets without much input from Harrisson, Mass-Observation's only resident anthropologist. Unlike Sommerfield's novel, which I discuss later in this chapter, *May the Twelfth* does not expound a particular message or allow the reports to function symbolically. This has earned it the approval of later critics, who tend to like it for exactly the reasons that Malinowski disapproved of it. For Malinowski, the 'essential difficulty' in the way of Mass-Observation is its openness to subjectivity and to different points of view. He is anxious about Madge and Harrisson's unapologetic statement that 'Mass-Observation has always assumed that its untrained Observers would be *subjective* cameras, each with his or her own individual distortion'.[30] According to Malinowski, these statements are at best 'the subject matter on which further scientific analysis is indispensable'; the 'standard or ideal towards which the movement must progress is that of objective work'.[31] Rod Mengham, returning to Mass-Observation in 2001, finds more to admire in the subjectivity of the observers. He suggests that the 1930s gaze polarised into two perspectives. Above there is the point of view of the 'hawk' or 'helmeted airman' which Auden assumes in his 1930 poem 'Consider this and in our time'. Here the poet's lofty role is to command reader, 'supreme Antagonist' and financier to 'look', 'pass on', 'join', 'view', 'mobilise'. He has privileged access to a sweeping bird's, aeroplane's or camera-eye view, and can announce authoritatively that 'The game is up'.[32] Below there is the Mass-Observer, 'the figure in the crowd, whose view is frequently obscured by other passers-by and by traffic'.[33] The observers in *May the Twelfth* are just such figures, jostling each other in a crowded text that refuses to allow precedence to any of its voices.

There are few 1930s left-wing writers, filmmakers or photographers who did not aspire to be the figure in the crowd, though it is debatable how many succeeded. 'The men, I loved them', announced Henry Green in a rather embarrassing interview for the *Star* about his work in the factory. 'They are . . . splendid pals.'[34] 'The working classes, who are always spoken of as something apart, are really very like other people', Isherwood later recalled thinking, when about to plunge himself into life in the Berlin slums.[35]

At best, the observer who becomes the figure in the crowd avoids the problem of seeing the masses as masses. The notion of the 'mass' was problematic within an English liberal context, even if the Communist leaders themselves were happy to define the proletariat as masses. In Germany in the late 1930s, Benjamin used 'masses' favourably, contrasting this new class of empowered workers – the 'newly created proletarian masses' – with the nineteenth-century working classes.[36] For Benjamin, the German working class had been 'corrupted' by the notion that it was moving with the current, while the 'masses' were the hopeful inheritors of a decaying civilisation, whose mass-produced art could provide a redemptive political force.[37] But few British writers in the 1930s can have identified with Lenin's statement, quoted favourably by Spender in his 1935 *Left Review* article, that art ought to 'extend with deep roots into the very thick of the broad toiling masses'.[38]

Raymond Williams has pointed out that in England at least the word 'masses' was a new term for 'mob', retaining the traditional characteristics of the mob with its 'gullibility, fickleness, herd-prejudice, lowness of taste and habit'. According to Williams, 'mass-thinking, mass-suggestion, mass-prejudice would threaten to swamp considered individual thinking and feeling'.[39] This is certainly true in Mass-Observation's account of the mass-suggestions of the newspapers and the mass-thinking they occasioned.[40] Madge, as well as Harrisson, saw himself as investigating the 'inarticulate masses'.[41] In seeking to reclaim the masses, Harrisson and fellow observers did not avoid stereotypes. While doing their best to enjoy the mass playground of Blackpool, the middle-class Mass-Observers who followed the Bolton workers there in 1937 were appalled both by the size of the crowds and by their homogeneity. On a fine day in September they found 10,000 people on the beaches; on bank holidays they estimated 40,000. They were troubled by these numbers and by the reported seven million people who visited Blackpool each year. 'No other place in England can show a comparable scene', said Tom Harrisson, who found it all the more disturbing that the crowds were an attraction rather than a deterrence to potential visitors. Blackpool even used its 'crush photos for publicity'.[42] Harrisson was bothered that Blackpool attracted a crowd who accepted their mass identity; few Mass-Observers would have disagreed with Williams that 'the masses are always the others, whom we don't know, and can't know' and that we do not think of ourselves as masses.[43]

For Williams, 'there are in fact no masses; there are only ways of seeing people as masses'.[44] Orwell might have agreed, arguing that the Auden brigade evinced this patronising mode of seeing. The Communist critic of the *Daily Worker* in turn would accuse Orwell of committing the sin he condemned and remaining merely 'a disillusioned little middle-class boy'.[45] The Mass-Observers put into practice one way of 'seeing people as masses' in their choice of name and project.

Defenders of one or other aspect of the 1930s documentary project tend to see the books, films or photographs in question as escaping this way of seeing and allowing a degree of individuality to emerge. In his defence of Mass-Observation, Ben Highmore proposes that it is where Mass-Observation fails on its own terms that it avoids seeing its subjects as masses. He argues that in combining surrealism with anthropology, they failed as anthropologists, blurring the boundary between 'native informant' and 'participant observer'. He sees Mass-Observation as being 'most productive' when engaged in the 'radically democratic project' of treating the natives themselves as ethnographers.[46] Where Malinowski's projects relied on the cultural separation between the observer and observed, this separation was impossible in Bolton where everyone became an observer. As a result, the Mass-Observation publications were more collages than anthropological studies. Rather than commenting on everyday life, they provided 'conditions for participation in the alteration of everyday life'.[47] For Highmore, at its best, Mass-Observation enabled every member of the crowd to become an autonomous, observing individual. The masses could avoid being the subjects of a Foucauldian surveillance by gazing back, surveying the surveyer in a more equal battle.

Elizabeth Cowie has defended Anstey's *Housing Problems* in similar terms. Detractors of *Housing Problems* have pointed out that the working classes may speak for themselves, but they are still seen as part of the mass. The film begins with a high-angle shot of the slum area, with the camera moving the viewer slowly into the slums from the outside, and we are never given the visual point of view of the occupiers (see Figure 2.3). Kathryn and Philip Dodd write:

> the camera keeps a discreet distance, it simply looks and allows its audience to examine poor people in their own houses. What the film shows is that these people need our help and that we have nothing to fear if we provide them with better homes.[48]

In this reading, *Housing Problems* is a lesson in surveillance. We learn to survey the working classes, who in turn internalise the surveillance and behave benignly. Cowie has defended the filmmakers from these Foucauldian charges on the grounds that the documentary film 'does not simply and wholly control the terms of its own reading' and therefore cannot be aligned with the scopic regimes of the prison or medical gaze.[49] She suggests that the verisimilitude of *Housing Problems* is undermined by the awkwardness of the speakers and the strangeness of the decorative objects that surround them. The social reality that

2.3 *Surveying the slums*
E. H. Anstey, Arthur Elton, *Housing Problems* (1935)

emerges is 'not fully contained by the film's documentary discourse' and the actors speak poetically through gesture and intonation.[50] For Cowie, documentary is a '*performance* of the specular through film as discourse'; we learn about looking in the process of looking, and in doing so we abandon our lofty viewing point.[51]

The split between the helmeted airman and the figure in the crowd was not a simple dichotomy. Many filmmakers and writers who wanted to mingle with the crowd were anxious that this would be a disingenuous position to adopt. In a sense Mengham's formulation of the Mass-Observer's gaze is more idealistic than that of most 1930s documentarists. Several middle-class writers were anxiously aware of their own hawk-like status and made clear their privileged vantage point in their texts. In MacNeice's 1933 poem *Birmingham*, the poet identifies himself in the first person plural with the working classes who indulge in 'Saturday thrills':

> Next week-end it is likely in the heart's funfair we shall pull
> Strong enough on the handle to get back our money.[52]

But in his 1939 *Autumn Journal*, MacNeice exposes his own separation from the workers during his time in Birmingham, making himself the subject of his own cross-class montage. 'We lived in Birmingham through the slump', he says, contrasting his own 'comfortable' life, 'with two in a bed and patchwork cushions', with the life of the unemployed who surround him and who is he only half aware of:

> the queues of men and the hungry chimneys . . .
> Little on the plate and nothing in the post. (pp. 115–16)

Spender grapples with the question of the poetic gaze when surveying the poor who beg 'In railways, on pavements near the traffic' in his 1933 Poem XXX. 'No, I shall weave no tracery of pen-ornament', he proclaims here, 'To make them birds upon my singing-tree'. He refuses to join the crowd, knowing that any sense of mutual struggle will be false when he will always wield both pen and singing-tree. At the same time, he rejects the hawk's view, refusing the wider picture 'Traced on our graphs through history', recognising that time 'never heals, far less transcends'.[53]

I shall suggest in Chapter 3 that the loftiness of the camera eye in Auden's 'Consider this and in our time' is less straightforward than it seems. Moreover, nine years later, writing in a war zone in China,

Auden would make the dangers of the position of the helmeted airman explicit. In the sonnet sequence in *Jouney to a War*, Auden and Isherwood's account of their travels round China during the Sino-Japanese war, Auden condemns the pilots who reduce the 'breathing city' into a 'target which / Requires their skill'.[54] This book came after Auden's involvement in Grierson's film unit in the mid-1930s, after he had lost his enthusiasm for the documentary film. This enthusiasm should in itself not be forgotten. Auden takes undeniable joy in the fast, train-like rhythm of his commentary in *Night Mail*, and seems to have thrown himself wholeheartedly into translating Vertov's *Three Songs about Lenin* (1934) for a London Film Society showing in 1935.[55] David Collard suggests that Auden relished the peculiar challenges of 'composing verses timed to accompany a rapid, headlong montage sequence' for his subtitles.[56] It also seems that Auden was able to bring together a 1930s enthusiasm for cinema with a similarly timely 1930s enthusiasm for Leninist socialism. There is an apparent sincerity in his liberally translated verses, which describe a slave escaping from darkness to light once he has learnt the 'truth' from the great leader, who gave 'his brain, his blood, his heart'.[57]

But by the time of *Journey to a War*, Auden's disillusionment with the documentary film movement had set in. His distrust is made explicit in his 1937 *Letters from Iceland*, discussed in Chapter 4. In *Journey to a War*, it is evident in Auden's and Isherwood's mutual recognition of the dangers inherent in the hawk-like camera eye view of the documentary form, with both writers problematising their position as observers in the text and photographs. This is apparent in Auden's harrowing photograph of a toothless old woman begging by a train, part of a sequence called 'Train Parasites'. Here he positions the woman at the bottom of the frame, giving the bulk of the space to the rails of the track. This reminds the viewer that Auden himself is seated in the train above the woman, shielded from her poverty by the walls of his first-class carriage. He makes his role in the situation more visible in the two photographs grouped by the heading 'Refugees in camp'. The first includes a portion of a sleek black car at the edge of the frame, which contrasts with the shanty huts and rags, reminding us that Auden and Isherwood will get back in the car and drive off to their comfortable living quarters. There is also the implicit suggestion of power in the car, which seems taller than the huts because of the perspective. We are aware that the car has the strength to run over the entire settlement. The photo below this shows a group of children, smiling curiously at the camera. Here Auden highlights his own presence by reflecting it in his subjects' smiling faces, refusing to play the part of the figure in the crowd. It is clear that they are welcoming the mysterious foreigner with a camera into their lives, and this makes Auden appear disingenuous, as he is there merely to observe and not to help.

In the cross-class montage in *Journey to a War*, Auden and Isherwood place themselves firmly on the side of the privileged bourgeoisie, implicitly questioning their right to speak for the suffering masses. In sonnet 19, Auden contrasts the 'lawns and cultured flowers' of the International Settlement in Shanghai with the 'land laid waste, with all its young men slain' which is the reality of the city, juxtaposing garden and waste land (p. 277). Later, he makes it clear that they themselves reside in the gardens:

> in an international and undamaged quarter,
> Casting our European shadows on Shanghai . . .
> We are compelled to realise that our refuge is a sham. (p. 291)

Similarly, Isherwood states:

> In this city the gulf between society's two halves is too grossly wide for any bridge. There can be no compromise here. And we ourselves, though we wear out our shoes walking the slums, though we take notes, though we are genuinely shocked and indignant, belong, unescapably, to the other world. We return, always, to Number One House for lunch. (p. 252)

The journalist-poets, whom Valentine Cunningham has described as 'bright young [Baedeckers]', were self-conscious enough to realise their distance from the life they observed.[58]

The contradictions inherent in the documentary gaze come together in Orwell's 1937 *The Road to Wigan Pier*. Orwell himself was often keen to assume the position of the figure in the crowd. He disapproved of the surveillance of Grierson's documentary film unit almost as much as he disapproved of the chumminess of the Auden brigade, condemning films he saw as imposing a middle-class view on the working classes. In a caustic review of Jennings' *The Heart of Britain* (1941) he asked, 'what is the use, in the middle of a desperate war . . . of wasting time and money on producing this kind of stuff?' He went on to criticise the type of documentary that was in fact more characteristic of Grierson than of Jennings:

Some day perhaps it will be realised that that dreadful BBC voice, with its blurred vowels, antagonises the whole English-speaking world except for a small area in southern England, and is more valuable to Hitler than a dozen new submarines.[59]

Orwell was more inclined to appreciate the revolutionary potential of slapstick cinema than socialist documentary. In 1940 he lauded Chaplin's *A Great Dictator* as being 'good at almost every level', despite some technical faults.[60] Clearly, some films were worth spending money on, even in wartime. Orwell took pleasure in the fact that Chaplin's message would reach a wide audience, gaining 'the nationwide success it deserve[d]'. And he saw this message, in the guise of Chaplin's 'peculiar gift', as noticeably Orwellian:

> It is his power to stand for a sort of concentrated essence of the common man, for the ineradicable belief in decency that exists in the hearts of ordinary people . . . Chaplin's appeal lies in his power to reassert the fact, overlaid by Fascism and, ironically enough, by Socialism, that *vox populi vox Dei* and giants are vermin.[61]

Whatever he might say about the pink boy scout brigade in 'Inside the Whale', Orwell was optimistic about the chances of a genuine popular art. Correspondingly, he was generally enthusiastic about Mass-Observation. *The Pub and the People* (1943), Sommerfield's Mass-Observation account of Bolton pubs, came in for particular praise. Orwell described it as a 'large and careful survey', finding that one woman's explanation of why she liked beer 'impresses itself upon the memory like a poem'.[62] In 1947 he remarked that 'it is curious to remember with what hostility [Mass-Observation] was greeted at the beginning' and decided that this must have been 'from people of Conservative opinions'.[63]

In *The Pub and the People* Sommerfield, a working man among the workers, was the Mass-Observing figure in the crowd. 'These are the things that people do in pubs', he says enthusiastically, proceeding to list standing, drinking, talking, thinking, smoking, spitting, playing games, betting, singing and listening to singing as typical pub activities.[64] By praising this book, Orwell salutes Sommerfield as a fellow-traveller, and in *Wigan Pier* he does go far beyond someone like James Greenwood in attaining a perspective of equality with his subjects. The habitual tense used in parts of the book helps here; he has spent long enough experiencing the life he describes to become accustomed to its details: 'I used to get to know individual crumbs by sight and watch their progress up and down the table from day to day.'[65]

Nonetheless, after this first scene, where Orwell is merely one of the many working-class lodgers in the Brookers' house, he does not often claim to be a figure in the crowd. For Orwell, as for Grierson, it would be unrealistic, and un-Marxist, to pretend to be one of the workers. Indeed, this is what he had done in *Down and Out in Paris and London* (1933), where he gives no explanation for his change in fortune, and risks being perceived as misleading. In the second part of *Wigan Pier* he dismisses his earlier experiences on the road, stating that 'you do not solve the class problems by making friends with tramps' (p. 143). The working classes, he informs the reader, are less willing than tramps to be approached on equal terms. A few 'scoutmasterish bellows of good will' cannot solve the problem, and no middle-class intellectuals actually want to join the working class (p. 149).

In *Wigan Pier* Orwell, like Isherwood and Auden in *Journey to a War*, makes clear his own position as the helmeted airman. Like *Coal Face*, Orwell's book is peppered with statistics and facts, most notably in the breakdown of the miners' wages, the estimate of the tonnage of coal a miner produces and the statistics about a miner's likelihood of sustaining injury or death (pp. 37–9). The second half of the book, which was dismissed by Jameson and included with great reluctance by its publisher, Victor Gollancz, incorporates an extended discussion of Orwell's own 'lower-upper-middle-class' attitude to the workers.[66] Although he fails to keep himself out of the picture, he succeeds in making his distanced viewpoint explicit. He also goes out of his way to make clear that his visual perspective is that of the distant camera eye and not a figure in the crowd. Looking out of a train window, he sees a girl 'poking a stick up the leaden waste-pipe', observing her from a distance and then in close-up. Seen at close range, her face exhibits 'the most desolate, hopeless expression' he has ever seen (p. 15). In fact, in the original diary account of the incident, Orwell walks past the girl. In choosing to move his location to a train and attain a cinematic distance, he emphasises his own distance from his subject.

Orwell can also be less deliberately hawk-like. Orwell's observation of the miners' bodies parallels the camera's perspective in *Coal Face* and has occasioned fierce critical debate. Nearly all of the miners, Orwell says,

> have the most noble bodies, wide shoulders tapering to slender supple waists, and small pronounced buttocks and sinewy thighs, with not an ounce of waste flesh anywhere (p. 20)

As in *Coal Face*, these victims who can barely afford to live on their wages and who face death on a daily basis become heroes when seen in the act of labour. John Roberts describes *Wigan Pier* as a satire on the documentary movement, suggesting that 'the book is largely a passionate critique of the *idealisation* of the working class', which Orwell sees as being 'pervasive within the new documentary'.[67] Certainly, in the second half of *Wigan Pier* Orwell dismisses the 'scoutmasterish' attempts of middle-class intellectuals to 'pal up' with the working class as 'pernicious rubbish' (p. 149). Nonetheless, here he seems to adopt an unironic, idealised gaze. 'Noble' and 'sinewy' do seem to be serious. Observing the miners too closely, Orwell reveals his distance. Caught between the positions of the figure in the crowd and the self-consciously helmeted airman, he exemplifies the difficulties inherent in assuming the documentary gaze.

Analysis versus observation

Storm Jameson found fault with Orwell for over-analysing; for interfering too much with his material. For Jameson, when the observer started to analyse himself in the process of observing, documentary witnessing was no longer possible. And for several 1930s commentators, the ideal documentary would present slices of working-class life without subjecting the material to analysis. For the *Left Review* editor Montagu Slater, 'to describe things as they are' could be 'a revolutionary act in itself'.[68] According to Michael Roberts, simply by including working-class characters, writers could give new life and value to their work.[69] If this was true, it was unnecessary to do more than merely record.

Thus a film like *People on Sundays,* though radical and undeniably socialist (not least because of its collective production methods), does not present us with any obvious political message. The film seems to enact the camera's love for its subjects and the beauty of the everyday, without overstating the point that the everyday in question is working class. Benjamin has pointed out that the traditionally ordinary becomes extraordinary on film. The camera is 'incapable of photographing a tenement or a rubbish-heap without transfiguring it', rendering everything it touches beautiful.[70] The 1920s and 1930s viewer could be entranced by a picnic and a swim in the same way that the viewer of early cinema was captivated by the feeding of a Lumière baby.

Where *People on Sundays* can be described as socialist despite its lack of a message, the politics of the films of Charlie Chaplin or Gracie Fields tend to be less easily classifiable. Chaplin is always on the side of the underdog, and the underdog is usually working class. Dressed as a policeman, he will steal vegetables for a poor woman; confronted with a poverty-stricken damsel in distress, he hands over all the money he has won at cards.[71] But he does ultimately marry the damsel, suggesting less straightforwardly heroic motivation, and the money he hands over he has won through cheating. Perhaps he is a Robin Hood figure, and certainly his heart tends to be in the right place, but it seems a laboriously fruitless process to try to pin down his politics.

This is true even of *Modern Times,* which the contemporary critic Meyer Levin thought showed that 'we should have known all along that Chaplin was meant to be the average man, the average worker'.[72] While undoubtedly mocking factory life, the film also seems to mock Lang's *Metropolis*, itself a more bitter and straightforwardly political indictment of the same sorts of mechanised work. Graham Greene warned in his review that though the Marxists would claim it as '*their* film', it was in fact 'a good deal less and a good deal more than socialist in intention'.[73] Similarly, Gracie Fields is rarely used as a vehicle for direct class comment. *Sing as We Go* may be a film set in the Depression, but ultimately the bosses are seen to toil on behalf of the workers and Fields is happy to resume her place as a millworker. Although the critic of the *Manchester Evening News* lauded Fields as 'one of the people', Caroline Lejeune reminded readers of the *Observer* that 'we have an industrial north that is bigger than Gracie Fields running round a Blackpool fun fair'.[74]

The desire to portray the working classes to the working classes was driven as much by market forces as by left-wing ideals. If the majority of the audiences were working class, it was profitable to give them at least some working heroes on screen. Chaplin and Fields were both bankable box-office sell-outs. For one reason or another, a significant tranche of film portraying the working classes did not make overt political statements or analyse the material politically. This tended to be less true of books in the period, perhaps because literature had less of a genuinely working-class audience. Any writer deciding to portray workers was probably doing so for political rather than economic reasons. More obviously, despite Jameson's hopes for the documentary novel, the written word more overtly interprets and analyses, even if the film is unable to avoid doing this implicitly.

For a number of commentators in both media, the left-wing artist must find some way of analysing the material presented. In 1939 Spender insisted that 'realism to-day involves not an imitation of but an analysis of the society in which we are living'.[75] Paul Rotha concurred:

> Observation alone is not enough. Camera portrayal of movement, no matter how finely observed, is purely a matter of aesthetic good taste. The essential purposes of documentary lie in the ends applied to this observation. Conclusions must be indicated and the results of observation must be put across in a manner that demands high creative endeavour.[76]

Similarly Grierson disapproved of both Ruttmann's *Berlin* and Vertov's *The Man with a Movie Camera* for piling up the 'little daily doings' without offering sufficient analysis.[77] In the terms of a series of documentary categories proposed by Rotha, Grierson is condemning the naturalist, realist and newsreel traditions of documentary and accepting only the propagandist tradition practised by Eisenstein.[78]

In fact, as suggested in the previous chapter, both *Berlin* and *The Man with a Movie Camera* do seem to offer a specifically socialist analysis of the situation through their use of (albeit playful) cross-class montage. The writer or filmmaker intending to document and interpret society had two main alternatives. He could provide analysis alongside the textual or filmic footage by way of commentary; alternatively, he could use the editing process to replace commentary. This is the method proposed by Jameson in her 'Documents' essay. Here, although she dismisses commentary on the grounds that 'the document is a comment' itself, she accepts the role of the documentary artist in 'presenting, arranging, selecting, discarding' (pp. 15–16). Specifically, she suggests that the novel, like the film, should attempt a 'double-sided record', setting an account of 'the life of a family of five living in one of the wealthier residential districts of the West End' opposite an account of a 'Paddington, Hoxton, Lambeth family' (p. 15).

This debate was played out forcefully in the German press, where the Frankfurt School cultural theorists Georg Lukács and Ernst Bloch engaged in a heated public discussion about Expressionism in 1938. Whereas Bloch defended Expressionism as a valid protest against an imperialist war and a movement capable of speaking to more than just the elite, Lukács condemned it as distorted, elitist and ultimately fascist. His criticism extended to the entire avant-garde, and he saw the decadence of the bourgeois artist as crystallised in the technique of montage. According to Lukács, while the good photomontage was as valuable as a good joke, as soon as montage became three-dimensional and attempted to 'give shape to reality' or 'totality', 'the final effect must be one of profound monotony'. Objective reality is forgotten and art loses touch with the 'life of the people'.[79] In this orthodox social realism, Lukács seems to be outside the literary current of the 1930s. Most British writers were more aligned with Lukács's colleagues Benjamin and Brecht in thinking that montage was the ideal socialist art form. Brecht himself later criticised Lukács for seeing Balzac as an ideal proponent of socialist art, arguing that society had changed too much for Balzac to remain relevant. He claimed that the working classes found his own montage theatre more exciting and accessible than they found Balzac's long-winded novels.[80]

It was film's capacity for cross-class montage that appealed to writers who were grappling with wanting to allow their subjects to speak for themselves at the same time as wanting to analyse their material; wanting to keep themselves out of the picture without being misleading. Although Jameson seems to present cross-class montage as a novel idea, it is clear that it comes from the socialist cinema (and indeed by this point from the British cinematic novel including, as we shall see, her own 1930s trilogy). For Eisenstein and Vertov, as for Jameson, cross-class montage can be used to illustrate conflict in a changing society, providing an alternative to commentary.

At one point Grierson, downplaying the aesthetic element of the 'representation of the real', suggested that the medium itself was arbitrary. The documentary filmmakers could easily have ended up working with written material rather than film:

if we were jealous of [film's] myth-making influence and made film the instrument of our door-step drama, it was partly by accident. We were interested in all instruments which would crystallise sentiments in a muddled world and create a will toward civic participation.[81]

But this is misleading. Grierson's choice of film was not arbitrary; throughout his career he saw film as the art form best placed to convey his message, largely because of its capacity for montage. In 1934 he lauded his own filmmakers, together with Ruttmann himself, as 'masters of *montage*', and he was a great exponent of the political potential of cutting.[82]

Rotha was clearer in attributing to film a potent capacity to attract mass audiences and engage in hard-hitting propaganda. He made this explicit in the foreword to his 1936 *Documentary Film*: 'I look upon cinema as a powerful, if not the most powerful instrument for social influence to-day.'[83] Rotha would later recommend that 'some critical assessor' might do well to

compare the documentary film people and their work in the 1930s with a similar generation growing up at the same time in Britain in the field of literature. Auden, Isherwood, Day Lewis, Warner, Spender, Graham Greene, Calder-Marshall and others were all exploring poetry and the novel at the same time as we were exploring the cinema medium. Without wishing in any way to denigrate their work, it is worth considering if anything written by this group of authors could compare in social influence to the work of the documentary film group.[84]

Rotha's criterion for influence here is the size of the audience, although he does also suggest that it is a question of the depth of 'social meaning'.[85] The film emerges in his account as the better vehicle for social realism, with literature well advised to learn what it can from its sturdier cousin.

In fact, the comparison that Rotha recommends (and enacts) is just the comparison attempted by Jameson some thirty years earlier in the 'Documents' essay. Writing in the thick of the battle, she is able to advocate that literature should follow film's example, and specifically should emulate filmic montage. Similarly, Raymond Spottiswoode, the author of an influential early exercise in film theory, *The Grammar of the Film* (1935), described cinema as 'the ideal weapon of Marxist art'.[86] Spottiswoode, not himself a Marxist, thought that cinema had a special capacity 'to see society in terms of the facets of organisations and institutions which, abutting on one another at different angles, compose layer by layer the body of the social structure'.[87]

Echoing Eisenstein, Spottiswoode suggests that cinema comes into its own in representing conflict, reflecting the division and reconciliation present throughout society. The layers that he describes are going to 'abut' on the screen through the process of montage. The sometimes 'proletarian' documentary novel developed in tandem with the documentary film, but writers such as Jameson were inclined to try to emulate the techniques of the more successful medium when portraying what increasingly was seen as specifically cinematic subject matter. Socialist class contrasts called for a cinematic mode of presentation.

Cross-class montage in British film and photography

GPO films, Picture Post, Bill Brandt

Although British writers wanting to experiment with cross-class montage had plenty of models in Soviet and German film, there is surprisingly little use made of this kind of contrast in the British documentary films of the period. It is implicit in the Auden-scripted *Night Mail* (1936), directed by Harry Watt and Basil Wright, where the poor in 'working Glasgow' are juxtaposed with the rich in 'well-set Edinburgh', with the film cutting from a construction site in Glasgow to a shot of Edinburgh castle.[88] The cross-class montage is more overt in *Today We Live* (1937), directed by Ralph Bond and Ruby Grierson, John Grierson's sister, where the depressed unemployed are cross-cut with a stream of top-hatted businessmen who walk by, oblivious to the suffering around them (see Figure 2.4). It is also used in the overtly Communist films produced under the auspices of the Workers' Film Movement. The 1935 film *Jubilee*, made by H. A. and R. Green, contrasts the East End Jubilee tour of the King and Queen, shown in the newsreels, with the everyday slum life of the East End. Here an intertitle announcing that 'The National Government Celebrates' is followed by flags being waved after the royal carriage. In the succeeding shot, the intertitle finishing the sentence with '25 Years of Progress' is ironically followed by images of slum dwellings and their inhabitants. This is a message that Grierson would be happy to second, and the absence of such overt cross-class montage in mainstream British 1930s documentary perhaps stemmed from the editors' fear of the censors' more powerful scissors.

By 1930, the British Board of Film Censors had ninety-eight commandments, including a rule prohibiting films whose subject dealt with 'Relations of Capital and Labour' and another concerning 'Subjects calculated or possibly intended to ferment social unrest or discontent'.[89] Although organisations such as the London Film Society and Kino Films had exploited loopholes enabling them to screen socialist films, according to Stephen Jones 'the State had greater controls over the British cinema industry by the end of the 1930s than it had ever had before'.[90] As the novel was rarely censored, it was better placed than the film to take on the techniques of Soviet cinema. So too was the photo

2.4 *Class contrasts*
Ralph Bond and Ruby Grierson, *Today We Live* (1937)

documentary. Combining the camera eye with the editor's ordering, the photo documentary provided a powerful vehicle for 1930s
cross-class montage and became increasingly popular throughout the
decade.

In 1938 *Picture Post* was founded by Stefan Lorent, also the editor
and founder of *Lilliput*, another potent source of documentary photography. From the start, *Picture Post* was political and made great use of
the contrasts between succeeding shots. The second issue in October
1938 included an exposé of 'London By Night', which opened with the
announcement that 'at the words "London by Night", a double picture
comes before one's mind – the inside of an expensive night-club,
brightly lit and noisy, and not far away, a public seat where a crumpled
figure sleeps covered with an unwanted newspaper'.[91] The writer goes
on to suggest that the picture is 'false', or at least 'misleading'; there are
only about forty homeless Londoners sleeping outside on any given
night. But the photo sequence belies this caution, juxtaposing a group
of dancers in a plush London restaurant with an old woman, slumped
on a pile of newspapers as she sleeps on a London street corner.[92] More
comically, a November 1938 issue followed Ruttmann in juxtaposing
the faces of the human 'speakers in Hyde Park', open-mouthed in mid-
oration, with the similarly incensed 'Speakers in the Zoo', even attributing Speakers Corner-like rants to the animals: 'What we all want is
an animal with claws', roars the bear.[93]

Perhaps the prime example of 1930s cross-class photo montage is Bill
Brandt's 1936 *The English at Home*, which provides a cross-section of
English life. Raymond Mortimer, in his introduction to the collection,
praises Brandt as 'not only an artist but an anthropologist', suggesting
that he 'seems to have wandered about England with the detached curiosity of a man investigating the customs of some remote and unfamiliar tribe'.[94] Here Brandt is rather misleadingly figured as the participant
observer, able to be as detached as his camera. For Mortimer, the political message comes from the photographic subjects themselves. 'Is there
any English man or woman', he asks, 'who can look at these without a
profound feeling of shame?' (p. 7). 'If every Member of Parliament had
to spend one week in each year living in such slums, there would very
quickly be no such slums left for them to go to' (p. 7).

Mortimer's contrast between the MP and the slum-dweller is
made manifest in the book. Whether or not Brandt succeeds in being
detached as a photographer, he is decidedly involved as an editor and
makes the most of unlikely contrasts. Early on, a foggy shot of the
English countryside headed 'November in the Country' is juxtaposed

with 'November in the Suburb', showing row after row of dark crowded housing (pp. 13–14). This contrast is used to introduce a series of harrowing shots of working-class life. A picture of 'Miners Returning to Daylight' shows the inhuman-looking dark faces of a group of miners, their white staring eyes and ghostly teeth gazing out of the picture as though in a German expressionist film (p. 15). In the bleakly titled 'Their only Window', three children look miserably out of the tiny window from their basement slum flat, most of the shot taken up by the inhospitable dark wall (p. 16).

These shots are followed by some overt cross-class montage. An austere 'Workmen's restaurant' is set against a plush 'Clubmen's sanctuary', where two men read in front of a roaring fire (pp. 17–18). The scenes are linked by the facial expressions; both display a figure who stares vacantly down, apparently unaware of his surroundings. Brandt seems to play with the natural tendency of the photograph to defamiliarise and render deathly; it is as though the artificiality of the class roles have dehumanised both figures. Abrupt contrasts like this appear throughout the book. More humorously, the 'Circus Boyhood' of a rakish-looking small boy is contrasted with the more self-satisfied 'Nursery Girlhood' of an innocent-looking, well-fed girl (pp. 39–40). Brandt follows these scenes with a series of enticing snapshots of relaxed English leisure, before returning to a more harrowing contrast. He juxtaposes the gleaming carriage that enables 'Travel for the Highest' with the dishevelled bed of a man in a Salvation Army hut. Frightened eyes peek out above a dirty pillow, implying that 'Rest for the Lowest' provides anything but rest (pp. 53–4). Here the ironic counterpointing of text and image matches the counterpointing of the two images, as in the disjunctive pictures and captions in the *Jubilee* film.

Reading Brandt's book in the context of 1930s political montage, the message behind these contrasts seems clear. Yet Brandt himself was politically ambivalent. Looking back on his documentary work in 1959, he said that he had been 'inspired to take these pictures because the social contrast of the Thirties was visually very exciting for me', insisting that he had never intended them 'for political propaganda'.[95] His biographer, Paul Delany, suggests that Brandt was more intrigued than horrified by the class contrasts:

One could even say that he was grateful to the class system for giving him so much to see . . . moving as his pictures of the poor might be, Brandt did not contemplate them with anything like Orwell's sense of intimate discomfort and self-reproach.[96]

Delany sees Brandt as less politically hard-hitting than his American counterparts, Dorothea Lange and Walker Evans, although Evans himself was aware that his photographs in the ironically entitled portrait of tenant farmers *Let Us Now Praise Famous Men* (1937) were also not without their own surreal beauty.[97] While there may be no political manifesto behind Brandt's work, Mortimer's introduction to *The English at Home* seems to entitle readers then and now to read it into the 1930s political canon. Whether or not the photographs themselves induce 'intimate discomfort', the contrasts alone seem to be enough to give the book a political charge.

Inspired by Brandt, or by Lange and Evans, several British writers included photo sequences in late 1930s textual documentary. The two most obvious examples are the series added to Orwell's *The Road to Wigan Pier* (1937) and the sequence of Auden's own photographs included in Auden and Isherwood's account of the Sino-Japanese conflict, *Journey to a War* (1939). We do not know whether Orwell himself wanted photographs in his book, but it was the day after a meeting between Orwell and his publisher, Norman Collins, that Collins sent a letter to Reverend Gilbert Shaw, asking him to send any photographs he had 'dealing with life in the distressed areas'.[98] The photographs themselves do not display the 'self-reproach' Delany found in Orwell's text. The focus tends to be external. Like Brandt, Shaw plays with the deathliness inherent in the photographic image to suggest the dehumanising effect of the slums and the pits. In a photograph of a South Wales miner taking a bath, we see a thickly blackened man leaning over a hopelessly small bucket on the carpet by the fire, presided over by his competently maternal wife. Her sympathetic expression contrasts with his more animalistic one, indicating that the dirt has reduced him to an unnecessary condition of bestiality.

The photographs in *Journey to a War* make more of the potential for abrupt montage between images, as well as for disjunction between text and image. The prime example of this is the 'Innocent'/'Guilty' montage. Here 'The Innocent' is a dead or unconscious body covered with a cloth, and 'The Guilty' is a mutilated arm sticking out of the earth.[99] Both are clearly the victims of a brutal war and the two are levelled by their fate. Auden implicitly asks if it matters whether they are innocent or guilty when they are both dead, challenging the arbitrary moral distinctions which follow the lines of battle. A similar effect is brought about by the 'With legs' and 'Without' montage, grouped together under the emotive heading 'Children in uniform'. In both images we see the torsos of teenage boys and it is only from the caption that we know that the grimly smiling boy in the lower picture is an amputee. The presence of a limping man with a walking stick in the background seems to confirm the general decay, but also serves to emphasise the apparent youth and health of the figure in the foreground.

Cross-class montage in British literature

John Sommerfield, Henry Green, Storm Jameson, James Barke
Cinematic documentary writing in the 1930s often bears more resemblance to serial photography than to film. This is a question of the mode of analysis. Where Valentine Cunningham has seen the documentary film as 'more powerfully truth-telling still than the . . . "picture essay"', with more potential to make 'revelatory and accusative connections' through montage, Blake Stimson suggests that serial photography analyses more overtly.[100] According to Stimson, serial photography enables images to exist simultaneously, on top of each other, where the film replaces each image in an inflexible temporal sequence.

> Whether it wants to be or not, film makes itself over into a one-sided conversation . . . by collapsing the analytical, atemporal space opened up by the abstraction of serial photography back into a false synesthetic naturalism of time.[101]

In line with Benjamin, Stimson sees the radical power of film and photography to reside partly in the way they force the viewer into a haptic identification with the subject. But he sees film as making this identification too easy – the movements are so natural that it is easy to forget we are moving at all. Serial photography, by contrast, requires a jerky movement from one shot to the next, forcing a more active process of viewing and bodily identification which necessitates analysis.

These disjunctive contrasts are often found in literature. Writers such as Jameson, Green, Sommerfield and James Barke drew fairly explicitly on the cinema in their 1930s cross-class montage. In 1928 Green described his novel-in-progress, *Living*, to his former tutor, Nevill Coghill, as 'a kind of disconnected cinema film'.[102] He would assert in 1950 that the English novel would never again emulate its 'three-decker' Victorian predecessor because the cinema had 'taught the modern novelist to split his text up into small scenes'.[103] The advertisement for *May Day* in *Left Review* drew attention to the mobile nature of the cross-class montage: 'A cross-section of the social pyramid, from the factory to the managing director's luxury flat ... and it *moves* – it's got technique'.[104] But Green's use here of 'disconnected' is telling. The disconnected film is in effect serial photography, and these novels often bear more resemblance to serial photography than to film. There is jerkiness in Green's *Living* (1929), Jameson's *Mirror in Darkness* trilogy (1934–6), Sommerfield's *May Day* (1936) and Barke's *Major Operation* (1936) which forces the reader to supply the gaps between the scenes, analysing as we go.

All four writers make great use of cross-class montage as a way of portraying working- and upper-class lives in a society that is changing and being changed. Green's own politics were always ambiguous, and he was hesitant in labelling *Living* either a socialist or a 'proletarian' work. In response to Isherwood's commendation of *Living* as the best 'proletarian novel ever written', Green grumbled that 'the workers in my factory thought it [*Living*] rotten ... I don't think that [Isherwood] ever worked in a factory'.[105] He did, though, admit in the same interview that he 'wanted to make that book as taut and spare as possible to fit the proletarian life I was then leading', and as late as 1952 he told Nigel Dennis that 'the *real* intellectual is the workingman', whom the writer is obliged to meet and observe.[106]

Throughout *Living*, Green cuts between the happy but anxious homes of working-class characters and the selfish, unloving home of the Duprets, using a simple montage technique comparable to Lang's in *Metropolis* or Ruttmann's in *Berlin*. As in these films, the montage takes us beyond the world of the characters, introducing a wider social framework. At the beginning of Chapter 4, an eight-line scene between the factor owner's wife, Mrs Dupret, and their son, Dick, is cross-cut with a page-long scene between the working-class Tarvers. In the Dupret scene, mother and son talk to each other across the barrier of their engagement books, behind which Dick surreptiousstly picks his nose. The first evening Mrs Dupret has free to see her son is in a fortnight's time. In the scene between the Tarvers, Green includes the dialogue within the paragraph, rather than setting it out with separating indents, typographically enacting the close communion of husband and wife:

'It's low' said Mrs Tarver. 'Low' said Mr Tarver, 'low' he said.[107]

The two are discussing the extreme measures introduced in the factory and come together sympathetically in the face of oppression. They are so close that it is often unclear which of them is actually speaking, and we see a totally different mode of family life at work from the Duprets'.

John Russell has noted the duplicate structures in the book, with plot-lines doubled between working- and upper-class characters, which strengthen the cross-class montage.[108] The most obvious example is the doubling of love triangles between the working-class Lily and Jim Dale/Bert Jones and the upper-class Hannah Glossop and Dick Dupret/Tom Tyler. Both girls choose the superficially sophisticated but ultimately unloving suitor and both girls are disappointed. Lily and Hannah are influenced in their choice by their position as unworking, unmarried women, with no sense of higher purpose. The two are cross-cut together when Hannah's 'Her mother said work? What work could she do?' is followed by Lily's 'Another night. She had cleared table after supper' (pp. 88–9).

Not only Lily and Hannah but also Lily and Dick are montaged in their disappointment and boredom. Lily's desperate internal cry 'I am I, why do I do work of this house, unloved work . . . Why may I not work for mine?' is followed by Dick's 'Why, he said in mind, why could not the old man die?' (p. 82). Dick, again picking his nose, is seen as less valid in his plea here. Where he is longing for the death of a parent, Lily is longing for the new life of a child, which comes across as a more generous and natural desire. The unwitting connection between the two is made explicit when Dick passes Lily in the street. Walking through a poor district, he contemplates the poverty of the neighbourhood, seeing 'a kind of terrible respectability on too little money', and wonders why people focus so much on having children:

> you were born, you went to school, you worked, you married, you worked harder, you had children . . . What had you before you died? Grandchildren? The satisfaction of breeding the glorious Anglo Saxon breed?

At the gate of a recreation ground, he passes Lily and does not notice her because 'she was so like the others'. He looks around at the children playing and continues in his misanthropic musings about Anglo-Saxon breeding before becoming distracted and thinking about himself. Immediately, the camera shifts to Lily who watches the same children and longs to be a mother: '"I must have babies," she said then, looking at baby in mother's arms' (pp. 140–1). Green uses the children as cinematic objects, focusing the contrast between the two points of view and again showing Lily's to be more human – more 'living' – than Dick's.

In 1930, Jameson declared her intention 'to write henceforward with the most unromantic plainness'.[109] Two years later, she began *The Mirror in Darkness,* which was originally intended to comprise five or six novels depicting 'the contemporary scene'.[110] She later described its inception in her autobiography:

> I was seized by the ambition to write a *roman fleuve.* I had its title: *The Mirror in Darkness,* and my brain spawned like a salmon scores of characters, politicians, ex-soldiers, financier, industrialist, newspaper proprietor, scientist, writers, labour leader, embryo Fascist, the rich, the very humble, the ambitious who knew where they were going, and the confused, the ruined, the lost.[111]

The rich and the very humble are juxtaposed throughout the trilogy, which seems to have spawned the ideas that would go into the 'Documents' article. Chiara Briganti has pointed out the influence of Vertov and Ruttmann on Jameson's trilogy, which can be read as an extended city symphony.[112] London is as much a character as a location. Alienating, hectic, unforgiving, it repels Jameson's heroine, Hervey Russell, who yearns for her family's country home but is drawn repeatedly to the anonymous city. Jameson's reader, like Vertov's viewer, is led round the city on a succession of buses and cabs, which journey frenetically from place to place and from class to class. Near the end of *Love in Winter* (1935), Jameson uses a bus to montage the lives of rich and poor and to glide from the consciousness of the socialist writer, Earlham, to the thoughts of the factory worker, Frank Rigden.

Earlham is on the bus briefly but then jumps off to catch a cab – a sign of his new social aspirations as well as his lateness. After following Earlham to an upper-class dinner where he finds it 'impossible' that he can be in the room 'as the equal of these people', Jameson moves abruptly to the bus he has left behind.[113] In a rare, omniscient authorial voice, she contrasts the bus passengers with the occupants of the comfortable cabs below, which overtake the buses as they rush to the stations to deposit the upper classes on their way to the 'playgrounds of Europe'. She states explicitly that each cab passes 'at least a hundred persons' more in need of rest and fresh air than the people it holds. She then enters the consciousness of the bus driver, who thinks wistfully that 'if our Gert could get out there' to the ski resorts 'she'd be saved' (p. 366). The narrator follows the bus driver as he drives down Piccadilly, the 'treasure-house' of 'underclothes of silk and fine

wool, winter strawberries' and 'gold-mounted bags', spotting, with the
driver, a 'man holding up a handful of boxes of matches and a card
inscribed LAST HOPE', ignored in the midst of the women in fur
coats 'as though he were not there' (p. 367). The bus crosses the river
into south London, the land of 'sunken cheeks and hands holding the
lapels of coats over the garment underneath' (p. 367). In Deptford a
man gets on, clutching a bundle. He turns out to be Frank Rigden, on
his way home to his wife armed with hard-earned but meagre apples
and oranges for his children's Christmas stockings. This is the contrast
between districts that Jameson would demand in her 'Documents'
article. The bus rattles through a London that seems arbitrarily divided
between hardship and luxury.

Sommerfield and Barke were two genuinely working-class 1930s
writers to use cross-class montage in overtly Communist novels.
Barke, a Scottish Communist, makes explicit the socialist nature of his
montage project in an authorial statement:

> crowds no more than individuals mix. The crowd in Sauchiehall Street
> was a middle-class crowd: the crowd in Argyle Street was a working-class
> crowd. In Dubmarton Road the crowd was more finely divided. On the
> north side paraded the better working class: on the south side the slum
> dwellers. Between, ran two sets of tram lines. They might have been a
> barbed wire entanglement.[114]

Here he combines montage with commentary, explaining the significance of the divide through the image of barbed wire. Both *May
Day* and *Major Operation* assert their status as documentary works
by including factual detail as a form of commentary throughout. Ian
Haywood writes that 'sections of *May Day* read like the voice-over
for a documentary', and certainly *May Day* incorporates the kind of
statistics about working-class lives that we would expect to find in a
GPO film.[115] We are told that there are 322,000 unemployed people
in London (p. 193), that 7,283 'souls' fall asleep in a particular three-
second window (p. 109), and given three pages of detailed statistics
about the number of Communists in London (pp. 193–5). In fact,
these statistics are inaccurate – exaggeration licensed by the novel's
claim to be set 'three years hence' – but they give the book an air of
reportage.

Both Sommerfield and Barke combine documentary with analysis-
inducing cross-class montage through the use of newspaper headlines.
Early on in *Major Operation*, Barke informs the reader:

> At 11.45 am prompt, gangs of newsboys skailed from the office of *The Glasgow Evening Star* with bundles of noon editions carrying banner headings:
>   King Sol to Reign at Coast and Country today.
>   And in slightly lower case:
>   Weather Experts Predict Glorious Weekend. (p. 22)

The headline serves to unite the disparate reactions of upper- and working-class characters to the heat as housewives 'cast off winter combinations', windows are 'flung open' and 'the better class pubs' arrange displays of beer on ice (p. 18). The newspaper headlines in *May Day* are less integral to the plot but more integral to the montage. The most important headlines in the book relate to the air race. We first hear about it when Langfier, the upper-class factory owner, is leafing through the newspapers during breakfast. Because 'today was the start of the great round-the-world air race', he finds that 'there was little else in the news' (p. 17). Quite a while later, the working-class James, back from his time as a sailor and unaware of the race, sees the newsbills of the evening papers and reads 'uncomprehendingly' 'AIR RACE – THOMPSON LEADING' (p. 35). Sommerfield makes his montage explicit here, stating:

> To one long from home the newspaper headlines speak a foreign language. But a million looks glanced upon these words understandingly, with varying thoughts, no two quite the same yet no two altogether different. (p. 36)

Immediately, the camera cuts to Langfier's son, Peter, who is riding in the park. Peter finds the captions 'a spur to the imagination', which leads him to think of 'the romance of modernity and the heroics of technology' (p. 36). Peter's romanticism makes him seem naïve and reminds us that only the rich have the luxury of gazing in wonder at new technology. He may share his enthusiasm for technology with Soviet Russia, but, like most British Communists, Sommerfield was more sceptical about the machine. The working-class characters in the book see technology as a threat that is depriving them of their jobs and making their work more hazardous.

We next hear of the air race when Peter and his girlfriend, Pamela, riding in the park, see the subsequent headline – 'THOMPSON HAS FORCED LANDING' – and read it disappointedly. Pamela's lament 'What a shame' is echoed later on the same page, when the working-class Martine reads an almost identical headline on the way to go shopping: 'Thompson down, she said to herself. What a shame' (p. 41). Immediately, she gets caught up in her shopping list ('marg, lard, sugar, cheese') and in looking after her baby and dog. Through this juxtaposition we see the way that the same external events punctuate the lives of the rich and the poor, and even affect them in the same way. Because Martine and Pamela have the same reaction, Sommerfield makes clear that both are English women who respond to the world in similar ways. It seems unfair that one has money and the other does not.

In their subject matter and message, all four books are strongly aligned with the 1930s documentary film. But the kind of analysis they induce is, I would suggest, more akin to that induced by serial photography than by film. The literal blank spaces between sections mean that the reader is given a chance for conscious reorientation as we are asked to identify with another character, in a disjunctive social position. Barke's flashing between the crowd in Sauchiehall Street and the crowd in Argyle Street has the effect of the disconnected film described by Green, rather than the continuous flow of images found in Eisenstein or Ruttmann. Similarly, Sommerfield's abrupt cuts between upstairs and downstairs require a readerly adjustment of position. At one point John watches a 'maid bending to scrub the lordly doorsteps' of the Langfiers' house and then cycles onwards, thinking about his courtship with his wife (p. 13). After a dotted pause, Sommerfield cuts to Jean, 'the bending maid', straightening herself up. The description of her sleepy body, stretching and yawning, gives way after another dotted pause to Peter Langfier, asleep two flights above, 'dreaming to waltz time' (p. 15). The positioning of Jameson's camera in the bus with the driver is cinematic, but the driver's view of the world is photographic. Caught in traffic, he experiences his surroundings as a series of snapshots:

> To his right he caught glimpses of the deep mist of trees; on the left he had a clear view into a high wide room, filled with a yellow light, in which some several persons were lolling in elbow-chairs. (p. 366)

The reader does not have access to a cinematic panning shot, only to these abrupt scenes.

As in Stimson's account of serial photography, the disjunction between montaged scenes in literature is often bodily. In Stimson's formulation,

> rather than a simple identification with the image of the other, a simple replacement of one image by the next and the next and the next, the

movement of the beholder's eye, head and body in the interstices between pictures came to be a central factor in the design concept as the photographer or exhibition designer came to orchestrate those patterns of bodily movement and with it the affective range of responses.[116]

It is this movement between interstices that the reader of *May Day*, *Love in Winter* and *Living* is required to perform. Sommerfield emphasises the bodily positions of his characters as he cuts between the cycling John, the stretching Jean and the sleeping Peter. Jameson's shift from the point of view of the driver to the point of view of Frank Rigden does not occur seamlessly. We first see Rigden from the outside, climbing 'awkwardly' onto the bus, and then standing 'leaning against the end rail' (p. 367). We then return to following the movement of the bus itself as it descends a hill, before switching abruptly to Frank, who steps out, 'holding the bag carefully away from him' (p. 368). Frank's progress is now separated from the progress of the bus, and the reader is left following him, as the bus moves on, unnoticed.

A pronounced example of bodily disjunction in *Living* occurs within the doubling of the love triangles. Lily, kissing Bert, is caught in a remarkable moment of mutual embodiment, 'their bodies straining against each other', becoming 'one warmth':

> They walked from cone of light into darkness and then again into lamp-light, nor, so their feeling lulled them, was light or dark, only their feeling of both of them which was one warmth, infinitely greater. (p. 99)

Here the cinematic experience of flickering light and dark becomes subjugated to the physical feeling of warmth. Touch exceeds sight, requiring the reader to engage in a haptic rather than a visual identification with the characters. This sentence is immediately followed by a blank space between sections, before lurching into the absurd physical antics of Tom Tyler, 'the life of the house-party':

> Before dinner he stood on his head, put a pin in the back of a chair and sitting on the chair leaned round it, bending his body into an arc and took the pin out in his mouth. (p. 99)

This is a disjunctive reading experience. Just when we are languidly imagining shared physical warmth, we are suddenly called upon to put our bodies through an impossible-sounding physical contortion. How can his mouth be in same place as the middle of his arched torso? As in Stimson's formulation of serial photography, the reader is prevented from continuous identification, interrupted between the interstices of the montaged scenes and required to supply the analysis omitted between the gaps. This is, of course, the analysis demanded by Eisenstein, who intended his conflict montage to impress on the spectator an analytical interpretation of the situation and implicate the spectator phsyically. But in *Living* the clunkiness of the changing of scenes necessitates a conscious analysis that remains merely desirable in film.

CHAPTER 3

The Documentary Movement and Mass Leisure, 1930–1945

The ideal documentarist emerges in the 1930s as someone able to straddle the contradictions inherent in social realism. He allows the workers to speak for themselves, at the same time as analysing them; and maintains an objective, camera-like distance, at the same time as mingling, when need be, with the crowd, blurring the boundary between observer and observed. Subsequent commentators, such as Mengham, Cowie, Williams and Highmore, all indicate that the best documentary creates a perspective that allows viewers to understand the social context while simultaneously allowing the workers to emerge as individuals.

The subject matter best suited for these virtuosic contortions of perspective was leisure. Leisure-time offered 'a chance to be ourselves', as Humphrey Jennings put it in the brief opening commentary to *Spare Time* (1936), his enthusiastic romp through working-class leisure activities. There was more scope for individuality in group singing or amateur dramatics than in descending into a darkened coal mine or battling with dirt in the slums. Leisure showcased the working classes at their most generous and least downtrodden. It was easy to stop seeing them as heroes or victims when they were bent merely on having fun.

And the cinema was ideally placed to capture the working class at play. It had emerged as victorious in Rotha's battle between the arts both because of its potency as a medium and because it had a series of radical techniques at its command. For Jameson, Rotha and Spottiswoode in Britain, as for Benjamin and Kracauer in Germany, cinema was the ideal medium for social realist art, at least in part because it could juxtapose the classes through montage and alternate between long shots of crowds and close-ups of individuals. Both techniques were useful in depicting leisure activities.

Several commentators extolled cinema's ability to represent crowds.

In 1927 Benjamin had described the proletariat as a 'collective', stating that 'no other medium [but film] could reproduce this collective in motion'.[1] Later, Kracauer linked the development of the crowd with the development of cinema: 'the instrument of reproduction came into being almost simultaneously with one of its main subjects.'[2] Even the least class-conscious of filmmakers had experimented with the medium's capacity to include a vast number of people within a single frame. From the start, crowds of workers appealed to directors as both an attraction and a worthy cause. For the Lumière brothers and Griffith, as well as for Eisenstein, crowd scenes showcased the filmmaker's art, shocking and thrilling the audience with their verisimilitude.

The crowd at play was particularly attractive to documentarists, who wanted to avoid seeing their subjects as a mass. Watching a football match or lazing on the beach, the workers seemed to unite as a community while retaining their individuality. Jennings in particular experimented with alternating point-of-view and documentary shots, slotting in and out of the individual perspectives. He also made the most of the community-forming aspects of working-class leisure. This became particularly important in wartime documentary and realist feature films, when a form of what might be termed across-class montage was useful for depicting communities forming across the class boundaries.

1930s leisure: the individual in the crowd

Dziga Vertov, W. H. Auden, Henry Green
For the socialist documentarist, part of the attraction of working-class leisure was that it was still a relatively new phenomenon in the 1930s. Its genesis lay in the 1880s, when the conditions of workers first started to improve, leaving them with some free time and a little spare money to enjoy themselves. In 1919, 6.3 million workers experienced cuts in weekly hours.[3] The workers' movements came to prominence in this period, with the Eight Hours movement demanding

> Eight hours work, eight hours play,
> Eight hours rest, eight 'bob' a day.

As workers found themselves with more spare time thanks to reductions in their working hours, their less fortunate counterparts faced endless hours of enforced leisure through unemployment. This is the darker side of the rise in working-class leisure, touched on by

Sommerfield in *May Day*, where John spends several demoralising months out of work. Between the two world wars, unemployment averaged 14 per cent of the insured workforce. In 1932, Delisle Burns, a reformist Christian, wrote a book called *Leisure in the Modern World*, in which he describes 'the spare time of the millions of unemployed' as 'itself a cultural problem'.[4] His sentiments were echoed more forcefully in 1934 in *Industrial Welfare*:

> enforced leisure is an embarrassment which only those who have experienced it can possibly understand. It is an imposition, and should be treated as such . . . The hopelessness and weariness of 'going after the job you know isn't there' imposes a stern self-discipline . . . Work is fundamental, there is no leisure without it.[5]

Now that so many of the workforce had more spare time on their hands, the government began to increase state funding for leisure. The expenditure on libraries and museums doubled in the 1920s and public spending on parks and open spaces increased threefold.[6] The Physical Training and Recreation Act of 1937 made available modest amounts of public money to aid voluntary organisations in the provision of facilities for 'physical training and recreation', partly in order to arm the country with a fitter nation in the event of war. Burns saw the government funding of leisure as motivated by civilised, socialist aims:

> the expenditure of public funds on facilities for recreation may be a first sign of returning civilisation, after the barbaric concentration on wealth-getting in the earlier industrial period.[7]

For Russophile socialists, the appeal of leisure was enhanced by its topicality in the Soviet Union. More stridently than the British government, the Soviet government had devoted itself to funding and supporting working-class leisure from the time that Lenin proclaimed the eight-hour day in 1917. From 1928 to 1940, Stalin promoted fitness and leisure through official sponsorship, holding the first Physical Culture Day parade in Red Square in 1931. Leisure plays an important role in Vertov's *Man with a Movie Camera*, which ends with a triumphant montage of happy, healthy workers enjoying the pleasures of sport and recreation.

In Cowie's terms, this sequence is performative. Vertov joins his subjects in producing a spectacle of leisure. The focus moves from observation to celebration, avoiding the question of surveillance altogether. The potential of leisure activities to produce a filmic show was exploited by several British documentary filmmakers in the 1930s. Most obviously, the seaside spectacles in *Hindle Wakes* and *Sing as We Go* also appealed to the documentarists. The seaside crowd is presented enthusiastically in the Rotha-produced documentary *The Way to the Sea* (1936), scripted by Auden and directed by J. B. Holmes. 'We seek a spectacle', announces Auden's commentary, as the train speeds from London to Portsmouth, aligning himself with the seaside visitors on the way to the Isle of Wight. The viewer is offered a montage of seaside exuberance, celebrating the graceful divers, a surreal puppet show and a girl dressed up as a queen.

The image of the teenage girl, regally facing the camera, illustrates the lure of the popular seaside resort in 1930s Britain. She is a garish queen and does not fool anyone for a second, but in her ecstatic smile she is an enticing seaside spectacle (see Figure 3.1). Auden's commentary exhorts us to

> Be extravagant,
> Be lucky,
> Be clairvoyant,
> Be amazing,
> Be a sport or an angel,
> Imagine yourself as a courtier, or as a queen.
> Accept your freedom.

By revelling in the excesses of the seaside, the girl has accepted its freedom – the freedom to be an individual amidst the crowd. Unlike Mass-Observation, *The Way to the Sea* consistently presents the seaside as a place where the masses can become individuals. The camera focuses first on a series of individual families playing and laughing, before drawing back to show a faceless mass of holidaymakers. The way

3.1 *A queen*
J. B. Holmes, *The Way to the Sea* (1936)

3.2 *A happy athlete*
Dziga Vertov, *The Man with a Movie Camera* (1929)

3.3 *A cheerful cyclist*
Humphrey Jennings, *Spare Time* (1936)

to the sea leads to liberty; the seaside is a charmed and dreamy land where even the lonely can '[dare] to look for an amazing romance'.

The individuality possible within mass leisure activities is also celebrated by Vertov in *The Man with a Movie Camera*. This is a film whose focus is consistently on the unique or special; the energetic swimmers and dancers seem to appeal to Vertov as individuals. The camera lingers lovingly on a female athlete smearing her face and body with mud, who then smiles cheerfully at the viewer (see Figure 3.2). She seems to find a direct successor in a cyclist eating a bun in *Spare Time* (1936), Jennings' montage of the leisure activities of workers in three industries, steel, cotton and coal. Here, in describing leisure as 'a chance to be ourselves', Jennings unites with his (individualised) subjects. His cyclist eats her bun and then leans back laughing, allowing her personality to emerge from the scene (see Figure 3.3).

The cycling expedition is a topical way to illustrate socialist leisure. One of the most successful voluntary organisations to spring up in the wake of the new government spending on leisure was the Clarion Cycling Club. This was rejuvenated in the 1930s for the 'Propagation of the Principles of Socialism, along with the social pleasures of Cycling', and boasted in excess of 8,000 members in 1936. In many ways, the bicycle is a convenient symbol of the contented labourer. It is a cheap, functional form of both transport and exercise, which grants the individual a measure of independence from the crowds. Happy cyclists populate *The Man with a Movie Camera* and *Berlin* as well as *Spare Time*.

These cyclists are consistently marked out as individuals, at the same time as they are seen as part of a community. The same is true of the groups of musicians and singers who come together in a kazoo band and a singsong in *Spare Time*. These communal activities bring out the goodwill of individuals, so that people help their fellow workers or neighbours. As the men assemble around the pianist at the choir practice in *Spare Time*, they collectively help her remove her coat so that she can carry on playing.

Leisure was both a time for the individual and a time for the community to come together democratically after a hard week's labour. Burns praised the rise of leisure activities such as football matches or community singing because they were teaching people how to enjoy being in a crowd:

> the modern man is learning to be at ease with all sorts of strangers. He is much less frightened of strangers than his grandfather used to be, and is therefore more companionable.[8]

He saw the new leisure-time as breaking down the division between workers and the upper classes:

> the displacement of the leisured class as the preservers and promoters of culture is the most significant of all the changes in our traditional social system, which are the results of the new uses of leisure.[9]

The early twentieth century saw the end of the age in which, according to Thorstein Veblen, labour was felt to be 'debasing' and leisure-time was used solely 'to show that one's time had not been spent in industrial employment'.[10] Now leisure and labour went hand in hand.

The working-class football match, lauded by Burns, is a popular set-piece scene in 1930s literature and film. J. B. Priestley, visiting a football match on his English journey, was impressed by the crowd's behaviour and their knowledge of the game. Much has been done to spoil football, he laments, with the heavy financial interests and the 'monstrous partisanship' of the crowds, 'but the fact remains that it is not yet spoilt, and it has gone out and conquered the world'. He lauds the crowd specifically for its community feeling, finding that it is

> good, when the right side has scored a goal, to see that wave of happiness break over their ranked faces, to see that quick comradeship engendered by the game's sudden disasters and triumphs.[11]

In *Living*, the male characters are brought together by a football match at the end of the book. At this point, the community is in danger of being wrenched apart by Lily's desertion and Craigan's illness, but Lily's father and his friend, Mr Connolly, escape to the football match for a few hours' pleasure. As they walk towards the football ground, 'more and more men' join the crowd from the surrounding roads, forming 'on each side of the street long lines of men walking, many of them still in blue overalls' (p. 199). At the gates,

> men are coming in, lines of them coming in are thicker and thicker . . . you see nothing but faces, lozenges, against black shoulders. As time gets nearer so more rattles are let off, part of the crowd begins singing. The drunk man, who has a great voice, roars and shouts and near him hundreds of faces are turned to look at him.

The visual abstraction of this description of the thick lines and lozenges gives the crowd an order that makes it unified and unthreatening. Cunningham describes this crowd as 'an obviously good place to be. The warmth of the tone announces that this is a text that's on the same side as those people, as ordinary persons.'[12]

As in Jennings' films, the communal singing serves to unify the crowd, who are then brought together by the excitement of the match itself: 'everyone is shouting'. Lily's father, who has been a largely unhappy figure throughout the book, loses his voice as he wails and sobs with his fellow men. As the game gets going, '30,000 people waved and shrieked and swayed and clamoured at eleven men who play the best football in the world'.

Wartime: leisure, class, national identity

The propaganda film, Humphrey Jennings, Henry Green, Elizabeth Bowen and the Lambeth Walk

In wartime, leisure became a symbol of hope. It offered propaganda filmmakers a chance to show the British having more fun than the

Germans and therefore as better equipped to win the war. It also allowed them to present the working classes as the worthy inheritors of a new and better world. Once Germany had started bombing Britain in 1940, the community value of leisure became more urgent. It was particularly important to show communities forming across classes, so that the working classes felt integrated in the war effort.

This became easier as class boundaries began naturally to break down. A. J. P. Taylor has written that 'everywhere in England people no longer asked about a man's background, only what he was doing for the war'.[13] The average income during the war rose considerably, and government initiatives such as the 1943 Beveridge Report, which provided for unemployment and poverty, helped to convince people that their situation was improving. Angus Calder has shown the limitations of both the Beveridge Report and the whole notion of the People's War. However, even if the consequences of the war were less revolutionary than people hoped for, the notion of the People's War certainly had currency in the literature and cinema of the period.[14] Filmmakers and writers experimented with what I have termed across-class montage, uniting the classes in shared leisure activities. They also contrasted the quirkiness of English leisure activities with the more uniform German varieties in a form of cross-national montage.

Jennings' war films are dominated by leisure. The importance of it to wartime propaganda enabled Jennings to continue the attempt he had made in *Spare Time* to combine the public gaze of the documentary with the private gaze of the individuals under scrutiny. In *Listen to Britain* (1942), his poetic sound montage of wartime life, a woman clearing a meal hears a child's voice call 'Mummy' and then turns to look out of the window. From her point of view, we see children dancing in a circle in a school playground. In a typical Hollywood shot-reverse-shot pattern, the camera then moves back to the woman, who looks at a photograph of a soldier on the wall, presumably her husband. This is essentially a private moment, but the introduction of the soldier reminds us of the context of Britain at war. As though to confirm this, the roar of tanks merges with the noise of the children's dance and we see troop carriers coming down a village street (see Figure 3.4). As the public, documentary aspect of the film intrudes on the private moment, we are reminded that these private, everyday moments are threatened by the encroaching war.

In the Second World War, a whole spectrum of directors attempted to merge private and public viewpoints. If they were going to attract a wider audience to 'realist' films about wartime Britain, they needed to

3.4 *War intrudes on village life*
Humphrey Jennings, *Listen to Britain* (1942)

enable the spectator to identify with individual points of view within the film. Looking back on the war in 1947, the filmmaker Roger Manvell celebrated documentary-style feature films like *Millions Like Us* and *The Way Ahead*, which 'resolved the personal equation, and showed us people in whom we could believe and whose experience was as genuine as our own'.[15] At the same time, these films needed to implicate the individuals in the wider story, making people aware of their role within society. Andrew Higson writes that in wartime, it was 'necessary that the individual citizen was in no doubt as to the importance of the assigned role which he or she must play'. The individual must therefore be 'allotted a place within the public sphere'.[16]

Directed by Frank Gilliat and Sidney Launder in 1943, *Millions Like Us* offers a cross-section of wartime life at the same time as allowing the viewer to identify with a handful of individuals. A bombardier, reporting for Mass-Observation, celebrated it at the time as 'the best film since Bank Holiday' on the grounds that it 'presents Britain and life as it is', and 'we must have truth and integrity in our films'.[17] In its attempt to reproduce life as it is, the film includes actual factory, canteen and hostel interiors. It also provides people of every age, sex and class with a character to identify with. Following the members of a single lower-middle-class family and their acquaintances, the narrative cuts between the points of view of Celia, the main heroine of the film, who is sent to work in a factory, her sister, Phyllis, who joins the Auxiliary Territorial Service, and their father, a home guard, who is left to fend for himself while his daughters are away. Through Celia, we meet the upper-class Jennifer, who arrives at the factory with expensive clothes and snobbish views, only to fall for the northern foreman, and Fred, Celia's pilot fiancé. Increasingly, as Fred is called into battle and killed, the film's focus is with Celia, whose point of view is often given. Nonetheless, her story is always seen in the context of the public life going on around her. Andrew Higson writes that the film's narrative system

> is able to represent precisely a community of people, rather than star individuals; it is able to develop a variety of limited egos, even if one of them, Celia, is developed into a more central and ideal ego.[18]

Millions Like Us makes much of the community-forming aspect of leisure. The girls in the factory bond through social dancing and singing. After Fred dies, Celia is unable to share the cheerfulness of her friends, but she is brought back into the group by a communal singsong so convivial that she finds herself joining in. Similarly, in *Listen to Britain* (1942), Jennings celebrates the community-minded aspects of working-class leisure which he had explored in *Spare Time*. He portrays a wide range of voluntary groups engaged in community singing, amateur dramatics, music and sport. Again, people help each other through these collective leisure activities. An ambulance worker sings 'The Ash Grove' to entertain her sister workers.

These propaganda films are explicit in showing leisure as breaking down the boundaries between classes. In *Millions Like Us*, it is the leisure activities that create a space in which the hostility between the upper-class Jennifer and the foreman Charlie Forbes can dissipate. The dancing and singing enable a romance to develop, albeit one that they both know will not survive the war. In *Fires Were Started* (1943), Jennings's documentary of life in a wartime fire station, the upper-class auxiliary fireman Barrett is integrated into the group of working-class firemen by playing the piano for a group rendition of 'One Man Went to Mow'. We see class divisions being broken down through the common purpose of fire-fighting as we do in Henry Green's *Caught* in the same year, where the upper-class Roe gradually learns to feel at home among the other firefighters. Like Gilliat in *Millions Like Us*, both Jennings and Green portray the democracy engendered by war through the sharing of leisure activities between classes.

While filming *Fires Were Started*, in which he was working with ordinary firemen rather than with trained actors, Jennings wrote to his wife that he was learning that class distinctions were 'total rubbish'. Crucially, he dismissed 'not merely the distinctions made by the famous upper classes but also those made [by] the grubby documentary boys'.[19] For Jennings, the upper-middle-class, hawk-like view was at last made impossible by war and he had come, like Woolf, to hope for a world with fewer classes and towers. Spender, recording the life of an imaginary, 'ordinary' fireman, Jim Braidy, saw this world as not merely desirable but urgently necessary if the government was to avoid full-scale revolution. *Jim Braidy, The Story of Britain's Firemen* is a 1943 account of the life of a typical fireman during the Blitz. Co-authored by Spender, William Sansom and James Gordon, it shows how the role of the fire service changed during the different phases of the Blitz and considers the impact of the Blitz on society. 'Jim Braidy', Spender states at the end of the book,

> is not a revolutionary. Not yet. He is something more dangerous than a revolutionary: a human being. Dangerous, because he is not a mechanical force, he is a living organism, offering the governing classes the opportunity for their salvation.[20]

According to Spender, Jim Braidy is open to democracy and, granted democracy, will help transform society 'on a human basis'. But if the opportunity is lost, he will cease to be 'an individual human being, and become a political force of overwhelming strength: a revolutionary politician'.

Spender is less idealistic than Jennings, who sees society as already transformed by the war. For Spender, the war is a 'people's war' only in the sense that it is creating the conditions for a people's society. Similarly in *Caught*, Green is ultimately ambivalent about the effects of the war, and the fire service in particular, on class. On one level, Green portrays a 'people's war'. He takes on the cross-class montage he had developed in *Living* and *Party Going* and adapts it into an across-class montage, emphasising the inherent similarities between classes in wartime. There is no straightforward dichotomy between classes in *Caught*. Richard, the hero, is a country house-owning, taxi-taking upper-class auxiliary fireman, while his wartime lover, Hilly, seems upper-middle-class (she is looked down on by Richard's sister-in-law, Dy, and is clearly never seen as wife material by Richard). Richard's boss, Pye, is aspirationally lower-middle-class. He puts in heroic efforts with his accent, but drops his 'h's in moments of stress. The rest of the fire station crew are broadly working-class, but there are still gradations of power between Piper, Mary Howells and Chopper that seem to reflect their social position. And Ilse and Prudence, two foreign 'tarts' with expensive tastes whom Richard introduces to Pye, seem to elude class altogether by being European.

Green uses a quick-cutting technique to juxtapose all these characters and to show their resemblances. From the start, we are encouraged to see the connection between Richard Roe and Pye by the lexical union of their names, which combine to mean 'fire' in Greek. They have been brought into a strange and unwilling alliance by their mutual secret knowledge of the abduction of Richard's son, Christopher, by Pye's mentally-ill sister prior to the action of the novel. When Richard first enters the fire service, he and his boss are far apart in character and in lifestyle, but over the course of the book they come to frequent the same expensive night-clubs, using their cachet as firemen to impress women. Shortly after Pye condemns Richard for indulging in 'champagne pressed out of the skin of the grape by the feet of starving peasant women', we see Richard and Pye visiting the same club later that evening (p. 106). Pye arrives with Prudence just after Richard has taken Hilly home to bed.

In one of the most sustained montage passages in the book, Richard and Hilly, in bed together, are cross-cut with Prudence and Pye in the night-club, and with the working-class Brid, who is crying about her wayward husband, Ted, and her baby. The narrator moves between consciousnesses, echoing the vocabulary of the characters he describes. Richard and Hilly lie on the sofa,

> a pleasant brutal picture by the light of his coal fire from which rose petals showered on them as the flames played, deepening the flush spread over contented bodies. She wriggled over on top. (p. 119)

Here the narrator speaks in both of their voices at once. The rose imagery is Richard's and is reminiscent of an earlier meeting with his wife in the rose garden. At the same time, the emphasis on bodies and the choice of 'wriggled' come from Hilly's sensual vocabulary, and the paragraph continues from her point of view: 'she murmured to herself, "This man's my gondola"'. The mingling of vocabulary serves to emphasise both the mutuality of their union and the virtuosity of Green's roving camera.

Immediately afterwards, the Brid narrative cuts in, using working-class syntax in the description of her husband as 'feckless with money and all but he loved her', and her own names for her family in 'something to do with mum, and of course there was baby'. We then see Pye, boring Prudence with his over-repeated stories, and finding himself reminded of the time 'so long ago, over that hill the time his sister put her hand inside his boy's coat because he was cold, to warm his heart' (p. 121). The sentimental language here is Pye's, as is the sexual/ fraternal confusion. The montage in this section serves to illustrate the fundamental similarity between the emotions in the three scenes. Hilly, Pye and Brid are falsely romantic in their attachments to people who they know will throw them over, and in their conflation of lust and love. All the characters lie to themselves and to each other, uttering the 'lies which give the underlying truth away', which Green described in his autobiography as characteristic of war.[21]

The ultimate elision of Roe and Pye is illustrated by Roe's impassioned defence of Pye to Dy at the end of the novel. He insists that 'a man can be responsible, somehow, for his wife, can't he, but never for his sister', with the sentence structure echoing Pye's 'a man's sister is sacred to 'im' earlier in the book (pp. 196, 76). This is indicative both of the doubling between Pye and Roe and of the general coming together of the men in the fire service over the course of the novel. At the start, Richard is aloof and is told by Pye that 'there's a prejudice against you lads' (p. 16). He gradually becomes friends with his colleagues, and Chopper agrees with him that 'It brings everyone together, there's that much to a war' (p. 46). He finds that

> In his dirt, his tiredness, the way the light hurt his eyes and he could not look, in all these he thought he recognised that he was now a labourer, he thought he had grasped the fact that, from now on, dressed like this, and that was why roadman called him mate. (pp. 48–9)

The other firemen now address Richard as 'Dick', and he even begins to use their language, horrifying Dy when he tells Shiner that Christopher is only his 'nipper' (p. 145).

However, this blurring of class boundaries is not complete. Keith Odom writes:

> In the barracks . . . especially through Piper's gossiping, each man's class is discovered; and Roe, who is from a higher social class, is paid odious deference. Also the lower classes adapt more easily to new life and skills, but Roe suffers because he is clumsy at manual labour.[22]

Roe's colleagues may come to like him but they are never able to forget his class. Pye may frequent the same night-clubs, but he still feels able to condemn Roe for frequenting them because he is jealous that they are Roe's natural habitat. Michael North has pointed out that the proletarian world of firefighting is ultimately unavailable to Roe, and that his last action is to send others away, 'to demand solitude even from his own family'.[23] By the end of the novel, Richard has been removed to the country, where his memories of the fire service come to seem increasingly unreal. Although *Caught* does endorse the popular myth of the Blitz as community-forming, it illustrates the limitations of the new classless society. Like the romance between Jennifer and Charlie Forbes in *Millions Like Us*, these newfound bonds are unlikely to survive the war.

In *The Heat of the Day* (1949), Elizabeth Bowen's postwar wartime novel, Bowen presents the wartime bonds between the classes as even more fragile and transient. Here there is a brief alliance between Stella, the upper-middle-class heroine of the book, and Louie, a working-class woman living alone in London while her husband is in the army. Meeting at a dinner with Harrison whom both women, for different reasons, dislike, the two develop a rapport, and Louie accompanies Stella home. Louie now starts to hero-worship Stella, who in turn feels some affection for her new admirer. Louie seems to counteract the world of intrigue and danger that Stella is led into by Harrison and Robert, by being 'ungirt, artless, ardent, urgent'.[24]

The two women come together again when they unwittingly stand on almost the same spot in Stella's street within hours of each other. Louie has returned hoping to see Stella, and Stella later comes 'out of a door and down steps not far from where Louie had stood' (p. 292). They never cross paths again, even unknowingly, but the course of Louie's life is nonetheless influenced by Stella. Reading of the apparent depravity of her heroine in a newspaper, Louie feels that virtue has become 'less possible now it was shown impossible by Stella, less to be desired because Stella had not desired it enough' (p. 306). As a result, she allows herself to become pregnant, and the novel ends with Louie's new life as a mother, wheeling a perambulator occupied by her son, Thomas Victor. The baby's name brings together the names of Louie's and Stella's dead husbands, eerily linking the two women.

By producing Thomas Victor, this random intersection of two lives has had permanent consequences. Nonetheless, it seems to be more a series of coincidences (and misunderstandings) than a genuine union. From the start, Louie mistakes Stella's relation with Harrison, thinking that they are courting and that he is treating her badly. She then underrates Stella by accepting (as always) everything that she reads in the newspapers as factual. Bowen, like Mass-Observation, disapproves of this frenzied and gullible newspaper reading. In the end, Louie is wrong about Stella because 'virtue' means something different for Louie; Stella saw nothing shameful in having a lover in the first place. Union between the classes is difficult when even their language is incompatible. This is a postwar novel and Bowen goes further than Green in presenting a quite different take on the wartime relations between the classes from the one we find in wartime films, where a more hopeful view prevails. In wartime, forming a sense of community was seen as a first step in beating the enemy. It is vital that Jennifer and Charlie Forbes learn to work together in *Millions Like Us* because otherwise the war effort will go short of supplies.

British propaganda films and literature also used cross-class montage to emphasise the superiority of British leisure activities to their German counterparts. Leisure plays a crucial role in a 1939 documentary propaganda film *The Lion Has Wings*, directed by Michael Powell and others. This alternates newsreel footage with acted accounts of the effects of the war in an individual family. The film begins by introducing us to Britain 'where we believe in freedom', illustrating the beauty and progressiveness of interwar Britain. The commentary then contrasts British and German leisure through a fast montage. 'While we played or cycled or walked, others preferred to march', announces the commentator, while the film cross-cuts between the good-natured frolicking of the British and the marching of the German storm-troopers (see Figure 3.5). British rowers and horse racers are contrasted with the German cavalry, with the commentary informing us that 'the chief use of our horses was to exercise, not to carry the cavalry'. 'What is your idea of a holiday?' he asks pointedly. 'This' – a joyful merry-go-round – or 'this' – a Hitler rally?

The contrast between British and German perambulation was a frequent feature of documentary in this period. A favourite for documentarists was the Lambeth Walk, which brought together questions of nation and of class. This began as a song in the 1937 musical *Me and My Girl*. The tune and dance that accompanied it became instantly popular, spreading from Britain to America. As early as 1938, *The Times* contrasted the jollity of the Lambeth Walk with the more miserable politics in Europe, quipping that 'while dictators rage and statesman talk, / All Europe dances – to The Lambeth Walk'.[25]

The middle classes embraced the Lambeth Walk because they saw it as a quintessentially working-class leisure activity which enabled its dancers to emerge as quirky individuals. In their popular 1939 Mass-Observation book *Britain*, Harrisson and Madge lauded the individuality of the Lambeth Walk, which they saw as uniting the community in a manner far superior to any upper-class pursuit, and even as a possible source of resistance to fascism. Here they take the rather

3.5 *'While we played or cycled or walked, others preferred to march'*
Michael Powell, Brian Desmond Hurst, Adrian Brunel, Alexander Korda, *The Lion Has Wings* (1939)

contentious step of identifying the upper classes with the fascists. They inform readers that anti-fascists broke up a Mosleyite demonstration in the East End by 'doing the Lambeth Walk' (p. 175). For Harrisson and Madge, the Lambeth Walk is superior to the ballroom dance of the upper class because

> ballroom dancers sleep walk to [ballroom dance music's] strains with the same surrender of personal decision as that of uniformed Nazis. These Lambeth Walkers are happy because they find they are free to express *themselves* without the hypnosis of a jazz-moon or a Führer. (p. 182)

Where Mass-Observation had disapproved of mass leisure in Blackpool, here they applaud it for creating individuals who will think independently. If people can keep dancing the Lambeth Walk, it might challenge the uniformity of the fascist goosestep.

This potently ridiculous contrast found its way into popular parlance, helped by the Nazis themselves. By 1939, the Lambeth Walk had reached Berlin and a Nazi official derided it as animalistic 'Jewish mischief'.[26] In 1942, Charles Ridley of the British Ministry of Information capitalised on the contrast in a short propaganda film, *Lambeth Walk – Nazi Style*. Ridley manipulated existing shots of a German rally in Leni Riefenstahl's *Triumph of the Will* (1935) to make it appear that Hitler and his soldiers were doing a goosestep version of the Lambeth Walk. In this context, Bill Brandt's iconic photograph of an East End girl dancing the Lambeth Walk took on a political significance. First published by *Picture Post* in mid-war in 1943, this cheerful snapshot of East End leisure found an enthusiastic home in a documentary culture that privileged the spontaneity and apparent authenticity of the Lambeth Walk.[27]

Mass culture

James Barke, John Sommerfield, Henry Green

Mass-Observation was not alone in distinguishing between good and bad mass leisure pursuits. The contrast between the Lambeth Walk and the Blackpool promenade finds parallels in a range of discussions of leisure in the period. At its best, working-class leisure was wholesome and hearty, in contrast to the more pretentious elements of middle-class culture. In 1935, Jennings professed relief that 'there are still certain things in England that have just not been culturised; examples: beer ads, steam railways, Woolworths, clairvoyants'.[28] Four years later, Orwell summed up the 'good civilisation' of wartime Britain in a remarkably similar list:

> the England of totes, dog-races, football pools, Woolworth's [*sic*], the pictures, Gracie Fields, Wall's ice cream, potato crisps, celanese stockings, dart-boards, pin-tables, cigarettes, cups of tea, and Saturday evenings in the four ale bar. [29]

And halfway through *Wigan Pier*, Orwell breaks into what seems to me to be a wholly earnest eulogy of the working-class hearth:

> Especially on winter evenings after tea, when the fire glows in the open range and dances mirrored in the steel fender, when Father, in shirt-sleeves, sits in the rocking chair at one side of the fire reading the racing finals, and Mother sits on the other with her sewing, and the children are happy with a pennorth of mint humbugs, and the dog lolls roasting himself on the rag mat – it is a good place to be in, provided that you can be not only in it but sufficiently *of* it to be taken for granted. (p. 108)

Orwell's middle-class envy (he is not *of* it) is paralleled by Sommerfield's, Greenwood's and Barke's working-class pride. The workers portrayed by these novelists may be the victims of a capitalist regime, but there is no doubt that they have more fun than their employers.

The only genuinely happy character in Greenwood's *Love on the Dole* is Larry Meath, who is both a Communist and a rambler. He takes his girlfriend Sally on walking expeditions 'Over mountains as high as y' never saw' which give her a new insight into life's potential for happiness.[30] The working-class love for hiking makes them a target for the mockery of George Anderson's wife, Mabel, and her upper-class friends in Barke's *Major Operation*. However, once Anderson has gone over to the working classes he goes for a walk in the country with his former secretary, Sophie Grant, and finds he is happier than he has ever been: 'My God, Sophie! I never believed I could know such happiness' (p. 434). It is clear that this is far more wholesome entertainment than the louche partying indulged in by Mabel and her acquaintants.

Jennings, Orwell, Barke and Sommerfield shared an appreciation of working-class food. As in *Berlin: Symphony of a Great City*, where the workers chew more vigorously and enjoy their food more wholeheartedly than the corpulent upper-class diners, in Jennings' *Spare Time* and *Listen to Britain* the workers are seen to eat hearty food and to be more energetic and industrious because of it. A woman serves an enormous pie to her happy working-class family at the beginning of *Spare Time*. At the Flanagan and Allen concert in *Listen to Britain*, the working classes gather for a meal that includes fried cod and chips, sausages, greens and lemon. The viewer is shown two separate close-ups of the concert menu, and it is notable that the more refined Myra Hess lunchtime concert is entirely devoid of food.

Jennings' lemon pudding would also have pleased Orwell. In his wartime essay 'The Lion and the Unicorn', Orwell finds:

> However much you hate [England] or laugh at it, you will never be happy away from it for any length of time. The suet puddings and the red pillar boxes have entered into your soul.[31]

Orwell's love of working-class food is tempered by his awareness that the millions of unemployed are lucky if they can get some dry bread or dripping. He makes it clear in *Down and Out in Paris and London* that people should not be expected to survive on such food. But the scarcity of working-class food only makes it more appealing. The same is true for Sommerfield, who contrasts James, out of work and hungry, with his brother, John, whose wife, Martine, has a wholesome stew ready for him, 'gently bubbling out delicate smells' (p. 44).

In Barke's *Major Operation*, MacKelvie and his family have great trouble finding food while MacKelvie is unemployed, and George Anderson lives for weeks on bread alone after his willing descent from upper class to working class. It is very much an unemployment novel, and we learn with Anderson of the impossibility of eating sufficiently on the limited unemployment funds available. However, some relief is brought to everyone by the fish suppers enjoyed by all the working-class characters. The narrator announces that 'there were few things MacKelvie liked better than an occasional fish supper' and that 'there was no home he knew of which did not provide a hearty welcome to the visitor bearing the savoury smelling, greasy paper package' (p. 98). Later, Sophie is able to take her mother for a fish supper on the way home from the cinema and feel briefly that 'the world was very beautiful and full of joy' (p. 216). Anderson himself finds his fish supper unpalatable as a result of his weak stomach, which makes the upper-class constitution seem generally weaker and less made for simple pleasures.

The hearty working-class appetite for stodge is matched by a wholesome appetite for sex. In *May Day*, the upper-class Peter and Pamela are presented as awkwardly unsure of themselves and each other, and Peter's father wakes up 'distastefully regarding his sleeping wife' (p. 15). Martine and her husband, John, are very much in love, despite all they have suffered through months of unemployment. Even after they have been married for eighteen months, they look at each other every morning 'full of a surprised gratitude that they should be together in the same bed' (p. 10). Their love-making is an idyllic, even innocent, activity: 'in the act of love these two achieved a perfect mutual adjustment, a complete mental and physical absorption and balance that was as beautiful as it was rare' (p. 106).

Barke explicitly contrasts upper- and lower-class love and sex in the chapter headed 'Erotic Nocturne over the Second City'. Here, as 'hot flesh, sweet flesh, young flesh, sweating, smelling flesh . . . and diseased flesh' come together, Barke cuts between Mabel telling George that they will never have sex again and the general 'coming together in union: in erotic closeness' of everyone else. George, turning and tossing unhappily, is juxtaposed with Jock MacKelvie, who is in the 'depths of deep oblivion' with his wife, presumably after sex (pp. 115–17). We hear later that, unlike Mabel, Jean loves her husband: 'there wasn't another like him in the world' (p. 203).

But in these novels too, the more wholesome aspects of working-class leisure are contrasted with the drug-like inanity of consumer culture. Hiking, the Lambeth Walk and love-making are active pursuits, requiring the individual volition of the participants. Cinema-going and newspaper-reading, on the other hand, require a passive spectatorship which disturbed the writers even of these self-consciously cinematic texts. Eisenstein, Vertov and Grierson may whip up the passions of the audience, forcing them into an analytical, even embodied spectatorship, but popular cinema was often represented in 1930s documentary as a mass drug, hypnotising its spectators. 'You may have three halfpence in your pocket and not a prospect in the world', says Orwell in *Wigan Pier*, apostrophising his apparently working-class reader:

> but in your new clothes you can stand on the street corner, indulging in a private daydream of yourself as Clark Gable or Greta Garbo, which compensates you for a great deal. (pp. 81–2)

But elsewhere he dismisses these same cinema audiences, stating that they 'swallowed' absurdities 'with ease'.[32] He blames those same producers who had brought Gable and Garbo to the screen for holding their audiences in 'intellectual contempt'.[33]

In *May Day* Jean, the Langfiers' maid, 'sees herself at the cinema, always triumphant, young and lovely, undergoing a thousand miseries and misunderstandings, but always winning the rich young man in the end' (p. 14). Sommerfield does not allow her to remain deluded, stating that when she comes out 'into the open air afterwards', she realises that rich men may look at her, 'but the embraces proffered in their eyes would bring her no triumph', awakening her to the reality of the capitalist society she lives in. Later he generalises about 'the millions that were sucked in through the doors of the cinemas' and are 'ruled, exploited, cheated, and swindled' by 'dope' (p. 143). In *Major Operation* Barke shows the MacKelvies watching terrible films because only then is Jean 'able to forget she lived in Walker Street' for two hours (p. 95); and George Anderson goes to the cinema not because the films engage his attention but because they distract him from the horrors of his new life (p. 419). Barke specifically condemns the 'American domination of this mightiest of cultural institutions', lamenting that 'had the citizenry seen a film of their own lives, of their own country, they would have been amazed and possibly have felt cheated' (p. 93); the Scottish public is not yet ready for the documentary film.

The debate about the effect of cinema on the working classes was played out heatedly throughout the 1930s. From its inception, cinema was seen as both a radical, transformative medium and a pernicious drug. In *Close Up* in 1928 the novelist Dorothy Richardson defended the cinema in the slums. 'It is said', she complained, 'that the cinema offers nothing to nobody save spiritual degradation'. But 'Imagination fails', she insisted,

> in attempting to realise all that is implied for cramped lives in the mere coming into communication with the general life, all that results from the extension of cramped consciousness . . . insensibly they are living new lives. Growing.[34]

Two years earlier, the cinema critic Caroline Lejeune had begged her readers not to

> grudge these folk their dream, you children of the older arts. Let them sit in the tuneful darkness, splendidly alone, yet with every feeling intensified by the consciousness of mass support, and extract from that white oblong of screen all the romance and adventure that their own lives have missed . . . Let them identify their own faces with the heroine's beauty and be content.[35]

Laura Marcus has pointed out that Lejeune defends the significance of the (female) audience's fantasies and dreams, while at the same time 'critiquing the film industry's cynical manipulations of those fantasies'.[36]

In the 1930s, these critiques became fiercer, as socialists became more anxious about the messages propounded by the capitalist studios. 'The cinema today is a weapon of the class struggle', announced the Communist critic Ralph Bond; 'so far this weapon has been the exclusive property of the capitalists'. His answer was to expose 'in a Marxist manner, how it is used as an ideological force to dope the workers' and to exhibit more Russian films.[37] In *The Condition of the Working Class in Britain* (1933), Allen Hutt listed cinema as one of the powerful cultural instruments which the bourgeoisie had perverted 'to its own class ends'.[38] Edward Upward, always more red than his pink comrades in the Auden Gang, described the picture house as 'concealing danger and misery, fraudulent as vulgar icing on a celebration cake rotten inside with maggots, sugary poison to drug you into contentment'.[39] Exiled in Oxford, Theodor Adorno chastised Benjamin for his attempt to appropriate cinema for the Left, insisting that 'the laughter of the audience at a cinema . . . is anything but good and revolutionary; instead it is full of the worst bourgeois sadism'.[40]

It is noticeable that where the filmmaker was usually gendered as male, the audience members were consistently gendered as female. In

Germany, Kracauer, when he wasn't celebrating the cult of distraction, was dismissing 'the little shop girls' who go to the cinema, suggesting that what these 'Little Miss Typists' really crave is not 'an unmasking of social practices', but an escape from identity in the dark as they 'grope for their date's hand and think of the coming Sunday'. [41] In Britain, the film critic Iris Barry tried to make the femininity of the audience a positive aspect of cinema, reminding her readers that 'three out of four of all cinema audiences are women'. She advocated that women should play a role in the making as well as the watching of films.[42]

It is women who are figured as comprising the passive cinema audiences in *May Day* and *Major Operation*, and Lily who is the fanatical cinema fan in *Living*. Green, however, is more ambivalent about cinema in his novel and seems to use the representation of cinema as a way to test the limits of the cinematic itself. Michael North has seen Green as condemning Lily's dependence on what North views as cinematic opium, but I agree with Cunningham that *Living* 'does not disapprove of Lily's cinema-inspired visions of emigration, nor the tawdry touches of beauty that movies intrude into her existence'.[43] Certainly, Lily is no less drugged by the opium than Green himself in *Pack My Bag*, weeping 'with a hangover . . . at words of his own he put onto the lips of the girl reproving her drunken lover on the screen' (p. 137).

Priestley seems implicitly to contrast his happy football spectators with cinema-goers in his account of the match in *English Journey*. The football crowd, he says:

> are not mere spectators in the sense of being idle and indifferent lookers-on; though only vicariously, yet they run and leap and struggle and sweat, are driven into despair, and raised to triumph. (p. 110)

He grants the football fans the embodied spectatorship that he had denied cinema-goers in his 1929 novel *The Good Companions*, where Inigo Jollifant is 'condemned' to an afternoon in the cinema that is so passive he compares it to 'being forcibly fed with treacle'.[44] Priestley himself would see his own film scripts (and indeed *The Good Companions* itself) realised into some fairly non-treacly films. We have seen that *Sing as We Go* invites a bodily identification not dissimilar from the vicarious running and leaping at the football ground. Priestley does not make explicit the reasoning behind the superior embodiment of the football fan, but it seems to come back to the usual questions of absence and presence. A real man kicking a ball is easier to identify with physically than the image of a man kicking a ball on celluloid. Or perhaps the problem is that 1930s Hollywood film stars rarely do enough running, leaping and sweating.

Henry Green, on the other hand, grants Lily a fairly active embodiment in the cinema, not least because of the presence of the band. Entering the picture house, she is caught by the rhythms of the music, 'tum tum did dee dee', and 'jump[s] her knees to the time' (p. 20). Her companion, Dale, spoilsport that he is, does 'not budge'. Quickly, the tune is over and Lily

> clapped hands and clapped. Applause was general. But film did not stop oh no heroine's knickers slipped down slinky legs in full floor.
> eeeee Lily Gates screamed.
> OOEEE the audience.
> And band took encore then. Tum tum ti tumpy turn. (p. 20)

With that evocative 'eeeee' Green leaves us in no doubt that in Lily's mind her own knickers are falling down too. As in Armstrong's account, Lily finds in the cinematic body a prosthetic extension of her own. Clapping, screaming, jiggling her knees, she is as embodied as the football fans at the end of the novel. The community feeling engendered by the cinema is also comparably strong. Arriving in the darkened theatre, Lily and Bert Jones join a mass of people that extends across the world:

> A great number were in cinema, many standing, battalions were in cinemas over all the country, young Mr Dupret was in a cinema, over above up into the sky their feeling panted up supported by each other's feeling, away away, Europe and America, mass on mass their feeling united supporting renewed their sky. (p. 44)

These panting audiences may be drugged, but there is an ecstatic freedom in the image of the unbounded sky. Knowing that she is watching the same films as audiences across the world, Lily's own horizons expand. With the 'away away' she seems to fly beyond the confines of her world, like the pigeons whose flight is intertwined with hers throughout the book.

It is notable that in a book Green himself described as a 'disconnected cinema film', these descriptions of cinema spectatorship are not particularly cinematic. In Lily and Jim Dale's first trip to the cinema, Green gives a subjective account of the opening sequence of the film:

> Light rain had been falling, so when these two acting on screen walked by summer night down leafy lane, hair over her ears left wet on his cheek

as she leant head, when they on screen stopped and looked at each other. (*Living*, p. 11)

Here there is none of the abrupt cross-cutting we find in Green's version of cinema. It is more of a modernist poem, with a single moment on the screen extending into a lyrical description that is as tactile as it is visual. What is it that Lily actually sees? Not the light rain, which *had* been falling; not the summeriness of the night or the confusing wetness, which seems to apply to the heroine's hair but also implies tears on the hero's cheek.

In going beyond the visual to the tactile, the cinematic technique in *Living* seems to exceed the possibilities of the cinema. Films from *Hindle Wakes* to *A Cottage in Dartmoor* had implicated the viewer physically, but Green takes this much further in appealing to a wider sensorium. Green seems to fit neatly into Jonathan Crary's model of early twentieth-century perception in that his gaze encompasses three if not five senses. In one scene, everyone in the iron foundry is linked by the sound of Arthur singing after the birth of his son; we see the reactions of Craigan, Joe Gates and Jim Dale. This is a piece of early sound montage in a book that coincides with the advent of the sound film. But the senses quickly merge in a way that would be impossible on the screen. Everything in the iron foundry is 'black' with the at once literal and metaphorical 'burnt sound', and 'here was his silver voice yelling like bells'. The coloured noise contrasts with the grimy visual scene. For Jim the noise has a tactile, even gustatory effect, acting like 'acid' on the bitterness inside him, which becomes the girder it is compared to, dissolved by the acid (p. 68).

Later, Lily opens her eyes where she lies above town with Jones and sees 'in feeling'. She has a half-real half-imaginary vision of the labourers in the factories below:

> She saw in her feeling, she saw men working there . . . Racketing noise burst on her . . . Men and women thickly came from, now together mixed, and they went like tongues along licking the streets. (p. 81)

This is a vision that encompasses sight, sound and, most importantly, 'feeling'. By becoming tongues and licking the streets, the people seem to metamorphose from a mental vision to a bodily sensation. In this 'disconnected cinema film', Green goes out of his way to imbricate the senses, refusing to privilege vision, or turning it into a fully embodied sensorium. Green's cinematic novel is not so much a copy of cinema as a self-consciously literary response to a cinematic world.

CHAPTER 4

Camera Consciousness

If the world itself is cinematic, its inhabitants must play their part in creating as well as viewing cinema. Having accepted the cinematic quality of their surroundings, several 1930s writers figured consciousness itself as a camera or projector. These narratives take the cinematic as read and investigate the experience of living in a world whose subjects are absent actors mediated by the cinema screen. This is the darker side of 1930s cinematic writing; it is hard to be hopeful when you are not sure if you exist at all. It also offers a subjective alternative to the objectivity aspired to by documentary literature and film.

Isherwood would later gloss his infamous 'I am a camera' declaration in terms of feeling like a camera, rather than attaining a camera-like objectivity:

> what I really meant by saying 'I am a camera' was *not* I am a camera all the time, and that I'm like a camera. It was: I'm in the strangest mood at this particular moment . . . I just sit and register impressions through the window – visual data – without any reaction to it, like a camera. The idea that I was a person divorced from what was going on around me is quite false.[1]

Camera consciousness here involves a subjective experience of passive, mechanised vision; Isherwood is more victim than witness.[2] According to Stanley Cavell, cinema entered a world 'whose ways of looking at itself . . . had already changed, as if in preparation for the screening and viewing of film'.[3] For Cavell, as for Isherwood, 'film's presenting of the world by absenting us from it appears as confirmation of something true of our stage of existence'. The cinema's estrangement confirms our own.

North has read John Dos Passos's influential experiments with camera-eye narration in similar terms to Isherwood's. Dos Passos's socialist *USA* trilogy, published between 1930 and 1936, is punctuated by 'Camera Eye' and 'Newsreel' sections, which would inspire several British cinematic narratives. However, North has pointed out how surprisingly uncinematic both these sections tend to be. The newsreels, he suggests, seem 'to be misnamed, for they are not actually newsreels at all'.[4] Instead, they are textual collages, compiled from newspaper clippings and song lyrics. If they are visual, they are more like Cubist collages than films, exploiting the capacity for juxtaposition inherent in the newspaper as a visual medium. And, according to North, they are in fact more sonic than visual. Dos Passos himself described them as giving the 'clamor, the sound of daily life', and North suggests that he was less interested in representing the appearance of the visual than in representing its effects on social life.[5]

The camera-eye sections, like the cinematic passages in Green's *Living*, evoke the entire sensorium, juxtaposing sight with sound, touch and smell. 'The Camera Eye (4)' describes the haptic experience of 'riding backwards through the rain', feeling the horse's hoofs 'rattle sharp on smooth wet asphalt after cobbles', and 'The Camera Eye (9)' is dedicated to the odour of the fertiliser factories with their 'reek of rotting menhaden'.[6] As in Green's novel, vision here is embodied, and the literary 'camera eye' is human and subjective. Dos Passos would later describe the camera-eye sections as 'a safety valve for my own subjective feelings'.[7] Where the newsreels investigate the effects of the visual on social life, the camera-eye sections explore its impact on the individual. These effects, Dos Passos suggests, are necessarily political. According to North, Dos Passos uses the camera-eye narration to explore the inherently isolating nature of the visual.[8] Where the aural can create a socialised community, the visual creates a crowd of isolated, fragmented spectators, too scared of being looked at to make the most of the opportunities for spectatorship. Dos Passos's depiction of consciousness as camera-like therefore serves to emphasise the deathly indexicality of cinema, turning the inhabitants of the USA into automata. The mind as camera is engaged in a vampiric act, draining the real of life in order to revivify it eternally as film.

Clouds of irresponsible fantasy

Edward Upward, Christopher Isherwood, Stephen Spender
If the camera eye is vampiric, the potentially radical indexicality of cinema becomes conservative. To accept consciousness as cinematic is to accept life as a living death, in which political change is impossible

because everything has effectively already taken place. The cinematically conscious subject has been co-opted into passively experiencing
the world as spectacle. This is made explicit in *Journey to the Border*, a
1938 novel by Edward Upward, a school friend of Isherwood's and the
most overtly Communist of the Auden Gang. At the start of the novel
Upward's hero, an unnamed tutor, is financially trapped into employment with the narrow-minded and bourgeois Parkin family. The action
of the book takes place during a single day, when the tutor unwillingly
accompanies the Parkins and their friends to the races.

The tutor experiences the day as a series of tests and a series of corresponding experiments in vision.[9] He falls at the first hurdle, when
he fails to assert himself by staying away from the races altogether. He
then oscillates between going off on his own, eschewing the crowd, and
falling under the insidious spell of the Parkins' jovial friend MacCreath,
a tempter with an attractive daughter and an offer of a better job. The
experiments in vision tend to occur at moments when the tutor comes
closest to renouncing the world of the Parkins and the MacCreaths.
Gathering psychological strength to escape the day at the races, the
tutor tries to see the Parkins not as 'living people' but as 'freaks belong-
ing to the same order of reality as the characters in a Grimms' fairy
story or a cinema film'.[10] This attempt to turn himself into a filmic
spectator in order to avoid pain is intensified when he finds himself
coerced into going to the races after all. He now decides that he must
'kill the nerves, put an end to feeling' (p. 26). As he 'mechanically
follow[s]' his employer out of the hall, he metamorphoses from spectator to film actor, performing the role of the already dead cinematic
automaton. Indeed, the tense of his actions becomes cinematic so that
he finds he 'was already following them'. The action is simultaneous
with the thought, because independent will is denied to the automaton.
The tutor stares 'glassily' into the hall, his nerves dead, deciding that
'from now on there would be no more feelings'. Once they are driving
to the races, the mechanical motion of the car seems to participate in
his own mechanisation, so that he longs to be 'dead like the car itself,
even though it moves' (p. 30).

The experiment fails. Thinking and feeling return, and the tutor
becomes 'quite normal again', realising that 'the abnormality had
probably been a fake, a deliberate experiment' (p. 31). Now he decides
to try a new mode of vision, attempting to bring about a change that
will be 'immeasurably more far-reaching' (p. 32). This time he will not
only alter his 'so-called surroundings', he will 'see and touch and hear
differently, as he wanted to, happily'. Now he is a filmmaker, at once

spectator and camera. Like Benjamin's camera, transfiguring the tenement or the rubbish-heap, the tutor transforms the world he observes into something beautiful. Looked at, the landscape lengthens and broadens, becoming 'a tremendous panorama' like 'an infra-red photograph'. As in a photograph or a film, the tutor can see great distances, and the colours become 'far more vivid' than usual. Looking around, he notices details with unusual clarity, picking out 'white insulators on telegraph poles and new copper wires' gleaming on the road. However, this vision too is disappointing. Gazed at for too long, the racecourse marquee dims from white to grey and the shape becomes 'less distinct against the sky' (p. 33). As his vision returns to normal, camera eye and human eye are briefly juxtaposed. The tutor sees the cinematic marquee and the actual marquee at the same time, 'like a superimposed photograph', before the large one fades away. The same process then occurs with sound, and he realises that he has 'not yet conquered his old habits of perceiving' (p. 34).

Nonetheless, the tutor persists in his attempts, with the approach of a steamroller enabling a moment of visionary epiphany. This new vision goes beyond the traditionally filmic to embrace the metaphysical, as the tutor extols the power of the machine. At first the power is visual: it is 'crested in front with a rampant brass unicorn, thumping with its pistons like a thumping heart' (p. 36). But the thumping heart simile is the first in a series of metaphorical attempts to understand the steamroller's extraordinary power. It combines the boldness of engines 'stared at by children from a nursery window' with the 'naïve boldness of a child who sticks out his stomach and makes piston movements with his arms'; it has the 'chuffing indifferent power' of a train carrying an unwilling boy to school and the 'sun-glittering' power of a motor coach transporting a middle-class man to the just life of the countryside. The steamroller seems to journey through the tutor's own youthful fears and hopes, exhorting him to 'remember your past' and see how he has wasted himself. From now on, it says, 'you will go my way, will be iron, will be new' (p. 37). This new vision, which transcends the cinematic in embracing the human, is more 'solid and real' than his previous attempt and 'will not fade'. Now certain of his vision and of himself, the tutor's eyes fill with tears: 'he had triumphed'.

Again, this vision recedes, but it leaves a residue of its power. Although the marquee, in its physical actuality, now proves itself ordinary, the steamroller retains its extraordinary quality. The tutor becomes 'normally happy' (p. 41). He now has the courage to abandon his companions and walk into the countryside, where he finds himself at one with his surroundings, able to appreciate the ordinary pleasures of existence. But, as always, the contentment is too illusory to be long-lived. It is interrupted by the arrival of the burly MacCreath, making small talk and attempting to sympathise with the tutor's 'ideals' (p. 50). Re-entering the marquee, the tutor is frightened by the 'ordinary and indifferent' crowds (p. 53). Losing control of the situation, he loses control of his vision, finding that the lips of a man he is talking to fail to synchronise with the sound of his words, 'like a talking-film that had gone slightly wrong' (p. 54).

The tutor now has a series of increasingly bizarre encounters, which include two potentially redemptive love scenes with young women. However, each is revealed to be false in its promise of ordinary human happiness until finally, just at the moment where he decides that he is both 'insane' and a 'hopeless failure', the tutor engages in a hallucinatory dialogue with himself (p. 110). Again, this dialogue begins with the question of vision. A few moments earlier he has seen a short man in an overcoat walking away from the marquee and realised that the man has 'an extraordinary resemblance to himself' (p. 107). Now, surrendering to physical paralysis, he is told by his inner voice 'you *are* walking'; looking at his feet he finds that 'It looks as though I am' (p. 111). The voice informs him that he is in fact his black-overcoated double and that he is now engaged in a 'perfectly sane' internal dialogue (p. 112). 'Stop thinking that what you see around you might be delusory', the voice commands; 'face up to the actuality' (p. 113). He must escape both his cinematic and his metaphorical visions and become aware of his 'real situation'.

Somewhat predictably, the way to do this is 'the way of the Internationalist Movement for Working-class Power' (p. 116). Once he links his lot with theirs, the tutor will acquire 'a new thinking and a new feeling', 'concerned first with the world outside you and only secondarily with yourself' (pp. 118–19). He will cease to be spectator, camera, filmmaker or dreamer and become 'more vigorous, more normally human' (p. 119). At the end of the novel, he begins a walk to the newsagent where he will be able to find out about the Internationalist Workers' Movement. He has made the first step towards escaping 'the cloud of his irresponsible fantasies' and beginning to live (p. 135). Upward derides camera consciousness as the product of a bourgeois society that must be redeemed through a new sense of external reality. The tutor can only be human once he has stopped experimenting with cinematic modes of vision.

For Isherwood, this Communist transcendence of cinematic

consciousness is naïve and impossible. He may have stated in his belated manifesto that he was only 'in the strangest mood at this particular moment', but in fact this passive alienation is the prevailing mood of the Berlin novels and is presented as the dominant mood in fascist Germany. The narrator's experience of being a camera may be subjective, but it is constant nonetheless, and is shared by many of the people around him. The inhabitants of Berlin are typified by the girl the narrator observes in Bobby's bar, ostensibly attractive but in fact 'tired and bored' with a drooping mouth.[11] 'It's so dull here', says Otto, on Rügen Island, bored by his querulous lover; 'if you were to go out into the street now and be run over by a taxi', Sally tells Christopher, 'I shouldn't really *care* a damn' (pp. 347, 307).

The 'I am a camera' opening to the 1930 Berlin Diary typifies this bored alienation. Isherwood begins the section with a description of the shabby, dirty streets in his district, before characterising himself as characterless: 'I am a camera with its shutter open, quite passive, recording not thinking' (p. 243). He records a man shaving and a woman washing her hair, before styling himself not as cameraman but editor: 'some day, all this will have to be developed, carefully printed, fixed'. The implication here is that one day he will have to re-enter his world, interpreting and reacting to what he currently passively observes. For now, he wanders restlessly around his room, turning the street into a peepshow as he peers through the slats of the blind to make quite sure that the whistling below 'is not – as I know very well it could not possibly be – for me' (p. 244). As a camera-wielding film-maker, Isherwood has Upward's tutor's capacity to magnify and distort objects. The cinema, he would say in his 1938 autobiography, 'puts people under a microscope: you can stare at them, you can examine them as though they were insects'.[12] In the Berlin novels the same is true of objects; in the 'I am a camera' scene, everything in his room appears 'abnormally heavy and dangerously sharp' (p. 244). Surveying 'a pair of candlesticks shaped like entwined serpents, an ashtray from which emerges the head of a crocodile', the narrator feels threatened by the apparent invincibility of the animated objects that surround him. He surmises that they 'will probably remain intact for thousands of years' before apathetically condemning them to the fate of being merely 'melted down for munitions in a war'.

Isherwood's restless inhuman camera consciousness places him at the mercy of malevolently distorted objects throughout the Berlin novels. As in Eisenstein's formulation, he does not act with but through objects.[13] He is displaced by the larger-than-life objects that surround him. The objects are all the more frightening when they are metaphorical; camera consciousness can go further than the actual camera in multiplying layers of imaginary horror. Thus in *Mr Norris Changes Trains*, as the clock strikes in the beginning of 1931, there is a disorientating crash from the band and 'Like a car which has slowly, laboriously reached the summit of the mountain railway, we plunged headlong downwards into the New Year' (p. 30). The car precedes and supersedes the humans it represents, so that they seem to be caught in a driverless vehicle, plunged against their will into an uncertain future.

The immediate future is characterised by a plethora of disorienting objects.[14] The narrator is greeted by a dehumanised head in silhouette, spitting vigorously from a window (p. 31). Entering the house, 'one of the anaesthetic periods of [his] evening supervene[s]', with the passive construction denying agency, implying that an anaesthetised filter is pushed in front of his camera consciousness. The narrator's camera eye is now bruised and drunken, like the drunken camera inside the beer glass in Vertov's *The Man with a Movie Camera*. His glance

> reel[s] about the room, picking out large or minute objects, a bowl of claret-cup in which floated an empty match-box, a broken bead from a necklace, a bust of Bismarck on the top of a Gothic dresser – holding them for an instant, then losing them again in general coloured chaos.

Arthur Norris's head is included in the list of objects, 'its mouth open, the wig jammed down over its left eye'. At home in the disembodied world of cinema, the narrator happily wanders around 'looking for the body', before collapsing on a sofa, 'holding the upper half of a girl' (p. 32).

The disembodied synecdoche in *Mr Norris* is continued in the stories in *Goodbye to Berlin*, chiefly through the images of hands, always the body part favoured by 1920s radical film directors. The image of Sally's green fingernails, at once hedonistic and macabre, is dotted through the novel. The narrator spots her nails early on in their first encounter:

> I noticed that her fingernails were painted emerald green, a colour unfortu-nately chosen, for it called attention to her hands, which were much stained by cigarette-smoking and as dirty as a little girl's. (pp. 268–9)

By the time that he introduces Sally to Natalia Landauer, they have become a mutual joke: 'To-day, I specially didn't paint my toe-nails'

(p. 437). The narrator is increasingly appalled by both the hands and nails, which are separated not only from Sally's body but from each other:

> I noticed how old her hands looked in the lamplight. They were nervous, veined and very thin – the hands of a middle-aged woman. The green finger-nails seemed not to belong to them at all; to have settled on them by chance – like hard, bright, ugly little beetles. (p. 277)

In less than ten pages Sally's hands have aged from girlhood to middle age and the fingernails have become objects of derision rather than curiosity. With the hands dehumanised through synecdoche, the nails are animated and given the power to move with volition. Having animated the nails, Isherwood dehumanises them, comparing them to insects. This process of simultaneous dehumanisation and animation renders Sally alien and grotesque .

Sally's hands resonate with the 'great big black hand stretching over the bed' in the nightmare Otto recounts to Christopher (p. 376). This recurring waking nightmare is itself bizarrely cinematic. Before Otto can see the hand, the room has to go dark, even if it is in fact 'broad daylight' to start with. He then becomes the spectator of a horrific vision, unable to move or cry out, trapped in his role as viewer. The narrator, whose camera vision is now alert to the strange, animated significance of hands, then becomes aware of the oddness of the hands of Erna, a tuberculosis victim in the sanitorium where Otto's mother has been sent. He notices the wedding ring rattling on 'her bony finger' and sees that when she talks her hands flit 'tirelessly about in sequences of aimless gestures, like two shrivelled moths' (p. 402). Like Otto's nightmare hand, Sally's beetles and Erna's moths seem to creep up on their owners unaware. In this strange and alienated city, nothing is what it seems and even one's own body has the potential for violence.

The scene at the sanitorium echoes the party scene in *Mr Norris* in its bewildering cinematic intensity. The narrator it explicit in viewing this as another of his passive, 'I am a camera' days:

> Everything which happened to me today was curiously without impact: my senses were muffled, insulated, functioning as if in a vivid dream. In this calm, white room, with its great windows looking out over the silent snowy pinewoods . . . these four women lived and moved. My eyes could explore every corner of their world. (p. 402)

As in Dos Passos and Green, the literary experience of cinematic consciousness is multi-sensual. On first arriving, 'the smell of the warm, clean, antiseptic building' enters the narrator's passive nostrils 'like a breath of fear' (p. 401). His passivity is now a more explicitly political reaction than it was previously. The women, helpless in their poverty and sickness, are unable to control their lives, and the only appropriate response seems to be a corresponding helplessness. The scene turns into a ghostly parody of a party, with the visitors and patients dancing to the music of a gramophone. The narrator holds a shivering Erna in his arms in the dark and as he kisses her he feels 'no particular sensation of contact' (p. 406). Instead, it is merely part of the 'rather sinister symbolic dream which I seemed to have been dreaming throughout the day'.

As Christopher and Otto depart, the patients throng around them in the circle of light created by the anthropomorphised 'panting bus' (p. 408). Now that Isherwood is about to leave – about, he hopes, to be woken from his cinematic dream – the women take on the aspect of the already dead figures of cinema. Their 'lit faces' are 'ghastly like ghosts against the black stems of the pines'. Aware that this is 'the climax of my dream: the instant of the nightmare in which it would end', the narrator is guiltily afraid that the women will attack them. But this is merely an illusion. The spectres of cinema are not there at all: 'they drew back – harmless, after all, as mere ghosts – into the darkness'.

The narrator's helplessness in the face of both suffering and antagonism reflects a more general passivity in Berlin. The strength of the city itself has been undermined by years of poverty and it drains the strength of its inhabitants. 'Berlin is a skeleton which aches in the cold: it is my own skeleton aching' (p. 464). This is a dull, passive ache, with the iron throbbing and shrinking and the plaster 'numb'. With the Nazis' rise to power, the whole city lies 'under an epidemic of discreet, infectious fear', which the narrator can feel, 'like influenza, in my bones' (p. 224). The violence of the Nazis is too sudden and determined to evoke much of a reaction from the already passive populace. Watching three SA men stabbing Rudi, a boy of seventeen, a group of dozens of onlookers are 'surprised, but not particularly shocked' (p. 482).

Ultimately, the narrator recognises his camera-eye persona as helpless. He cannot offer documentary accuracy, because in a world where individuals are at the mercy of the whims of a fascist state, documentary accuracy is impossible. What is it that happens to Rudi, and the hundreds of boys like him, who are taken away? The narrator can only speculate: 'perhaps at this very moment Rudi is being tortured to death' (p. 489). All he can offer is a portrayal of camera consciousness, with its apolitical tendency to separate the observing self from the unreal world. At the end of the novel, about to escape poverty and fascism in England, the narrator watches the trams and the people, observing that they have an air 'of curious familiarity', 'like a very good photograph' (p. 490). Looking back from the safety of his writing desk, he finds that he 'can't altogether believe that any of this really happened'.

Upward would no doubt dismiss Isherwood's sense of life as a mediated photograph as a cloud of irresponsible fantasy. In the world of *Journey to the Border*, Isherwood's narrator would do well to join the Communist Party he flirts with in *Mr Norris* and to force himself into active participation with his surroundings. But the politically active characters in the *Berlin Novels* are presented as corrupt or merely naïve. Mr Norris and the Communist leader Bayer are too concerned with power to be genuinely engaged in societal reform; Otto and his fellow workers are too naïve to have an effect anything. The narrator's journalist friend, Helen Pratt, rushing around, combating indifference with 'vitality, success, and news', seems to miss the point of the human dramas she encounters (p. 230). In the end, she will achieve no more than the narrator in fighting fascism.

For Isherwood, Hitler's Berlin is an unreal, mediated city. Benjamin, in his 'Work of Art' essay, published three years before *Goodbye to Berlin*, observed the tendency of the fascists to introduce aesthetics into political life, pressing film into 'the production of ritual values'.[15] According to Benjamin, 'mass movements, including war, constitute a form of human behaviour which particularly favours mechanical equipment'.[16] By the time that Isherwood published *Goodbye to Berlin*, Hitler had made clear his commitment to cinema and to cinematic spectacle. 'The masses need illusion', he said in 1938, observing the crowds flocking to the cinema, 'but not only in theatres or cinemas. They've had all they can take of the serious things in life.'[17] According to Virilio, Hitler transformed Europe into a cinema screen, and his spectacular rallies were created foremost in order to be filmed.[18] Thus Riefenstahl and others were given unlimited budgets to film the Nazi rallies, and the rallies themselves were created as film sets. In 1937 Hitler's architect, Albert Speer, was given the use of 130 anti-aircraft searchlights (almost the entire German strategic reserve) to create 'the feeling' of a 'vast room, with the beams serving as mighty pillars of infinitely high outer walls'.[19] 'The result,' he said later, 'was to make the architecture of the building emerge sharply outlined against the night, and at the same time to make it unreal.'[20] In this 1965 diary, Speer professed himself to be 'strangely stirred by the idea that the most successful architectural creation of my life is a chimera, an immaterial phenomenon'.[21] What is more, this immaterial 'cathedral of light' was created largely for the purposes of being filmed.[22]

Isherwood evokes this sense of a chimeric world through his camera consciousness. Keith Williams has seen 1930s texts as foreshadowing Baudrillard's postmodern 'hyperreal', representing a 'transitional phase between Modernism and Postmodernism'.[23] For Baudrillard, in the postmodern world 'signs of the real' have been substituted for the real, and everywhere 'the hyperrealism of simulation is translated by the hallucinatory resemblance of the real to itself'.[24] This is the world created by Hitler at his rallies and the world experienced by Isherwood's narrator.

The hyperreality of 1930s Germany is also made explicit by Spender in his 1951 autobiography. Here he describes attending a party in Hamburg where a film is shown 'of another party just like the one at which I was now present and with some of the same people'.[25] 'It was as though,' he says, making the hyperreality explicit, 'this Germany were a series of boxes fitting into one another, and all of them the same.' The experience becomes even more unnerving when the setting changes to a party in the very room Spender is in:

> The camera passed through moving figures, surveying the room, occasionally pausing as if to examine someone's dress or figure. Boys and girls were lying on the ground embracing and then rolling away from one another to turn their faces towards the camera's lens. Willi lay stroking the head of a girl beside him. He turned, his face white in the light, and then he kissed her, the shadow first, and then his head, covering the light on her lips. I heard Willi laugh beside me.

In Spender's account, the party is not merely unreal because it is filmed. It is as though it happens in the first place only on film. Like Speer's pillars of light, Willi's kiss takes place in the hyperreal. He kisses her shadow and then covers the light on her lips, enacting a ghostly, illusionary imitation of a kiss. The actual Willi's laughter becomes as unreal as the filmic Willi's gestures. And at the end of the film, Spender sees the people around him as absent actors. They rise up 'with gestures as though they were yawning', with two or three couples dancing 'to no music in the half darkness' and then seeming 'to swoon away together' in the 'silence and shadow' of the corners of the room. For Spender, as for Isherwood, the experience of life as cinema is appropriate in a country of simulacra. He states that with the rise of Nazism, he and Isherwood became 'ever more aware that the carefree personal lives of our friends were facades in front of the immense social chaos' (p. 131).

Skeletons and shadows

John Sommerfield, Louis MacNeice, Walter Allen, Patrick Hamilton
As the decade progressed, not just Germany but Britain too was gripped by the hyperreal. For British Marxists this was endemic in mechanised labour itself. Where 1930s Soviet Russia was embracing a programme of increased mechanisation as a necessary step towards building a productive Communist society, British and German writers tended to adopt Marxism more romantically. Benjamin quoted Marx, who states in *Capital* that in working with machines, workers learn to coordinate 'their own movements with the uniformly constant movements of an automaton'.[26] Work turns the working classes into automata. In *Modern Times*, Chaplin makes explicit the link between the automaton in the factory and the automaton on the cinema screen, enacting the very passivity that Isherwood attributed to the cinematic consciousness. Sommerfield condemns the mechanisation of labour in *May Day*, where John's life in the factory is lived 'in hearing of the rhythm of the machines' (p. 174). The 'loose belt' in the 'big machine-shop' goes on with an 'interminable flap . . . flap . . . flap . . . setting an irritating, despondent rhythm to whose beat the girls continually [find] their thoughts going' (p. 213). Caught in these rhythms, the workers lose their individuality and their volition; there is 'a kind of strange numbing beauty in the rhythm of the work' (p. 214). They are overtaken by the machines, which the factory bosses set faster and faster so that it becomes 'impossible for the department to function as a whole'. A 'positive anarchy' reigns as they struggle to catch up with each other.

The hyperreality of life in Britain was also intensified by international politics. Britain like Germany was threatened by fascism from within and without, and with the onset of the Civil War in Spain the extent of the danger became clear. Several writers made explicit the connection between their helplessness in the face of political terror and their experience of life as a cinematic dream or nightmare. In his autobiography, MacNeice would recall the anxiety of the late 1930s in terms of a dream about a nightmarish film:

> Shortly after seeing the film of *Dr Mabuse* I had the following dream. I had been invited to a house party . . . on a little peninsula . . . The peninsula

consisted of a long neglected garden in the centre of which was a knoll on top of which was a house. This house was a skeleton . . . I found myself walking along an overgrown path and in the flower borders on either side there was growing, instead of flowers, regular rows of swords planted with the point up, as regularly as tulips, curving shining swords . . . there stood a soldier in khaki with a fixed bayonet. A terrifying imbecile cackle made me look behind and there at my left shoulder stood Dr Mabuse from the film, cackling and leering; he had a great bush of orange-red hair. On sight of him I awoke.[27]

He adds that 'Nineteen thirty-eight was like my dream of the skeleton house', suggesting that the horror of pre-war Europe is best captured by a filmic nightmare inspired by a nightmarish film.

Fritz Lang's 1922 film *Dr Mabuse: The Gambler* is a frightening portrayal of the machinations of the eponymous psychoanalyst-*cum*-hypnotist who drives a series of victims to gamble, cheat and commit suicide. Although it was made long before Hitler had made any impact on Germany, it is easy to see how, in the 1930s, MacNeice linked Lang's film with the threat of fascism and with his own helpless passivity in the face of world events. In the second part of the film, Dr Mabuse announces that he wants to become 'a giant – a titan – swirling laws and gods like withered leaves', and throughout both parts he evinces a megalomania and mad determination akin to Hitler's own. From the standpoint of the 1930s, the dangers inherent in Mabuse's easy manipulation of others are clear. His victims are lured half-willingly and half-protesting to their deaths, with one woman even laying down her life out of love for him. Lang is ahead of his time in revealing the threat to civilisation posed by persuasive dictators and by their gullible subjects.

In his 1938 *Autumn Journal*, MacNeice dramatises his own sense of helplessness in the face of world events. He learns about Hitler's ambitions through a series of visual and aural representations. Posters, 'flapping on the railings', tell the 'fluttered / World that Hitler speaks', and 'Hitler yells on the wireless' (pp. 108, 113). Unable to experience an unmediated world, MacNeice comes to feel that he 'must be dreaming' (p. 108). The individual is 'powerless' as the 'bloody frontier / Converges on our beds', invading sleep and dreams (p. 109). Violence is now making inexorable progress into everyday life, and that inexorability manifests itself visually through the image of

> A windscreen-wiper
> In an empty car
> Wiping away like mad[.] (p. 114)

The wiper itself is as unstoppable as a film or a filmic nightmare, continuing mechanically, irrespective of the lack of a spectator gazing through the windscreen. MacNeice uses the image to comment on the events he is describing, much as Eisenstein uses non-diegetic montage such as the waking lions. Throughout the poem, visual symbols and similes both provide a peculiar, cinematic commentary, juxtaposing the sights and sounds of 1938 London with external images. MacNeice finds that the 'carpet-sweepers' advance across tables in cafés 'Inexorably, like a tank battalion'; later, the 'wood is white like the roast flesh of chicken' (pp. 109, 113).

Faced with so much unreality, the poet finds that 'Nightmare leaves fatigue':

> We envy men of action
> Who sleep and wake, murder and intrigue
> Without being doubtful, without being haunted. (p. 131)

He comes to envy his Irish countrymen, who

> shoot to kill and never
> See the victim's face become their own[.]

Here the Irish, unlike MacNeice and his haunted generation, are able to separate self and other, viewer and object. These men of action resist the lure of the cinematic hall of mirrors. MacNeice himself yields to the charm of dreaming. 'Sleep, my body', he exhorts; 'sleep, my ghost' (p. 151). It is impossible to withstand the unreality and so it becomes easier to accept his own absent presence, to join the similarly ghostly 'Cagney, Lombard, Bing and Garbo', who 'Sleep in [their] world of celluloid' (pp. 151–2).

MacNeice's former Birmingham student Walter Allen shared the poet's fear that the ghostly, nightmarish aspects of cinema were rendering experience unreal. Allen, brought up in a working-class household in Aston, Birmingham, was educated at a grammar school before becoming MacNeice's student during the poet's six-year stint teaching Classics at Birmingham University in the 1930s. In Allen's 1939 novel *Blind Man's Ditch*, the violence and pain threatened by the blades in MacNeice's skeleton house materialise in a brutal and unnecessary murder. The epigraph to the book prefigures the murder, reproducing a passage from later in the novel in slightly different form:

The old man's shadow, spindled and contorted in grotesque parody, moved jerkily along the sun-bloomed surface of the wall. A green van rattled to a stop and obliterated it. When it emerged again the shadow bobbed up and down as though twitched violently by a string.[28]

Here the reader witnesses the murder, projected shadow puppet-like on the wall. The epigraph gives the murder itself a cinematic inevitability. It takes place textually before the characters have decided to enact it, which undermines their volition, suggesting that they are merely fulfilling their automaton-like roles in a predetermined scene.

Allen himself was as cinema-obsessed as his contemporaries in the 1930s. I have quoted his recollection that he was trying to 'get on the page the image as a film-director might present it' and his sense that the 1930s was the decade of the 'montage' novel. *Blind Man's Ditch* is built of a montage of quickly changing scenes from different points of view, which juxtapose the life and thoughts of the upper- and working-class characters and show the perspective of each on the other. But in this 1939 novel, published on the eve of war, he also makes the dangers of internalising cinema apparent. Like Isherwood, Allen presents his characters as gripped in a paralysing detachment from external events and from each other.

This detachment is typified by Rosamund, an attractive journalist, whose hard-won independence comes at the price of a cold heart. Rosamund's prize possession is her telephone, a symbol of independence which she values chiefly because it is always possible to ring off. When we first see her she is in a markedly Isherwood-like pose, looking into the street below her office. She surveys the crowds of shoppers, the cars, the amorous young men and listens to the sounds of 'people chattering, aimlessly, of gears being changed' (p. 51). Like Isherwood, she bemoans her own, apparently inevitable disengagement from the scene. The first words she utters are 'God, I'm bored', as she drifts from the window to her desk. During a languid coastal holiday with her mother, Rosamund's detachment is figured as explicitly cinematic. Her thoughts unravel lazily, 'like a film unwinding' (p. 246). She daydreams about her next holiday in Norway and sees it remotely, 'as though on a cinema screen, happening to somebody else'.

At the end of *Prater Violet*, Isherwood's 1946 account of his time in the film industry making *Little Friend* (1934), the narrator ponders the potential benefits of assuming a distanced, cinematic consciousness.[29] Longing for a holiday, for sex and for the death-like sleep that follows sex, he glimpses a mode of thought that leads to safety, 'to where there is no fear, no loneliness'.[30] For an instant this way 'is even quite clear', but he realises that to take it 'would mean that I should lose myself . . . I should no longer be Christopher Isherwood' (p. 125). Isherwood, like Upward, realises that voluntarily adopting the passive cinematic consciousness he evinced in the *Berlin Novels* would be to sacrifice too much. Rosamund, however, has chosen this way, allowing herself to live a life that is so cinematically mediated that it appears to be happening to someone else.

It is detachment that is the potentially fatal trap in *Blind Man's Ditch*; a trap which snares Eugene, the working-class hero of the novel. At the start of the book, Eugene is engaged in an improving course of study, excelling in his evening classes and intending to move on to better things. Passionate and engaged, he is not even aware that people like Rosamund exist. Indeed, when he first meets her, he figures her, more accurately than he realises, as a Hollywood character, 'a figure seen in a slick film or in an advertisement in the expensive shiny weeklies that you glanced at from time to time in the reading-room at the public library' (p. 65). After talking to her at the theatre and accompanying her home to her flat, Eugene recalls their encounter as a frozen photograph. She is 'framed in memory, in her dark blue jumper'; 'it was as though he had walked into the cinema and had seen himself upon the screen with Rosamund' (pp. 111–12).

Rosamund serves as Eugene's introduction to the hyperreal. Once he is caught in her mediated world, he himself becomes gradually more ghostly. When he writes Rosamund a naïvely impassioned declaration of love, she is frightened as though by a ghost:

> She was like one who has spent his lifetime passionately denying the existence of ghosts, has staked his life upon it, and then, turning a corner one night, has confronted a ghost. (p. 169)

In fact, it is Rosamund who is the ghost, confronting the living, but in this bizarre, cinematic world, she is the spectator and Eugene the absent actor who, ignored by Rosamund and drained of life, can only become a ghost himself.

Mourning his friendship with Rosamund, Eugene becomes embroiled with Bartholomew, a fairly hardened criminal, who involves the younger man in a plot to rob an old man on his regular trip to the bank. In a scene which is cross-cut with Rosamund's own filmic seaside musing, Eugene awaits the murder, feeling as he once did at the dentist:

He had been completely passive, as though he had been delivered into the hands of something very much more powerful than himself, something that it was futile to resist . . . It was as though inexorable machinery were in motion, and he part of it. Nothing he could do could arrest its progress . . . If, as the spanner descended, the machine stopped, his hand would freeze with it. (p. 251)

Looking down, he sees himself cinematically, 'a pillar of flesh erect in a jostling crowd of shadows' (p. 252). He knows that the people around him are figures in a dream world, who will 'disappear when he wakes up'. In figuring Eugene as a cog in an inexorable machine, Allen uses terms that are startlingly similar to those Isherwood would use to describe cinema in *Prater Violet.* 'The film is an infernal machine', Bergmann the film director tells Isherwood the narrator:

Once it is ignited and set in motion it revolves with an enormous dynamism. It cannot pause. It cannot apologise. It cannot retract anything. It cannot wait for you to understand it. It cannot explain itself. It simply ripens to it inevitable explosion. (p. 33)

Caught in this inexorable, cinematic dream, Eugene can do nothing but hit Mr Overs on the head and steal his money. Only he is dreaming too deeply to understand his actions and he hits him hard enough to kill him.

Eugene commits the murder in a cinematic trance. It therefore seems logical that when the murder itself starts to seem unreal, he tries to render it real by experiencing it in the hyperreal. Hiding in a hotel, unable fully to process what he has done, he is convinced 'that if only he could see the scene in its shabby horror, with himself an actor in it, then he would be free of it' (p. 269). For now he is existing 'in some half-world of dream'. He longs to witness the blood, 'to watch it trickle from beneath the cheap cap', so that he can convict himself of his guilt (p. 270). It is only in sleep that he seems to approach it; in that 'under-sea world, in which objects bulged distorted in heavy green water, flattened and foreshortened by the pressure of the water' (p. 278). As in MacNeice's nightmare, sleep mimics the distortions of the camera, magnifying and highlighting objects.

Lying half-awake, staring at the shadows on the wall, Eugene at last sees the murder played out cinematically in an echo of the epigraph. As in the epigraph, he watches the old man's shadow moving across the surface of the wall. This time his conscious thoughts interject: 'He wanted to shout out and warn him; but no words came' (p. 281).

Eugene has been transformed from passive camera to passive specta-tor, although he was originally responsible for creating the scene that is played out on the wall before him. He now sees the blood he has been longing for. A second shadow cuts across the first in 'mimic assault' and then hinges to the ground 'as though the string had been cut', decomposing 'into a pool of blood'.

Inevitably, this filmic re-enactment does not serve to make the crime seem any more real. Eugene finds that

> Everything was now outside him. He was quite empty, merely a pair of eyes watching an action that had been part of him and was now externalised; and the action went on continuously, like a section of a film that is projected time and time again in slow motion. The action went on, and he saw the action whether he closed his eyes or not. He did not need his eyes as a screen any longer. Anything served for the action to be projected upon. (p. 295)

He is satisfied, 'but only intellectually' (p. 296). He still cannot know 'how it felt when the steel of your spanner came into contact with the back of a man's skull' (p. 296). Until he knows this, he realises, 'he would be living in a story . . . unable to divorce it from reality'. The hyperreal replaying of the murder, projected onto brain or wall, cannot recreate it as a real experience. It is fitting that the book ends not with Eugene but with Rosamund. By a happy coincidence, Bartholomew has chosen to escape to the seaside resort where Rosamund is languidly dreaming away with her mother. Seeing his photograph in the newspa-per, she recognises him and realises that she can have her moment of triumph: 'it was the best scoop ever' (p. 317). Just as the murder itself takes place in the hyperreal, its consequences belong to the media and not the law courts.

This tendency for the media to appropriate and reduce human stories is mocked by Patrick Hamilton at the end of *Hangover Square* (1941). Hamilton, who had grown up in a world of genteel poverty, turned to Marxism in the 1930s, not so much out of sympathy with the working classes as out of antipathy to the petty bourgeoisie. According to his biographer, he

> followed the Marxist line that Fascism was the last gasp of capitalism; the final attempt by the bourgeoisie to preserve their power against the inevita-ble triumph of Socialism.[31]

Hangover Square is an account of life in the seedier parts of London and Brighton in the lead-up to war, which explores the fascist tendencies

Hamilton sees as endemic in the louche strata of society. The novel ends with the suicide of its hero, George Harvey Bone, a vulnerable schizophrenic, who is unable to survive in the cruel world in which he has found himself. Bone kills himself after murdering his callously manipulative beloved, Netta, and her fascist lover, Peter. 'Only one newspaper,' says the narrator, 'a sensational picture daily', gave Bone's murders and suicide any prominence.[32] The novel ends with the newspaper's 'crude epitaph':

SLAYS TWO
FOUND GASSED
THINKS OF CAT

For hard-hearted journalists like Allen's Rosamund, murder merely makes good, albeit brief, copy. Bone's murders, like Eugene's, are both a product of cinematic consciousness and a symptom of his time. *Hangover Square* can be read as an unwitting sequel to *Blind Man's Ditch*. Allen's novel too is pervaded by the vague threat of fascism, with Eugene's increasing detachment reflecting a more general malaise. Hearing that Hitler has marched into Vienna, Anderson, Eugene's tutor and Rosamund's lover, finds that 'the Common Room break, with the coffee, the hot milk, and the Horlicks, the music master . . . all seemed unreal' (p. 129). But, caught up in his obsession with Rosamund, Eugene himself seems increasingly oblivious to the political situation.

In *Hangover Square,* which Hamilton began writing in December 1939, in a country already at war, the dangers of fascism are more apparent. Hamilton would later explain his motivation for writing *Hangover Square* in explicitly political terms:

> What I was trying to present was a 'black' social history of my times. There were so many 'white' portraits of the Twenties and Thirties that I wanted to show the other side of the picture. After all, those were the decades in which Hitler rose to power. No one that I read was writing anything about him and the evil he represented.[33]

The political apathy he derides in fellow writers is reflected in the lazy fascist sympathies of Netta and Peter. Both are engaged in dissolute, hand-of-mouth Earl's Court living, sponging off strangers and friends, and both are attracted by the excesses and order of fascism. Peter sports a Hitler moustache and has been unashamedly involved with Mosley's Blackshirts, going 'about Chelsea in a uniform' (p. 32). Netta is too apathetic to join a political party. Born 'without any natural predilection

towards thought or action', she has 'become totally impassive', step-
ping over obstacles like a 'somnambulist' (p. 125). Nonetheless, she is
'physically attracted by Hitler' and likes 'the uniforms, the guns, the
breeches, the boots, the swastikas, the shirts' of fascism, though she is
'bored to distraction' by the idea of a war (p. 129).

A frequent cinemagoer himself, Hamilton links the easy acceptance
of fascism and of Chamberlain's ineffectual 'peace in our time' with
the complacency of popular cinema. Wandering through Leicester
Square, Bone's friend Johnny pauses in front of the Empire Cinema
with its 'bright advertisements of "Good-bye, Mr Chips", with Robert
Donat and Greer Garson' (p. 101). This 1939 British film, directed by
Sam Wood, portrays a shy schoolmaster finding unexpected happiness
with an implausibly beautiful young woman. Johnny links the film
with the unnaturally fine weather, reflecting that it is 'Fine for Hitler
in Czechoslovakia . . . Fine for Mr Chamberlain, who believed it was
peace in our time – his umbrella a parasol!' and 'You couldn't believe it
would ever break, that the bombs had to fall.'

In this context, the cinematic nature of Bone's schizophrenic 'dead
moods' is significant. From the start, Bone's lapses in consciousness are
figured as filmic. The novel opens with a photographic '*Click!*', which
Bone thinks might better be described as a '*snap*' or '*crack*' (p. 15). The
effects of this distortion of consciousness are presented as more aural
than visual here. Bone is faced with a sudden, deafening silence, though
he is not actually 'physically deaf'. Instead, it is as though 'a shutter had
fallen' on him like a 'sudden film'. At first, 'film' is figured as a covering,
but Bone seizes on the double meaning of his own simile and thinks
that 'it was like the other sort of film, too'. It is as though, he thinks, 'he
had been watching a talking film, and all at once the sound-track had
failed'. The figures continue to move, but life has 'all at once become a
silent film' with no music. It is not simply the dead mood that is cinematic here. Normal life itself is presented as a talking film, although it
is only when the talking stops that its cinematic nature presents itself.

The silent film, always more 'ultracinematographic' than the talkie,
asserts its own filmicness. And in the process it makes Bone aware
of the filmic aspect of ordinary life, so that the people around him
move 'like automatons, without motive, without volition of their own'
(p. 17). Bone, whom Netta later describes as acting like a 'somnambulist' in his dead moods, becomes aware that everyone else has been
somnambulists all along (p. 39). Walking as if in 'a dream', the viewer
but not the creator of this silent film, he comes to see that everything
he witnesses is nonexistent – lacking 'colour, vivacity, meaning';

already dead (p. 17). This becomes more extreme in a later dead mood, when Bone figures himself as a spectator imprisoned by the cinema screen. The world is now 'enclosed' behind a film; things and people move 'eerily, without colour, vivacity or meaning, grimly, puppet-like' (p. 165). He sees this click as the opposite of the camera's: an '*inclosure*' instead of an '*exposure*'. He and the world are both trapped, though on either side of the glass.

Once he reawakens, Bone always looks back on his dead moods with embarrassment. 'Really, it was awful', he thinks, 'wandering about like an automaton, a dead person, another person, a person who wasn't you' (p. 25). But in fact the situation is more complex. In *Blind Man's Ditch*, Allen followed Upward in presenting Eugene's cinematic detachment as an unfortunate aberration from conscious living, albeit one that he saw as symptomatic of the 1930s human condition. In *Hangover Square*, Hamilton suggests that cinematic detachment can be one way to escape delusion. Whereas Bone spends most of his life martyring himself to Netta, it is in his dead moods that he becomes aware of her true nature and sees that she brings him nothing but harm. However, as Isherwood suggests in *Prater Violet*, this kind of absolute cinematic detachment comes at the price of a loss of self and a corresponding loss of engagement. When caught in his 'dead moods', Bone becomes as apolitical as his hedonistic friends. Chamberlain's declaration of war on the radio dimly impinges on Bone's consciousness as he completes the murder of Peter and Netta: 'Oh, so they were at it, were they, at last! Well, let them get on with it – he was too busy' (p. 274). The phrase 'at it' is his usual dismissive shorthand for sex. The war becomes an extension of the sexual depravity that Bone has deplored and envied in Brighton and Earl's Court. In these moods, he becomes indifferent to death. He consigns Netta and Peter to death with the same callousness as he dismisses the war, and the thousands of deaths it will bring.

'Eyes are another signature of Spanish death'

Stephen Spender, Joris Ivens, George Orwell, Robert Capa, John Sommerfield

In his more alert moments, Bone looks forward to war, if only as a way out of his current passivity:

> The year was dying, dead – what had next year, 1939, in store for him? Netta, drinks and smokes – drinks, smokes, Netta. Or a war. What if there was a war? Yes – if nothing else turned up, a war might. (p. 31)

Though he views war itself as a 'bloody business' and the idea of welcoming it a 'filthy' one, at times Bone can 'find it in his heart to hope for a war'. He sees it, at any rate, as more real and therefore more desirable than the 'phoney business' of Chamberlain's 'peace in our time'. Hamilton presents Chamberlain's pact with Hitler as a cinematically detached gesture, an event experienced by Bone, as by most in Britain, in images:

> All grinning, shaking hands, frock-coats, top-hats, uniforms, car-rides, cheers – it was like a sort of super-fascist wedding or christening. (p. 32)[34]

War at least might turn out to be Arthur Keith's pruning hook, purging society of parasites like Peter and Netta and forcing Bone himself into active engagement with his surroundings.[35]

But what if war, too, should turn out to be merely filmic? What if war itself exists only in the hyperreal? During the Spanish Civil War it had become clear that war was no less mediated than other public events. If the 'peace in our time' agreement existed primarily through photographs, so, by 1938, did the battles in Spain. Initially in 1936, many British writers saw the Spanish Civil War as offering just the sort of awakening that Bone hopes to find in the Second World War. 'When the fighting broke out on 18 July', Orwell wrote in *Homage to Catalonia* (1938), 'it is probable that every anti-Fascist in Europe felt a thrill of hope'.[36] According to the editor and Auden cohort member John Lehmann, 'every young writer began seriously to debate with himself how he could be of use, by joining the Brigade, or driving an ambulance'.[37] Signing up with the International Brigade, Auden announced gleefully, 'here is something I can do as a citizen and not as a writer'; 'I shall probably be a bloody bad soldier but how can I speak to/for them without becoming one?'[38] For a generation of male writers who had missed the heroism of the First World War and were starting to doubt how even the redemptive power of cinema could save the day, war provided the great test of strength they had been looking for.[39] According to Cyril Connolly, the test was often successful. He looked back on the Spanish Civil War as a time when many young writers experienced a crucial 'moment of conviction that [their] future is bound up with that of the working classes' and 'came back with their fear changed to love, isolation to union and indifference to action'.[40]

In fact, for many writers, Spain was disappointing. Politically, it was less straightforward than it had at first seemed. In *Homage to Catalonia*, Orwell recounts his gradual disillusionment with the Communist cause, which he discovered was too faction-ridden to be true to any grand ideals. Here he bemoans the 'unmistakable and horrible feeling of political rivalry and hatred', observing that 'it was above all things a political war' in which the soldier was a 'pawn in an enormous struggle that was being fought out between two political theories' (pp. 97, 188, 189). More fundamentally, the British media was so saturated by photographs of the atrocities committed by both sides that many writers found it hard to disentangle photography from actuality, or the sign of the real from the real itself. 'Here comes the dead war', Baudrillard would say in 1991, 'everything in *trompe l'oeil*'.[41] 'We now have virtual war', Žižek announced ten years later; 'like coffee without caffeine'.[42] Baudrillard's sense that the deeds of the First Gulf War were merely constructed for the sake of the media might apply equally to either the Spanish Civil War or the Second World War.[43]

In a 1938 essay about Pablo Picasso's *Guernica*, Spender stated that Picasso's painting was not a response to personal horror but to 'horror reported in the newspapers, of which he has read accounts and perhaps seen photographs'.[44] 'This kind of second-hand experience', he adds, gleaned from the media, 'is one of the dominating realities of our time':

> The many people who are not in direct contact with the disasters falling on civilisation live in a waking nightmare of second-hand experiences which in a way are more terrible than real experiences because the person overtaken by a disaster has at least a more limited vision than the camera's wide, cold, recording eye, and at least has no opportunity to imagine horrors worse than what he is seeing and experiencing.

In Spender's formulation, war mediated by camera consciousness is worse than real war. Where for Žižek virtual war, like decaffeinated coffee, loses its sting, for Spender it only becomes more horrific – more warlike. According to Sontag, the Spanish Civil War photographs were 'a means for making "real" (or "more real") matters that the privileged might prefer to ignore':

> Look, the photographs say, *this* is what it's like. This is what war *does*. And *that*, that is what it does, too. War tears, rends. War rips open, eviscerate. War scorches. War dismembers. War *ruins*.[45]

At the same time as seeing the horrors of war as created by camera consciousness, Spender sees war itself as intensifying the existing camera consciousness through the proliferation of images. The 'second-hand experiences' are foisted on potentially unwilling viewers, who are thrust into a waking cinematic nightmare. Photography simultaneously renders war more horrifically real and turns it into a simulacrum of itself.

Keith Williams has called the Spanish Civil War the 'first fully modern media conflict', in the sense that people away from the battlefield learnt about events there almost as they took place.[46] Due to recent advances in photography, news photographers at the front were able for the first time to take thirty-six photographs before needing to reload their cameras. The cameras themselves were more portable than ever before, making the photographer almost as mobile as the soldier, and subject to the same dangers.[47] 'I am kino-eye', Vertov had announced in 1923. 'I outstrip running soldiers, I fall on my back, I ascend with an airplane, I plunge and soar together with plunging and soaring bodies.'[48]

By the time of the Spanish Civil War, the cameraman was able to realise Vertov's ambitions in both photography and film. A striking number of films were made in the early years of the war, several including footage of actual battles. As early as 1936, the Spanish government released *España*, written by Luis Buñuel and directed by Jean-Paul Le Chanois using a montage of still photographs and documentary footage. In 1937 the American Herbert Kline, self-styled 'foreign correspondent of the screen', recorded the indignities of civilian life in *Heart of Spain*. And the Dutch Joris Ivens depicted the civilians' and soldiers' struggle to survive in *The Spanish Earth* (1937), written and narrated by Ernest Hemingway.[49]

The Spanish Earth, which combined documentary reportage with acted scenes, is a film that is consistently aware of the unprecedented intimacy of its own war footage. Near the beginning, Ivens cuts from the work in the village irrigating the fields to the front line itself. The viewer comes face to face with a soldier, who himself shrinks from such intimate contact with the camera, looking into a pair of binoculars (see Figure 4.1). Hemingway informs us that 'man cannot act before the camera in the presence of death'. The act of killing may now be captured on film, but etiquette demands that the killers remain oblivious of the camera. This self-consciousness on the part of both soldier and filmmaker heightens the audience's awareness of the dangerous proximity of the film crew to the fighting. Shots are fired in the middle distance before the camera pans out to reveal the smoke-filled aftermath of the battle. Later, Ivens provides a series of close-ups of the faces of the soldiers who are taking aim (see Figure 4.2).

4.1 *Self-conscious viewing*
Joris Ivens, *The Spanish Earth* (1937)

4.2 *Close-ups*
Joris Ivens, *The Spanish Earth* (1937)

The focus of the film is shared between the heroism of the government soldiers and the brutality of the rebel forces. It is unsparing
in its depiction of horror, because this horror is the justification for
the mobilisation of government troops. At one point, Hemingway
announces that 'boys look for bits of shell fragments as they once gath-
ered hailstones', emphasising the youthful innocence of the children
we see peering into the rubble. In the next shot, the boys are lying dead
on the ground. 'So the next shell', Hemingway announces, 'finds them'.
Shells are more dangerous playthings than hailstones. From this point
onwards, Ivens piles horror on horror. The German planes streak across
the sky, wreaking destruction on the villages and cities. Meanwhile, the
camera reels jerkily from shots of dead bodies to images of bereaved
women, who fling out their arms in agonised despair. This camera is as
helpless in the face of devastation as Isherwood's or MacNeice's literary camera eyes.
    Meanwhile in London, newspapers and picture magazines competed
to show the most recent and most dramatic (most horrific) pictures of

the war. Gone were the taboos preventing the publication of gory representations of injury and death. Justifying the publication of a series of
photographs of mutilated children laid out under clinically numerical
labels, the *Daily Worker* reminded its readers that 'these dead children
are the cost of brutal, militaristic aggression against peaceful people',
insisting on the necessity of printing 'this awful page'.[50] Like the propaganda films, these photographs did not merely depict the war. In a
sense they were the war. They were weapons rather than mere representations – weapons used to inspire the foreign involvement that was
so crucial to both sides.[51]

In the Spanish Civil War, the events of war were distorted by and
even created for the media. Orwell later revealed that he had seen

> great battles reported where there had been no fighting and complete
> silence where hundreds of men had been killed . . . and I saw newspapers
> in London retailing these lies and eager intellectuals building emotional
> superstructures over events that never happened.[52]

Orwell was not alone in complaining in *Homage to Catalonia* that
newspapers rarely know or tell the truth about either side. The
Communist journalist Claud Cockburn, who was reporting on the
war in Spain for the *Daily Worker*, later recalled fabricating a battle
in Morocco in order to frighten Franco's troops into granting conces-
sions to the socialists.[53] And photographs, of course, are no more reli-
able than articles. Sontag has pointed out that photographs are always
paradoxically both an objective sign of the real and a reflection of
subjective choice.[54] The subjective aspect is open to easy manipulation;
once shot (in both senses), the corpses of socialist and fascist civilians
look much the same.

Robert Capa's controversial *Loyalist Militiaman at the Moment of
Death* or *The Falling Soldier* typifies the hyperreal aspect of the Spanish
Civil War. Capa himself was a figure constructed for and by the media.
Born André Friedmann, a Hungarian immigrant in France, he created
the Hollywood-inspired persona of the rich American photographer
Robert Capa in order to get better-paid work. In the right place at the
right time in the Spanish Civil War, Capa rose to fame and the persona
stuck. It seems appropriate that the photograph that brought him
renown should itself prove to be constructed.

Capa's photograph of a soldier supposedly taken just as he was
shot at the battle of Cerro Muriano was first published in the French
magazine *Vu* in September 1936 (see Figure 4.3). Headed *Loyalist*

4.3 Robert Capa, 'Loyalist Militiaman at the Moment of Death', 1936.
Courtesy of Robert Capa/Magnum Photos.

Militiaman at the Moment of Death, the commentary described the
soldiers running down the slope 'with lively step', when they were
interrupted by a whistling bullet – 'a fratricidal bullet – and their blood
was drunk by their native soil'.[55] Historians have since long debated the
exact circumstances behind the *Loyalist Militiaman at the Moment of
Death*. Most agree that the photograph was not taken at Cerro Muriano
and some even suggest that the soldier did not die.[56] Capa's biographer,
Richard Whelan, recently gave a comprehensive and thus far convincing explanation for the photograph. According to him, the soldiers
were playing around with their rifles for Capa's benefit, hoping to help
him manufacture some convincing shots. This was not an uncommon
phenomenon. In *Homage to Catalonia*, Orwell recalls photographing
some machine-gunners with their gun pointed directly towards him.
'Don't fire', he says, 'half-jokingly', as he focuses the camera, but the
next moment there is 'a frightful roar' as bullets stream past his cheek
(p. 36). Whelan speculates that Capa's soldiers 'indeed fired, and by
doing so attracted the enemy's attention'.[57] Federico Borrell Garcia, the
soldier in question, stood up so that Capa could photograph him from
below. But just as Capa was about to press his shutter release, an enemy
machine gun opened fire.

If we accept Whelan's account, the photograph becomes all the
more potent, straddling as it does the real and the hyperreal. The head
thrown back, the body about to hit the ground and the muscles flexed
in a final moment of strength can still be horrific, even if Borrell died
for the media and not for politics. And of course in this context the
media is politics. Borrell's death had a greater impact on the political
stage through being propagated by the media. The photographer has
entered the war not just as a would-be soldier, falling like Vertov with
the soldier he frames. Instead, he is a killer as well as a victim, initiat-
ing conflict. Capa later claimed to be haunted by the incident: 'then,

suddenly it was the real thing. I didn't hear the firing – not at first.'[58] But in the logic of the mediated war it was already real. The fascists were merely playing their part in a conflict set up by a photographer.

The British soldier-poet making his way to the Spanish Front was fully aware of his role in adding to the second-hand experiences of those at home. 'This is something I can do as a citizen and not as a writer', said Auden. But in fact it was as a writer that he contributed to the war. 'Spain' (1937), his strange, haunting poem about the inexorability of history, made far more impact than his activities as an ambulance driver. And it is a poem that is ironically aware of its status as a second-hand artefact. 'Tomorrow', the poet announces, inscribing the soldier-poets in a naïve vision of war, 'for the young the poets exploding like bombs'.[59] The poets explode like the bombs – and like the photographers' flashbulbs (and victims). They have condoned 'the deliberate increase in the chances of death' and accepted guilt in the so-called 'necessary murder', only to remain writers before they are citizens.

'I have an appointment with a bullet', begins Spender's poem 'War Photograph', written from the point of view of Capa's dead soldier in 1937.[60] Spender figures the dead man as

> that numeral which the sun regards,
> The flat and severed second on which time looks,
> My corpse a photograph taken by fate.

The already dead aspect of photography lends an inevitability to the death. War, like cinema, is an inexorable machine. Saturated in images of war, many soldiers found it difficult to situate themselves in the here and now. It was hard to throw off the habit of experiencing events second-hand and begin to make history for themselves. According to Carl von Clausewitz, the new soldier entering the battlefield always 'for a moment still thinks he is at a show'.[61] He then learns to appreciate the reality of his surroundings, although he does well to continue to see war as spectacle, because it will help him to believe he will come out alive. Virilio writes that 'to be a survivor is to remain both actor and spectator of a living cinema'.[62] For Virilio, cinema is a necessary aspect of war.

'Now we can walk into the picture easily', Bernard Gutteridge began his poem 'Spanish Earth' (1939), whose title was taken from Ivens' film.[63] Gutteridge sees the soldier's excitement entering the battlefield as inseparable from the actor's excitement entering the film set. He walks into the picture

> To be the unknown hero and the death;
> We who have watched these things as stunts
> And held our breath.

Gutteridge makes explicit the link between the deathly nature of cinema and cinematic death:

> Eyes are another signature of Spanish death.
> This evening in the cinema will kill
> This man we watch direct his troops;
> A man whose eyes are still
>
> Searching the landscape for his dying countrymen
> In buildings burning fast as celluloid[.]

The cinema here is both metaphor and actuality. Night after night, the cinema audience watches the man directing his troops, knowing that he will die – that in effect he is already dead, or at least absent. At the same time, entering the cinema that is the battlefield, Gutteridge knows that the man will die because he has watched the scene, or scenes like it, on film, and has learnt what to expect. War has caught up with cinema. The buildings burn as fast as they do on film; as fast as the highly flammable film-stock itself. Gutteridge ends the poem with the inevitable pun, never far away in the Spanish Civil War. 'Perhaps we will be killed', he muses. 'The shooting never stops.' If the photographer is Capa, the two shots are the same.

For Sommerfield, arriving in Spain, the mediated, cinematic aspect of the Spanish Civil War was dangerous for the soldier. In *Volunteer in Spain* (1937), Sommerfield first glimpses the war as a spectacle, reflected in the 'sea of faces and waving hands' of the audiences who welcome the soldiers to Spain.[64] On the train going to battle, he has an 'unreal' vision of a crowd of 'peasants dressed in their best clothes', illuminated by the headlights of a semi-circle of lorries, which form 'a brilliantly lit stage'. This scene, at once cinematic and theatrical, takes place in a ghostly past-present, 'like something remembered from a dream'. For Sommerfield, the war itself is best glimpsed in the eyes of the soldiers in the lorries which roar past them, returning from the front: 'their eyes had seen it, and mostly they had known death and retreat' (p. 45).

When they finally arrive at the front, Sommerfield welcomes the moment 'long expected, anticipated in dreams' (p. 69). His sense of the war now becomes explicitly theatrical. These soldiers are at last 'the main actors in the play', but the drama has gone on too long (p. 91). For the cheering audiences:

the illusion didn't work; they were like people who go to the theatre to forget some calamity in their own lives, and for whom the illusion doesn't work because however much they might be caught up in the action of the play they are remembering all the time at the back of their minds that when the last curtain descends they will have to go out into a cold night full of inescapable grief.

In Sommerfield's account, the problem with experiencing the war as mediated and illusionary is that it ignores the real suffering of the civilians on whose behalf they are fighting. These civilians, who have been taken in by the spectacle themselves, now feel that 'their play [is] nearly over, the reality of death and destruction and terror would soon begin'.

Sommerfield succeeds in overcoming the cinematic detachment described by Gutteridge. Awakened by the scream of a shell, he at first 'picture[s] its flight in the air, and death' (p. 96). But rushing out to fight, he is filled with 'an extraordinary strength and lightness and joy' (p. 97). Quickly, he learns the realities of 'the cold and the danger, the firing in the night, the expressions on the face of the dead' (p. 103). Baudrillad, Virilio and Žižek have suggested that the experience of being bombed from the air has rendered war inevitably hyperreal. When the aggressors are intangible, they might as well be invented. Sommerfield pre-emptively refutes their arguments, insisting that

> It made no difference that the perils that beset us were the product of a scientific age, that men had learned to fly so that our enemy could kill us from a thousand feet above our heads, that the poetry of mathematics had made it possible for him to direct death at us invisibly from behind the flanks of hills five miles away . . . In defending the advance of mankind we lived like men of the Stone Age.

The daily conditions of war, the new knowledge of 'the various ways of broken flesh' and of the 'precarious impermanence' of their own lives, prevent warfare from seeming unreal, however mechanised and impersonal it may have become (pp. 109, 110).

'I am Not a Camera'

W. H. Auden

In 2004 Sontag chastised writers like Baudrillard and Žižek who had accepted 'the death of reality':

To speak of reality becoming a spectacle is a breath-taking provincialism. It universalises the viewing habits of a small, educated population living in the rich parts of the world, where news has been converted into entertainment . . . It assumes that everyone is a spectator. It suggests, perversely, unseriously, that there is no real suffering in the world. But it is absurd to identify the world with those zones in the well-off countries where people have the dubious privilege of being spectators . . . just as it is absurd to generalise about the ability to respond to the sufferings of others on the basis of the mind-set of those consumers of news who know nothing as first hand about war and massive injustice or terror.[65]

For Sontag, to see war as taking place in the hyperreal is to ignore the 'Stone Age' aspects of suffering experienced by Sommerfield. Sontag is right to reprimand Baudrillard. His position, like Spender's in the *Guernica* essay, remains that of the privileged voyeur who is too engrossed in how interesting voyeurism is to make the imaginative leap that will render suffering as suffering. But Baudrillard's own sense of the unreal side of contemporary warfare stems not only from its hyperreal, mediated nature but also from its unfairness. In 'The Gulf War Did Not Take Place', he is partly making the conventional liberal argument that the Gulf War was unfair because it was 'won in advance' and 'we will never know what an Iraqi taking part with a chance of fighting would have been like'.[66] By using this moral argument, Baudrillard to some extent contradicts his own, more radical sense of virtual reality and virtual war. It is clear that Baudrillard, like Sontag, and like Sommerfield or Orwell, ultimately believes that there is a point where suffering breaks through the film of cinematic consciousness, forcing an engagement with the real.

'I am Not a Camera', Auden would announce in the title of a poem in 1969; 'It is very rude to take close-ups . . . lovers, approaching to kiss, / instinctively shut their eyes'.[67] By then it had become easier to dismiss the camera consciousness of the 1930s, although the world was as hyperreal and mediated as ever. But at the time, it was Auden, more than Isherwood or Spender, who was to be found behind a camera lens; Auden who lauded photography as '*the* democratic art' and insisted that you had to take a lot of photographs 'to make an effect'.[68] 'I walk among them taking photographs', he wrote in a 1937 letter from Iceland to R. H. S. Crossman:

> let the camera's eye record it:
> Groups in confabulation on the grass[.][69]

Here the camera enables specificity; he can see the figures from Iceland's sagas as clearly as 'The wraps of cellophane' which flit 'through the glass' of his lens. This specificity is set against 'the word of fate' and the forces of law and order. In contemplating fate, people forget 'The rusting apple core we're clutching still'. Photography is a way to remember it. Later, MacNeice, in his persona as Hetty, mocks Maisie/Auden 'who fancies herself with a camera' and goes round 'taking art shots of people through each others legs'.[70]

Yet even in Iceland Auden, keen photographer though he may be, himself mocks both the objective documentarist and the subjective camera consciousness. I have already said that in his 1930 'Consider', Auden had half-adopted, half-derided the panoptic perspective of the 'hawk' or the 'helmeted airman'.[71] As in the letter to Crossman, he delights here in observing the 'cigarette-end smouldering on a border'. But in using the airman and not the cameraman, he makes clear the antagonistic aspect of the panoptic perspective, which is used for bombing and surveillance and not just for objective observation. The hawk or helmeted airman metamorphoses into the 'supreme Antagonist', possessed of camera-like powers to roam around, observing, interrogating and spreading rumours. The Antagonist induces neuroticism through surveillance as everywhere people are 'Seized with immeasurable neurotic dread'.

Now, offering his former GPO film colleague William Coldstream 'a little donnish experiment in objective narrative', Auden easily reveals the documentary filmmaker to be pompous and false:

Let me pretend that I'm the impersonal eye of the camera
Sent out by God to shoot on location . . .
The whole place was slippery with filth – with guts and decaying flesh –
  like an artist's palette. [72]

The poet intrudes on the camera, forcing a moral reaction to the guts and decaying flesh, and then suggesting that painting is more appropriate than photography to describe the visual aspect of the scene. Auden goes through his own photographs as though they are stills in a film, and finds that they are inaccurate: 'Too confused to show much.' Having done with 'perceiving', he moves on to 'telling', providing the external, personal details that characterise Isherwood's camera eye. These too are confused; he ends up listing a jumble of trivia and personal gossip. He finds that both language and image are inadequate in describing the 'purely subjective feelings, / The heart-felt exultations and the short despairs'. Instead, they 'Require a musician'. 'The novelist has one way of stating experience,' he says, 'the film director another'; 'each man to his medium'.

As the epigraph to 'I am Not a Camera', Auden quotes the German philosopher Eugen Rosenstock-Huessey's statement that 'photographic life is always either trivial or already sterilised'. Both objections are already clear in his letter to Coldstream. Enthusiastic photographer he may be, but film is not his medium. As he would put it in his 1949 poem, 'Memorial for the City', 'The eyes of the crow and the eye of the camera open / Onto Homer's world, not ours'. The crow and the camera magnify earth, 'the abiding / Mother of gods and men', but only notice the men themselves in passing. They 'See as honestly as they know how, but they lie'.[73] In mocking the camera eye, Auden joins Upward and Sommerfield in suggesting that it is not enough just to observe, even if, like Isherwood, one observes oneself in the process of observing. For Isherwood, Allen or Hamilton, on the other hand, the writer has no choice; it is precisely the already sterilised or trivial aspect of the world that they want to record. These writers see the politics of the 1930s as creating a detachment best expressed through the dominant metaphor of the camera. For Spender and Gutteridge, even war has become a mediated, second-hand experience.

Like the argument between Baudrillard and Sontag, the 1930s argument goes round in circles. Is it politically irresponsible to embrace the hyperreal or merely politically accurate? When objective camera vision is the dominant subjective mode, how can you distinguish between subject and object, self and world, vision and action? It is easy to end up in a hall of mirrors – the boxes within boxes, or screens within screens, which Spender experienced in Berlin. And this hall of mirrors operates both within politics and outside it. Like Speer's chimeric buildings, which reconstitute architecture as light, the political itself has been redefined in terms of cinema.

CHAPTER 5

Framing History: Virginia Woolf and the Politicisation of Aesthetics

In *Three Guineas* (1938), Virginia Woolf attempts to reclaim Spanish Civil War photography from the realm of the hyperreal. Woolf goes against Spender's understanding of the war in Spain as a second-hand experience, where photographs of atrocities lose their power to shock through familiarity. Instead, she uses the photographs that the 'Spanish Government sends with patient pertinacity about twice a week' to create a consensus of 'horror and disgust' in her audience as she wages a feminist war against war (p. 125).

She does this, in the first instance, by incorporating the images in her text through descriptions rather than reproductions. Elena Gualtieri has argued that the pictures Woolf refers to are the same photographs of hideously maimed children printed in the *Daily Worker*, accompanied by an explanation justifying their inclusion.[1] If Gualtieri is right, in choosing not to follow the *Daily Worker*, Woolf seems to trust language to do a better job than the images themselves. According to Maggie Humm, the descriptions do not correspond to any of the photographs collected in the Marx library, and may well be imaginary.[2] They are linguistic portraits, and through language Woolf can admit the ambiguity of the represented reality at the same time as she insists on the power of its effect:

> They are not pleasant photographs to look upon. They are photographs of dead bodies for the most part. This morning's collection contains the photographs of what might be a man's body, or a woman's; it is so mutilated that it might, on the other hand, be the body of a pig. But those certainly are dead children.

Here Woolf harnesses the natural uncertainty of the photograph to emphasise the wanton destruction of war. In a reproduced image, the pig-like nature of the dead body would chiefly present a problem of identification. But in the text, Woolf uses the pig metaphorically, suggesting that war turns humans into animals.

Having assembled her sources, Woolf goes on to make explicit the function of these photographs as a call to (pacifist) arms:

> Those photographs are not an argument; they are simply a crude statement of fact addressed to the eye. But the eye is connected with the brain; the brain with the nervous system. That system sends its message in a flash through every past memory and present feeling. When we look at those photographs some fusion takes place within us; however different the education, the traditions behind us, our sensations are the same; and they are violent. You, Sir, call them 'horror and disgust'. We also call them horror and disgust.

Here the photographs (or their verbal representations) are pushed beyond the bounds of second-hand experience, fulfilling Sontag's sense of the war photograph as making '"real" (or "more real")'.[3] For Woolf, access to reality, with its horror and disgust, comes in a 'flash', which bursts through past and present, forcing us to reinterpret both. This flash, she adds later, demands appeasement. The viewers of the photograph are left seeking an 'energetic', 'active method of expressing our belief that war is barbarous' (p. 126).

The flash of the camera, producing a flash in the nervous system, forces an engagement with both politics and history. It therefore has the potential to overcome the numb, second-hand state of camera consciousness discussed above in Chapter 4. Woolf's flash evokes Benjamin's flash in his 1940 'Theses on the Philosophy of History'. For Benjamin, 'the true picture of the past flits by'; the past 'can be seized only as an image which flashes up [*aufblitzt*] at the instant when it can be recognised and is never seen again'.[4] In the *Arcades Project*, Benjamin figures this flash as a dialectical image in which 'the Then and the Now come together in a constellation like a flash of lightning' at the 'now of recognisability'.[5]

Benjamin's sense of the past flitting by is cinematic. He positions viewer and camera as static, recording and watching history as it rushes past like a moving train. In her 1926 essay 'The Cinema', Woolf situates her viewer in a similar relation to the world presented on screen in the ideal cinema of the future, which she depicts as flashing rather than flitting: 'the most fantastic contrasts could be flashed before us with a speed which the writer can only toil after in vain.'[6] For both Woolf and Benjamin, a redemptive engagement with the flitting world comes in a now of recognisability in which history ceases to be part of the dead past, instead coming together with the present. In 'Theses', Benjamin dismisses historians who attempt to 'blot out everything they know about the later course of history', escaping the present in their attempt to recreate the past.[7] Similarly Woolf, in her unfinished essay, 'Anon', written in the year that Benjamin's 'Theses' were published, laments that the printing press has brought into existence 'the settled recorded past'.[8] She calls for a more active engagement with the past, which sings at the back door of the present, stating that the 'thing that the writer has to say' is now 'only to be discovered in a flash of recognition' (p. 390).

I present Woolf and Benjamin side by side to suggest that Benjamin articulates the implicit links between the flash of photography, cinema and history that Woolf makes in her late essays and fiction.[9] Both Woolf and Benjamin are aware of the dangers inherent in adopting a camera consciousness. If the world is experienced in a second-hand hyperreal, events seem to have taken place before they actually occur. History becomes inevitable and politics illusionary. The hyperreality causes the aestheticisation of politics, overtaken by cinema, which Benjamin sees as explicitly fascist in his 'Work of Art' essay. For Benjamin, the left-wing solution to the aestheticisation of politics is to politicise aesthetics. The technologically reproducible media of cinema and photography provide the means with which to do this.[10] Benjamin, like Woolf, sees the numbness created by aestheticised politics as leading directly to war. The coerced viewers of the fascist spectacle 'can experience its own destruction as an aesthetic pleasure of the first order'.[11] This passivity is interrupted by the flash of recognition that both Woolf and Benjamin see as forcing an engagement with history. The nervous system sends its message in a flash through every past memory and present feeling.

This chapter is about the way that Woolf used cinematic (or ultracinematographic) technique to politicise aesthetics, creating fiction that engaged actively with politics and history. It is now generally accepted that Woolf was as politically engaged as her contemporaries in the 1930s. Here I argue that it was the cinema, or rather her vision of cinema's potential, that enabled Woolf to incorporate politics and history in her fiction and, crucially, to create a politicised aesthetic which combated passivity and forced an embodied, awakened mode of reception. I see Woolf as engaging with cinema in three, interrelated aspects of her work. Firstly, she made the most of the radical potential of montage in her photograph albums and scrapbooks, and in the interface between photographs and text in *Three Guineas*. Secondly, she assumed a cinematic vision in incorporating history and politics into the physical landscape of *The Years* (1937). Here she presents history spatially, as though it is making its way across the screen, and uses billboards to insert the news into the streets of London. Finally, she mimicked the cinema's Bergsonian capacity to collapse the distinction between past and present in her wartime memoir 'A Sketch of the Past' (1940) and in her final novel, *Between the Acts* (1941). Here she uses the fluidity of time as flux to allow the past to flash transformatively into the present.

I take Woolf as the focus of this chapter both because she is a representative writer of the period and because she is not. Woolf herself was quick to separate herself from the 1930s writers discussed in the previous chapter. This is clear in her 1940 'Leaning Tower' essay, read to the Workers' Educational Association in Brighton, and written to explain and criticise the Auden–Isherwood coterie. Planning the essay, Woolf distanced herself from the younger generation, alluding to the 'Leaning Tower school' in her diary as though they have nothing to do with her:

> The idea struck me that the Leaning Tower school is the school of auto-analysis after the suppression of the 19th Century.[12]

In the essay itself, she distances herself from the writers under discussion on the grounds of technique, politics, age and gender. This is a generation of writers whose excessive political involvement she sees as detrimental to their art. She criticises them for allowing the 'didactic, the loud-speaker strain' to dominate their writing.[13] She is scathing about MacNeice's 'feeble' *Autumn Journal* and labels Day Lewis's work as 'oratory, not poetry' (pp. 169, 172). And she is all the more dismissive because these writers have had privileges that she, as a woman, and her audience, as workers, have been denied. She aligns herself with her audience in placing herself outside the tower:

> we are not in their position; we have not had eleven years of expensive education. We have only been climbing an imaginary tower. We can cease to imagine. We can come down. (p. 168)

Spatially, she and her audience are securely removed from the writers she describes.

However, although Woolf is clear that she has never inhabited the tower that has now begun to lean, she does identify herself with the leaning tower generation in her anger and hopes. The feelings with which she imbues the 1930s writers are akin to the sense of betrayal and helplessness she expresses in her diary in the lead-up to war in 1939:

> First discomfort; next self-pity for that discomfort; which pity soon turns to anger – to anger against the builder, against society, for making us uncomfortable. (p. 168)[14]

Moreover, she credits the younger generation with realisations about the unfairness of their education:

> The tower they realised was founded upon injustice and tyranny; it was wrong for a small class to possess an education that other people paid for; wrong to stand upon the gold that a bourgeois father had made from his bourgeois profession. (p. 169)

This complaint resonates with her own views in *Three Guineas*, where she complains that 'the daughters of educated men' have paid 'with their own education for Eton and Harrow, Oxford and Cambridge' (p. 211). Although she endows the upper-class men with guilt on behalf of the working classes and not of their sisters, she suggests that their eyes are open to the same injustice as her own.

In addition, despite the difference in age, in her original exclusion from the tower Woolf seems to have more in common with the generation that is about to fall from an unstable tower than with her own complacent generation, which was 'raised above the mass of people upon a tower of stucco' (p. 165). At the end of the essay, Woolf becomes more complimentary about the younger writers, lauding the honesty of their autobiographies. She goes on, more generally, to outline what seem to be her own hopes for the future:

> There are two reasons which lead us to think, perhaps to hope, that the world after the war will be a world without classes or towers. Every politician who has made a speech since September 1939 has ended with a peroration in which he has said that we are not fighting this war for conquest; but to bring about a new order in Europe . . . That is one reason why, if they mean what they say, and can effect it, classes and towers will disappear. The other reason is given by the income tax. (p. 175)

In moving to the pronoun 'us' in an essay that has largely been about 'them', except when Woolf has included herself in the audience of outsiders, Woolf begins to share the ideals of the writers under consideration. She, like them, and unlike many of her own, safely towered generation, would like to see the hedges separating the classes pulled down. Throughout the essay she has carefully distanced herself from the male 'Leaning Tower' writers, but she now makes explicit her desire for a new social order.

In insisting on the genderedness of literature and politics, history and war, Woolf makes the 1930s picture of the world more complex. Woolf's view in the late 1930s was decidedly morbid and she was less hopeful than the younger, usually male, 1930s documentarists who believed that class divisions could be overcome. Nonetheless, Woolf's 1930s and 1940s politics are strongly aligned with the other writers discussed in this book. Although Woolf was often dismissive of the younger generation of women writers, which included Storm Jameson and Winifred Holtby, she, like them, was engaged in fighting for feminist and pacifist causes, and in the 1930s she was one of the most political of the prominent women writers of her own generation.[15] It is evident in Woolf's correspondence with Spender, her closest friend amongst the Auden coterie, that she shared his desire to influence the public and to integrate politics into literature. She wrote to the younger writer after the publication of *The Years* that she had intended 'to give a picture of society as a whole; give characters from every side; turn them towards society, not private life; exhibit the effects of ceremonies'.[16] This is a starker declaration of social engagement than we would expect in a writer described by a contemporary as an 'unpolitical aesthete', or from the author of parts of the 'Leaning Tower' essay.[17]

Woolf's engagement with cinema is as complex as her politics, and again she is both typical of and exceptional among left-wing writers of the decade. She was often dismissive of both the cinema and cinematic fiction, belittling Compton Mackenzie's *The Early Life and Adventures of Sylvia Scarlett* as a '"movie" novel' and seeing her trips to the cinema as unworthy of recording in her diaries.[18] However, it is clear from the cinema essay that she saw *The Cabinet of Doctor Caligari*, and in her diary and letters she mentions seeing Pudovkin's *Storm Over Asia* (1928), René Clair's *Le Million* (1931) and William Wyler's *Wuthering Heights* (1939), as well as about fifteen unnamed 'movies', which she doesn't comment on.[19] In addition to going to the cinema, in 1928 the Woolfs published Eric White's *Parnassus to Let*, a treatise on rhythm in film. White is in line with the writers of *Fact* and *Close-up* in his list of 'good' films: *Battleship Potemkin*, *The Cabinet of Dr Caligari*, *Warning Shadows* and *Berlin: Symphony of a Great City*. But the most obvious indication of Woolf's interest in film is the 1926 cinema essay itself, which is both an indictment of contemporary popular cinema and an acclamation of the ultracinematographic.[20] Although Woolf never claimed to be in any way a camera, she was always interested in the inherently cinematic phenomenon of absent presence (several of her novels feature empty rooms) and in the shifting dynamics of space and time. As Woolf became urgently interested in history in the 1930s, she engaged with a cinematic vocabulary in depicting time spatially and in picturing the flash of the past in the present moment. She also used cinematic devices to incorporate contemporary politics in her novels, often through the presence of newspapers.

Montage: Woolf's newspapers and photographs

In the 1930s, Woolf became increasingly obsessed with newspapers. Striving to understand a frightening world, she read *The Times* and *The Daily Telegraph* urgently. 'What about politics?' she asked Spender in a letter in 1934. 'Even I am shocked by the last week in Germany into taking part; but that only means reading the newspaper.'[21] Listening to the radio and reading the newspaper were Woolf's only ways to attempt to gain control of events, and so she did her best not to be one of the passive, duped consumers of news who were the target of Mass-Observation's campaigns. One way to do this was by keeping abreast of multiple newspapers and learning to distinguish between fact and interpretation.

In *Three Guineas*, Woolf asks an imaginary 'daughter of an educated man' why she feels the need to take six newspapers – three dailies and three weeklies (p. 220). 'Because,' the woman replies, 'I am interested in politics, and wish to know the facts'. But do the facts differ from paper to paper, Woolf asks naïvely? She receives a sharp retort:

> You call yourself an educated man's daughter, and yet pretend not to know the facts – roughly that each paper is financed by a board; that each board has a policy; that each board employs writers to expound that policy, and if the writers do not agree with that policy, the writers, as you may remember after a moment's reflection, find themselves unemployed in the street. (pp. 220–1)

'If newspapers', Woolf the narrator reflects, merging the two personae, 'were written by people whose sole object in writing was to tell the truth about politics and the truth about art we should not believe in war, and we should believe in art' (p. 222). In the meantime, the best the educated man's daughter can do is to use her many newspapers to gain a sense of perspective. She can then 'strip' the newspaper copy of 'its money motive, power motive, advertisement motive, publicity motive, vanity motive and so on', before unwrapping 'the grain of truth'. This 'grain of truth' is needed to combat both fascism and war; armed with truth, women can resist the coercion of male society. As soon as 'the mulberry tree begins to make you circle, break off', Woolf exhorts her readers; 'pelt the tree with laughter' (p. 205).

For Woolf, another way to take control of the newspaper copy was to press it into the service of her own message through montage. Throughout the early 1930s, Woolf was cutting and pasting newspaper clippings into her Monk's House scrapbooks, exploiting the collage techniques developed by photomontage artists such as Heartfield and Klutsis to create new meanings through juxtaposition.[22] Woolf had begun to experiment with collage much earlier, in her photograph albums. Always a keen photographer, she began to arrange her photographs into albums in the 1920s and 1930s.[23] Maggie Humm has pointed out the debt to cinematic montage in the ordering of the albums, which is rarely chronological.[24] In all six albums, stiff Victorian photographs, which Woolf had collected from family and friends, are juxtaposed with more playful photographs of her contemporaries. Her desire to mock the pomposity of the Victorian portraits is evident in a letter she wrote to Margaret Llewelyn Davies in 1940: 'I stuck all your photographs into a great book and called it Eminent Victorians.'[25] The contrast between the stateliness of the Victorians and the freedom of the younger generation is especially stark in a series of photographs in the first album. Here spontaneous shots of Woolf's nephews frolicking naked, engaging with the camera in their play, are juxtaposed with a formal Victorian photograph of Madge Vaughan, taken at the studios of Woolf's great-aunt, the renowned photographer Julia Margaret Cameron.[26]

In the Monk's House scrapbooks, Woolf takes the political possibilities of collage further than she had in the photograph albums, using it to undermine the surface message of the newspaper stories. Halfway through the second volume, she juxtaposes two articles from the *Daily Herald* on 1 August 1936, one where an MP urges the public to 'Stand up to Dictators', the other where a woman complains that her husband insists she 'call him "Sir"'.[27] By putting the two together, Woolf implicitly asks how people can be expected to stand up to dictators if there are petty dictators ruling homes throughout England. Soon after, she includes a quote from a CID official claiming that women are armed with a dastardly and nefarious cunning:

> The male crook is a specialist; he perfects a method and loathes to depart from it . . . Yet he seems unable to perceive that fresh ideas would probably give him a prolonged spell of freedom . . . But instinct and opportunity are the only guides of the woman crook. She is the slave of no rule, and so is dangerous.

This is immediately followed by a quote from William Gerhardi entirely dismissing the intelligence of women:

> Never yet have I committed the error of looking on woman writers as serious fellow artists . . . Their true role, therefore, is rather to ho,d [*sic*] out the sponge to us, cool our brow, when we bleed.[28]

Later, the poverty of a women's college in Oxford, receiving a gift of £7,000 with 'pathetic gratitude' is juxtaposed with a description of the wealth of male colleges. Hitler's boast that 'in battle we have won the German Reich and in battle we shall maintain and guard it' is then followed by an article about animals that advertise their fighting qualities to women.[29]

Although Woolf never intended her newspaper collages for publication, they can be read alongside both surrealism and the German montage tradition, which carried on beyond Heartfield into the 1930s and 1940s. At the same time as Woolf was compiling her notebooks, Benjamin was at work on his unfinished *Arcades Project* and Brecht was starting the collages that would eventually become his *War Primer*, published in East Germany in 1955. Like Woolf, Benjamin and Brecht were using two-dimensional collage to create the kinds of effect achieved by Brechtian theatre and Soviet cinema. Benjamin was explicit in seeing his collage of materials broadly relating to nineteenth-century Paris as a montage: 'method of this project: literary montage. I needn't *say* anything. Merely show.'[30] He saw himself as an Eisensteinian constructor, defining his aim as being 'to assemble large-scale constructions out of the smallest and most precisely cut components'.[31] Benjamin's mammoth compendium of quotations juxtaposes his own aphoristic statements with quotations from literature and politics, art and architecture. By bringing together the 'refuse' of history, he at once critiques bourgeois history and attempts to let a more accurate version of history flash into visibility in the present.[32]

Brecht's *War Primer* is a montage of photographs taken from newspapers, each collaged with a four-line poem by Brecht himself. The effect of the poems is to undermine the message of the photographs, much as Woolf was doing with the newspapers in her notebooks, or indeed with the photographs in *Three Guineas* itself. Brecht's second collage combines an imposing 1940 *Life* magazine photograph of the American steel industry at work with a poem in which Brecht asks the workers ('brothers') why they are making steel plates. The ensuing dialogue illustrates the Marxist argument against war:

> 'They're for the guns that blast the iron to pieces.'
> 'And what's it all for, brothers?'
> 'It's our living.'[33]

These workers are alienated from their labour and its effects; too passive to question the war that their efforts enable.

Like Woolf, Brecht is against not just Nazi aggression but war in general. The publication of the *War Primer* was delayed because the GDR felt that it did not portray the Allies any better than it portrayed the Germans. Like Woolf, he undermines the newspaper propaganda by stripping it of 'its money motive, power motive, advertisement motive'. Both writers are quick to spot the pomposity of the warmongers on both sides. Brecht's Collage 15 portrays a self-satisfied photograph of Winston Churchill, sporting a top hat, bowtie, cigar and gun. The poem is written from the point of view of Churchill himself:

> Gang law is something I can understand.
> With man-eaters I've excellent relations.
> I've had the killers feeding from my hand.
> I am the man to save civilisation.[34]

Brecht implies that Churchill can understand gang law and killers because he has personal experience, undermining his claims to stand for civilisation. Juxtaposed with the poem, the photograph seems to reveal the inherent links between capitalism and violence, wealth and war, top hats and guns.

Woolf had already mocked the sartorial pomposity of the Victorian man in her albums and she interprets photographs of men in public office in a Brechtian light in *Three Guineas*. Here, addressing her male interlocutor, she considers the attire of public men: 'Your clothes in the first place make us gape with astonishment' (p. 133). She takes the reader on a verbal cinematic fashion parade through the different varieties of men in high office: 'Now you dress in violet; a jewelled crucifix swings on your breast; now your shoulders are covered with lace; now furred with ermine . . . Now you wear wigs on your heads' (p. 134). Throughout, the narrator gazes at the men with mock amazement, marvelling at the strange, 'symbolical meaning' of their buttons and at 'the ceremonies that take place' when they wear them. By combining photographs of military men with men serving in the judiciary, the academy and the state, Woolf implies that all these venerable institutions are ultimately serving the same militaristic ends. Unlike the Spanish Civil War photographs, the photographs of men in high office do appear in the text. Woolf includes photographs of a general, a group of heralds, a procession of university dons, a judge and a bishop, all in their official costume. Here she goes further than she did in the notebooks, and further than Brecht does in the *War Primer*, in making the link between sartorial pomposity and war explicit by juxtaposing the two sets of photographs and asking:

> What connection is there between the sartorial splendours of the educated man and the photograph of ruined houses and dead bodies? (pp. 137–8)

Answering her own question, she asserts that the connection 'is not far to seek; your finest clothes are those you wear as soldiers'. She goes on to suggest that women can prevent war (can prevent the existence of the dead bodies and ruined houses) by refusing to wear such costumes themselves and by insisting that the male wearer 'is not to us a pleasing or an impressive spectacle'.

Sonita Sarker writes that Woolf uses the contrast between the two sets of photographs to show that where the dead bodies shatter the complacency of the private world, the pomp and show of 'preserved bodies and histories' evidenced by the male costumes 'keep the gentlemen's world intact'.[35] Costumes like these serve to make the male world impregnable, buttressed by years of history. The insertion of newspapers and photographs into a new context enables Woolf to engage actively with politics, rejecting the messages of the warmongering press conglomerates, symbolised by the ceremonial male costumes. This collage technique provides a way to experience or induce the awakening that both Woolf and Benjamin see as occasioned by the flash of history in the present moment. In the *Arcades Project*, Benjamin is explicit in seeing this as the role of his montage. Here he distances himself from the surrealists with his emphasis on montage as dialectic and his urgent interest in history:

whereas Aragon persists within the realm of dream, here the concern is to find the constellation of awakening. While in Aragon there remains an impressionistic element, namely the 'mythology' . . . here it is a question of the dissolution of 'mythology' into the space of history.[36]

Benjamin presents the space of history, accessed through montage, as one in which awakening is possible.

The past flits by: spatial history and politics in *The Years*

Benjamin's use of the word 'space' for what is essentially a temporal phenomenon is pertinent to Woolf's 1937 project in *The Years*. In this novel, history is continually intersecting with the present moment spatially, in the streets and houses of London. The present moment of contemporary politics is often figured through the newspapers, which pervade the interiors and exteriors of the novel, flying across streets and into railings, lying on doorsteps, folded to speed up the boiling of the kettle or hiding the face of a woman in a train carriage. *The Years* is Woolf's most political novel, written at the point when she was collecting newspaper clippings and campaigning against fascism.[37] 'There's a good deal of gold – more than I'd thought – in externality', she recorded in her diary, while writing the novel.[38] It is also explicitly a book about history, navigating its way through sixty years of London life, showing the changes in the Pargiter family in the context of changes in London itself and in British politics.

Three Guineas and *The Years* emerged simultaneously out of the novel-essay planned as *The Pargiters*, which was to alternate chapters of fact with chapters of fiction. In 1933, six months into writing *The Pargiters*, Woolf had outlined her hopes for the book in her diary, stating her intention

> to give the whole of the present society – nothing less: facts, as well as vision. And to combine them both. I mean, The Waves going on simultaneously with Night & Day . . . And there are to be millions of ideas but no preaching – history, politics, feminism, art, literature.[39]

By 1933 she had abandoned this compendious project, splitting it into its two halves. But this did not prevent history and politics from entering the novel half. Anna Snaith has shown that critics who find an irreconcilable tension between fact and fiction in Woolf's mind and in *The Years* lose sight of the palimpsestic layers within the text:

Whereas critics tend to map the fact/fiction dichotomy onto the essay/ novel division, thereby seeing the omission of the essays as a rejection of the fact, the fact/fiction divide was much more deeply rooted in the writing itself . . . Woolf abandoned the essay-novel idea not because fact and fiction were in conflict, but precisely the opposite, because she did not need the genre divide, she had already found a balance between fiction and the 'truth of fact' which supported it.[40]

Snaith is persuasive in arguing that both parts of the original project were retained in *The Years*, though the facts are presented more subtly than in the original version.

In the initial diary entry on *The Pargiters*, Woolf wonders 'what form is to hold . . . together' the satire, comedy, poetry and narrative in her new book. She asks if she should bring in 'a play, letters, poems'. Here she anticipates the form she would choose for her next novel, *Between the Acts*. In *The Years*, she ends up retaining a conventional novel form – so much so that Hilary Newman has classified it as a 'Victorian' 'Condition of England' novel.[41] Nonetheless, form is crucial to this book, and an understanding of Woolf's spatial engagement with cinema provides a way into her text. Snaith is one of what remains only a handful of critics to read *The Years* as simultaneously realist and formalist in its depiction of politics and history.[42] Here I argue that Woolf solves the problem of combining history and politics with poetry by incorporating them cinematically into the spatial landscape of her text. Woolf wanted to write a novel that was at once a perfectly crafted work of art and a document of history and politics. In order to do this she turned to cinema not, like her younger contemporaries, as a form of documentary, but as a way to bring the external world visually into the text. Through cinema, the political storms shaking the lives of individuals could be shown and not told; through cinema, Woolf could avoid the didactic, loudspeaker strain.

The London of *The Years* is a city of *flâneurs*. Almost every member of the extended Pargiter family walks through London or observes it through a window. But where the traditional *flâneur* observes the details of daily life, the Pargiters are granted visual access to the passing of time itself. Wandering through the streets, the characters turn into cinematic viewers (or cameras), observing the spectacle of the changing world. Woolf uses the experience of streetwalking to experiment with modes of vision and modes of spatialising time. Sometimes characters are stationary viewers, immobile witnesses of history in the making. This is the position assumed by the viewers of early panoramas

and dioramas, who would remain stationary while paintings or photographs sped past them, with the moving scene creating a sense of time
passing. It is also the position Woolf herself assumes, looking back
at her own past in her 1940 memoir, 'A Sketch of the Past'. Here she
finds that sometimes she can 'reach a state where I seem to be watching things happen as if I were there'. She wonders whether some day a
device will be invented enabling her to tap into the past, fitting a plug
to the wall to listen in.[43]

In other scenes, characters become moving cameras, walking alongside or even overtaking the history they are registering. In 1913 Martin
stands by the window, observing the world from a fixed vantage point
and watching 'the little figures slinking along the wet pavement',
passing him by (p. 212). He sees the family servant, Crosby, leaving his
room and trotting off into the snow, a symbol of the old order. On the
next page, it is a brilliant spring day in 1914 and the narrator draws our
attention to the passing of time through the 'old church clocks' that
rasp the hour in the country and the cacophony of irregular London
clocks (p. 213). One particular 'distant frail-voiced clock' is striking
within earshot of Martin, who is 'standing at his window', having
apparently remained motionless since 1913. Martin now abandons his
stationary position and steps out into the world, walking to the city. On
his way he passes shop windows full of summer dresses, a merry street
organ and a kitchen full of people drinking tea (p. 214). Rushing along,
keeping step with the changing seasons, he catches up with the history
that has passed by his window between the scenes. After lunch with
his cousin Sara, he relaxes, again assuming his stationary viewpoint.
Passed by a motorcar, he observes that it is 'odd how soon one got used
to cars without horses', making explicit a sense of history flitting by, as
it does in Woolf's 'Cinema' essay and Benjamin's 'Theses' (p. 223).

Woolf's play with the stationary and moving viewer of history parallels contemporary experiments in cinematic representations of moving
space and time. Woolf was prescient in the 'Cinema' essay in seeing the
spatial unrolling of the past as something that will happen in the ideal
cinema of the future. A year later, Walter Ruttmann was experimenting with a complex interplay of space and time in *Berlin, Symphony
of a Great City*. At the beginning of Ruttmann's film, the viewer is
aligned with the camera in a train, watching as the scenery flashes
forth. Although both camera and train are moving, it feels as though
we are stationary and it is the scenery that moves vertiginously past us.
Berlin begins with a representation of space, but it is a film dominated
by time. Because it is clear from the start that the film is set over the

5.1 *History flits by*
Michael Powell and Emeric Pressburger, *A Canterbury Tale* (1944)

course of a single day, the viewer is aware throughout of the ticking of
the clock that marks the hours from start to finish. Ruttmann's opening
foregrounds the importance of time passing through the movement of
the train. In the cinema, a visual medium, the sense of time flashing by
can best be conveyed by rapid movement through space.

Woolf's own experiments with unrolling time in *The Years* would
find a corollary in the cinema of the future. Powell and Pressburger's
Second World War film *A Canterbury Tale* (1944) is notable for its
imaginative attempt to convey the passage of time. The film begins with
the Prologue to Chaucer's Tales and shows a group of medieval pilgrims
engaged in a bucolic pilgrimage. The camera remains stationary, which
makes it seem like the pilgrims rush past us on the screen. Powell and
Pressburger cut from one angle to another, so that the pilgrims begin by
moving towards us, apparently processing out of the screen, and then
move on past to the left (see Figure 5.1). A man on horseback releases
a falcon which, far in the distance, metamorphoses into an aeroplane.
The camera returns to the man through a shot-reverse-shot, but he
has himself metamorphosed into a soldier, wearing a tin helmet. 'Six
hundred years have passed', the commentary announces, wondering
what Chaucer and his contemporaries would see if they were trans-
planted into England today. The countryside is largely unchanged,
though 'hedgerows have sprung' and 'the land is under plough'. At this
point the camera pans the countryside, as though it is taking the viewer
on a tour of the landscape and simultaneously traversing 600 years of
history. The commentary then makes explicit the passage of time: 'but
though so little's changed since Chaucer's day, another kind of pilgrim
walks the way'. And the poetry is drowned out by the rumble of tanks,
as they make their way onto the screen (see Figure 5.2). Once again, the
camera (and viewer) remains stationary, so that the tanks come into

5.2 *Time passes*
Michael Powell and Emeric Pressburger, *A Canterbury Tale* (1944)

view and then drive away. History has passed, only to flash forward into a present moment that is laden with the urgent danger represented by the insistent tanks.

Woolf makes her spatialisation of history explicit in the preludes, which she added late on in the writing process to each section in *The Years*.[44] In the 1880 prelude at the start of the book, the narrator observes the sky in which

> Slowly wheeling, like the rays of a searchlight, the days, the weeks, the years passed one after another across the sky. (p. 4)

When time is mapped onto space, the past can cyclically follow the present. This coexistence of past and present is made manifest both by the searchlights themselves and by the continuity within the descriptions of the searchlights, which cast their rays across the book. They take on a darker significance at the start of the 1917 section, where darkness presses on the windows and

> No light shone, save when a searchlight rayed round the sky, and stopped, here and there, as if to ponder some fleecy patch. (p. 266)

Here the black and white chiaroscuro of wartime searchlight and blackout prefigures the landscape of the Second World War literature I discuss in Chapter 6. This sinister searchlight evokes the earlier searchlight metaphor, conjuring a sense of the passing of time as it propels the characters into war. In the presentday section, North takes on the narrator's searchlight description as part of his own memory of the war, remembering 'the dark night; the searchlights that slowly swept over the sky; here and there they stopped to ponder a fleecy patch' (p. 297). The repetition of 'fleecy patch' implies that the boundary between North's and the narrator's consciousnesses is as permeable as the boundaries between the time periods, which pass back and forth across the sky.

The intersection of the three searchlight moments is typical of *The Years*, where characters frequently become aware of the passing of time (or history) through visual reminders. In 1911, Eleanor is confronted by her former suitor Dubbin, now Sir William Whatney, and is shocked by the 'crumpled red-and-yellow face of the boy she had known' (p. 190). 'Are we all like that?' she asks herself; 'had they all suddenly become old fogies like Sir William?' In 1910, Rose finds that her younger cousins talk as though her own past is a scene in a play. She feels as if she is 'living at two different times at the same moment' (p. 159). This is a theoretical proposition about time, but Rose envisages it photographically: 'she was a little girl wearing a pink frock; and here she was in this room, now.' Rose herself is experiencing her past as a cinematic flashback or a faded photograph. This is true also for the reader, because we too have seen Rose as a little girl in a 'stiff pink frock' with a green smudge at the opening of the novel (p. 10). The rapid passing of time leaves us too with the sense of history flashing past.

This image of Rose, stilled in time while the real woman ages, parallels the portrait of another Rose, which presides over the drawing room at Abercorn Terrace. The picture of the Pargiter children's mother in her youth is present in the first scene, when the Pargiter children make tea, wondering if their mother is going to die. Over the fireplace, 'the portrait of a red-haired young woman in white muslin holding a basket of flowers on her lap smile[s] down on them' (p. 10). She is at once a benign and a benevolent presence; she may be watching over them protectively, but she is also preventing them from getting on with their own lives. Delia, waiting for her mother to die, looks up at the picture of the 'girl in white', who seems to be 'presiding over the protracted affair' of her own deathbed with a smiling indifference that outrages her daughter (p. 44). Like Deborah Kerr in *Colonel Blimp*, this woman seems to be ageless and therefore immortal. The picture confronts Delia with its eternal youth, so that soon the girl seems not so much to smile as to 'simper down at her daughter with smiling malice' (p. 37). '"You're not going to die"', Delia cries, frustrated, 'clenching her hands together beneath her mother's picture'.

By the end of the book, the picture has assumed a more neutral, half-remembered status. Martin finds that 'in the course of the past few years' it ceases to be his mother, becoming instead 'a work of art', albeit a dirty one (p. 143). Rose's cousin, Maggie, vaguely remembers the presence in Abercorn Terrace of 'a picture over the fireplace, of a girl with red hair', leaving Rose to supply her mother's identity (p. 158). Once the picture has been cleaned, Eleanor fails to recognise her mother in the image of the girl. 'Was it like her?' Peggy asks her aunt. 'Not as I remember her', Eleanor replies (p. 309) Throughout the novel, Woolf builds a vocabulary of images that function as metonyms for the separate time periods or for the passing of time itself. The most obvious images to function in this way are objects: the kettle that will not boil, the spotted walrus brush, the gilt chair.[45]

Woolf had experimented with the formal potential of objects in *Mrs Dalloway* (1925), using the aeroplane to juxtapose multiple points of view. In *The Years*, the points of view are dispersed across the course of time. The kettle (which features in Lesley Stern's list of inherently cinematic objects) is at first representative of the pent-up frustration of the Victorian Pargiter home. The Pargiter children wait for the recalcitrant kettle to boil as they wait for their equally recalcitrant mother to die. '"But that doesn't do any good"', Delia says irritably, watching Milly attempting to fray the wick with a hairpin, much as she savagely reprimands her sleeping mother: '"You don't want to die"' (pp. 10, 21). By 1908 most of the children have left home, but Eleanor is still there, 'fumbling with the wick', irritating Martin who echoes Delia, thirty years earlier: '"that's no sort of use, Nell"' (p. 145). It is only after her father's death that Eleanor can escape the daily struggle with the wick. In the deleted First World War extract, Woolf shows Eleanor in her new flat, revelling in the 'ease and rapidity of the "modern conveniences"' (p. 426). As in Rodchenko's account, the object has become a comrade, metamorphosing from an inefficient commodity into a functional friend.[46] Eleanor has merely to 'light the gas ring and the kettle would be boiling in five minutes'.

The spotted walrus brush, which provides a *leitmotif* in *The Years*, is given far more significance in the published novel than in the draft of *The Pargiters*. In the manuscript, Eleanor thinks about the walrus brush in the 1911 section, noticing that the 'ugly object' has survived all these years, and musing that 'there was no reason why it should not survive forever'.[47] Two pages later, she bestows it on Crosby as a sign of affection when she pensions her off: 'the problem of the walrus was solved, or shelved. It occupied an honourable position on the mantelpiece of Crosby's room.'[48]

In *The Years*, the walrus brush crops up more often and becomes more overtly a reified symbol of the characters' sadness for the forgotten past. As in *The Pargiters*, its first significant mention is when Eleanor sees it at her writing table, and finds it 'awfully queer . . . that *that* should have gone on all these years' (p. 88). This happens in 1891, several years earlier than in *The Pargiters*, which leaves it longer to accrue associations in its absence. By 1908 it is not there: 'she glanced apprehensively at her writing-table. The walrus, with a worn patch in its bristles, no longer stood there' (p. 149). Five years later, we find Crosby hoarding 'odds and ends with a view to her retirement' and among these see 'the walrus that she had found in the waste-paper basket one morning, when the guns were firing for the old Queen's funeral' (p. 208). This dates the walrus brush's departure from the desk as occurring in 1901, many years after it disappears in the draft. It seems significant that its near-demise should coincide with the real demise of Queen Victoria. The walrus brush becomes a half-forgotten, half-treasured reminder of the Victorian era, and all that has been lost since then. It makes its final appearance at Delia's party when Eleanor wakes up,

> and again she was suffused with a feeling of happiness. Was it because this had survived – this keen sensation (she was waking up) and the other thing, the solid object – she saw an ink-corroded walrus – had vanished? (p. 405)

Here Eleanor asserts the supremacy of human feelings over solid objects, but in her mental image of the walrus brush she also reveals her regret for the forgotten past. This is reinforced because we remember the sadness of the walrus brush's appearance in the wastepaper basket and of its association with Crosby, as she fades away with her dying dog.

The crimson chair with gilt claws serves as a more ambivalent symbol of Victorian England. The walrus brush is harmless throughout, and only just resists being carelessly discarded. The chair is a more pompous and imposing object, and seems to survive through its own force. Its first appearance is in 1891 at Eugenie and Digby's house in Browne Street, when Abel takes his hat and looks 'vaguely at a great crimson chair with gilt claws that stood in the hall' (p. 123). Seeing the chair, he envies Digby 'his house, his wife, his children'. Abel unconsciously makes the chair into a symbol of male patriarchal power, akin to the male costumes in *Three Guineas*. In his case, as a patriarch himself, this makes the chair an enviable object, but for the women in the family the chair is more oppressive. Even when the house is silent and everyone is in bed, the narrative camera eye quakes before the chair, which now has gilt 'paws' rather than its customary claws:

> The chair, standing empty, as if waiting for someone, had a look of ceremony; as if it stood on the cracked floor of some Italian ante-room. (p. 126)

The use of 'paws' seems to domesticate the chair at the same time as the rest of the description makes it more imposing. A few pages later, Maggie, walking along the passage at night, sees 'the great Italian chair with the gilt claws' with her mother's evening dress on it, and hears the imposing voice of her father and her mother's apologetic responses (p. 139).

It is only some years later, as the women in the family begin to gain in confidence and power, that the chair can become a more reassuring symbol. In 1910 Rose recognises it in Maggie's room with 'relief' as a symbol of the old house: '"That used to stand in the hall, didn't it?"' (p. 158). The chair is at odds with its new setting, shabbily ostentatious amidst the impoverished, slum-like dwelling, which neutralises its power. By 1917 Eleanor, at last liberated from her role as the eldest daughter of a Victorian patriarch, is able to see the chair as radiating 'some warmth, some glamour, as she looked at it' (p. 274). She finds that 'things seemed to have lost their skins; to be freed from some surface

hardness'. Mitchell Leaska has argued that, because of the visual association with the claw of Abel Pargiter's hand, the chair's claws

> are not only the gilt claws of a masculine world of abstract ritual: these are
> also the *guilty claws* of a particular and a collective father – the guilty claws
> of a crippling paternalistic world.[49]

Given the prevalence of cinematic images, the two claws do resonate,
although Leaska perhaps stretches the point in making specific connections between Abel's guilt as a (sexually) abusive father and the gilt
claws of the chair. It is significant that Abel is not the only character
with a claw. In the present-day chapter, nearly all the characters are
described as animals. Patrick appears to North as a bear 'on which
coats are hung in a hotel' and shakes paws with him (p. 346). Eleanor
sees Nicholas as a 'loose-skinned, furry animal, savage to others but
kind to herself' (p. 350). Maggie is forced to put her hand into Hugh's
'shapeless paw' and North, fidgeting, observes that the older generation
are only interested in 'their own flesh and blood, which they would
protect with the unsheathed claws of the primeval swamp' (p. 359).
Like the surreal animals in Ruttmann's *Berlin: Symphony of a Great
City,* and the animals in *Between the Acts,* these images defamiliarise
the characters, deflating their upper-class airs, showing that they are
not that far removed from their savage forebears. In this sense all the
claws derive power from their association with the chair, and in turn
imbue it with power.

Maud Ellmann has contrasted the objects in the novels of Woolf and
Bowen, stating that where 'in Woolf's novels, objects serve as spring-
boards for flights of consciousness – a technique that emphasises the
superiority of mind to matter', in Bowen's novels 'things behave like
thoughts and thoughts like things'.[50] In *The Years*, objects function
like thoughts, impugning the supremacy of consciousness as Ellmann
suggests they do in Bowen's work. At the end of Delia's party objects
seem 'to be rising out of their sleep, out of their disguise, and to be
assuming the sobriety of daily life' (p. 409). These sleeping objects have
the potential for consciousness that Tzara attributed to the objects that
dreamed rayographs in their sleep. By taking cinematic centre stage
and refusing to fade into obscurity, the portrait, walrus and chair function as cinematic objects that remind the characters and the reader of
their powerlessness against decay, loss and brute power.

Through periodically sighting these objects, the Pargiters become
aware of the passing of time. When the objects appear before them in

familiar rooms or streets, the passive reception of history is interrupted as the flitting past flashes into being. They are also interrupted spatially by the newspapers, which punctuate the text, enabling politics to intrude upon the present moment, much as they do in Sommerfield's *May Day*. In 1891, Eleanor steps briefly out of the stuffy courtroom where she has been watching her barrister brother at work into the freedom of the streets. 'The uproar, the confusion, the space of the Strand came upon her with a shock of relief . . . a rush, a stir, a turmoil of variegated life came racing towards her' (p. 108). She is a camera-like *flâneur*, watching as life passes her by, expanding 'as if something had broken loose – in her, in the world'. But Eleanor's escape is short-lived. She sees the newsboy at the gate, 'dealing out papers with unusual rapidity' and learns from a placard crumpled across the boy's legs that the Irish leader Charles Stewart Parnell is dead. '"Death" was written on the placard in very large black letters.' Even in 1891, the individual reverie is interrupted by politics. The city provides only a temporary escape from the demands of society because society is always there in newspaper headlines, inserted into the space of the streets.

Newspaper placards play an important role in Woolf's writing in the 1930s. They make politics un-ignorable and therefore frightening through their insistent visibility, imposing on the mental sensorium as they are flashed before it. Already in 1920 Woolf had wondered in her diary why life was 'so tragic' and had found the answer not in her personal problems (the labour of going to London, the lack of money) but in 'life itself': 'no newspaper placard without its shriek of agony'.[51] Nonetheless, in *Mrs Dalloway* (1925) she presents newspaper placards as providing a kind of excitement for Rezia, reminding her that it is a 'silly dream, being unhappy', and in *The Waves* (1931) she portrays Bernard as able to ignore newspaper placards and look at paintings instead.[52] It is in *The Years* that she voices her own thought, in the final, 'present day' 1930s section, at the end of Delia's party. Far away Peggy hears 'the sounds of the London night'; a horn hooting, a siren wailing (p. 369). The sense of 'people toiling, grinding, in the heart of darkness' makes her wonder how it is possible for Eleanor to be happy:

> How can one be 'happy'? she asked herself, in a world bursting with misery. On every placard at every street corner was Death.

In 1937, the placards have become impossible to ignore. For Peggy, they are linked with the cinema itself. Thinking about the unhappiness of the world, her mind returns to the 'faces mobbed at the door of a picture palace' they passed on their way to the party, 'apathetic, passive faces; the faces of people drugged with cheap pleasures; who had not even the courage to be themselves' (p. 369). Peggy's cinemagoers are Sommerfield's drugged dreamers; the picture palaces, like the newspapers, mislead and cheapen their audience.

Peggy's 1937 musings follow on from Eleanor's anger at a newspaper seen on the floor, on the way to the party. Here it is a photograph of a dictator that prompts her anger, much as photographs provoke Woolf's own scorn and anger in *Three Guineas*. She is accosted by a fat man, gesticulating from the evening paper on Peggy's doorstep.

'Damned ––' Eleanor shot out suddenly, 'bully!' (p. 313)

Surprising Peggy with her venom, Eleanor rips the paper and throws it on the floor. The newspaper has brought a dictatorial man onto the threshold between the house and the street, threatening to cross the border between private and public. She must react physically, banishing the newspaper from the house. 'You see', she interrupts, in the cab to the party, 'it means the end of everything we cared for . . . Freedom and justice' (p. 315). The conversation then meanders between war, contemporary fashion and the Victorian past, as Eleanor reminisces about life in Abercorn Terrace and Peggy finds that the past is 'so interesting; so safe; so unreal . . . so beautiful in its unreality' (p. 316). The unreality of history is interrupted by the frightening reality of the present. Just as they start to discuss North, Peggy's brother, who has survived the war, 'a newspaper placard, with large black letters' intervenes, completing Eleanor's sentence for her (p. 320). This time Woolf does not reveal what it says, but it seems to provoke Peggy's later sense of the placards as *memento mori* and to resonate with the previous inscription of 'death' on the Parnell placard. The placards that flash before the characters bring both death and history crashing in on the present.

'A mere cut made by thought in the universal becoming': Bergson and 'A Sketch of the Past'

Once we spatialise time, we grant it simultaneity. There is no linear succession between past, present and future in two- or three-dimensional space. The searchlights in *The Years* pass 'one after another' in a continual, cotemporaneous flux that resembles the philosophy of time as becoming propounded by the influential early twentieth-century philosopher Henri Bergson. According to Bergson in his 1910 *Time and Free Will*, humans are deluded in figuring time as occurring in the equal intervals mapped out by the clock. We live with 'the mistaken idea of a homogeneous inner duration, similar to space' and mistakenly picture successive states of consciousness through the movement of clock hands or, as he had put it in *Creative Evolution* (1907), the successive snapshots of the cinematograph. [53] Bergson insists that consciousness should instead be understood as a *durée*, or flux, in which every moment involves a complete transformation of the previous state and each successive state is 'a mere cut made by thought in the universal becoming'. [54]

Although Woolf claimed in 1932 never to have read Bergson, several critics have linked her exploration of time and consciousness with the work of the French philosopher. [55] According to Humm, to take Woolf's statement at face value is to ignore her cultural context; several of the people around her (most notably Duncan Grant) gave serious consideration to Bergson's work. [56] Woolf's most obvious echoes of Bergson are in her disruption of temporality in *Mrs Dalloway*, where the clocks, 'shredding and slicing, dividing and subdividing', are seen to distort and belie the inner experience of time. [57] Laura Marcus suggests that Woolf's early novel *Jacob's Room* (1922) also contains 'some significant echoes' of Bergson's critique of cinematographic consciousness. [58] Here Woolf, like Bergson, is interested in the relationship between the 'successive attitudes' of her characters, exploring how the movement between these states might best be figured. [59]

In *The Years*, Woolf seems to engage more abstractly with the relationship between space and time. For Bergson, the delusion in figuring time spatially is that the space remains untransformed by time. He criticises the cinematographic model of consciousness for assuming that the snapshots are projected at regular intervals and that each one is independent of the next. Rebutting Bergson's dismissal of cinematographic consciousness *per se*, one might say that cinema as a medium enables this delusion to be corrected. The film is perhaps the art form best placed to create dreamlike landscapes that are reconfigured at every moment. We may be wrong in experiencing consciousness as cinematographic, but in its more experimental incarnation, the cinema itself has revealed to us Bergson's own conception of consciousness as flux.

However, Bergson does not go any further in exploring the potential implications of cinema for consciousness or consciousness for cinema. It is Gilles Deleuze who has tested the cinematic ramifications of Bergson's theories in his two influential cinema books. According to Deleuze, in *Cinema II*, avant-garde, late twentieth-century cinema has exploited the film's potential to transform and distort time. From neo-realism onwards, cinema has provided us with flashbacks, dream landscapes and time-crystals, in which the present and the virtual past (the present as the memory it will become) coexist.[60]

Deleuze sees these effects as occurring primarily after the 1950s, but in fact this is what is going on in *The Man with a Movie Camera*, with its exploration of cinema's power to suspend or reanimate time and, as Deleuze recognises, in Buñuel's films. In Buñuel's 1929 *Un Chien Andalou*, captions announcing that events take place 'eight years later' or 'six years earlier' only serve to emphasise the dreamlike simultaneity of the action.[61] Within the atemporal logic of a dream, a character can be killed years before he is found kissing a woman. Woolf's spatialisation of time, predicated as it is on the division between 'actual time' and 'mind time', as she puts it in *Between the Acts*, recognises time's power to transform space.[62] Martin may look out of the same window in 1913 and 1914, but it is a totally different window, because both he and the world have changed in the interim.

Woolf's mode of spatialising time is very different from the delusory spatialising of time condemned by Bergson. By writing cinematically, Woolf gives time a spatial existence that allows separate moments to exist simultaneously. This becomes explicit in 'A Sketch of the Past', where Woolf self-consciously explores her sense of her individual past as a cinematic vision. Here she attempts to give 'a rough, visual description of childhood':

> Many bright colours; many distinct sounds; some human beings, carica-
> tures; comic; several violent moments of being, always including a circle of
> the scene which they cut out; and all surrounded by a vast space. (p. 91)

Woolf's sense of time as a vast space in which intense moments are momentarily 'cut out' seems to echo Bergon's sense of the immobile cuts of time, wrought out of the *durée*. Woolf's cuts retain a circle of the scene which engendered them; the successive states are figured as overlapping spaces, though each is transformed beyond recognition. 'This is how I shape it', Woolf goes on; 'and how I see myself as a child, roaming about, in that space of time which lasted from 1882 to 1895'. She makes the problem of the movement between the scenes explicit. Somehow into that picture must be brought, too, the sense of movement and change. Nothing remained stable long. One must get the feeling of everything approaching and then disappearing, getting large, getting small, passing at different rates of speed past the little creature; one must get the feeling that made her press on, the little creature driven on as she was by growth of her legs and arms, driven without her being able to stop it, or to change it, driven as a plant is driven up out of the earth, up until the stalk grows, the leaf grows, buds swell. That is what is indescribable, that is what makes all images too static, for no sooner has one said this was so, than it was past and altered. How immense must be the force of life which turns a baby, who can just distinguish a great blot of blue and purple on a black background, into the child who thirteen years later can feel all that I felt on May 5th 1895 – now almost exactly to a day, forty-four years ago – when my mother died.

As in *The Years*, Woolf figures herself as the viewer of history; everything passes the little creature cinematically. She sees the past as a series of scenes, but does not fall into Bergson's delusionary state of conceptualising a 'homogeneous inner duration'. Like Bergson, Woolf observes that consciousness does not register the passing scenes at an even pace: they arrive at 'different rates of speed'. Woolf also captures Bergson's sense of growth as flux, rather than as a series of discrete states. The child, driven on by the inexorable process of becoming – the growth of her legs and arms – emerges like a plant out of the earth. In *Creative Evolution* Bergson considers the transition from the child to the man and decides that there is more in the becoming – in the transition – than in the stops.[63] Similarly, Woolf finds that 'all images' are 'too static', because the image of any individual state has disappeared, to be replaced by the next, before it can be observed. Her sense of the 'force of life' that turns the baby into the child seems to parallel Bergson's sense of the power of the transition itself. It is in the process of becoming that life is to be located.

This notion of becoming seems to underlie both Woolf's and Benjamin's conception of the flash of history. For both writers, the history that flits by is not a series of discrete, finished states, but a flux, in which immobile cuts from the past can flash into being in the present, disrupting temporality much as in Deleuze's time-image cinema. In 'A Sketch of the Past', Woolf explains her decision to record the date of writing within the text on the grounds that

> I write the date, because I think I have discovered a possible form for these notes. That is, to make them include the present – at least enough of the present to serve as a platform to stand upon. It would be interesting to make the two people, I now, I then, come out in contrast. And further, this

past is much affected by the present moment. What I write today I should not write in a year's time. (p. 87)

The past, which has been superseded by the present, is reinterpreted in the light of the present. Its significance is a present significance and the present in question is the war. In June 1940 Woolf returns to the memoirs while 'the Germans fly over England' (p. 109). Contemplating a potential German victory, she finds that the future of writing has become doubtful and 'one solution is apparently suicide'. Yet she wishes 'to go on' with the memoir, returning to the past deaths of her family while she contemplates her own death in the present.

In wartime the 'now of recognisability' invests both the individual and the national past with significance. Woolf has a strong sense of the simultaneity of the past and the present, and of the continuity between the personal and the collective histories. This simultaneity of time is made explicit in a wartime poem by T. S. Eliot, who may well have been Woolf's conduit to Bergson. Eliot, who later admitted to 'a temporary conversion to Bergsonism', finds in 'East Coker' that there is

> a lifetime burning in every moment
> And not the lifetime of one man only
> But of old stones that cannot be deciphered[.][64]

For Eliot, as for Woolf and Benjamin, the past and the present are mutually transfiguring. The past, he finds in 'The Dry Salvages', ceases 'as one becomes older'

> to be a mere sequence –
> Or even development: the latter a partial fallacy
> Encouraged by superficial notions of evolution,
> Which becomes, in the popular mind, a means of disowning the past.[65]

Eliot envisages a past that does not segue neatly into the present with the ticking of the clock.[66] The 'past experience revived in the meaning', he says again,

> Is not the experience of one life only
> But of many generations[.]

To understand the past, it is necessary to look beyond 'the assurance / Of recorded history', 'towards the primitive terror'.[67] Comforting or terrifying, the past flashes up, unassimilable, in the present.

The flash of history

Pageants, Between the Acts and Humphrey Jennings

The wartime engagement of the individual with history is the subject of Woolf's last novel, *Between the Acts*. Like Eliot, Woolf looks back beyond recorded history to the primitive. At the start of the novel, Mrs Swithin is reading H. G. Wells' popular *Outline of History* (1920) and has spent the afternoon 'thinking of rhododendron forests in Piccadilly' (p. 8). She is briefly unable to separate the paraphernalia of modern life from the 'barking monsters' of the 'primeval forest'. Although the pageant itself is dedicated to the span of recorded English history, the villagers pass in and out of the trees singing of Babylon, Nineveh and Troy, looking back to Agamemnon and Clytemnestra (p. 125). When the stage empties for the interval, the 'yearning bellow' of the cows takes up 'the burden', with the 'primeval voice sounding loud in the ear of the present moment' (p. 126).

Woolf herself shares Mrs Swithin's expansive sense of history in her essay 'Anon', composed while she was writing *Between the Acts*. In this unfinished essay, intended as the introduction to a book called *Reading at Random*, she sees the pageant as the art form best placed to put us in touch with our primeval ancestors. Looking back to the time when Britain first became an island, Woolf traces the origins of English literature to Anon, the sometimes male, sometimes female 'common voice singing out of doors' (p. 382). Woolf sees Anon's most free and provocative work as taking the form of the pageant itself. He was sometimes to be found 'acting the Mass in the church' but, finding his 'own art', he 'left the church, and staged his pageant in the churchyard' (p. 383). According to Woolf, the printing press has caused the demise of Anon, and of the public art he represents, chiefly because it has 'brought the past into existence' (p. 385). By past here she means the recorded history propounded by historians, the past, seen independently of the present, which both Woolf and Benjamin found stultifying.

'Anon' is not hopeful about the future of public art. Woolf sees it as re-emerging briefly with the Elizabethan theatre and then receding into the background. I have already quoted Woolf's sense that the 'cumbered' message of the writer can now emerge only occasionally in 'a flash of recognition'. Yet emerge it does. 'Some say', Woolf notes, 'that their beards bristle when they come upon it; others that a thrill runs down the nerves of the thigh' (p. 390). We can read this as both an observation and a rallying cry. Woolf seems to be asking for a form of public art that will inscribe the audience physically as well as intellectually. The thrill of the thigh is not unlike the 'bodily collective innervation' demanded by Benjamin. It is also in line with Woolf's demands in her 'Letter to a Young Poet', where she criticises younger male poets for writing as though they had 'neither soles to their feet nor palms to their hands, but only honest enterprising book-fed brains, unisexual bodies'.[68] Public art, it is clear, will restore the body to the sexless brain. It will reinstate a collective engagement with history, while preventing the possibility of the 'settled recorded past'. The new art will appeal to a large and noisy audience, watching in a state of distraction.

Just such an audience is found watching the pageant in *Between the Acts*, which enables a collision between history and the present. Woolf's pageant is part of a more general vogue for pageants in the 1930s, with Forster and Eliot both trying their hand at reviving the form.[69] Jed Esty has read the 1930s British revival of the pageant form as a sign of fear (as war became expected) and of hope (as the end of empire enabled a new kind of nationalism). According to Esty, as a village rite the pageant was

> perfectly suited to the tenets of English civic nationalism, likely to promote and express just enough collective spirit to bind citizens together but not to trip over into the frightening power of fascist mob fever. At a time when the masses began to assert themselves on both the literary and political stages of Europe, the English pageant-play was refitted to perform insular and interclass harmony.[70]

Here the pageant takes on the power that Mass-Observation accredited to the Lambeth Walk, bringing together the community without requiring them to relinquish their individuality. Like Benjamin's cinemagoers, the Lambeth Walkers and the pageant spectators overcome the passivity that Mass-Observation (and Woolf herself) saw fascist society as inducing in the masses. In its ideal form, the pageant can therefore participate in counteracting war through a British version of Benjamin's politicisation of art.

The peculiar relevance of the pageant form in wartime is made explicit in Anthony Asquith's 1943 comedy *The Demi-Paradise*. Asquith's film, which celebrates Englishness through depicting the gradual anglicisation of a Soviet inventor, contains two pageants, both directed by a redoubtable Margaret Rutherford. The first takes place in the summer of 1939, in a time of uncertain peace. The Soviet inventor Ivan (played by Laurence Olivier) is new to England, a country he finds decidedly lacking in highmindedness. Escorted to the pageant in the resonantly named Barchester by the famous engineer he is trying to interest in his revolutionary propellers, Ivan sees the scenes from English history as both parochial and ludicrous. 'We English have a tendency to indulge in matters historical', the elderly engineer tells him, by way of explanation. At this stage, Asquith seems to share Ivan's view. Rutherford's character is presented as the maddest kind of English woman as she exhorts her cast to be soldiers, not tax inspectors, and roars 'shame on you' at a fleeing horse. The climax of the pageant comes when Ivan starts an offstage fight with a rival for Ann, the engineer's granddaughter. The fight moves onstage and the Russian ends by pushing the Englishman into the lake, breaking up the pageant.

A year later, Ivan returns to Barchester to find the small town heroically resisting the war. The Russians and British are now allies, so he is greeted enthusiastically by the locals, who are now involved in constructing his propellers. This time the pageant takes place just after the German invasion of Russia. The villagers show their support for Ivan by using the pageant to raise funds to help his home town. He now attends enthusiastically, laughing at the jokes, which are the same as the previous year's, and cheering as the stagecoach brings news of the victory at Waterloo. At the end, Rutherford gives a rousing speech, pledging British support to Russia, and Ivan gratefully receives a generous cheque to take back home. The film ends with the successful production of the propeller and the engagement of Ivan and Ann. Ivan announces that he now understands the English penchant for not taking things seriously. If you can laugh at yourselves, he declares, you can be tolerant and you can love freedom. 'There is no laughter where there is no freedom.' This is precisely the message of the pageant itself, which has shown English history meandering from past to present, always humorous and always free.

In the pageant in *Between the Acts*, history flits by cinematically; it comes in 'scraps, orts and fragments', provoking a form of distracted spectatorship (p. 169).[71] As in Woolf's cinema essay, the past is unrolled and distances annihilated. The effects of the pageant on the audience are so similar to the effects attributed to the early cinema that Michael Tratner has entitled an essay 'Why Isn't *Between the Acts* a Movie?'[72] The audience members are frequently distracted; they gossip, fidget, powder their noses and watch each other. Mrs Lynn Jones, pushing a chair forward and 'humming the tune', could be Lily, jigging her knees to the tune of the band in Green's *Living* (p. 141). Patricia Joplin writes that for the first time in Woolf's career, the interrupted structure acts not as a 'terrible defeat' but as a 'positive formal and metaphysical principle'.[73] The distraction enabled by the disruptions prevents the Debordian passive reception of spectacle that Woolf fears in *Three Guineas*.

Most cinematic of all is the climax of the pageant, when the audience members are revealed to themselves through a series of artfully positioned mirrors. For Michael Tratner, the mirrors provide a 'visceral moment of mechanical reproduction, very much as if the frames of a film featuring them were magnified and assembled into a shifting collage on stage'.[74] In 1935, the director Arthur Robison had made a sound version of *The Student of Prague*, this time with the mirror reflection visible only to Balduin himself. A year later, Benjamin had made explicit the connection between the actor's feeling of strangeness before the camera and the comparable 'estrangement felt before one's own image in the mirror'.[75] The audience of Miss La Trobe's pageant is a 1930s audience, whose experience of public viewing comes more from films than from mirrors. 'You can't get people, at this time o' year, to rehearse', the 'old cronies' say; 'There's the hay, let alone the movies' (p. 178). Their anxiety in front of the mirror is comparable to the anxiety of the subject, looking back on a moment that is subsequently revealed to be photographed. Like Spender's friends, watching the party within a party in Hamburg, or like Balduin, watching his reflection-*cum*-film image perform, Woolf's characters are subjected to the experience of absent presence. Seeing themselves in the mirrors, they come face to face with their own reproducibility. At the same time as they become aware of their own bodies in a visceral moment of embodied spectatorship, they begin to doubt the authenticity (or presence) of their original selves: 'scraps, orts and fragments, are we, also, that?' (p. 170).

In 'Anon', Woolf describes the effects of anonymous art in terms that resonate with the mirror scene in *Between the Acts*. She finds that although the printing press killed Anon, it also preserved his voice in the form of the *Morte D'Arthur*. Contained in the twenty-one volumes of the Arthurian chronicles, she locates an earlier version of 'ourselves':

> save that self-consciousness had not yet raised its mirror, the men and women are ourselves, seen out of perspective; elongated, foreshortened, but very old, with a knowledge of all good and all evil. (p. 385)

Here she suggests that the *Morte D'Arthur*'s power derives from its capacity to involve the audience by revealing its members to themselves. But for the original audience, self-consciousness had not yet raised its mirror. It is only for subsequent readers that the potential of recognition exists. It takes a post-mirror-stage self-consciousness to recognise its own distorted self. In *Between the Acts*, this self-consciousness is a given. Faced with the horrifying predicament of 'Ourselves! Ourselves!', the audience is 'caught' in an unforeseen self-recognition that is 'distorting and upsetting and utterly unfair' (p. 165). It is as though they are forced to watch themselves in a German Expressionist film that reflects the existing distortion of their world.

Karen Jacobs sees this exposure of the audience as providing the first stage in a Benjaminian 'politicisation of art':

> before the audience members are able to recognise themselves in the stages of history, they must recognise the varied parts of themselves and grasp fully their roles as historical actors in the present.[76]

Like Benjamin, Woolf (and Miss La Trobe) evokes the now of recognisability. Miss La Trobe wants 'to expose them, as it were, to douche them, with present-time reality' (p. 161). Catherine Wiley sees Miss La Trobe as concerned 'to upset rather than mirror reality', confronting the audience with a feminist version of Brecht's epic theatre.[77] Radical theatre seems to come together with radical cinema in language that evokes the flickering screen. The mirrors begin by 'flashing' the audience into being, darting and dazzling (p. 165). They then come to a halt, enabling the audience to see themselves 'not whole by any means, but at any rate sitting still' (p. 167). The audience members confront themselves in the present: 'The hands of the clock had stopped at the present moment. It was now. Ourselves.' The flash of insight in the present compels them to see themselves as implicated in history. Earlier in the day, Giles had a vision of Europe 'bristling with guns, poised with planes', on the brink of war (p. 49). In facing themselves in the 'now', the audience members are forced to see history as intersecting with this present. The old cronies, chattering afterwards, admit that the aeroplane 'made one think' of invasion and find that 'there's a sense in which we all, I admit, are savages still' (p. 179). Woolf and Miss La Trobe set the cinematic mirror against the camera. The mirrors induce a cinematic consciousness of absence at the same time as they preclude a passive, cinematic mode of perceiving the world. An Isherwood-like, alienated camera eye is prevented by the scraps, orts and fragments.

But the politicisation of art and the moment of awakening are not unequivocally successful. Critics who see Woolf as engaging in a wholeheartedly Benjaminian awakening in the pageant tend to lose sight of Miss La Trobe's sense of failure, and of the book's insistent sense of itself as a novel. 'A failure', Miss La Trobe groans, stooping to put away the records (p. 188). Her 'gift' means nothing because the audience has failed to understand 'her meaning', and the actors to know their parts. Woolf may show us the characters briefly awakened by the end of the pageant, but throughout the book the reader is too enlightened – too distant – to share their engagement, even in its distracted form. Woolf does not invite a Benjaminian distracted spectatorship so much as present an attempt to create it which she shows to have failed.

In answer to Tratner's question, *Between the Acts* is not a film because Woolf did not set out to write one, any more than she set out to write an actual pageant. Tratner suggests that she did not write a film (or pageant) herself because, as a female outsider, she considered it her role to work against fascism not in public but in private.[78] He argues that by amalgamating genres, she presents an ideal portrait of combined private–public artistic consumption, 'bringing the crowd into the private reader and bringing the private reader into the crowd'.[79] But this is to ignore the tedious inanity of much of the pageant, which is largely written as a parody. The exploits of Flavinda and Valentine may induce a moved reverie on the part of the audience, but we have to take Woolf's word for it. For the reader, one step removed from the pageant, interest is sustained through the passions offstage rather than onstage. The pageant's radicalism lies in its rejection of traditional, masculine history in favour of a meandering trail through the everyday, and, crucially, in its formal properties, as interrupted public art.[80]

The pageant form itself extends beyond the play to the fabric of the novel itself. The 'orts, scraps and fragments' that compose Woolf's texts are located not just within the pageant but also within the wider frame. In this respect, Woolf's novel can be aligned with two pageant-like films by Humphrey Jennings: *Words for Battle* (1941) and *Listen to Britain* (1942). Where Asquith presents a pageant within his film, Jennings is more like Woolf in turning his films into pageants, celebrating England past and present through a series of episodic vignettes.[81]

Words for Battle is a montage of English words and images. The text, spoken by Laurence Olivier, is taken from poetry by John Milton, William Blake and Rudyard Kipling and speeches by Churchill. Like Woolf, Jennings uses a selective history of English literature to create a history of England and, like Woolf, shows history as transformed through its intersection with the present moment. He does this through juxtaposing the historical texts with images from wartime Britain. Blake's chariot of fire is a train bringing evacuees to an idyllic English village, where they play in boats on a river. This is an England in whose 'pleasant land' Jerusalem has already been built (see Figure 5.3). Milton's 'Methinks I see her as an eagle, mewing her mighty youth' is juxtaposed with a shot of a spitfire propeller, which then flies into the distance as the eagle's 'undazzled eyes' are kindled 'at the full midday beam' (see Figure 5.4). In making a pageant using the techniques of avant-garde film, Jennings finds a potent way to combine past and present, using a new medium to present a historical form. Jennings' juxtaposition of birds and aeroplanes, carriages and tanks, would be echoed by the decidedly pageant-like opening of *A Canterbury Tale*. Here the developments of history are made manifest in the falcon that metamorphoses into an aeroplane, the pilgrim who turns into a soldier, and the horses which evolve into tanks. The film uses English history to show the continuity of the English countryside and to juxtapose this cyclical continuity with the threat of the present, reminding the audience how much it has to lose.

A year after *Words for Battle*, Jennings made *Listen to Britain*, a montage of everyday sounds in wartime. Here he creates a new form of

5.3 *'Bring me my chariot of fire'*
Humphrey Jennings, *Words for Battle* (1941)

5.4 *'Methinks I see her as an eagle'*
Humphrey Jennings, *Words for Battle* (1941)

present-day pageant. Although this time Jennings does not stray from the wartime present, he brings in details of perennial English life which enable him to make the same kinds of surreal contrasts he made in *Words for Battle*. A horse goes under industrial chimneys; a tank roars as it sweeps through a small village and is juxtaposed against a typical village teas sign. Through presenting the audience with defamiliarised versions of everyday details that it would traditionally take for granted, Jennings illustrates the fragility and specialness of the everyday.

Like Jennings, Woolf incorporates pageant-like qualities within the fabric of her text. Her search for a new form that would interweave fact and fiction is realised in *Between the Acts* through the incorporation of radio effects and newspaper extracts, as well as through the poems and plays. And, as in her photograph albums and scrapbooks, she uses montage to force an awakening on the part of her characters. Although newspapers are less omnipresent than in *The Years*, Woolf goes further in the detail she includes for specific stories. Early on we see Isa, for whose generation 'the newspaper [is] a book', reading scraps of a story about rape in her father-in-law's copy of *The Times* (p. 18). This is a true story, recorded in *The Times* in June 1938, which begins with a 'fantastic' opening describing a 'horse with a green tail' and then has a 'romantic' reference to a 'guard at Whitehall'.[82] It is only as Isa concentrates harder and pieces together the fragments that she realises the terrible truth of the story:

> The troopers told her the horse had a green tail; but she found it was just an ordinary horse. And they dragged her up to the barrack room where she was thrown upon a bed. Then one of the troopers removed part of her clothing, and she screamed and hit him about the face. (p. 18)

Isa finds this so 'real' that she can see the girl 'screaming and hitting him about the face' and then the door opens 'and in [comes] Mrs Swithin carrying a hammer' (p. 19).[83]

The juxtaposition of Mrs Swithin and the hammer with the terrible story introduces bathetic humour and also suggests that even the most apparently benign humans are capable of violence. This is made explicit as Isa muses on the sound of hammering:

> Every summer, for seven summers now, Isa had heard the same words; about the hammer and the nails; the pageant and the weather. Every year they said, would it be wet or fine; and every year it was – one or the other. The same chime followed the same chime, only this year beneath the chime she heard: 'The girl screamed and hit him about the face with a hammer.' (p. 20)

Here the chiming evokes the hammering and together they suggest both of the notions of time explored in this novel which, like *The Years*, consistently sets a vision of historical continuity against the relentless ringing of bells or ticking of clocks. Mrs Swithin, for whom heaven is 'changeless' and mammoths still roam in Piccadilly, does not believe, as William Dodge puts it, 'in history' (p. 156). She sees the Victorians as 'only you and me . . . dressed differently'. Her vision finds expression in the song of the villagers passing through the trees: '*Digging and delving . . . for the earth is always the same, summer and winter and spring; and spring and winter again; ploughing and sowing, eating and growing*' (p. 112). This is a comforting vision in a time of war, suggesting that Britain will survive another few years of destruction, but it is belied by the urgent 'chuff, chuff, chuff' of the gramophone, signifying that 'time was passing' (p. 135). Even Mrs Swithin is prompted by the 'machine' chuffing in the bushes to recognise that 'time went on and on like the hands of the kitchen clock' (p. 156). In the scene with the hammer, the repetition from year to year is cyclical, but the insistent chiming takes on the quality of the ticking of the clocks, pushing forward through history towards the anxious present. For Isa, 'the age of the century, thirty-nine', an escape into Mrs Swithin's timeless world is impossible, even through poetry (p.18). She cannot shake off the chimes of temporality or the cry of the rape victim, which act as a timely reminder of the imminent destruction in Europe.

This newspaper extract is incorporated in the text not physically but aurally.[84] It is part of a cacophony of sounds which are montaged within the novel. According to Laura Marcus, it is clear in *The Years* that Woolf is writing in 'the period in which sound film was becoming fully established', at a time when 'the technologies of sound – wireless radio, gramophone, loudspeaker – were central' to Woolf's own life.[85] Arguably, this is even truer of *Between the Acts*, a novel that is structured around sound.[86] The screaming and the hammering blend with the noise of the pageant, the drone of the aeroplanes and with the implied noise of the radio, which Jane Lewty has seen as permeating the novel through Woolf's use of the disjointed, collective voice. After the play, we hear the conversation of the audience as a series of bizarrely unified fragments:

> The aeroplanes, I didn't like to say it, made one think . . . No, I thought it much too scrappy. Take the idiot. Did she mean, so to speak, something hidden, the unconscious as they call it? But why always drag in sex . . . It's true, there's a sense in which we all, I admit, are savages still. Those women

with red nails. And dressing up – what's that? The old savage, I suppose . . .
That's the bell. Ding dong. Ding . . . Rather a cracked old bell. (p. 179)

The bell combines with the voices, as Mrs Swithin's hammer did earlier.
In its fragmentation, the dialogue evokes the crackling obfuscation of
radio in this period. Lewty writes that

> Twisting the dial of her radio set, like any listener of the time, Woolf would
> have encountered shards of unconnected dialogue, the hissing of static and
> superheyerodyne screeching, all enveloping the 'genuine' message from a
> disembodied voice at the opposite end of the circuit.[87]

As the audience members try to ascertain the 'genuine' meaning of the
play, which itself was subject to the disruptive sound of aeroplanes,
their own voices seem to crackle through the waves to the reader, who
has to piece together the disembodied voices to find a meaning. The
radio functioned for Woolf in this period as an ever-present reminder
of the precarious state of her world, even when she was listening to
music: 'Bach at night. Man playing oboe fainted in the middle. War
seems inevitable.'[88] At times the radio seemed not only to announce
the war, but to cause it: 'Are we at war? At one I'm going to listen in . . .
One touch on the switch & we shall be at war'.[89]

The sound montage in *Between the Acts* is reminiscent both of
Brechtian theatre and of cinematic sound montage. Jennings' virtuosic
sound montage in *Listen to Britain* had its predecessor in Vertov's 1931
Enthusiasm. Here Vertov uses the figure of the sound editor much
as he had used the cameraman in *The Man with a Movie Camera*,
showing her gathering together sound from different sources. As the
Communists march through Russia, desecrating churches and install-
ing their own icons and plans, Vertov montages the sounds of church
bells and priests chanting mass with the triumphant music of the
marching band and the mechanical noises of the new industrialisation.
Like Vertov (and Jennings), Woolf montages diegetic and non-diegetic
sound, creating meaning through juxtaposition, as much as through
the specific sounds. In this respect she continues what she had done
in *The Years*, where she experimented with the fragmented sound
created by the one-sidedness of the telephone conversation or by the
surrounding noise of the street.[90] Although the collective dialogue
and the drone of the planes are part of the audience experience of the
pageant, the sound montage goes beyond the audience experience to
be part of the reader's experience of the novel as a whole. Whether the

sound montage is a version of Brechtian theatre, Vertovian cinema or just a reflection of 1930s radio, it serves to induce a form of distracted reading, leaving the reader responsible for constructing connections, like the spectator of montage cinema. It also serves as a way to connect past and present, forcing a connection between history and the present moment as it enables the past to flash into being. Where in *The Years* Woolf turned history itself into a cinematic visual landscape that characters could explore as cameras, in *Between the Acts* history flashes past, visually and aurally, crashing into the present-day thoughts of the distracted audience.

In a decidedly pageant-like 1941 poem, 'I see London', Jennings used the kind of history experienced by Mrs Swithin to belittle the agonies of war. 'I see the great waters of the Thames', he announced:

> like a loving nurse, unchanged, unruffled, flooding between bridges and washing up wharf steps – an endlessly flowing eternity that smoothes away the sorrows of beautiful churches – the pains of time – the wrecks of artistry along her divine banks – to whom the strongest towers are but a moment's mark and the deepest-cleaving bomb an untold regret.[91]

Here history flits past, flowing like the water, unruffled by these brief troubles. London is going to be strong enough to survive the Germans. Woolf's cinematic mode of writing in the 1930s did not offer such consolation. Her pageant may offer us a version of Eliot's vision of continuity between past and present, individual and collective. But neither wandering through history nor reeling from it in confusion provides an escape from the bristling guns. Ultimately, the connection between history and the present moment in *Between the Acts* is unsatisfactory. History will not redeem the present, and the novel ends on the brink of a war whose destruction is going to be unmitigated by either Miss La Trobe's or Mrs Swithin's attempts to create oneness through historical continuity. But in an anxious age, the pageant, with its sweeping view of the past, offers history as a radical alternative to fascism. Viewed in a state of embodied distraction, it enables an active form of spectatorship. Presenting history cinematically, Woolf could mobilise the 1930s camera consciousness and in the process overcome the helpless passivity which that same camera consciousness often induced. The urgent insights provided by history were not always sustainable. But, in an age when words themselves had become cumbered, it was enough for the beard to bristle briefly, for the thrill to run down the nerves of the thigh.

CHAPTER 6

'The savage and austere light of a burning world': The Cinematic Blitz

Fire and blackout

Stephen Spender, Henry Green William Sansom
The London Blitz brought a cinematic end to a decade of camera consciousness. When the first bombs fell on London in September 1940, the blaze of the fire and searchlights joined the flicker of the camera and the flash of history in a spectacular vision of apocalypse. Stephen Spender experienced an early raid as 'the end I seemed now to have been awaiting all my life', not least because the writer was now the photographer and viewer of an already photographic conflagration.[1] In his 1945 poem 'Abyss', Spender positions himself as the unwilling photographer of the destruction:

> When the foundations quaked and the pillars shook,
> I trembled, and in the dark I felt the fear
> Of the photograph my skull might take
> Through the eye sockets, in one flashlit instant[.][2]

The camera has infiltrated the poet's brain so that even in the dark he has no escape from vision. He awaits the potentially fatal flash of the camera-like bombs.

Unsurprisingly, wartime photographers and filmmakers made the most of the inherently cinematic aspects of the Blitz. According to Virilio, the bombing raids were 'a *son-et-lumière*, a series of special effects, an atmospheric projection designed to confuse a frightened, blacked-out population'.[3] Black-and-white photography and cinema came into their own in capturing the darkness of the blackout, punctured by the fire. Week after week, photographs in *Picture Post* showed London lit up against the blackout. In February 1941 the magazine broke its usual rule of anonymity to laud the photographer of a particularly

6.1 *Wartime chiaroscuro*
Humphrey Jennings, *Fires Were Started* (1943)

powerful picture of a silhouetted fireman, leaning vertiginously over a burning building, caught in a nimbus of white light.[4] The fire sequence in Jennings' 1943 film *Fires Were Started* is dominated by sharp chiaroscuro. Jennings presents the viewer with dark images of burning buildings, lit only by the piercing brightness of the fire within or the briefly illuminated faces of the firemen (see Figure 6.1). Throughout the war, filmmakers exploited the visual and dramatic potential of the blackout, not least, Antonia Lant suggests, because in an era of shortages, the fewer carbon rods needed the better.[5] According to Lant, the cinema itself enhanced the 'metaphoric power' of the blackout, which itself had become a synecdochic shorthand for war.[6] It is in the shadowy light of the blackout that Candy sees the illuminated face of his driver, Johnny, in *Colonel Blimp*, realising her striking resemblance to his two dead loves. In *A Canterbury Tale*, Powell and Pressburger portray the blackout as allowing a bizarre form of sexual licentiousness. The gentleman farmer Mr Colpepper uses the darkness to throw glue into the hair of unsuspecting young women, hoping to scare them from going out at night and falling into the exploring hands of the soldiers.

The cinematic properties of the Blitz were perhaps best captured in literature by three wartime firemen: Stephen Spender, Henry Green and William Sansom. The last doubled as both an actual and a cinematic fireman, playing Barrett, the new recruit, in *Fires Were Started*, a film in which Jennings himself was drawing on his own experiences as a wartime fireman. In 'A Man-made World', Spender pictures himself as shut off 'from the light' in the 'gloom' of a 'windowless night' in the blackout, trapped in a cinematic 'black, malicious box'.[7] When the siren wails, he sees 'white rays gleaming', punctuating the darkness with 'sudden flashes'. Watching a raid across the sea in 'The Air Raid across the Bay', Spender experiences the bombs and the fire as a distant, cinematic spectacle. He observes the 'high / Searchlights probe the centre of the sky', 'fusing in cones of light' and 'Projecting tall phantom / Masts' above the sea. As the bombs thud, 'pink sequins wink from a shot-silk screen'.

In his autobiographical short story 'A Rescue', published in 1941, Green was explicit in seeing the lighting effects of the Blitz as cinematic:

> By the cinema light of our electric torches we could see fifteen feet down this opening another cover swinging on a shaft or pivot through the centre of its length.[8]

Trained to frame scenes photographically, Green, like Spender, is sensitive to the natural photographic framing provided by the war. Searching for the lost man in the manhole, Green figures the hole itself as a screen, with the man's figure illuminated (or projected) by the 'cinema light' of the torches. The torches themselves provide a spotlight amidst the darkness of the blackout, as they do for Jennings. Like the cinema image, this man looks 'flat' in the 'shrouded' torchlight, 'grotesquely caught up, dreadfully still, most like a rag doll made full size he was so limp'.

Green depicts the chiaroscuro of the Blitz at greater length in *Caught* (1943), where the acres of dark timber that catch fire are like a 'dark mosaic aglow with rose', and 'the distant yellow flames [toy] joyfully with the next black stacks which softly [merge] into the pink of that night' (p. 181). Like Spender's pink sequins, Green's fire is black and rose rather than black and white, which introduces heat visually into the picture. Cinematic writing can exceed the capacities of the black-and-white film. In this respect, Green's writing has more in common with the chiaroscuro of wartime paintings and drawings than with cinema. Graham Sutherland, employed as an official war artist during the bombing raids, captured the peculiarly hallucinogenic aspect of the fires with a more colourful palette than that of wartime photographers. His 'Devastation 1941: An East End Street' contrasts the darkness of the blacked-out night with an unearthly yellowish row of house façades. The rusty yellow, cut out from the solid blackness, conveys the dreamlike unreality of the scene more eloquently than most photographs in the period (see Figure 6.2). In *Caught*, as in Jennings' film, the firemen's faces are lit up against the night:

> the firemen saw each other's faces. They saw the water below a dirty yellow towards the fire; the wharves on that far side low on black, those on the bank they were leaving a pretty rose. (pp. 177–8)

6.2 Graham Sutherland, 'Devastation 1941: An East End Street' (1941). Courtesy of Tate.

Green's typically ambiguous syntax enables the phrase 'a pretty rose' to elide the fiery colour with the flower that it resembles, evoking the actual roses that pervade the novel and intensifying the strange beauty of the play of light and dark.

Now that the city has become the set for a film, Green experiments with other lighting effects, bathing Pye's childhood encounter with his sister in moonlight and Richard's son Christopher's abduction in the pink and red filters of gaudy shop lighting. For Pye, the troubled sub-officer of Richard's station, the moonlight becomes a sinister force that he sees as prompting his (falsely recollected) incestuous childhood encounter with his sister: 'So in the blind moonlight, eyes warped by his need, he must have forced his own sister' (p. 140). He starts haunting moonlit streets in an attempt to recreate the conditions of this apparent lapse, and the moonlight seems to accompany and induce his downfall. It is in the moonlight that he himself comes close to abducting a small boy, bringing him back to the fire station:

> He came back out into full moonlight holding at arm's length, thrashing with legs, struggling, not the lost girl with flaxen hair he had imagined . . . but a small, rough boy. (p. 168)

The description of the lighting in the shop where Christopher is abducted by Pye's sister is a cinematic set-piece scene. Lyndsey Stonebridge suggests that 'Christopher is abducted not so much by a woman posing as his mother but by phantasmatic colour'.[9] He becomes dazzled by 'the pink neon lights', 'caught in another patch of colour', just as Richard, revisiting the scene of the crime, finds himself lured into unconsciousness by the 'deep colour spilled over' the objects in the shop (pp. 9–10).

The firefighting novelist Sansom offers an inventory of the lighting effects of the air raids in his 1947 account of the London bombing, *The Blitz, Westminster at War*. This book, intended 'to provide a record of the war years for the citizens of this City', explores the technological and military developments of the bombing war alongside its social effects on London.[10] Sansom is keenly aware of the visual qualities of the fire. In a passage that calls to mind the ghostly light of Sutherland's 'Devastation 1941', Sansom finds that a city 'bereft of electric and neon light took on a new beauty' in the moonlight, though on clouded nights 'nothing could be seen' (pp. 49–50). He observes the same prismatic spectrum of colours as Green and Sutherland. The artificial 'flash and luster'

> permutated into many freakish effects – the searchlights above turning to turquoise in the fireglow, the faces yellow in the gaslight, the perpetual sunset coppered and orange above any black roofscape. (p. 175)

Two effects in particular stand out: 'the 'bombed house cold and away from all firelight' and the 'warm and garish' quality of the 'pantomime light of the fire'. Sansom finds the fires less cinematic than theatrical; they have the constructed quality of the 'garish set-piece' (p. 176). The bombed houses are pictured more cinematically. They are

> lit by the moon; or on darker nights by the starlight of searchlights, the whitish beams of masked torches, the blue lamps of the incident officer, and emphasised by here and there a red hurricane lamp lit to advise a roadblock. (p. 175)

As in Spender's raid across the bay, the scene appears as a black screen, flashed into relief by the lighting effects.

Sansom had explored the visual qualities of fire in the wartime short stories collected in *Fireman Flower and Other Stories* in 1944. The fireman narrator of 'The Wall' contrasts the red fire inside the rooms with the blackness of the outside walls, finding that

> like the lighted carriages of a night express, there appeared alternating rectangles of black and red that emphasised vividly the extreme symmetry of

the window spacing: each oblong window shape posed as a vermilion panel set in perfect order upon the dark face of the wall.[11]

Here Sansom echoes the visual imagery of *Fires Were Started*, with its sharp contrasts between the light seen through the windows of the burning buildings and the darkness of the blackout outside. These are potent images partly because they reverse the usual order of vision, making the gaps and spaces more visible than the solid bricks. In Sansom's title story, Fireman Flower experiences the bombing as a colourful lighting effect. He watches as 'a peculiar light, iridescent – mostly very white but interspersed with beams of pinkish orange and livid blue' flickers over the helmets and buttons of the firemen like a 'rotating spotlight' (p. 139).

Cinematic objects

William Sansom, Elizabeth Bowen

Sansom's firemen find that the firelight bizarrely illuminates objects. Fireman Flower surveys the smoke clearing 'to reveal some object of the surrounding chaos', glimpsing 'a sodden drape of flowered wallpaper hanging listless' and 'a burnt out fire extinguisher, empty, its red paint blistered and blacked' (p. 134). Highlighted and exposed, these tattered objects acquire the numinous quality of objects in cinema, taking over the frame. The group of mysterious observers who collectively narrate 'The Witnesses' watch the night flaring up and everything 'flash[ing] into being':

> Light evaporated the mist, so that each corner of the architecture, each detail of the pump, each line of the operator's uniform leapt into abrupt definition, like objects switched suddenly onto a screen. (p. 85)

The link between fire and cinema is made explicit in the screen simile; fire shares the cinema's capacity to intensify objects.

Projected onto a ghostly cinema screen, objects become animated. Recording the raids in his diary, the novelist Hector Bolitho found that he did not remember 'ever seeing inanimate objects become so human' as they seemed the morning after an attack: 'there was expression on the faces of the old houses. Even the trees were wounded.'[12] This effect is particularly pronounced in the wartime fiction of Elizabeth Bowen, whose objects had always had an unnerving propensity to stir into life. In Bowen's wartime short story 'Mysterious Kôr', the lighting effects of the London blackout create a world in which body parts are objectified and people are usurped by the objects that surround them. Pepita sees her lover's 'eyeballs glitter', separated from his head in the shadows of the 'full moonlight' that drenches the 'moon's capital'.[13] Waiting at home for the lovers, Pepita's jealous flatmate Callie allows the moon to flood into her room through a crack in the blackout blind. All her possessions are transfigured:

> out stood the curves and garlands of the great white marble Victorian mantelpiece of that lost drawing-room; out stood, in the photographs turned her way, the thoughts with which her parents had faced the camera. (p. 734)

She returns to bed and allows one hand to lie, 'until it [is] no longer her own'. The eyeball and the arm seem to be less living than the mantelpiece; her parents' thoughts, objectified through the photograph, encroach upon her own.

Here the Blitz lighting recreates the lighting effects of the cinema, which Bowen had explored in the cinema scene in her 1938 novel *The Death of the Heart*. Holidaying at the seaside, Portia, the teenage heroine of the novel, is accompanied to the cinema by the crass children of her host and by her own rather caddish London suitor, Eddie. In the darkness of the auditorium, Portia finds that Eddie is distorted by the bright light of the cinema screen itself, which illuminates only details of his body: 'on her side, one of his hands, a cigarette between the two longest fingers, hung down slack'.[14] It is in the artificial, spot-lighting gleam of Dickie's cigarette lighter that Eddie's shadowy liaison with Daphne is revealed. A host of objects, or parts of objects, are illuminated by this tiny but piercing source of light:

> It caught the chromium clasp of Daphne's handbag, and Wallace's wristwatch . . . It rounded the taut blond silk of Daphne's calf and glittered on some tinfoil dropped on the floor . . . The light, with malicious accuracy, ran round a rim of cuff, a steel bangle, and made a thumb-nail flash.

Portia now sees that Eddie is holding hands with Daphne, and her own, tormented mood is reflected by and reflects the maliciously piercing light.

The perpetual darkness of wartime replicates the darkness of the auditorium, lit up briefly by different forms of artificial light. In Bowen's *The Heat of the Day* (1949), Stella finds that at dinner with Harrison 'wherever she turned her eyes detail took on an uncanny salience' (p. 225). Here the effects of the fire and moonlight have extended to an interior scene. The restaurant is lit by 'bald white globes screwed aching to the low white ceiling' which destroy shadow, and highlight odd, synecdochic detail, quite apart from being bizarrely sentient themselves. Indeed, even the shadows they eliminate have a living quality: they have been 'ferreted out and killed'. Like Pepita, Stella no longer sees the whole of Harrison but merely his eyes, his eyelids red with fatigue, his pupils 'mapped round with red-brown lines on a green-brown iris', and his eyelashes strangely touching in 'their generic delicacy' (p. 227). The eye takes over her field of vision like the famously slit eye in Buñuel's *Un Chien Andalou*, pierced by a razor sharpened by the director himself, or the eyes that pervade *The Man with a Movie Camera*, merging with the camera to form Vertov's 'Kino-Eye'. According to Jean Epstein, the film is a 'cyclopean art, a unisensual art, an ecnoscopic retina', and 'all life and attention are in the eye'.[15] Vertov takes this further in superimposing the camera and the human eye through a series of special effects. At one point the human eye looks out of the camera as the lash-like shutters close gradually round the pupil; later, the cameraman himself is reflected in the human eye that he is apparently filming. At the end of the film, the shutter closes over the eye, which nonetheless peers through from beneath the camera; empowered by cinema, the human eye can now continue to gaze out at the world even when the camera is switched off (see Figure 6.3). In Bowen's novel, the wartime gaze mimics the bizarre intimacy of cinematic viewing in which the viewer can look straight into the magnified eye of the stranger on the screen. And, as in cinema, the intimacy is at one remove. Stella finds the eyelashes 'touching', but her feeling has 'no more than an echo of intimacy about it, as though transmitted from someone else'.

'I have isolated,' Bowen said in the postscript to her wartime stories. 'I have made for the particular, spot-lighting faces or cutting out gestures'.[16] She describes her stories as 'disjected snapshots – snapshots taken from close up, too close up, in the middle of the melee of a battle'. As a narrator she mimics the effects of the searchlights and torches, piercing the blackout. By spotlighting and cutting out, Bowen exposes and even breaks the objects she highlights, exacerbating the literal breakages of war. Her objects take on the peculiar charge that Heidegger attributed to the broken thing, which reveals its Thingness at the moment when it is broken and form is severed from function.[17] Bowen's and Sansom's objects are potent because they have been broken by war, either literally (the burnt-out fire extinguisher)

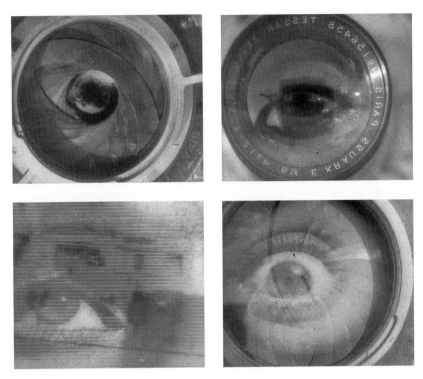

6.3 *A cyclopean art*
Dziga Vertov, *The Man with a Movie Camera* (1929)

or visually (the curves and garlands of the mantelpiece). Broken and partially illuminated objects become more treasured. 'In the savage and austere light of a burning world, details leap out with significance', Bowen announces in a 1963 afterword to her wartime *Bowen's Court* (1942).[18] The savage light is the literal blaze of the fire, with its visual tendency to highlight details. It is also the tendency of wartime to make everything more fragile and therefore more precious. Callie's parents face the camera with unusual pertinacity both because their faces are highlighted by the moonlight and because either they or she may soon be killed. They take on the ghostly quality that Kracauer ascribed to the photograph, reminding us of the death that they are attempting to defy through their presence.

Bowen's Court, like Woolf's 'Sketch of the Past' and Green's *Pack My Bag*, is written in the face of imminent death. Green finds in *Pack My Bag*, which he began in 1940, that 'we who must die soon, or so it seems to me, should chase our memories back, standing, when they are found' (p. 92). The threat of death wakes 'what is left of things remembered into things to die with' (p. 33). Bowen followed Green's injunction in tracing her memories back to their origins, which she locates not in the people who brought her into the world, but in the houses they brought her to. In 1942 she published two autobiographical books. *Bowen's Court* is a biography of her ancestral home and *Seven Winters* a short, impressionistic record of her first seven years. Both are focused on the details illuminated by the savage light of war. In *Seven Winters*, Bowen finds that her childhood home was characterised less by talk than things; it was 'gently phenomenal' (p. 469). As a result, her early memories are 'visual rather than social'. It is 'things and places rather than people that detach themselves from the stuff of my dream' (p. 470). Like Green, Bowen seems to be faithfully recording the facts and objects of her past, as something to hold on to in the wake of destruction.

Reflecting on *Bowen's Court* in the 1963 afterword, Bowen situates the book as wartime writing and finds that in the light of war, 'the past – private just as much as historic – seemed to me . . . to matter more than ever: it acquired meaning; it lost false mystery (p. 454). In that savage and austere light, 'nothing that ever happened, nothing that was even willed, planned or envisaged, could seem irrelevant'. Because 'war is not an accident' but an 'outcome', 'one cannot look back too far to ask of what?' In *Seven Winters*, the details rendered relevant by war seem to include ordinary household objects, such as the brass plates of doors, which merit a whole section (pp. 491–4). Later in this book she describes the rooms of her childhood home in careful, loving detail:

> The Herbert Place drawing room, as I remember it, had a doubly watery character from being green in tone. On the light-green 'trickle' (or moiré) wall-paper hung Florentine mirrors, not bright, wreathed in spiked gilt leaves. Between the mirrors hung sketches in gilt frames. (p. 511)

These objects from the past take on the metonymic quality of the walrus brush and the gilt chair in *The Years*, visually serving to summon up a whole era. At the same time, there is an obsessiveness in the garnering of detail here that seems to live up to Green's injunction in *Pack My Bag* that 'we who must die soon . . . should chase our memories back, standing, when they are found', telling themselves, 'as the siren goes', 'how we did once find this or the other before we go to die to take with us like a bar of gold' (pp. 92, 33). Tracing the house and its occupants to their origins in *Bowen's Court*, Bowen at once mourns and treasures the passing of a lost tradition. In the afterword, she speculates that everyone, fighting or just enduring, carried within him one private image, one peaceful scene. Mine was Bowen's Court. War made me that image out of a house built of anxious history (p. 457)

The long history contained within the house brings a comforting sense of the continuity of past and present.

It is the imminence of death, as much as the lighting effects of the fire, that gives Bowen's wartime London its cinematic charge. And the objects take on their bizarre potency partly because they may be about to disappear. 'Objects exist', Jean-Luc Godard once said,

> and if one pays more attention to them than to people, it is precisely because they exist more than these people. Dead objects are still alive. Living people are often already dead.[19]

This is particularly true of Bowen's wartime fiction, where the living people often operate as cinematic automata – or as ghosts – and the objects are animated to the point of malignity. Later in *The Heat of the Day* Louie's chair, once occupied by her husband, Tom, whom she has betrayed, seems to gaze at her (p. 146). 'It directed something at her whichever way she pushed, pulled or turned it, in whatever direction she turned herself.'

Because literature has consciousness readily at its disposal, it can go further than the cinema in elevating objects. Ellmann's sense that in Bowen 'things behave like thoughts and thoughts like things, thus impugning the supremacy of consciousness' captures what is most cinematic in her writing but also what is most literary.[20] In Bowen's wartime fiction, objects don't just share a democratic centre stage, they take over, so that no character feels safe from the physical world. In most accounts of cinema, the viewer is present and the actor is absent. But in Bowen's fiction everyone has become both viewers and actors, so that the viewers themselves are absent ghosts. The only tangible presence comes from the objects.

This is clear in the opening scene of *The Heat of the Day*, which is a virtuosic exercise in observation. According to Cavell, in cinema we glimpse the world as seen in our absence.[21] Reading Bowen, we are invited into the scene before we are presented with its inhabitants, granted the cinematic perspective denied to the characters themselves. The action takes place in a theatre, the open-air theatre in Regent's Park, and Bowen describes the light as 'low' and 'theatrical' (p. 7). But, lacking any actors, it becomes cinematic. The first thing we see is leaves drifting onto the grass stage, 'crepitating as though in the act of dying'. These are the leaves that Lesley Stern regards as exhibiting an acute example of cinema's capacity 'to register a world as if caught "off-guard"'.[22]

When we first see Harrison, he is introduced merely as an example, part of the panoramic cross-section of characters inhabiting the theatre: 'for instance, an Englishman in civilian clothes' (p. 9). Denied a name, he is viewed from the outside; he is part of the world caught off-guard, 'body bent forward, feet planted apart on the grass floor'. Harrison starts the novel as an absent actor but, at the same time, he is revealed as the watcher he will remain throughout the book. Forced to confront Louie, who is attempting to initiate a conversation, he turns towards her: 'He more than looked, he continued to look, he stared at this person.' He is disturbed by her presence precisely because she too is a watcher. And she has been watching him long before he deigned to notice her: 'she had given him, the watcher, the enormity of the sense of having been watched' (p. 14).

The reader here, granted the privilege of registering the world from outside, is in the position of watching the characters watch each other. This experience continues into the next scene, where we see Stella setting up her first sight of Harrison, or rather her first sight of his presence, through the movement of the door. Stella positions herself as an absent viewer, attempting to survey her room and her visitor caught off-guard. Hearing Harrison's footsteps on the stairs, she looks in the mirror, 'not at herself but with the idea of studying, at just one remove from reality, the door of this room opening behind her, as it must' (p. 24). In fact, she is unable to sustain the position and swings round to face him, 'stood stock still, arms folded'. As she stands, 'watching Harrison make his entrance', she is both an actor in her own right and the viewer of the man who now comes in and brings himself 'face to face with the mirror and the photographs', turning himself into a figure seen in the mirror (p. 28).

Harrison surveys the photograph of Robert, Stella's lover, which becomes the topic of the conversation, taking over the room like the photograph of Callie's parents, as it will continue to do throughout the book. In Bowen's wartime fiction, the photograph is an extreme example of an animated object. These pictures carry the full force of Kracauer's sense of the photograph as the failed '*go-for-broke game* of history' or Sontag's sense of photographs as a *memento mori*, which enable the photographer 'to participate in another person's (or thing's) mortality, vulnerability, mutability'.[23] As in *Sally in Our Alley*, they are used metonymically to stand in for the absent beloved, but they are inadequate symbols, unable to sustain the burden of presence. At this stage, the photograph of Robert enables Harrison to tell Stella that he knows 'the original', and that it's a face that interests him. Over the course of the scene, Harrison informs her that Robert is a traitor, whose life is in her hands. As if to illustrate his power over his rival, he turns the photograph round. In a moment of defiant anger, Stella restores it to its correct position:

> 'And another time', she said, 'leave my things alone!' She then turned full on him, from less than a yard away: they were eye to eye in the intimacy of her extreme anger. (p. 42)

Stella is angry that Harrison claims to have power over Robert, now symbolised metonymically by the photograph. In turning it back, she attempts to restore him to life, but he remains nonetheless unnervingly absent for her. He is caught in Barthes' 'has-been-there'.[24]

Robert himself makes clear this association of photography and death when Stella and Robert visit his childhood room. Stella is horrified to find herself confronted with 'sixty or seventy photographs', hung 'in close formation' on two walls of Robert's room, all featuring Robert himself 'at every age' (p. 116). '*You* didn't hang all these up?' she asks, alarmed. 'No,' he replies, 'though, as you see, I haven't taken them down'. Looking round, Stella finds that 'this room feels empty' despite the insistent presence of the images. 'It could not feel emptier than it is', Robert replies:

> Each time I come back again into it I'm hit in the face by the feeling that I don't exist – that I not only am but never have been. So much so that it's extraordinary coming here with you . . . I now only have no idea [what I was doing] but must have had even less idea at the time. Me clawing at that fur rug as a decently arranged naked baby seems no more senseless, now, than me smirking over that tournament cup. (pp. 117–18)

The photographs of Robert render him ghostly in the present. Stella observes that they have 'made this room as though you were dead'. His mother and sister have used the photographs to construct a shrine to the living; by freezing the past they are evoking a funereal future in which Robert has ceased to exist.

Stella finds her own photograph of Robert equally unreal when she stares at is during their final encounter. Now Robert is revealed both as the traitor he has been and as a man condemned to imminent death. Listening to his explanations, Stella finds that 'in something more powerful than the darkness of the room the speaker had become blotted out' (p. 269). She has an arrest of memory in which she finds it 'impossible to conceive not only what the look on the face might now be but what the face had been, *as* a face, ever'. Resigning herself to his imminent absence, she seems to have pre-emptively consigned his face to the fate of the photographs in his bedroom at home. She has turned him into an absent ghost in the present.

Getting out of bed, Stella goes into the sitting-room, which she feels has the 'look of no hour' (p. 277). She now finds absence from Robert as impossible as presence, and comes 'to a stop in front of the photograph'. Gazing at the 'black-and-white of what was for ever dissolved for her into the features of love', she finds only 'the face of a late-comer'. As a physical object, this particular photograph has come to accrue a disturbing power. It functions as what Lesley Stern has called an 'accursed object', referring to objects in films that have a functional purpose within the narrative at the same time as they generate 'an excess of affect'.[25] Stella now turns the photograph round, imitating Harrison's gesture, banishing it to face the wall 'in order to try to picture life without him'. Again, the effect is in excess of the physical object:

> At the look of that blank white back of the mount the ice broke; she had to hold on to the chimneypiece while she steadied her body against the beating of her heart.

The reversed photograph is enough to make her feel the force of her grief at life without Robert – to give her a taste of the death that it already signifies. Unable to speak, she calls out his name in her mind, looking at the door, which now takes over from the photograph as a metonym for his absence: 'it was incredible that anyone loved so much should be still behind it.' Defying this pre-emptive ghostliness, Robert appears. Apparently he has heard her silent call. Grieving for the future in the present, Stella falls into his arms and the photograph, 'bent into unaccustomed reverse', topples forward, crashing to the floor (p. 278).

Ghosts and time

Elizabeth Bowen, Stephen Spender, Powell and Pressburger, William Sansom

The deathly charge of the photograph-as-object is shared by the photographic slow-motion scenes in Bowen's novel. Bowen is explicit in seeing the scene where Stella and Robert first meet as taking place in a suspended, photographic present. Their relationship begins with a glance in which they see 'in each other's faces a flash of promise' (p. 95). The metaphorical 'flash' heralds a series of cinematic lighting effects, with the blue of his eyes, as they glance at Stella, intensified by the 'mirror-refracted lighting'. Even Stella's hair invites wartime chiaroscuro; Robert fixes his gaze on the 'one white lock' in her hair as he studies her. At this point, Stella turns to wave goodbye to the friend who has brought her across the room and her 'gesture of goodbye' freezes immediately as a photographic memory in their minds, so that

> Remembered, her fleeting sketch of a gesture came to look prophetic; for ever she was to see, photographed as though it had been someone else's, her hand up. The bracelet slipping down and sleeve falling back, against a dissolving background of lights and faces, were vestiges, and the last, of her solidity.

Her hand, removed and animated, takes on its own agency and becomes a symbol of solidity in an unstable wartime world. The motion of the bracelet introduces movement into the photographic image, making it seem like a brief section from a film that is continually rewound and replayed in her mind. According to Stern, gestures are inevitably enhanced by the cinema. Where 'the gestural often goes unnoticed in the everyday, in the cinema (where it travels between the quotidian and histrionic) it moves into visibility'.[26] Stella's gesture is doubly visible because it is both cinematic and suspended in time.

This is a scene that fulfils the fate of the photograph in Kracauer's essay, attempting and failing to resist death. Their relationship is posited in the past before it has had a chance to begin. This first meeting is photographically indexed as a farewell gesture and, significantly, their first words remain unspoken. Bombs interrupt them just at the moment when they begin to speak and '[fix] their eyes expectantly on each other's lips' (p. 96). In the insistent fixing of their eyes, they attempt to still time; to turn their gazes into cameras that will hold the moment still and to defy the insistent drumming of the bombs. They succeed in the attempt, experiencing a present suspended in time. But, like Kracauer's photographers, they fail to defy death. The deathliness of the photographic stillness comes together with the very real threat of the bombs, tainting the beginning of love with the promise of its extinction.

It is significant that this photographic image is in fact a tiny section of a slow-motion film, stopped in mid-flow as the bracelet slips slowly down her arm. In 1933, Rudolf Arnheim had described the slow-motion film as producing a 'curious gliding, floating, supernatural effect', suggesting that it could be 'a wonderful medium for showing visions and ghosts'.[27] More uncannily than the photograph, the slowed film attempts to bring the past to life by intricately dissecting and reconstructing it in the same manner as human memory. And, like the photograph, it fails. In feeling like a slow-motion film as it takes place, their experience seems to be consigned to the deathliness of memory before it has a chance to live. As in *People on Sundays*, the photographic suspension of movement is more unnerving than the stillness of a photograph. Knowing that movement can be mechanically stopped makes all subsequent movements seem automated and mechanical.

Their dehumanised faces are then juxtaposed with the enemy aeroplane overhead. The plane itself is eerily animated, 'dragging, drumming slowly round in the pool of night, drawing up bursts of gunfire – nosing, pausing, turning, fascinated by the point for its intent'. The gerunds become gradually more human as 'dragging' morphs into 'nosing', with the plane's human qualities made explicit in 'fascinated'. Even the night itself is given a physical existence as a 'pool', threatening the incipient lovers alongside the bombs. As the danger increases, their more local environment, 'in here', becomes threateningly alive:

> With the shock of detonation, still to be heard, four walls of in here yawped in then bellied out; bottles danced on glass; a distortion ran through the view.

The dancing bottles and the yawping wall seem to have a life and agency of their own. The bizarre 'yawped' invokes the fear of the walls as they yelp inwards; apparently the scream is enough to induce physical movement.

Irrevocably interrupted, Stella and Robert's first words remain unspoken and 'from having been lost [begin] to have the significance of a lost clue'. Andrew Bennett and Nicholas Royle describe this first meeting as taking place 'in a blitz-riven fictionality and absence . . . in the phantom of an exchange which can never be known or forgotten'.[28] There is a fundamental lack of both meaning and self in Stella and Robert's world, which stems partly from the cinematic ascendancy of objects that thwart communication and decentre human identity and partly from the fact that, experienced in slow motion, their encounters begin as memories.

Stella's meetings with Robert are again and again pictured as slow-motion, stilled films. When she meets him after a night of bombing in which each has feared for the other's life, she is aware of the stilling of time as they freeze, a cigarette suspended in her mouth and a lighter in his hand. Stella observes that 'so in the cinema some break-down of projection leaves one shot frozen absurdly, onto the screen' (p. 98). In seeing this suspended moment specifically as a paused film rather than a photograph, Bowen invokes precisely the deathly stilling of motion that is exploited in *People on Sundays*. This is cinematic writing at its strangest. The narrator brings the cinema into play in order to turn it back into a photograph. But, as Garrett Stewart has observed, the photogram is all the more cinematic for being still.[29] The lack of motion draws attention to the previous motion, just as Stella's premonition of Robert's absence makes her aware of the strength of her love.

Gazing at Robert, Stella confronts 'the face of before she opened her eyes'. The usual 'flame-thin blueness' of his eyes is missing. She is experiencing Robert himself as absent and the result is uncanny because 'in the unfamiliar the familiar persisted like a ghost'. The effect of presence and absence here is more peculiar than that in conventional cinema. Instead, they are more like the almost interchangeable student and his reflection in *The Student of Prague*. Both Stella and Robert are at once present viewers and absent actors. This means that they are also absent viewers and present actors. Like the student and his reflection, both have an apparently corporeal ability to interact with the world, but neither exists fully and neither believes fully in the existence of the other. Both are given a premonition of absence.

During Stella's ill-fated tea with Robert's family, the sun starts to set and its 'chemically yellowing light' has the same effect as the evening light in Regent's Park at the opening of the book. This time, its chemical, cinematic properties are explicit:

> Reflections, cast across the lawn into the lounge, gave the glossy thinness of celluloid to indoor shadow. Stella pressed her thumb against the edge of the table to assure herself this was a moment *she* was living through – as in the moment before a faint she seemed to be looking at everything down a darkening telescope . . . she dared look again at Robert . . . Late afternoon striking into the blue of his eyes made him look like a young man in Technicolor. (p. 114)

Here indoor and outdoor lighting are both film-like. The outdoor lighting is chemically yellowing; it has the cinematic power of the lighting effects in the park, spotlighting and highlighting like the lights in an exterior shot in a black-and-white film. The indoor lighting is shadowy and flimsy in contrast: it is the muted glare of an early Technicolor interior shot. Aware of the unreality of the celluloid world, Stella feels herself and Robert become unreal; he is merely a Technicolor actor. She seems to be observing the scene through a telescope – as in the moment before a faint – with the reference to fainting evoking the ghostly, floating quality that Arnheim ascribed to the slow-motion film. This makes the whole scene seem to take place in a deathly slow motion, which also gives it simultaneously the hindsight of memory. The image of the telescope, intruding on the film conceit, separates Stella from the cinematic screen and places her in the role of both viewer (observing) and filmmaker (focusing). She is constructing the film as it plays. Telescopes by their nature magnify detail, so Stella becomes aware of the horror of every facet of the tea table, 'with its china and eatables'. With each slow-motion scene, she moves a step further away from the world she observes and, crucially, a step further from Robert himself, who takes on the form of the absent ghost he is destined to become.

The suspension of time in the tea scene seems to echo the effects of the bombing in Stella and Robert's first meeting. It is as though the war has created an atmosphere in which time is apt to be stilled at any moment. This is partly the result of the physical effect of the bombs, which were well known to stop clocks, literally cutting off the flow of Woolf's 'recorded past'. In *the Heat of the Day*, the ghostly timelessness of wartime London is accentuated by the 'shock-stopped' clocks (p. 99). Their lack of time-telling becomes a kind of bizarre presence, so that Stella and Harrison come face to face in 'the unbounded night in which no clock struck' (p. 141). Other clocks are more wilfully single-minded. Stella's and Robert's wristwatches come to 'some kind of relationship of their own by never perfectly synchronising' (p. 99).

The bizarre distortion of time created by the war is made explicit in Bowen's wartime story 'The Inherited Clock'. Clara, the heroine of the story, is the joint heir of her cousin Rosanna's fortune; she is also set to receive the special bequest of a 'skeleton clock', which has kept time unrelentingly for a hundred years. The story opens in the wartime present, when Clara hears from her aunt about the clock and realises that she has absolutely no recollection either of her alleged love for the clock or of the clock itself. It becomes clear that she has forgotten chunks of her own past; her aunt observes that 'I remember you before you remember yourself' (p. 624). On her next visit to her cousin, Clara makes a point of seeking out the clock and is terrified by its blatant portrayal of the anatomy of time. The clock is all the more unnerving because it demonstrates its invincibility by being 'none the worse' for the bomb that Rosanna informs her has recently come close to it (p. 628).

Rosanna dies soon after, leaving Clara in possession of a large fortune. But Clara is unable to enjoy her newfound wealth because the newly arrived clock, 'chopping off each second to fall and perish, recalled how many seconds had gone to make up her years, how many of these had been either null or bitter', making her anxious that the past can 'injure the future irreparably' (p. 631). Clara's sense of the tyranny of time, demonstrated by the clock, resonates with Henry Green's wartime recollection of the Oxford clocks in *Pack My Bag*. Here he finds that the Oxford bells tolling the hour are 'so overdone they soon lost their charm', adding to the recognition that 'every day one died a little' (pp. 129–30). Looking back on the bells in the context of the war, he finds that the 'bells chime the death of time which is always passing, but the sirens warn that they may be no more, that the watch may stop' (p. 134). War has made the clocks more pernicious, but also more vulnerable.

Fearing the clock, Clara telephones her married lover Henry, who is with his wife and carefully formal. His distance, as she tells him about the clock and the inheritance, makes her hysterical. Just as he is able to hang up, she screams out in fear: 'I can't bear this clock! I dread it; I can't stay with it in the room' (p. 632). Putting the phone down, she steps into the street for a walk in the blackout. Now the wartime lighting exacerbates the distortion of time imposed by the hundred-year-old clock. She walks 'at high speed into the solid darkness' and is 'surprised all over her body to feel no impact: she seemed to pass like a ghost through an endless wall' (p. 632). She is a ghost partly because of her relationship with time; she is unable to inhabit her own past. The blackout lighting effects are at their most extreme. Unlit by moon or stars, Clara can only 'spy with her torch', illuminating 'a post-box, a corner with no railing, the white plate of a street-name'.

Realising that she is lost, Clara asks the way and, 'for either a second or an eternity', forgets where she lives. Time seems to be suspended both because she has escaped the clock and because of the cinematic lighting, which renders the scene ghostly and the viewer absent. Clara returns home to find Paul, her rivalrous co-heir, who at last reveals the truth about the clock. As a child, he taunted her, forcing her to '[see] a minute' by putting her finger inside the clock (p. 639). The finger interfered with the clock's mechanism and, unbeknown to Rosanna, the clock stopped for half an hour, until a man came coincidentally to wind it. Learning to re-enter her own past, Clara starts to find the clock less demonic. Now that she knows it can be stopped, it becomes less threatening.

The pre-war stilling of the skeleton clock seems to prefigure the more general stilling of time by the war, warning, like Green's bells, that the watch may stop. In Clara's case, the disruption of recorded history provides a release from time. She is no longer aware of each second as an irrevocable step in the process of ageing. For Stella, the suspension of time is more unnerving, making her ghostly in the present. This is also true for both Spender and Sansom, who see the flash of the bombs as echoing the flash of the camera, trapping the moment in a suspended present, and endowing it with the ghostly quality that Kracauer attributed to the photograph.

Spender fears the photograph his 'skull might take' in 'Abyss' primarily because it can obliterate past and future. In that 'flashlit instant',

> the crumbling house would obliterate
> Every impression of my sunlit life
> With one impression of black final horror
> Covering me with irrecoverable doom.

The flash of the bombs, unlike the flash of history, does not enable the past to be redemptively present in the now. The impressions of his sunlit life are merely eliminated. Spender himself was keenly alive to the deathly power of photography. In Spender's then unpublished 1930s novel, *The Temple*, Joachim, a photography enthusiast, says that he likes photography because it 'fixes a time which rapidly recedes into the past'.[30] Echoing Kracauer, he observes that

> A photograph of you when you were a baby looks older than you will ever look, even at ninety. It is embalmed in the moment when the photographer took it. I like that. That is very FUNNY. Photography is comedy of life and death. Terrible comedy sometimes. Under the flesh the white skull of slaughtered soldiers.

In Spender's poem the bombs, like the photograph, will trap the scene in an eternal present that is itself immediately in the past, with the black horror remaining 'final' and 'irrecoverable'.

Similarly, in Sansom's 'The Wall', the moment of destruction occurs in 'a timeless second' before the wall falls down towards the fireman narrator, wreaking deathly destruction (p. 109). In this 'simple second', his brain takes in 'every detail of the scene'. 'New eyes' opening at the sides of his head he, like Spender, becomes a camera: 'from within, I photographed a hemispherical panorama'. The 'shutter' closes on his mind so that the 'picture appear[s] static to the limited surface senses', even through he knows on one level that the scene is moving:

> Even the speed of the shutter which closed the photograph on my mind was powerless to exclude this motion from a deeper consciousness. (p. 111)

As in *The Heat of the Day*, the stilled photogram testifies to the motion that precedes it. And, as in Spender's poem, the bombing at once evokes the photograph in its deathliness, and is more deadly because it is already visually photographic.

After mentally photographing the bombed scene around him, Spender goes out into the city night. Here he sees 'The dead of all time float on one calm tide'. He encounters the 'London prophets', saints of Covent Garden and Parliament Fields, who cry in 'Cockney fanatic voices' that 'In the midst of loif [*sic*] is death'. The poet realises that the 'walls of brick and flesh' are merely 'transitory dwellings of the spirit / Which flows into that flooding sky of death'. The bombs, through their destructive ease, have revealed houses and bodies alike to be transient, rendering the dead as tangible (or intangible) as the living. Spender's viewer, like Bowen's, becomes as absent and ghostly as the viewed scene. The bombs, unlike the photograph, make no distinction between observer and observed. 'Most of all', observes the narrator of *The Heat of the Day*,

> the dead, from mortuaries, from under cataracts of rubble, made their anonymous presence – not as today's dead but as yesterday's living – felt through London. (p. 91)

For the dead, this today is a 'tomorrow' they had expected – 'for death cannot be so sudden as all that'. 'Absent from the routine which had been life, they stamped upon their routine their absence.' They have an eerie presence, turning today into an impossible tomorrow. In this respect they are not unlike the figures in a film, who move in front of the audience, reminding us, by our presence, that they are absent – that we are experiencing their past as our present.

The amorphous interchange between the living and the dead is made explicit in Powell and Pressburger's *A Matter of Life and Death*. This 1946 film opens with Peter, an RAF pilot played by David Niven, saying his final words to a love-struck American radio operator, June (Kim Hunter). As Peter brings his burning plane down to his inevitable death, the two declare that they could have loved each other, and Peter promises to appear to June as a ghost after his death. In fact, their relationship is given a chance to begin in a more embodied vein. Peter awakens on the beach, apparently unharmed, and finds June. But the burgeoning wartime love affair is rudely interrupted by a visit from a heavenly messenger, a victim of the French Revolution who has been sent as a conductor from the 'other world'. It is the messenger who is responsible for Peter's unexpected survival; sent down to scoop him up to heaven, he missed him in the fog. The messenger comes from a realm in which there is space but no time, much like in the moment of bombing. As a result, he can talk to Peter for lengthy periods while all his earthly companions remain suspended mid-action, caught at the moment of leaping for a table-tennis ball or reaching for a cup.

Peter takes the unusual step of demanding a heavenly appeal. He insists that his earthly circumstances have changed solely as a result of heavenly error; June will now mourn his death as a lover. The film proceeds with Peter preparing for his trial in heaven at the same time as his earthly friends prepare him for urgent brain surgery to save him from his apparent hallucinations. The two worlds are initially kept totally separate; only Peter is able to migrate between the living and the dead. But by the time of the trial, the line between the two realms is increasingly blurred. Peter's doctor, Frank, dies in a road accident just before the now simultaneous earthly operation and heavenly trial, and is drafted in at the last minute as Peter's heavenly lawyer. Halfway through the trial, the jury decides that it needs to interview June herself, and the entire court descends the steps to earth. Here they enter the surgery in which Peter is being operated on, where June steps forward into the arms of the heavenly version of Peter. Together they convince the court that love must win the day and Peter is given a lengthy reprieve on earth.

The film is light-hearted throughout and never makes any serious attempt to assert the existence of the heaven that it frivolously depicts. Nonetheless, its huge appeal at the time was surely partly the result of its suggestion that the dead are not as far away (or as dead) as they may seem; that war, in making death increasingly common, had also brought the dead closer to the living. And the cinema is well equipped to illustrate this merging of heaven and earth. With special effects at their disposal, Powell and Pressburger were able to separate visually between black-and-white heaven and colourful earth ('one is starved for Technicolor up there', says the messenger) and then to fade between one and the other. Sent to gather evidence on earth, Peter's friend Bob Trubshawe comes down to earth in black-and-white and

6.4 *From heaven to earth*
Michael Powell and Emeric Pressburger, *A Matter of Life and Death* (1946)

then gradually emerges in colour (see Figure 6.4). As in *People on Sundays*, the frozen photograms enable the living to look more dead than the living. And, at its most basic level, the cinema is always able to resuscitate the dead. As *Colonel Blimp* had shown, the filmic dead are in fact no more absent (or no less present) than the filmic living.

Although both *Colonel Blimp* and *A Matter of Life and Death* are fairly conventional narrative films, they exhibit the awareness of the coexistence of past and present that Deleuze sees as characteristic of late twentieth-century avant-garde cinema. For Deleuze, cinematic flashback memories and dream landscapes foreground shards of time: moments that resist assimilation within a measurably, chronometric time. He sees avant-garde directors such as Alain Robbe-Grillet as taking these techniques further and accessing 'a simultaneity of a present of past, a present of present and a present of future'.[31]

Here Deleuze is influenced by Bergson's theories of temporality, or more precisely of time and memory. According to Bergson in *Matter and Memory* (1896), for memories to be formed, every actual moment must be doubled by a coexisting virtual past moment. The virtual past itself extends as a single domain from the present point in time into the vast reaches of the past. Normally, we do not perceive the coexistence of actual present and virtual past, but in experiences of déjà vu and automatism we receive faint intimations of time's double nature:

> There comes a moment when the recollection thus brought down is capable of blending so well with the present perception that we cannot say where perception ends or where memory begins.[32]

This is just the effect of these two wartime Powell and Pressburger films. When half the cast is living in a timeless other world, as in *A*

Matter of Life and Death, or dead characters are apt to be resuscitated in the present, as in *Colonel Blimp,* the past is apt to crash into and coexist with the present. And when we know that life in the present can be suspended at any moment and that the fates of the characters on earth are preordained in heaven (where a clerk cheerfully looks up June's subsequent date of death), the present takes on its own aura of already pastness, and the film actors seem more than usually absent.

The presence of ghosts in cinema was always apt to create this Deleuzian or Bergsonian effect, long before the development of the avant-garde tradition investigated by Deleuze. Balduin's mirror image in *The Student of Prague* is both his uncanny double and the ghost of his past. Unlike the evil mechanised double of Maria in *Metropolis,* who has no connection with the real woman, Balduin's image may be in thrall to an evil master, but also seems to spring authentically from Balduin's former life. Still clad in the costume of a homely student, the image insists on the continued presence of a more authentic past persona. Balduin, in choosing frivolous finery over the more whole-some ways of his student days, has exposed himself to being haunted by his own past.

It is not surprising that war writing should be populated by ghosts or that it should be so often explicitly or implicitly cinematic when depict-ing the incursion of these ghosts into the world they have recently and reluctantly left behind. Once the world is destroyed by 'Apocryphal fire', the imagist poet H. D. finds in her 1942 *Trilogy* that 'ruin opens / the tomb'; 'like a ghost, / we entered a house through a wall'.[33] After a raid in which the 'dark dove with the flickering tongue' passes over the horizon, T. S. Eliot meets a 'familiar compound ghost' amidst the ruins in 'Little Gidding'.[34] The ghost shares its 'intimate and unidentifiable' aspect with its setting, in which the prosaic 'dead leaves' and 'asphalt' are transformed by the bombing into a silent, uncertain landscape, 'Between three districts'. Where the ghosts in *The Heat of the Day* tend to be metaphorical, Bowen's wartime short stories bustle with more tangible ghosts. The ghosts, she announces in the preface to the stories, are 'the certainties'; 'hostile or not, they rally, they fill the vacuum for the uncertain "I"'.[35] A definite ghost, as she says, in 'Green Holly', and more questionable ghosts (for they may be subjective) in 'Pink May', 'The Cheery Soul' and 'The Demon Lover'. Ghosts drive off into the night, wander round houses and destroy marriages.

From the start of 'The Demon Lover', Mrs Drover is haunted by ghosts. Returning to her abandoned London house, she is eclipsed by the animated objects on her 'once familiar street' (p. 661). Absently present, she is watched by a cat but by 'no human eye' as she pushes her key into an 'unwilling lock'. Inside the house, she is greeted by the 'dead air' which comes 'to meet her' and, looking around, she is confronted by a 'bruise' in the wallpaper and by the 'claw-marks' of an absent piano. Into this haunted setting, where even the objects have left ghostly traces behind, comes a letter, mysteriously unstamped, which awaits her on the hall table. A former lover, abandoned in the previous war twenty-five years earlier, announces that he will be there to collect her at the ordained hour, later in the day.

Assailed by this ghost from her past, Kathleen Denver looks back on a previous wartime parting that was itself every bit as ghostly as the present scene. She pictures, as though in a cinematic flashback, 'the young girl talking to the soldier in the garden'; a soldier who for some reason is caught in a film so noirish that she 'had not ever completely seen his face' (p. 663). Like Stella, the youthful Kathleen is struck by the absence of her lover. It feels, 'from not seeing him at this intense moment, as though she had never seen him before'. As Stella pinches herself to reassure herself that she is alive in the present moment, Kathleen puts out a hand towards her lover, which he presses onto the buttons of his uniform. She is left with an indexical souvenir of his presence, carrying away the 'cut of the button on the palm of her hand'. Mourning his future absence as though it is already in the past, Kathleen longs to run inside and to tell her family he is gone:

> Being not kissed, being drawn away from and looked at intimidated Kathleen till she imagined spectral glitters in the place of his eyes.

She imagines him prematurely as a wartime ghost. Foolishly, she pledges to wait for him, even after his death, aware as she says it that 'she could not have plighted a more sinister troth' (p. 664).

Soon afterwards, the lover is reported dead and Kathleen herself becomes ghostly. Dislocated 'from everything', she fails to be present enough to attract men. She is grateful to be courted and married by William Drover. Now, threatened by the letter-writer, 'dead or living', she is struck by the 'hollowness' of her wartime London house. Remembering her lover, the twenty-five years 'dissolv[e] like smoke' and she feels for 'the weal left by the button on the palm of her hand' (p. 665). The weal turns out to be the only trace of the man whose face she has never been able to remember. His face is a 'white burning blank as where acid has dropped on a photograph'. Her memory of her lover is a ghostly photograph that itself records only his absence, framing his missing face. Terrified, Kathleen attempts to suspend the present: 'the thing was to get to the taxi before any clock struck what could be the hour.'

Watched in the 'intense' silence by the 'damaged stare' of the 'unoccupied houses opposite', she descends to the street, where she finds a taxi 'alertly waiting for her' (p. 666). But it is too late. The clock strikes seven and she is plummeted into a future in which the past is revived. The driver spins round and she faces him 'for an eternity eye for eye'. Time is suspended once more as she 'continue[s] to scream', and the demon lover makes off with her 'into the hinterland of deserted streets'. According to Rod Mengham, Bowen's story depicts the 'invasion of the self by a memory that cannot be brought into a manageable relation with the past'.[36] By breaking down temporal boundaries, the war has forced the two time-periods together, reviving Bergson's sheets of the past in the present. Bowen juxtaposes two wartime encounters, resurrecting a man rendered ghostly by one war as a literal ghost in the next.

Like *A Matter of Life and Death* and like Bowen's wartime fiction, Sansom's 'Fireman Flower' turns both the living and the dead into ghosts. Here Sansom explores the psychological ramifications of the ghostliness induced by the fires. From the start, the visual effects of the fire are associated not just with death but with the long-dead past. The objects photographically highlighted by the smoke seem to emerge out of a 'half-remembered episode from the dreamed past' (p. 133). As he becomes drunker on the fire, Flower sees faces smiling out of the fire glow, 'wholly sensual' (p. 143). He is then confronted by what appears to be 'another fireman flying towards him – a dark shape helmeted, with buttons aflash in the glow' (p. 146). Stopping 'dead' in front of the mirror, he realises that it is in fact 'the ghost of himself standing in the bare corridor'. It is 'the reflection of his past masqueraded as the darkling ghost of the future' (p. 146). Here Kracauer's photographic timeframe is reversed. Where Kracauer's young girl poses as a figure from the past but in fact reminds us of the future, Flower's reflection poses as his future but serves only to resuscitate his past.

Flower escapes into a wardrobe and, hacking his way through, emerges into a fantasy room where he is greeted rather prosaically by the ghost of an old friend. The friend takes it upon himself to point out the relics of Flower's past arrayed around the room (his father's bowl, his mother's sewing bag, his own French grammar) and then recounts the story of a shared picnic from long ago. Lulled into sleepiness, Flower wonders if the afternoon is lost, but finds that it is returning:

'The photograph was brilliantly clear, a bright circle of summer yellow framed by the grey mists of memory' (p. 149). Indeed, he finds that 'the past was more real than the present because the picture was clearly defined'. The photographic wartime present has evoked the clearer photographs of the past, making Flower himself ghostly in the present. For Flower, as for Mrs Drover, the cinematic wartime lighting effects give a visual reality to the likely imminence of death. Ghosts are the natural inhabitants both of wartime and of cinema; it was perhaps inevitable that they would take over in this most cinematic of wars.

Ghostly politics

Stephen Spender, Louis MacNeice, Graham Greene, Elizabeth Bowen
The second that the flash of the bombs becomes the flash of a camera, the experience is aestheticised. The bombing itself forms an abstract, cinematic spectacle. Recording the November 1943 bombing of Berlin, Hitler's architect, Albert Speer, observed:

> I had constantly to remind myself of the cruel reality in order not to be completely entranced by the scene: the illumination of the parachute flares, which the Berliners called 'Christmas trees,' followed by flashes of explosions which were caught by the clouds of smoke . . . no doubt about it, this apocalypse provided a magnificent spectacle.[37]

According to Virilio, Speer's is the only possible reaction. For Virilio, the entrancing spectacle is the purpose of war:

> War can never break free from the magical spectacle because its very purpose is to *produce* that spectacle: to fell the enemy is not so much to capture as to 'captivate' him, to instil the fear of death before he dies.[38]

Captivated and fearful, Spender ends by turning the raid into a decontextualised religious experience in 'Abyss', with the poet himself going forth as 'a prophet seeking tongues of flame'. Here Spender takes on the imagery of Eliot's 'Little Gidding', where the fire of the Blitz becomes the 'flame of incandescent terror'.[39] In his autobiography, Spender is explicit in seeing the raid described in 'Abyss' as exhilarating. This is the raid he welcomes as 'the end I seemed now to have been awaiting all my life', sensing that this 'tremendous' explosion could be 'powerful enough to destroy the whole of London'.[40]

Here Spender wills the raid into being, urging on the fire. MacNeice responds with similar frightened enthusiasm in an article on 'The

Morning after the Blitz', where he is 'half appalled and half enlivened by this fantasy of destruction'. Making it clear that 'people's deaths were another matter', he admits that the damage to the buildings is an enlivening 'spectacle, something on a scale which I had never come across'.[41] As he watches London blaze, there is a voice inside him which keeps saying,

> as I watched a building burning or demolished: 'Let her go up!' or 'Let her come down. Let them all go. Write them all off. Stone walls do not a city make. Tear all the blotted old pages out of the book; there are more books in the mind than ever have got upon paper.' (p. 118)

In his 1942 poem 'Brother Fire', MacNeice makes explicit his complicity with the fire. Here the destructive fire is figured as a 'brother', having his dog's day as he 'slavers' and crunches at the human rooftops.[42] The poet presents the fire as the 'enemy and image of ourselves'; a worthy nemesis whose thoughts Londoners echo, encouraging the conflagration with a cry of '"Destroy! Destroy!"'

This aestheticisation is ultimately the aestheticisation of politics described by Benjamin in the 'Work of Art' essay. Speer, Spender and MacNeice resemble the coerced viewer of the fascist spectacle who experiences his 'own destruction as an aesthetic pleasure of the first order'.[43] By welcoming their own destruction, they divorce themselves from the war as a political phenomenon. In the moment of aestheticisation, the personal experience is detached from the national. Recalling the raids in his autobiography, Spender states that 'we lived in a trance-like condition', witnessing events as 'in a dream'.[44] In this state, countries like France become 'mental concepts only'; he is unable to gain a clear sense of the political situation. Crucially, the enemy is forgotten. For both Spender and MacNeice, the raids seem to be a personal test, whose ground was prepared long before the war.

Spender later criticised the Bowen-like wartime stories of the German writer Wolfgang Borchert for exhibiting an entranced detachment. 'The war which he described', Spender wrote, 'is not the one for which German leaders bore, in the opinion of the rest of the world, a certain responsibility'.[45] Spender might be describing his own war writing here, or that of MacNeice or Sansom. According to Adam Piette, British Blitz literature tends to

> defuse the bombardment as Luftwaffe action. The bare fact of real German bombers dropping sticks of bombs on real Londoners is translated into solitary politics and aesthetics, as though the enemy did not exist. The

apocalypse falls from the empty sky into the waiting imagination, which claims it for its own.[46]

The detachment Piette described results partly from the aestheticised beauty of the Blitz and partly from the writers' sense of themselves as ghostly automata. If, as in *The Heat of the Day*, people are absent ghosts, they cannot be held responsible for their actions. The deathly ghostliness created by the cinematic lighting effects also turns people into mechanised automata.

In his account of the lighting effects of the Blitz, Sansom sees the cold moonlight as making everyone pale and ghostly:

> with the pale plaster crumbled out on the street, with the puppety figures of rescue workers in their flat bowlerish hats covered also with pale dust, with the dead and wounded collapsed and unmoving – there was some of the atmosphere of the doll-shop, the shop for making plaster figures or people of wax.[47]

Here the Blitz changes all Londoners into doll-like automata, like the dangling man in Green's 'A Rescue', who is still alive but takes on the appearance of a ghostly, projected 'rag doll made full size he was so limp'. It is only a small step to see the bombers themselves as lacking agency. Later, Spender would recall that all the bombers appeared as 'automata controlled by the mechanism of war', unequipped with 'wills of their own'.[48] This seems true in several films of the period. In Noël Coward's 1942 *In Which We Serve*, the bombs seem merely to drop from the sky and there is no visual reference to the enemy planes themselves. And the actuality of war followed the imaginative fantasies. Near the end of the war, the Nazis introduced pilot-less flying-bombs, which Sansom records were 'particularly disliked for their automatic nature, their unpleasant unreality'.[49] These mechanised toys of war are the dark successors to Benjamin's Parisian dolls or Vertov's animated cyclist. The planes continue inexorably, oblivious of their audience, resembling Bergman's description of the film itself as an 'infernal machine' that 'cannot pause' in Isherwood's *Prater Violet* (p. 33). Like the false Maria in *Metropolis*, the planes are set in motion with the single goal of wreaking havoc in the skies. And once you see the planes as mindless automata creating abstract visual spectacles, it becomes immaterial which side they are on. Indeed, it was difficult to tell them apart in the first place. The planes flew so high that people on the ground often had trouble working out if they were friends or foe. This is reflected in Harry Watt's 1941 RAF documentary *Target for Tonight*, where it is impossible to assign the flashes of attack and defence to the British or the Germans.[50]

Brecht warns against this viewpoint explicitly in his *War Primer*. In collage 25, Brecht introduces a Swedish photograph of the ruins of the 1940 bombing of Berlin, which depicts a veiled woman, bent over to stare at the rubble. 'Stop searching, woman,' the quatrain commands:

> you will never find them
> But woman, don't accept that Fate is to blame.
> Those murky forces, woman, that torment you
> Have each of them a face, address and name.[51]

Here Brecht directly challenges the attitude of people like Borchert or Spender, who divorce the destruction from politics, accepting the raids as an apocalyptic dream. He reminds the woman that the planes may seem like murky spectacles but are in fact driven by individual human beings, each with his own background and history.

But Brecht experienced the raids at a distance, reading the newspapers while exiled in Scandinavia and America. It seems that it was more difficult to retain a sense of the political situation while experiencing the bombing on the ground. And it was doubly difficult to avoid aestheticising a war that was cinematic not just in its effects but in its execution. The Second World War, even more than the Spanish Civil War, took place on film. It was increasingly hard to distinguish between cinema and actuality. The bombs fell into the waiting imagination partly because they had been imagined in literature and film before they had been invented. From H. G. Wells' *The Shape of Things to Come* (1933) to Frank McIlraith and Roy Connolly's *Invasion from the Air* (1934), interwar literature predicted the apocalyptic destruction that would be realised in the bombing war. In 1936 *Things to Come*, Alexander Korda's film version of Wells' novel, gave a spectacular visual reality to the predicted air war.[52]

During the conflict itself, both sides used cinema to advance the war and to imagine its end. Hitler in particular devoted large tranches of his dwindling resources to the hyperreal depiction of the war. Between 1942 and 1943, when the military successes of the Nazis were becoming rather scarce, he proposed providing the German public with flashbacks to earlier victories and ordered the director Veit Harlan to go to Norway to re-enact the fighting between the British and the Germans that took place at the beginning of the war.[53] The spectacle was to include a mixture of direct re-enactment and filmic exaggeration, with General Dietl asked to play his own role in capturing and occupying Narvik. At a point in the war when all resources were severely strained, Hitler promised Harlan several warships and 100 aircraft, which would parachute in thousands of men. The British, learning about the plan, decided to save Hitler the expense of casting the enemy. They announced over the radio that they would be happy to provide some especially bloody scenes for the cameras, in the hope of overturning the original German victory. At the last minute, the plan was aborted following protests from German soldiers. According to Harlan, 'to die for the fatherland struck them as more logical than to die for the cinema!'[54]

Hitler himself carried on with his plans to win the war in the hyper-real if not in reality. In October 1943, the Germans began filming a re-enactment of the medieval battle of Kolberg.[55] Just when the army was retreating on almost all fronts, Hitler issued a military order demanding that it should be placed at the disposal of the filmmakers, who were provided with 6,000 horses and 2,000 men. This time the film was finished but, by the time it was ready to screen, the cinemas of Germany had been reduced to rubble.

The Allies, although less willing to invest in fantasy than Hitler, also made the most of cinema's potential as a war weapon. The success of cinema as a form of morale-boosting propaganda in wartime Britain is well known.[56] What is less documented, and stranger, is cinema's role as a tool in the theatre of war itself. Virilio describes how Whitehall, learning that German intelligence was filming the UK, decided to take part in constructing the film.[57] Enemy cameras were offered a series of visual illusions, with Shepperton film studio producing fake armoured vehicles and landing ships. Like Hitler, the Allied leaders joined in the subterfuge. Montgomery and Eisenhower visited spurious docks and building sites and a Churchill look-alike was sent on various bogus plane trips. Through cinematic illusion, the enemy is first captivated and then captured.

The political implications of the cinematic, aestheticised aspect of the war are taken to their furthest extreme in Graham Greene's 1943 *The Ministry of Fear* and Bowen's *The Heat of the Day*. Both novels expose the arbitrary nature of international politics in a war that is fought by automata in the sky and by ghosts on the ground, a war in which there is little difference between the living and the dead, and there may well be little difference between actuality and illusion. In *The Ministry of Fear*, Greene creates a comically complicated thriller plot, involving a fortune-teller, a cake, a séance and a tailor, in order to parody the genre. He uses the ridiculousness of the detective story to highlight the ridiculousness of war itself. Halfway through the novel, the hero, Arthur Rowe, loses his memory and gains a defamiliarised perspective on the world. He realises that

> Jones and the cake, the sick bay, poor Stone . . . all this talk of a man called Hitler . . . your files of wretched faces, the cruelty and meaninglessness . . . It's as if one had been sent on a journey with the wrong map. [58]

In the context of large-scale cruelty and meanness, it is pointless to try to condemn one side more than the other, or to hunt down murderers when the murders themselves take place 'in the middle of a daily massacre' (p. 70).

Arthur himself understands and fits into wartime London partly because he was existing as a ghost among ghosts before the war. Several years earlier, he killed his wife in an ambiguous mercy killing for which he has been acquitted but condemned to constant self-reproach by his Catholic conscience. Like Candy in *Colonel Blimp*, Arthur is haunted by the ghost of his wife, waiting at street corners 'because of a small resemblance, just as though the woman he loved was only lost and might be discovered any day in a crowd' (p. 42). He therefore finds comfort in the ghostliness of wartime London. In this 'strange torn landscape' he can become 'part of this destruction as he was no longer part of the past', moving 'like a bit of stone among the other stones' (p. 40).

Because he accepts the ghostliness of the war, Arthur can also accept it as a personal rather than a national phenomenon. In the end, Arthur and his lover, the double (or triple) Austrian agent-*cum*-refugee Anna Hilfe, end by buying happiness at the price of truth or national loyalty. This is a novel that condemns all idealism, with its easy sacrifice of the lives of individuals, coming down on the side of the specific. 'I don't give a damn about England', Anna tells Arthur, in a statement neither supported nor condemned by the narrative voice. 'I want you to be happy' (p. 201). Ultimately, Arthur is ambivalent about his sacrifice. In the final sentence of the book, he finds that 'after all one could exaggerate the value of happiness' (p. 221). But he never engages sufficiently with the political events around him to think in national rather than personal terms.

Arthur's ghostlike, nervy detachment is very different from the cool confidence of Stephen, the protagonist of Fritz Lang's 1944 film of Greene's novel. Indeed, the ambivalence of Greene's novel as a whole is highlighted by a comparison with the film which, as befits a war picture made by a German exile, draws the line between right and wrong more clearly. Stephen is the worthy hero of a *noir* thriller, energetically whipping out his gun at every turn. The set makes full use of the ghostliness of the blackout, using it to enhance the usual chiaroscuro of *film noir*, but the characters are no longer ghostly. Stephen is unequivocally innocent of his wife's murder, and is only briefly haunted by her when a medium takes on her persona at a séance. In Greene's novel, Arthur kills his wife because he himself is unable to bear the pain of her illness, and he does it in secret, leaving her to die alone. In the film she begs him to kill her, and he holds her hand as she dies. The film presents murder as straightforwardly punishable, even in wartime, using the war as a dramatic background for a fairly conventional thriller. The scriptwriter Seton Miller simplified the plot, removing its parodic element. Even the cake, shining white against the darkness of the blackout, is convincing as one of Stern's 'accursed objects' (see Figure 6.5). Where in the book its attempted theft takes place in the humorously mundane setting of Arthur's shabby lodgings,

6.5 *The cake*
Fritz Lang, *The Ministry of Fear* (1944)

in the film the scene is transposed to a moving train. Here, amidst the crashing of the bombs on a stormy night, a filmic hand creeps monstrously across the screen to purloin the glistening cake. The film endows Stephen with a political responsibility that Arthur lacks in the novel. In his ghostly detachment, Arthur abstains from politics. Although he continues to believe in justice, he urges on the destruction of a world that seems to become with each day of bombing more like his own annihilating vision.

In her novel published four years after the end of the war, Bowen goes further than Greene in permitting Robert to pursue the logical consequences of this kind of ghostly, detached vision of the world. Where Greene makes his spies villains, Bowen allows Robert to remain the hero of *The Heat of the Day*, even though he has committed to a worldview so annihilating that he goes over to the Nazis. Critics then and now have found that the revelation of Robert's defection to fascism stretches the bounds of credibility, making Bowen herself either a flawed novelist or a fascist sympathiser. The critics who see Bowen as flawed wonder why she didn't make Robert a Communist sympathiser instead. It would be more palatable and leave fewer unexplained gaps.[59] Alan Sinfield has taken the opposite approach and suggested that Bowen wholeheartedly endorsed Robert's decision. In his view, Bowen, like Robert, was troubled by the increasing power of the masses and the tendency for democracy to cater for the lowest common denominator.[60] For Sinfield, *The Heat of the Day* is better read as a postwar than a wartime novel; it was published in a period when the upper-middle classes had come to doubt the benefits of a fully democratic welfare state.

I think that both readings take us too far from the texture of the novel, or rather from its strange, photographic surfaces. Robert's decision makes sense only if we read it in the context of a cinematic, ghostly, aestheticised and hyperreal war. If we see the whole novel as operating in a death-driven, eerily deanimated world, the political itself is undermined by a history that operates as memory. Amy Bell has suggested that the hallucinogenic wartime fear provided a '"counternarrative" to the positive and patriotic images of the People's War', producing a portrait of 'a darker and more sinister London'.[61] The same seems to be true of the war's photographic ghostliness. In committing himself to the fascists, Robert is behaving logically in a world he experiences as a living death, in which he, like Arthur, is a ghost surrounded by ghosts.

The scene in Robert's family home is crucial for understanding his decision, but not just, as Sinfield suggests, because we see his horror of the mediocrity of the lower-middle classes. Even more important is Robert's reaction to the photographs in his bedroom; his sense that 'each time I come back again . . . I'm hit in the face by the feeling that I don't exist – that I not only am not but never have been'. He seems to be rebelling against this as much as anything else; this feeling that, like Clara in 'The Inherited Clock' or Arthur in *The Ministry of Fear*, he has moved as a ghost through his own life, failing to inhabit his past. Wartime has made this stronger, so that he has become an absent onlooker of his own life, always in danger of being already dead, like the moments in the photographs. And as far as he is concerned, he lives in a world of ghosts. 'What country', he asks Stella, 'have you and I outside this room? Exhausted shadows, dragging themselves out to fight' (p. 267). Robert, like Anna Hilfe, refuses to believe in countries.

Where Arthur accepts his role as a ghost, Robert attempts to rebel against the photographic ghostliness of his life. In this respect, his decision to go over to the other side can be seen as a Brechtian attempt to reverse the aestheticisation of politics. Like Brecht, he insists that you should fight fate rather than accept it. But ultimately, Robert is powerless against the cinematic ghostliness of wartime London. It is as a ghost that Robert makes his decision to sympathise with the Nazis, who are never actually named as such. They seem to exist in his mind merely as just the vague, almost supernatural other that Brecht tried to endow with specificity. Stella herself comments on the shadowiness of his explanation:

> You know, Robert, for anybody *doing* anything so definite, you talk vaguely. Wildness and images . . . to me it's as though there still were something you'd never formulated. (p. 282)

Robert has crossed to the other side in an attempt to overcome his ghostliness, to hit the currents of his world full-on. But in fact he is never more ghostly than at the end of the novel. He disappears onto the roof and, as far as Stella is concerned, never materialises again. He slips, as Harrison will slip, into immateriality. In Britain, Benjamin's sense of fascism as aestheticising politics and leading to war seems to have been reversed. War has aestheticised politics and numbed the Left through its cinematic beauty. It has turned its victims into ghostly echoes of themselves, moving as automata through the blitzed cities. In *The Heat of the Day*, Bowen suggests that there is no way to escape this condition.

Wartime witnessing

William Sansom, Henry Green

The ghostly spectators of the London bombing were far removed from Benjamin's or Grierson's embodied cinematic viewers. Just when life became most cinematic, the cinematic mode of writing became redundant. Second World War writing makes little use of the cinematic techniques developed by the 1930s documentarists. The spectatorship induced by the Blitz was a markedly disembodied, often passive experience. As a result, the war magnified the apolitical tendencies inherent in 1930s camera consciousness. To view the world cinematically was no longer to attempt objective reportage or even documentary witnessing. It is difficult to witness when the spectacle before you might prove to be an illusion, when, as in Green's *Caught* or Sansom's 'Fireman Flower', the dancing colours of the fire may turn out to be dangerously seductive, hypnotising even the fireman into complicity with the fire he is meant to be fighting.

Sansom makes explicit the problematic aspect of wartime witnessing in 'The Witnesses', a story told by a ghostly crew of observers. In self-consciously ascribing the narrative voice to a plural, chorus-like witness, Sansom undermines the concept of witnessing. The chorus draws attention to the specific fallibility of visual observation in wartime conditions:

> We, the witnesses, were of course present throughout the episode, although it would be difficult ever to determined whether what we saw was the final truth or indeed if we viewed the matter in its right perspective at all, for at the time there was a great deal of smoke blurring the air. (p. 81)

Objectivity proves impossible; the witnesses see a fireman floating 'in mid-mist' but are aware that he is actually sitting astride a broken wall (p. 82). Photographic vision is shown to be rendered inaccurate by the cinematic effects of the bombing.

The witnesses venture into more subjective territory when they invent a feud between the pump operator and the fireman as a prelude to the fireman throwing himself away from the wall. This moment, the climax of the story, takes place in the 'malicious instant of blinding light' in which 'everything flash[es] into being . . . like objects switched suddenly onto a screen' (p. 85). In the witnesses' account, the fireman's gesture follows a sinister smile from the pump operator, who then sets about attempting to murder the fireman by increasing the pressure of his pump. But the narrative voice makes clear that this is mere speculation: 'We never saw the pump operator's hand move the throttle' (p. 86). The story ends with the suggestion that both the firemen and the witnesses have been deluded by the visual:

> A moment's fear transformed into a smile of hatred by the fireman's brain, the unreliable agent that informed us, the witnesses, his eyes. (p. 86)

The fireman's own eyes here are described as unreliable. But the ambiguous syntax also enables Sansom to suggest the unreliability of the witnesses themselves who have acted as his eyes, reflecting him back to himself. They, like him, have been blinded by the light, seduced by the 'brilliant red glare' of the fire (p. 85).

In *Caught*, Green tests both the cinematic and the literary as modes of witnessing the wartime fires. He had found in *Pack My Bag* that film was the medium best suited to capturing the real. Trying to remember his childhood, he stated that the impressions stored in his memory were 'inaccurate and so can no longer be called a movie, or a set of stills', seeing film as the art form that best corresponds with present experience (p. 3). In the final section of *Caught*, Richard returns home shell-shocked after being knocked out by a bomb and attempts to describe his experiences in the fire to his sister-in-law, Dy. He complains that 'one's imagination is so literary', when in fact 'what will go on up there to-night in London, every night, is more like a film, or that's what it seems like at the time' (p. 175). It is only later that it becomes unreal, 'as you begin building again to describe to yourself some experience you've had'. In a novel visually dependent on the techniques of cinema, Green seems to encourage us to question the reality of the scenes we have read. Are they more real for being more filmic, or are they filtered through the unreal web of literary language?

Richard goes on to say that half the time he was in the fire he was so tired he was 'in a fog' (p. 176). He seems to re-enter that fog now, confusing the living and the dead as he addresses Dy as though she were his ex-wife, her dead sister. From this point, his recollections take the form of two separate voices, one that speaks out loud to Dy and a mental one that is inserted into the narrative in parenthesis, correcting the inaccuracies of his spoken memories. The spoken voice over-generalises: 'it was fantastic, the whole of the left side of London seemed to be alight.' The mental voice corrects: '(It had not been like that at all. As they went . . . the sky in that quarter . . . was flooded in a second sunset, orange and rose, turning the pavements pink . . .)' (p. 177). This second voice at first limits itself to describing the colours in a filmic chiaroscuro, but quickly becomes as literary as the spoken voice, if not more so. Mentally, Richard tries to recapture the lighting effect that 'stretched with the spread of a fan up the vertical sky' under which two men and a girl resemble 'grey cartridge paper'. The conflagration of the fire is a 'pandemonium of flame' which,

> a roaring red gold, pulsed rose at the outside edge, the perimeters round which the heavens, set with stars before fading into utter blackness, were for a space a trembling green. (p. 178)

The lighting effects here are cinematic, but the narrative that describes them is decidedly literary. The simile of the cartridge paper and the 'roaring' and 'trembling' of the colours show Richard reworking the scene at the same time as he attempts to remember it visually.

Dy is bored by this point, so Richard attempts to make the story more interesting with self-consciously literary language, describing their taxi as looking 'like a pink beetle drawing a pepper corn' (p. 180). She finds this 'vivid' and gives him her attention, suggesting that 'the real thing is the picture you carry in your eye afterwards, surely? It can't be what you can't remember' (p. 181). Richard is reluctant to accept this because it suggests too easy a submission to the limits of the imagination, which refuses to be easily pictured. The 'point about a blitz', he informs her, is that 'there's always something you can't describe'. The memory, he suggests, vanishes because it evades description even as it happens. The parenthetic voice then becomes more and more intensely colourful, seeming to move beyond Richard's thoughts into a more authorial literary realm:

> (It had not been like that at all. What he had seen was a broken, torn-up dark mosaic aglow with rose where square after square of timber had been burned down to embers, while beyond the distant yellow flames toyed joy-fully with the next black stalks which softly merged into the pink of that night.) (p. 181)

This is still a colourful version of the chiaroscuro we find in Jennings' film, but it goes beyond the filmic in its interjection of the imagination. Mengham writes:

> The prismatic style exceeds the range of 'literary' description by the sheer exorbitance of its effects, disconcerting the ambition of clear reportage.

Its intensity is girded in with brackets, which aggravate the discordancy between two competing idioms.[62]

Mengham suggests that Green sets up a dichotomy between literary description and filmic reportage and deconstructs it in a process of derationalising 'historicisation' that disperses 'the fog of "wishful thinking"'. I think that Green deconstructs not only the literary and the filmic, but the cinematic text itself. He continues the process he had begun in *Living* by suggesting that the mind, even in mid-experience, combines visual observation with imaginative transformation that is neither filmic nor literary.

Like Upward's experiments in consciousness in *Journey to the Border*, the lighting effects of wartime London seem to test the limits of possible modes of perception. The unreal, ghostly quality of both the firelight and the darkened streets makes photographic witnessing impossible at the same time as it induces a mode of cinematic vision that seems to place the observers outside time and therefore outside history. For Upward, this kind of detached camera consciousness is false; the socialist must fight against aestheticisation and open his eyes to the realities of his time. In the Blitz, Upward's awakening seems to be impossible. The long-expected bombs have accelerated the flight into the hyperreal. The flash of the bombs proves stronger than the flash of history. The air raids bring the apocalypse that writers like Spender and MacNeice have been awaiting and create the ghostly, mediated world of Bowen's and Sansom's wartime fiction. The Blitz literature was necessarily cinematic because the bombing, like the film and the photograph, thrust its victims into the deathly tense of the has-been-there. But literature could exceed the capability of film in capturing the cinematic strangeness of the war. It could be more eerie in its ghostliness, more prismatic in its lighting effects, and could do more to blur the boundaries between observer and observed, living and dead.

Afterword

Victory Bonfire

On 7 May 1945, London was again in flames. William Sansom watched apprehensively as the citizens celebrated 'joy, the fireworks of victory, the bonfires and songs of deliverance'.[1] Those Londoners who had urged on the Nazi fires in their destruction could now legitimately kindle their own victory bonfires. As in the days of the Blitz, the small fires spread, until each 'cast its coppery glow on the house-rows, on glassy windows and the black blind spaces where windows once had been' (p. 201). Higher up, the sky blazed with fireworks – a curious luxury for a nation that had cowered from the explosions of the bombs and the rattle of the guns. And of course, as the fire reignited memories of wartime conflagration, it also awakened the ghosts of the dead. 'The ghosts of wardens and fire-guards and firemen were felt scurrying again down in the redness.'

These fires were built on the wreckage of other fires, not just in Britain but throughout Europe. The British had valiantly survived the air war. But the German ruins would be harder to rebuild, their dead too many to commemorate. And as well as the ashes in Dresden or Hamburg, there were the even less thinkable vestiges of the bodies systematically burned in the Nazi gas ovens. Ruth Pitter weaves together the fires of a European war and an English peace in her poem 'Victory Bonfire', which describes a VJ day bonfire burning in 'a sweet September twilight'.[2] Here, in the middle of a village bonfire, the locals plant an image of Hitler himself, 'forlornly leering'. The scene is idyllic – children pile themselves 'lovingly on each other' and wisps of smoke rise at the four corners of the pile. Then 'she's away'. In 'a matter of seconds' there are 'Sheets of orange flame' and then, in a few 'hypnotised minutes',

> Vast caverns of embers, volcanoes gushing and blushing,
> Whitening wafts on cliffs and valleys of hell,

Quivering cardinal-coloured glens and highlands,
Great masses panting, pulsating, lunglike and scarlet,
Fireballs, globes of pure incandescence
Soaring up like balloons, formal and dreadful,
Threatening the very heavens.

The English countryside is transformed by the flames into hell; the fire is 'lunglike' in its scarlet redness. Through their very formality – their aestheticised, incandescent beauty – the fireballs threaten the heavens. In what Adam Piette has described as 'a parody of the Blitz-inspired apocalyptic writing', Pitter insists that fire cannot be an abstract spectacle.[3] There are bodies at stake, and the moon, climbing, is 'Hitler's ghost'. The villagers have unleashed the evil of the war into their cliffs and valleys.

Stoking up their fires in May and September 1945, the British had clearly come to appreciate the value of cinematic spectacle. But British writers had learned their lesson from the wartime cinematic hyperreal. Cinema, which had promised a means of literary political engagement, had always threatened merely to induce passivity. Now, the writers who had so violently committed themselves both to left-wing politics and to cinema tended to withdraw from both. The literary tradition of self-consciously cinematic, politically engaged literature that began in the early 1930s and flourished at the end of the decade was brought to an abrupt halt by the end of the war. In the early postwar period, the literary climate in Britain was divided between the hedonist nostalgia of Nancy Mitford or Evelyn Waugh and the gloomy portrayal of a broken world of Green's *Back* (1948) or Greene's *The End of the Affair* (1951). Writers such as Sommerfield, Greenwood or Allen never again regained the popularity they had enjoyed in the 1930s, and left-wing tendencies were no longer prerequisites for acceptance in the literary world.

The postwar novel was written in an age of austerity described by Arthur Marwick as 'rock-hard and grey'.[4] Soon after the end of the war, it became apparent that the standard of living in Britain would not quickly improve. Rationing continued into the 1950s; between 1946 and 1948 even bread was rationed. This was an age in which upper-class writers were beginning to see the effects of the revolution they had so fervently desired. In a late stage of the war, a Conservative minister, R. A. Butler, shaped a new Education Act, making secondary education available for all; with the election of a Labour government in July 1945, the essential tenets of a Welfare State were put in place. 1946 saw the foundation of a National Health Service and a Social Security system, and the government quickly nationalised coal and electricity. While there was a broad consensus throughout Britain that these changes were necessary, the upper classes began to fear the demise of the world they had grown up in. Andrzej Gąsiorek writes that the 'move towards a democratisation of society' provoked 'fears of massification among what was a predominantly conservative intelligentsia'.[5] Waugh compared the period of the first Labour government to enemy occupation, while the upper-class politician and writer Harold Nicolson complained that the destruction of class would lead to the destruction of 'learning, scholarship, intelligence and the humanities', and predicted that 'we shall have to walk and live a Woolworth life hereafter'.[6] Where for Jennings and Orwell Woolworths had been a symbol of the wonderfully 'unculturised' British everyday, it now became a symbol of the mass mediocrity being foisted on the upper classes.

Fear of the new world was not limited to bastions of the old school, right-wing establishment. In 1950, Bowen assessed the new mood of nostalgia in contemporary literature and found that the natural human longing for the past was 'aggravated to malady-point' by the uneasiness of the postwar climate. She was particularly disturbed by the 'soaring blocks of flats' and 'mushroom housing estates', which dismayed 'creatures of feeling' and left no place for 'fancy to dwell'.[7] Green found his already unsteady socialist convictions challenged by the high levels of taxation. His biographer writes that 'what rankled particularly' was that 'tax was depriving him of a good part of his income' just when his business was booming.[8] I quoted his dismissive 1975 'Damn all politicians' in the Introduction. Even in the 1952 interview with Nigel Dennis where he championed the proletariat as the true intelligentsia, he stated that he always remembered his business interests and voted Conservative.[9]

At the same time as the upper classes remembered their own interests, support for Communism in Britain died a natural death with the increasing vilification of the Soviet Union. In 1945 Orwell popularised the term 'Cold War' to describe relations between the superpowers, and in 1946 Churchill announced that an 'Iron Curtain' had 'descended across the Continent'.[10] In this climate, Orwell in particular became rabidly anti-Communist, disillusioned in part by his experiences in Spain. In 1949 he aided his friend Celia Kirwan, then working for the Information Research Department, by producing a list denouncing 125 writers and artists he considered dangerously pro-Communist, including many former friends.

Five years earlier, two stalwarts of the left-wing establishment in Britain, Auden and Isherwood, had abandoned not only their support for socialism but their political commitment itself. At the end of *Christopher and His Kind*, Isherwood records a conversation on a boat bound for America in which Christopher 'heard himself say', 'You know, it just doesn't mean anything to me any more – the Popular Front, the party line, the anti-fascist struggle. I simply cannot swallow another mouthful', and Wystan answered, 'Neither can I.'[11] Peter Parker has pointed out the disingenuousness of Isherwood's report, as he follows the statement with 'those were not our words'.[12] Nonetheless, the spirit of the decision the two writers made on the boat remains clear. Once in America, both men abandoned politics, channelling their idealism into new sexual relationships and religious devotion, Isherwood turning to Vedanta and Auden to Christianity. Auden later dismissed his socialism of the 1930s, stating that there was 'a larger element of old-fashioned social climbing than we care to admit'. He claimed to have listened to 'the voice of the Tempter' who insisted that 'unless you take part in the class struggle, you cannot become a major writer'.[13]

For Isherwood, Auden, Orwell, Green and Bowen, the postwar world ushered in a new political climate in which political commitment was no longer simple and not necessarily even desirable. In this context, cinematic technique, which had been tested and naturalised by the fires of the Blitz, also became less urgent. The literary establishment came to share Auden's view that he was not a camera and that it is rude to take close-ups. It is significant that Green's 1950 statement about the legacy of the cinema for the novel refers to cinema in its broadest sense. He does not mention the montage that pervades his early forays into cinematic writing, stating only that the cinema has 'taught the modern novelist to split his text up into small scenes'.[14] Conversely, Walter Allen's statement about the '"montage" novel' is firmly embedded in the past. The self-conscious cinematic technique he describes is a mode of writing he 'used to do', and not a mode that has become character-istic of the modern novel.[15] By the end of the war, cinematic technique had become endemic in the novel but was rarely used overtly with a political purpose. In *Back* (1946), Green abandoned the cross-class montage he had used in his work over the previous fifteen years, and wrote a more austere and simple tale of one man's quest for personal postwar reconstruction.

The postwar world was, as Woolf had predicted, a world with fewer towers, if not with fewer classes. The literary intelligentsia politely welcomed but rarely championed the conservative version of welfare capitalism that emerged. The quest to expose social inequality through cross-class montage and documentary accuracy ended as abruptly as it had begun. Nonetheless, the sudden ending of a movement does not make it any less significant. The fact that Raymond Williams could still ask in 1985 for films that continued the work of the 1930s in portraying 'the lives of the great majority of people' who 'have been and still are almost wholly disregarded by most arts', is testament to the movement's power, if only as an historical memory.[16]

We need not, with Auden, dismiss the 1930s as a decade of inverse social climbing and false temptation. We need not, with Sontag, separate ourselves from that moral universe so unlike our own. Where, in the 1920s, Russian and German cinema ushered in new possibilities of innovative socialist art, in the 1930s, the literary tradition examined here realised those possibilities in a wealth of politically engaged, cinematic texts. In 1908, Leo Tolstoy allegedly predicted that a revolution in the life of writers would be wrought by the 'little clicking contraption' that was the cinema.[17] This revolution took place in Britain in the years between 1930 and 1945, uniting writers across the classes in framing a new kind of literature. Broadly, and briefly, the creation of this tradition enabled the 1930s to contain a moment of hope. In an era defined by both the disappointments of the postwar and the anxiety of the pre-war, socialism and cinema came together in offering the possibility of change.

It was a tradition that deconstructed itself even as it began. In the early years of the politically engaged, cinematic text, Green was rendering the cinematic as tactile and olfactory as it was visual and showcasing the literariness of his novels. From the start, the danger of passivity was inherent in the cinematic vision. Isherwood's bruised camera eye could only reel from the events he described; writers in the Spanish Civil War found themselves caught in a world where the cinema seemed to precede actuality. The Second World War cast doubt on the cinema-driven Benjaminian politicisation of aesthetics, which many British writers had embraced in the 1930s. It now seemed that the cinematic spectacle of the Blitz completed the aestheticisation of politics begun by the fascists. The flash of history was superseded by the flash of the bombs. Surveying a London distorted by smoke, Green found it hard to believe as confidently in vision as he had in the 1930s. The camera-eye witness had been left helpless by war; the cinematic was now as shadowy and ghostly a realm as the bombed streets of London. Ultimately, the cinematic text, like Pitter's victory bonfire, consumed itself, leaving only 'blushing and whitening embers', 'fading and falling'.

Endnotes

Introduction

1. In his 1926 essay on the 'Cult of Distraction', the German cultural critic Siegfried Kracauer branded the large picture houses in Berlin 'palaces of distraction', but suggested that viewing in a state of distraction need not be a passive, reactionary process. Instead, the picture houses should 'aim radically toward a kind of distraction that exposes disintegration instead of masking it'. Like his colleague Walter Benjamin, Kracauer saw cinema's mass appeal as a potential source of radicalism. In his 1936 'The Work of Art in the Age of Mechanical Reproduction', Benjamin contrasted the concentrating man, who was 'absorbed' *by* a work of art, with the 'distracted mass', who themselves absorb the work of art. He found that 'reception in a state of distraction, which is increasingly noticeable in all fields of art . . . finds in the film its true means of exercise. The film with its shock effect meets this mode of reception halfway'. Siegfried Kracauer, 'Cult of Distraction: On Berlin's Picture Palaces', 1926, in *The Mass Ornament, Weimar Essays,* edited and transl. Thomas Y. Levin (Cambridge, MA: Harvard University Press, 1995), pp. 323, 328. Walter Benjamin, 'The Work of Art in the Age of Mechanical Reproduction', 1936, in *Illuminations, Essays and Reflections,* edited with an introduction by Hannah Arendt, transl. Harry Zohn (New York: Schoken Books, 1968), pp. 239–40.
2. Walter Allen, letter to Andy Croft, 1982, quoted in Andy Croft, *Red Letter Days, British Fiction in the Thirties* (London: Lawrence & Wishart, 1990), p. 256.
3. Virginia Woolf, 'The Leaning Tower', 1940, in *A Woman's Essays,* ed. with an introduction by Rachel Bowlby (Harmondsworth: Penguin Books, 1992), pp. 164, 169.
4. Woolf, 'The Leaning Tower', pp. 172, 171.
5. Woolf, 'The Leaning Tower', p. 175.
6. Eric Hobsbawm, *Age of Extremes, The Short Twentieth Century 1914–1991* (London: Michael Joseph, 1994), p. 144.

7. George Orwell, 'Inside the Whale', 1940, in Sonia Orwell and Ian Angus (eds.), *The Collected Essays, Journalism and Letters of George Orwell* (Harmondsworth: Penguin Books, 1970), vol. 1, p. 563. All subsequent references to this collection will appear as *CEJL*.

8. Stephen Spender, *World Within World*, introduction by John Bayley (New York: The Modern Library, 2001), pp. 375–6. Subsequent references are incorporated in the text.

9. Michael Roberts, 'Poetry and Propaganda', *London Mercury*, vol. 31, January 1935, p. 231; quoted in Samuel Hynes, *The Auden Generation* (London: Faber and Faber, 1976), p. 171.

10. Stephen Jones, *Workers at Play, A Social and Economic History of Leisure 1918–1939* (London: Routledge & Kegan Paul, 1986), p. 37.

11. 1936 postscript in C. Day Lewis, *A Hope for Poetry* (Oxford: Basil Blackwell, 1936), p. 98. Day Lewis admits here that poetry can probably 'never be popular again to the degree that the cinema is popular at the moment'.

12. Alexander Korda, 'British Films: Today and Tomorrow', in Charles Davy (ed.), *Footnotes to the Film* (London: Lovat Dickson, 1937), pp. 162–3.

13. Benjamin, 'The Work of Art', p. 231. Similarly, H. D. praised film in *Close Up* as 'a universal art open alike to the pleb and the initiate' (H. D., 'Conrad Veidt, The Student of Prague', *Close Up*, vol. 1(3), September 1927, p. 4).

14. W. H. Auden, letter to Erika Mann Auden, in W. H. Auden and Louis MacNeice, *Letters from Iceland* (London: Faber and Faber, 1937), p. 137.

15. John Grierson, 'Flaherty', 1931, in Forsyth Hardy (ed.), *Grierson on Documentary* (London: Faber and Faber, 1966), p. 140.

16. Storm Jameson, 'Documents', *Fact*, vol. 4, July 1937, p. 15. Subsequent references are incorporated in the text.

17. Valentine Cunningham, *British Writers of the Thirties* (Oxford: Oxford University Press, 1988), p. 334.

18. For the appearance of montage in little magazines of the period, see Michael North, *Camera Works: Photography and the Twentieth-century Word* (Oxford: Oxford University Press, 2005), chapter 2. The September 1928 issue of the avant-garde film journal *Close Up* was dedicated to Russian cinema. The editor, Kenneth MacPherson, announced in his editorial that Russian films were on a 'level of intellect, spiritual value and truth which has never been approached in any medium'. See Kenneth Macpherson, 'As Is', *Close Up*, vol. 3(3), 1928, p. 8.

19. For a fuller discussion of censorship see pp. 18, 85.

20. Dziga Vertov, 'The Council of Three', 1923, in Annette Michelson (ed.), *Kino-Eye, The Writings of Dziga Vertov*, transl. Kevin O'Brien (London: Pluto Press, 1984), p. 17. Of course, speed was appropriated by the Right as much as by the Left, if not more so, and the Left remained ambivalent about the desirability of the increased speeds. Benjamin explicitly

connected the shocks of the modern metropolis with Marx's comments about the new speeds of machine production, though Benjamin was more enthusiastic about speed in cinema. See Walter Benjamin, 'On Some Motifs in Baudelaire', 1939, in *Illuminations*, pp. 176–7. For an extended discussion of the early twentieth-century attitude towards speed, see John Tomlinson, *The Culture of Speed: The Coming of Immediacy* (London: Sage, 2007).

21. Henry Green, *Pack My Bag*, ed. with an introduction by Alan Ross (London: Vintage, 2000), p. 137. Subsequent references are incorporated in the text.

22. Quoted in Cunningham, *British Writers*, p. 322.

23. Walter Allen, *As I Walked Down New Grub Street* (London: Heinemann, 1981), p. 134.

24. Henry Green, 'A Rescue', 1941, in *Surviving, The Uncollected Writings of Henry Green,* ed. Matthew Yorke (London: Chatto & Windus, 1992), p. 79.

25. Green, *Pack My Bag*, p. 125.

26. Henry Green, *Caught,* introduction by Jeremy Treglown (London: Harvill, 2001), p. 175. Subsequent references are incorporated in the text.

27. David Lambourne, '"No Thundering Horses": The Novels of Henry Green', *Shenandoah*, vol. 26(4), Summer 1975, p. 63. For Auden's and Isherwood's repudiation of politics, see the Afterword. In 1978, Spender dismissed his generation as 'ill-equipped to address a working-class audience, and . . . not serious in their efforts to do so', although he emphasised that there was 'nothing despicable' about the 'middle-class *crise de conscience*' ('Background to the Thirties', in *The Thirties and After, Poetry, Politics, People (1933–75)* (London: Macmillan, 1978), pp. 23–4). In her 1969 autobiography, Jameson looked back on her own 1930s work as 'flawed' and admitted that she had been 'secretly bored' by the proletarian enthusiasms of fellow writers at the time. Storm Jameson, *Journey from the North* (London: Virago, 1984), vol. 1, pp. 301, 297.

28. Susan Sontag, 'America, Seen Through Photographs, Darkly', *On Photography* (London: Allen Lane, 1978), p. 31.

29. Richard Overy, *The Morbid Age, Britain Between the Wars* (London: Penguin Books, 2009), p. 1.

30. Overy, *The Morbid Age*, p. 2.

31. George Orwell, 'Inside the Whale', p. 548.

32. Michael Roberts (ed.), *New Signatures, Poems by Several Hands* (London: Hogarth Press, 1932), pp. 12–13.

33. Louis MacNeice, *The Strings Are False, An Unfinished Autobiography* (London: Faber and Faber, 1965), p. 169. Subsequent references are incorporated in the text.

34. Spender, *World Within World*, p. 145.

35. Orwell, 'Inside the Whale', p. 559.
36. Raymond Williams, 'Cinema and Socialism', 1985, in *Politics of Modernism, Against the New Conformists,* ed. Tony Pinkney (London: Verso, 2001), p. 107.
37. Williams, 'Cinema and Socialism', p. 108.
38. Williams, 'Cinema and Socialism', p. 115.
39. Williams, 'Cinema and Socialism', p. 116.
40. Susan Sontag, 'In Plato's Cave', *On Photography*, p. 12.
41. Stephen Spender, *The New Realism: A Discussion* (London: Hogarth Press, 1939), p. 15.
42. Williams, 'Cinema and Socialism', p. 118.
43. Benjamin, 'The Work of Art', p. 252.
44. Tom Harrisson, Humphrey Jennings and Charles Madge, 'Anthropology at Home', *The New Statesman and Nation,* 30 January 1937, p. 155.
45. Mass-Observation, *Britain by Mass-Observation* (Harmondsworth: Penguin Books, 1939), p. 32. Subsequent references are incorporated in the text. In 1937 Madge had complained that 'newspapers which belong to one class are largely sold to another class'. 'Press, Radio and Social Consciousness', in C. Day Lewis (ed.), *The Mind in Chains* (London: Frederick Muller, 1937), p. 155.
46. Virginia Woolf, *A Room of One's Own/Three Guineas,* ed. with an introduction by Michèle Barrett (London: Penguin Books, 2000), p. 220 (subsequent references are incorporated in the text); Iris Barry, *Let's Go to the Pictures* (London Chatto & Windus, 1926), p. 73: John Sommerfield, *May Day,* introduction by Andy Croft (London: Lawrence & Wishart, 1984), p. 143 (subsequent references are incorporated in the text).
47. Walter Benjamin, *The Arcades Project,* transl. Howard Eiland and Kevin McLaughlin (Cambridge, MA: The Belknap Press of Harvard University Press, 1999), [N3a, 3], p. 464.
48. Leo Charney, 'In a Moment: Film and the Philosophy of Modernity', in Leo Charney and Vanessa R. Schwartz (eds.), *Cinema and the Invention of Modern Life* (Berkeley, CA: University of California Press, 1995), p. 282.
49. Benjamin, *Arcades Project* [N1a, 8] p. 460.
50. Benjamin, 'The Work of Art', p. 242.
51. Michel Foucault, *Discipline and Punish: The Birth of the Prison,* transl. Alan Sheridan (New York: Vintage), 1977.
52. Jonathan Crary, 'Spectacle, Attention, Counter-Memory', *October,* 1989, vol. 50, p. 105. For a discussion of Foucault, Debord and Crary, see Karen Jacobs, *The Eye's Mind: Literary Modernism and Visual Culture* (Ithaca, NY: Cornell University Press, 2001), pp. 13–15.
53. In their report on Mass-Observation's first year's work, Madge and Harrisson included reports from observers detailing what they had gained from their experiences. A hospital nurse stated: 'I find already that

it has increased my appreciation of the life around me, because I observe it in more detail', while an infant school teacher felt confident that 'the frank expression of thought encouraged by Mass-Observation does more for the individual than an expensive course of Psycho-Analysis'. Charles Madge and Tom Harrisson (eds.), *First Year's Work, 1937–38, by Mass-Observation*, with an essay on 'A Nation-wide Intelligence Service' by Bronislaw Malinowski (London: Lindsay Drummond, 1938), pp. 76, 72–3.

54. For a fuller discussion of Mass-Observation and the Lambeth Walk, see pp. 112–14.
55. Jacobs, *The Eye's Mind*, p. 22.
56. David Trotter, *Cinema and Modernism* (Oxford: Blackwell, 2007), p. 8.
57. In 1927 the British government passed the Cinematograph Films Act to promote and encourage the British film industry. This introduced quotas for British films of 7.5 per cent for renters and 5 per cent for exhibitors, both rising to 20 per cent by 1936. See Margaret Dickinson and Sarah Street, *Cinema and State: The Film Industry and the Government, 1927–1984* (London, British Film Institute, 1985), pp. 5–6.
58. Virginia Woolf, 'The Cinema', 1926, in *The Crowded Dance of Modern Life*, ed. with an introduction by Rachel Bowlby (Harmondsworth: Penguin Books, 1993), p. 58.
59. Elizabeth Bowen, 'Why I Go to the Cinema', in Davy, *Footnotes to the Film*, p. 220.
60. André Bazin, *What Is Cinema, Essays Selected and Transl. Hugh Gray* (Berkeley, CA: University of California Press, 2005), vol. 1, pp. 63–4.
61. Trotter, *Cinema and Modernism*, pp. 4, 9.
62. Laura Marcus, *The Tenth Muse, Writing about Cinema in the Modernist Period* (Oxford: Oxford University Press, 2007).
63. For Baudrillard, see p. 132. Slavoj Žižek, *Welcome to the Desert of the Real, Five Essays on September 11 and Related Dates* (London: Verso, 2002), p. 19.
64. Sara Danius, *The Senses of Modernism: Technology, Perception, and Aesthetics* (Ithaca, NY: Cornell University Press, 2002); North, *Camera Works*; Keith Williams, *British Writers and the Media, 1930–45* (London: Macmillan, 1996).
65. David Seed, *Cinematic Fictions, The Impact of the Cinema on the American Novel up to the Second World War* (Liverpool: Liverpool University Press, 2009).

Chapter 1 Radical cinema

1. Trotter, *Cinema and Modernism*, p. 8.
2. René Clair, *Réflexion faite, Notes pour servir à l'histoire de l'art cinématographique de 1920 à 1950* (Paris: Gallimard, 1951), p. 112.

3. Kenneth Macpherson, 'As Is', *Close Up*, vol. 5(4), October 1929, p. 262.

4. For the London Film Society, see *The Film Society Programmes: 1925–1939*, introduction by George Ambert (New York: Arno Press, 1972).

5. Ralph Bond, 'Labour and the Cinema: A Reply to Huntley Carter', *The Plebs*, August 1931, p. 186.

6. *Sunday Worker,* 24 November 1929, p. 5.

7. Carlo Rim, 'On the Snapshot', 1930, in Christopher Phillips (ed.), *Photography in the Modern Era, European Documents and Critical Writings, 1913–1940* (New York: The Metropolitan Museum of Art, 1989), p. 38.

8. Siegfried Kracauer, 'Photography', 1927, in *The Mass Ornament, Weimar Essays*, transl., ed. and with an introduction by Thomas Y. Levin (Cambridge, MA: Harvard University Press, 1995), p. 59.

9. Quoted in the introduction to Robin Kelsey and Blake Stimson (eds.), *The Meaning of Photography* (Williamstown, MA: Sterling and Francine Clark Art Institute, 2008), p. xxiii.

10. See Kelsey and Stimson, *The Meaning of Photography*, p. xix.

11. Humphrey Jennings, 'Who Does That Remind You Of?', 1938, in Kevin Jackson (ed.), *The Humphrey Jennings Film Reader* (Manchester: Carcanet, 1993), p. 230.

12. Sergei Eisenstein, 'The Problem of the Materialist Approach to Form', 1925, in Richard Taylor (ed.), *The Eisenstein Reader*, transl. Richard Taylor and William Powell (London: British Film Institute, 1998), p. 59.

13. For Vertov, the task of the filmmaker was 'to see and hear life, to notice its curves and sudden changes, to catch the crunch of old bones under the press of the Revolution'. Dziga Vertov, 'Fiction Film Drama and the Cine-Eye. A Speech,' 1924, in Richard Taylor and Ian Christie (eds.), *The Film Factory, Russian and Soviet Cinema in Documents 1896–1939* (London: Routledge & Kegan Paul, 1988), p.115.

14. Sergei Eisenstein, 'The Dramaturgy of Film Form (The Dialectical Approach to Film Form)', 1929, in Taylor, *The Eisenstein Reader*, p. 93.

15. Quoted in David Bordwell, *The Cinema of Eisenstein* (Cambridge, MA: Harvard University Press, 1993), p. 121.

16. 'Eisenstein's Lectures in London: A Reconstruction by Basil Wright and J. Isaacs', Saturday 17 December 1949, Third Programme 10.05–10.45pm, transcript in Film Society Collection.

17. For early British reactions to Eisenstein that ignored his politics, see Marcus, *The Tenth Muse*, p. 338.

18. Herbert Read, 'Towards a Film Aesthetic', *Cinema Quarterly*, vol. 1, 1932, p. 10.

19. Siegfried Kracauer, *From Caligari to Hitler, A Psychological History of the German Film* (London: Dennis Dobson, 1947), pp. 184–5.

20. David Macrae, 'Ruttmann, Rhythm and "Reality": A Response to Siegfried Kracauer's Interpretation of *Berlin. The Symphony of a Great City*', in Dietrich Scheunemann (ed.), *Expressionist Film, New Perspectives* (New York: Camden House, 2003), p. 253.

21. Indeed, Roberts goes so far as to argue that *The Man with a Movie Camera* can be viewed as a cinematic affirmation of 'Stalinist policies'. See Graham Roberts, *The Man with the Movie Camera* (London: I. B. Tauris, 2000), p. xiv.

22. Christine Gledhill, *Reframing British Cinema, 1918–1928, Between Restraint and Passion* (London: British Film Institute, 2004), p. 111.

23. See Gledhill, *Reframing British Cinema*, p. 11.

24. Sergei Eisenstein, 'Dickens, Griffith, and the Film Today', 1944, in *Film Form, Essays in Film Theory and The Film Sense*, edited and transl. Jay Leyda (New York: Meridian Books, Inc, 1959), p. 234.

25. Arthur McCullouch, 'Eisenstein's Regenerative Aesthetics: From Montage to Mimesis', in Jean Antoine-Dunne and Paula Quigley (eds.), *The Montage Principle, Eisenstein in New Cultural and Critical Contexts, Critical Studies* (Amsterdam: Rodopi, 2004), p. 51.

26. Walter Benjamin, 'What Is Epic Theatre', 1939, in *Illuminations*, p. 153.

27. Walter Benjamin, 'The Author as Producer', 1934, in *Understanding Brecht*, transl. Anna Bostock, introduction by Stanley Mitchell (London: Verso, 1998), pp. 100, 99.

28. Eisenstein, 'The Montage of Attractions', 1923, in Taylor, *The Eisenstein Reader*, p. 30.

29. Bertolt Brecht, 'The Modern Theatre is the Epic Theatre', 1930, in Bertolt Brecht, *Brecht on Theatre, The Development of an Aesthetic*, ed. and transl. John Willett (London: Eyre Methuen, 1978), p. 37.

30. Bertolt Brecht, 'Notes to the Threepenny Opera', 1937, in *Collected Plays: Two*, ed. with an introduction by John Willett and Ralph Manheim (London: Methuen, 1994), p. 315.

31. Bertolt Brecht, *The Threepenny Opera*, 1928, in Brecht, *Collected Plays: Two*, p. 133.

32. V. F. Perkins, *Film as Film, Understanding and Judging Movies* (London: Penguin Books, 1972), p. 103.

33. Eisenstein, 'The Dramaturgy of Film Form', p. 103.

34. Eisenstein, 'The Dramaturgy of Film Form', p. 103.

35. Vsevolod Pudovkin, 'S. M. Eisenstein (From *Potemkin* to *October*)', 1928, in Taylor and Christie, *The Film Factory*, p. 199.

36. Eisenstein also uses non-diegetic animals to comment on the action in *Strike*, where spies with nicknames such as 'the fox' and 'the owl' are juxtaposed with images of the actual animals, and the brutal carnage of the police is illustrated through an image of a bull being killed, linked through the intertitle 'they behaved like wild animals'.

37. John Grierson, review of *Kameradschaft*, March 1932, in Forsyth Hardy (ed.), *Grierson on the Movies* (London: Faber and Faber, 1981), p. 65.

38. Russell A. Berman, 'A Solidarity of Repression: *Kameradschaft* (1931)', in Eric Rentschler (ed.), *The Films of G. W. Pabst* (New Brunswick, NJ: Rutgers University Press, 1990), p. 117.

39. Karl Marx, letter to Ruge, 1843, quoted in Benjamin, *The Arcades Project*, p. 456.

40. Walter Benjamin, 'Eduard Fuchs: Collector and Historian', 1937, transl. Knut Tarnowski, *New German Critique*, no. 5, Spring 1937, p. 34. See Miriam Bratu Hansen, 'Benjamin and Cinema: Not a One-Way Street', *Critical Inquiry*, vol. 25, 1999, p. 312.

41. Walter Benjamin, 'Surrealism, the Last Snapshot of the European Intelligentsia', in *Selected Writings*, ed. Marcus Bullock and Michael W. Jennings (Cambridge, MA: Belknap Press of Harvard University Press, 1996–2003), vol. 2, p. 217. For Buck-Morss, see Hansen, 'Benjamin and Cinema'; Hansen links this with Benjamin's 'self-regulated' attempts to negotiate the historical confrontation between human sensorium and technology through 'autoexperiments with hashish, gambling, running downhill and eroticism' (p. 321).

42. See Sabine Hake, *The Cinema's Third Machine: Writing on Film in Germany, 1907–1933* (Lincoln, NB: University of Nebraska Press, 1993), pp. 82–3.

43. For Marx, see Jacobs, *The Eye's Mind*, p. 16.

44. Sergei Eisenstein, 'The Filmic Fourth Dimension', 1929, in *Film Form*, pp. 71, 70.

45. Sergei Eisenstein, 'Dickens, Griffith and the Film Today', 1944, in *Film Form*, p. 233.

46. Bordwell, *The Cinema of Eisenstein*, p. 79.

47. Both quoted Siegfried Kracauer, *Theory of Film, The Redemption of Physical Reality*, introduction by Miriam Bratu Hansen (Princeton, NJ: Princeton University Press, 1997), p. 160. Analysing the ideal qualities of the cinema, Grierson wrote that he looked 'to register what actually moves: what hits the spectator at the midriff: what yanks him up by the hair of the head or the plain boot-straps to the plane of decent seeing'. John Grierson, 'What I Look For', June 1932, in Hardy, *Grierson on the Movies*, p. 38.

48. Kracauer, *Theory of Film*, pp. 159–60.

49. Tim Armstrong, *Modernism, Technology and the Body: A Cultural History* (Cambridge: Cambridge University Press, 1998), p. 5.

50. Bazin, *What Is Cinema*, vol. 1, p. 150.

51. Trotter, *Cinema and Modernism*, pp. 192–3.

52. Gilles Deleuze, *Cinema 1, The Movement-Image*, transl. Hugh Tomlinson and Barbara Habberjam (London: Continuum, 2005), p. 2. For further discussion of Bergson's theories of cinematographic consciousness, see p. 178.

53. Lynda Neade, *The Haunted Gallery, Painting, Photography, Film c. 1900* (New Haven, CT: Yale University Press, 2007), p. 15.

54. Bottomore has suggested that the early accounts of audience panic were exaggerated, although early viewers did speak of 'starting' or 'flinching'. See Stephen Bottomore, 'The Panicking Audience? Early Cinema and the "Train Effect"', *Historical Journal of Film, Radio and Television*, vol. 19(2), 1999, p. 177.

55. Tom Gunning, 'The Cinema of Attractions: Early Film, Its Spectator and the Avant-Garde', in Thomas Elsaesser and Adam Barker (eds.), *Early Cinema, Space, Frame, Narrative* (London: British Film Institute, 1990), pp. 57–8.

56. Alistair Cooke, 'The Critic in Film History', in Davy, *Footnotes to the Film*, p. 252.

57. Andrew Higson, *Waving the Flag: Constructing a National Cinema in Britain* (Oxford: Clarendon, 1995), p. 146.

58. Higson, *Waving the Flag*, pp. 165–6.

59. Higson, *Waving the Flag*, p. 170.

60. See Crary, *Suspensions of Perception*, p. 3; Danius, *The Senses of Modernism*, p. 19.

61. Jean Epstein, 'Magnification', 1921, in Richard Abel (ed.), *French Film Theory and Criticism: A History/Anthology, 1907–1939* (Princeton, NJ: Princeton University Press, 1988), vol. 1, p. 235.

62. Epstein, 'Magnification', p. 239.

63. Kracauer, *Theory of Film*, p. 47.

64. Kracauer, *Theory of Film*, p. 48.

65. Fernand Léger, 'The Machine Aesthetic: Geometric Order and Truth', 1925, in Fernand Léger, *Functions of Painting*, ed. Edward F. Fry, transl. Alexandra Anderson (London: Thames & Hudson, 1973), p. 65.

66. In *The Mother*, the factory boss's aggression towards the strikers is emphasised by a close-up of one of them banging his fist on the table. The announcement of the arrival of the soldiers to arrest the young revolutionary, Pavel, is heralded by a close-up of a hand on the knocker, which turns out to be the hand of Pavel's friend who has come to warn him. Pavel's eponymous mother raises her hands to her head in horror, and her ravaged and fragile hands are contrasted with the expensively gloved hands of the colonel, who runs one hand over the other in satisfaction as they arrest Pavel. This gesture resonates with the comforting stroking of the mother's hands by a supporting friend after Pavel has been sentenced and taken away.

67. Robert Bresson, *Notes on the Cinematographer*, transl. Jonathan Griffin (London: Quartet, 1981), p. 101.

68. Cited in Naum Kleiman, 'Arguments and Ancestors', in Ian Christie and Richard Taylor (eds.), *Eisenstein Rediscovered* (London: Routledge, 1993), p. 35.

69. Graham Greene, review of *October,* 1936, in Graham Greene, *Mornings in the Dark: The Graham Greene Film Reader,* ed. David Parkinson (Harmondsworth: Penguin Books, 1995), p. 87. Béla Balázs also emphasised the animation of Eisenstein's objects in his description of *Potemkin* in his *Theory of Film,* ascribing physiognomies to the boots: 'not men, mere boots trample down those human faces. The boots have such oafish, stupid, base physiognomies that the spectator clenches his fists in anger. Such is the effect of picture-metaphors'. See Béla Balázs, *Theory of Film, Character and Growth of a New Art,* transl. Edith Bone (London: Dennis Dobson, 1952), p. 112.

70. Fernand Léger, 'A New Realism – the Object', 1926, in Herschel B. Chipp (ed.), *Theories of Modern Art, A Source Book by Artists and Critics* (Berkeley, CA: University of California Press, 1969), p. 279.

71. Siegfried Kracauer, Marseilles Notebook, 1940, quoted in Miriam Hansen's introduction to Kracauer, *Theory of Film,* p. xvii; Kracauer, preface to *Theory of Film,* p. l.

72. Walter Benjamin, 'Unpacking My Library, A Talk about Collecting', 1931, in *Selected Writings,* vol. 2, p. 492.

73. Walter Benjamin, 'Dream Kitsch, Gloss on Surrealism', 1927, in *Selected Writings,* vol. 2, p. 4.

74. Tristan Tzara, 'When Objects Dream', 1934, in Phillips, *Photography in the Modern Era,* p. 51.

75. See Christina Kiaer, *Imagine no Possessions, The Socialist Objects of Russian Constructivism* (Cambridge, MA, MIT Press, 2005).

76. Boris Aratov, 'Everyday Life and the Culture of the Thing', 1925, transl. Christina Kiaer, *October,* vol. 81, summer 1997, p. 126.

77. Jean Epstein, 'On Certain Characteristics of Photogénie', 1924, in Abel, *French Film Theory,* vol. 1, p. 317.

78. Leo Charney, 'In a Moment', p. 288.

79. Martin Heidegger, 'The Thing', 1950, in *Poetry, Language, Thought,* transl. Albert Hofstadter (New York: Harper Colophon Books, 1975), p. 167.

80. Heidegger, 'The Thing', p. 174.

81. Epstein, 'On Certain Characteristics', p. 317.

82. Lesley Stern, '"Paths That Wind through the Thicket of Things"', in Bill Brown (ed.), *Things* (Chicago: University of Chicago Press, 2004), p. 411.

83. Heidegger states that when its 'unusability is . . . discovered, equipment becomes conspicuous'; Thingness or what Heidegger terms 'readiness-to-handness' reveals itself in 'the conspicuousness of the unusable' (Martin Heidegger, *Being and Time,* transl. John Macquarrie and Edward Robinson (Oxford: Basil Blackwell, 1985), pp. 103–4. For the relationship of this Heidegger passage to cinema, see Stanley Cavell, 'What Becomes of Things on Film?', 1977, in *Themes Out of School, Effects and Causes* (San Francisco: North Point Press, 1984), p. 174.

84. Bazin, *What Is Cinema*, vol. 1, p. 145.

85. See Trotter, *Cinema and Modernism*, p. 9.

86. See Sheila Fitzpatrick, *The Russian Revolution* (Oxford: Oxford University Press, 2008), pp. 130–5.

87. Jean Baudrillard, *The System of Objects* (London: Verso, 1996), p. 112.

88. Kracauer, original preface to *Theory of Film*, p. xlix.

89. Charles Sanders Peirce, *Collected Papers*, ed. Charles Hartshorne and Paul Weiss (Cambridge, MA: Harvard University Press, 1931–35), vol. 2, p. 281.

90. Bazin, *What Is Cinema*, vol. 1, p. 15.

91. See Paul Virilio, *War and Cinema: The Logistics of Perception*, transl. Patrick Camiller (London: Verso, 1989), p. 29.

92. Noël Simsolo, 'Le cinéma allemand sous Guillaume II', *La Revue de cinéma*, September 1982, quoted in Virilio, *War and Cinema*, p. 30.

93. Benjamin, 'The Work of Art', p. 229.

94. Benjamin, 'The Work of Art', p. 230.

95. Henri Lefebvre, *The Critique of Everyday Life* (London: Verso, 1991), p. 110. For a discussion of surrealism versus realism in photography, see John Roberts, *The Art of Interruption, Realism, Photography and the Everyday* (Manchester: Manchester University Press, 1997), pp. 98–112.

96. John Roberts argues against Lefebvre, suggesting that the surrealists were in fact investing in photography 'as a resistance to the abstractions of their epoch', insisting on the realist power of photography 'to bring the contradictions of social reality into view' (Roberts, *The Art of Interruption*, p. 112).

97. André Breton, *What Is Surrealism?*, transl. David Gascoyne (London: Faber and Faber, 1936), p. 49.

98. André Breton, *Nadja*, transl. Richard Howard (New York: Grove Press, 1960), pp. 65, 154.

99. Salvador Dali, 'The Object as Revealed in Surrealist Experiment', 1931, in Chipp, *Theories of Modern Art*, p. 11.

100. Walter Benjamin, 'Surrealism: The Last Snapshot of the European Intelligentsia', 1929, in *One Way Street and Other Writings*, transl. Edmund Jephcott and Kingsley Shorter (London: Verso, 1997), p. 229.

101. Benjamin, 'Surrealism', p. 229.

102. See Kracauer, 'Photography', Sontag, *On Photography* and Roland Barthes, *Camera Lucida, Reflections on Photography*, transl. Richard Howard (New York: Hill & Wang, 1981). I will discuss the deathly element of photography in more detail in Chapter 6.

103. In the late nineteenth century, the English photographer Eadweard Muybridge had used multiple cameras to capture motion, breaking down the movement of a horse into its component scenes.

104. Rudolf Arnheim, *Film*, transl. L. M. Sieveking and Ian F. D. Morrow with a preface by Paul Rotha (London: Faber and Faber, 1933), pp. 120–1.

105. Garrett Stewart, *Between Film and Screen: Modernism's Photo Synthesis* (Chicago: University of Chicago Press, 1999), p. 13.

106. Stewart, *Between Film and Screen*, note 342.

107. See Stewart, *Between Film and Screen*, p. 16.

108. Deleuze, *Cinema 1*, p. 85.

109. The narrator's grandmother, reading a book, fails to notice the entrance of her grandson, who becomes 'the spectator of [his] own absence'. He compares the process to a photograph and, viewing her as a photograph, sees signs of her impending death. She has become 'red-faced, heavy and vulgar, sick, day-dreaming . . . an overburdened old woman whom I did not know'. See Marcel Proust, *The Guermantes Way, In Search of Lost Time*, transl. Terence Kilmartin, C. K. Scott Moncrieff, vol. 3 (London: Vintage: 2000), pp. 155–6. For a discussion of this passage, see Danius, *The Senses of Modernism*, pp. 13–14.

110. Woolf, 'The Cinema', p. 55.

111. Stanley Cavell, *The World Viewed: Reflections on the Ontology of Film*, enlarged edition (Cambridge, MA: Harvard University Press, 1979), p. 41.

112. Alexander Bakshy, 'The Road to Art in the Motion Picutre', *Theatre Arts Monthly*, vol. 11, June 1927, p. 455. See Marcus, *The Tenth Muse*, p. 115.

113. Stern, '"Paths that Wind"', p. 415.

114. Marcus, *The Tenth Muse*, p. 114.

Chapter 2 Mass observing

1. Stephen Spender, 'Writers and Manifestoes', *Left Review*, vol. 1, February 1935, p. 146.

2. Paul Rotha, *Documentary Film* (London: Faber and Faber, 1936), p. 8.

3. Higson, *Waving the Flag*, p. 190.

4. Rotha, *Documentary Film*, p. 122.

5. See Higson, *Waving the Flag*, p. 191; John Grierson quoted in Paul Rotha, *Documentary Diary, An Informal History of the British Documentary Film, 1928–1939* (London: Secker & Warburg, 1973), p. xvi.

6. Fredric Jameson, *Signatures of the Visible* (New York: Routledge, 1992), p. 158.

7. For an extended discussion of the reaction to socialist realism in Britain, see Peter Marks, 'Illusion and Reality: The Spectre of Socialist Realism in Thirties Literature', in Keith Williams and Steven Matthews (eds.), *Rewriting the Thirties: Modernism and After* (London: Longman, 1997), pp. 23–36.

8. Maxim Gorky et al., *Soviet Writers' Congress 1934: The Debate on Socialist Realism and Modernism* (London: Lawrence & Wishart, 1977), p. 20.

9. Julian Bell, 'On Roger Fry – A Letter to A', 1936, *Essays, Poems and Letters*, ed. Quentin Bell (London: Hogarth Press, 1938), p. 259.

10. Amabel Williams-Ellis, 'Report on the Competition', *Left Review*, vol. 1, March 1935, p. 217. The editorial in *Left News* in October 1938 described the Left Book Club, founded in 1936, as 'the most successful political adventure of our generation', suggesting that its success testified to the fact that 'people *want* to know . . . people, when they once learn the truth, have a burning desire to open the eyes of those who have also been blind' (Editorial, *Left News*, no. 30, October 1938, p. 995).

11. *Sunday Worker*, April 7, 1929, p. 8.

12. Kathryn and Philip Dodd, 'Engendering the Nation: British Documentary Film, 1930–1939', in Andrew Higson (ed.), *Dissolving Views: Key Writings in British Cinema* (London: Cassell, 1996), p. 40.

13. Quoted in Peter Keating (ed.), *Into Unknown England, 1866–1914: Selections from the Social Explorers* (London: Fontana, 1976), p. 15.

14. James Greenwood, *A Night in a Workhouse*, 1866, in Keating, *Into Unknown England*, p. 38.

15. Greenwood, *A Night in a Workhouse*, p. 39.

16. George Sims quoted in Keating, *Into Unknown England*, p. 107; John Grierson, obituary for Tom Harrisson in *The Times,* quoted by Stuart Hood, 'John Grierson and the Documentary Film Movement', in James Curran and Vincent Porter (eds.), *British Cinema History* (London: Weidenfeld & Nicolson, 1983), p. 107.

17. Tom Harrisson, Introduction to Bob Willcock, 'Poles Apart', unpublished survey of Mass-Observation, 1947, p. 2.

18. See Ben Highmore, *Everyday Life and Cultural Theory* (London: Routledge, 2002), p. 79.

19. Grierson, 'The Story of the Documentary Film', p. 121.

20. Madge and Harrisson, *First Year's Work*, p. 94. See Highmore, *Everyday Life*, p. 100.

21. See p. 7.

22. See p. 122.

23. For the relationship between objectivity and aesthetics in Jameson's article see Keith Williams, 'Post/Modern Documentary: Orwell, Agee and the New Reportage', in Williams and Matthews, *Rewriting the Thirties*, pp. 166–7.

24. Higson, *Waving the Flag*, p. 194.

25. Elizabeth Cowie, 'Working Images: The Representations of Documentary Film', in Valerie Mainz and Griselda Pollock, *Work and the Image II, Work in Modern Times* (Aldershot: Ashgate, 2000), p. 183.

26. See Madge and Harrisson, *First Year's Work*, p. 96, and for *May the Twelfth* in particular p. 113.

27. Mass-Observation, *May the Twelfth,* ed. Humphrey Jennings and Charles Madge (London: Faber and Faber, 1937), p. 90. Subsequent references are incorporated in the text.

28. Stuart Laing, 'Presenting "Things as they are": John Sommerfield's *May*

Day and Mass Observation', in Frank Gloversmith (ed.), *Class, Culture and Social Change, A New View of the 1930s* (Brighton: Harvester Press, 1980), p. 157.

29. Highmore, *Everyday Life,* p. 93.
30. Madge and Harrisson, *First Year's Work,* p. 66.
31. Madge and Harrisson, *First Year's Work,* p. 96.
32. W. H. Auden, 'Consider This and in Our Time', 1930, in *Collected Poems,* ed. Edward Mendelson (London: Faber and Faber, 1994), pp. 61–2.
33. Rod Mengham, 'Bourgeois News: Humphrey Jennings and Charles Madge', *New Formations*, no. 44, Autumn 2001, p. 32.
34. Green, *Star,* 15 June 1929, quoted in Jeremy Treglown, *Romancing, The Life and Work of Henry Green* (London: Faber and Faber, 2000), p. 99.
35. David Lambourne, '"A Kind of Left-Wing Direction": An Interview with Christopher Isherwood', *Poetry Nation*, vol. 4, 1975, p. 53.
36. Benjamin, 'The Work of Art', p. 241.
37. Walter Benjamin, 'Theses on the Philosophy of History', 1940, in *Illuminations*, p. 258.
38. Spender, 'Writers and Manifestoes', p. 147.
39. Raymond Williams, *Culture and Society, 1780–1950* (London: Hogarth Press, 1987), p. 298.
40. See Mass-Observation, *Britain by Mass-Observation*, pp. 30ff.
41. According to Madge's then wife Kathleen Raine, for Madge Mass-Observation 'was less sociology than a kind of poetry, akin to Surrealism. He saw the expression of the unconscious collective life of England, literally, in writings on the walls, telling of the hidden thoughts and dreams of the inarticulate masses'. See Kathleen Raine, *The Land Unknown* (New York: George Braziller, 1975), p. 81.
42. 62C, *The Mob,* Mass-Observation Archive, Sussex University.
43. Williams, *Culture and Society*, p. 299.
44. Williams, *Culture and Society*, p. 299.
45. Harry Pollitt, 'Mr Orwell Will Have to Try Again', *Daily Worker*, 17 March 1937, p. 7.
46. Highmore, *Everyday Life,* p. 87.
47. Highmore, *Everyday Life,* p. 111.
48. Dodd and Dodd, 'Engendering the Nation', p. 43.
49. Elizabeth Cowie, 'Giving Voice to the Ordinary: Mass-Observation and the Documentary Film', *New Formations*, no. 44, Autumn 2001, p. 106.
50. Cowie, 'Giving Voice to the Ordinary', p. 108.
51. Cowie, 'Giving Voice to the Ordinary', p. 106.
52. Louis MacNeice, *Collected Poems* (London: Faber and Faber, 1979), p. 18. Subsequent references are incorporated in the text.
53. Stephen Spender, 'XXX', 1933, in *New Collected Poems,* ed. Michael Brett (London: Faber and Faber, 2004), pp. 22–3.

54. Sonnet XV in W. H. Auden and Christopher Isherwood, *Journey to a War* (London: Faber and Faber, 1939). Subsequent references are incorporated in the text. The photograph section is unnumbered.

55. Auden's poem echoes the rhythm of the train throughout, as is evident in the opening: 'This is the Night Mail crossing the border, / Bringing the cheque and the postal order' (1936), in W. H. Auden and Christopher Isherwood, *Plays and Other Dramatic Writings by W. H. Auden, 1928–1938*, ed. Edward Mendelson (Princeton, NJ: Princeton University Press, 1988), p. 423. Christopher Innes emphasises the cinematic and socialist elements of Auden's hopeful poem, which he states 'exactly matches the thrusting rhythms of the clacking wheels over the track as the railway engine of the title surges northwards, and gives a strong human – and socialist – dimension to the images of pounding machinery and empty landscape'. Christopher Innes, 'Auden's Plays and Dramatic Writings: Theatre, Film and Opera', in Stan Smith (ed.), *The Cambridge Companion to W. H. Auden* (Cambridge: Cambridge University Press, 1994), p. 91.

56. David Collard, 'Comrade Auden', *Times Literary Supplement*, 20 May 2009, p. 14.

57. Collard, 'Comrade Auden', p. 14.

58. Cunningham, *British Writers*, p. 450.

59. George Orwell, review of *Eyes of the Navy; The Heart of Britain; Unholy War*, 1941, in Peter Davison (ed.), *Orwell's England*, introduction by Ben Pimlott (London: Penguin Books, 2001), p. 249. It is worth noting that Jennings himself did not use a middle-class commentator in his most successful documentaries, *Listen to Britain* (1942) and *Fires Were Started* (1943).

60. George Orwell, review of *The Great Dictator*, 1940, in Peter Davison (ed.), *The Complete Works of George Orwell* (London: Secker & Warburg, 1991–99), vol. 12, p. 314. All subsequent references to this collection will appear as *CWGO*.

61. George Orwell, review of *The Great Dictator*, 1940, *CWGO*, vol. 12, p. 315.

62. George Orwell, review of *The Pub and the People* by Mass Observation, 1943, *CEJL*, vol. 3, pp. 61, 62.

63. George Orwell, 'As I please', 1947, *CWGO*, vol. 19, p. 91.

64. Mass-Observation, *The Pub and the People, A Worktown Study* (London: Victor Gollancz, 1943), p. 20.

65. George Orwell, *The Road to Wigan Pier*, introduction by Richard Hoggart (Harmondsworth: Penguin Books, 1989), p. 5. Subsequent references are incorporated in the text.

66. In the original foreword to the Left Book Club edition of the book, Gollancz complained that 'the whole of this second part is highly provocative, not merely in its general argument, but also in detail after detail' (*CWGO*, vol. 5, p. 218).

67. Roberts, *The Art of Interruption*, p. 66.

68. Montagu Slater, 'The Purpose of a Left Review', *Left Review,* vol. 1, June 1935, p. 365.
69. Michael Roberts, in his preface to his anthology *New Country* in 1933, wrote that the novelist must 'turn for his subject-matter to the working class, the class which is, he thinks, not utterly corrupted by capitalist spoonfeeding and contains within itself the seeds of revolution' and in so doing would 'give new life and value to his work'. Michael Roberts (ed.), *New Country, Prose and Poetry by the authors of* New Signatures (London: Hogarth Press, 1933), pp. 15–16.
70. Walter Benjamin, speech to the Institute for Fascism in Paris, 1934, quoted in Caroline Brothers, *War and Photography: A Cultural History* (London: Routledge, 1997), p. 170.
71. See *Easy Street* (1917) and *The Immigrant* (1917).
72. Meyer Levin, review of *Modern Times,* 1936, in Alistair Cooke (ed.), *Garbo and the Night Watchmen, A Selection from the writings of British and American Film Critics* (London: Jonathan Cape, 1937), p. 328.
73. Graham Greene, review of *Modern Times,* 1936, in Cooke, *Garbo and the Night Watchmen,* p. 345.
74. Both quoted in Higson, *Waving the Flag,* p. 104.
75. Spender, *The New Realism,* p. 19.
76. Rotha, *Documentary Film,* p. 132.
77. 'The little daily doings, however finely symphonised, are not enough. One must pile up beyond doing or process to creation itself, before one hits the higher reaches of art' (Grierson, 'First Principles of Documentary', 1933, in Hardy, *Grierson on Documentary,* p. 150).
78. According to Rotha, the naturalist tradition comprised the films of Griffith, together with Flaherty's *Nanook,* the realist tradition comprised films offering ordinary snapshots of life (such as *Rien que les Heures* and *Berlin*), the newsreel tradition was characterised by Vertov's *The Man with a Movie Camera* and the propagandist tradition included Eisenstein's films, Grierson-produced films such as *Coal Face,* together with German films such as *The Triumph of the Will* (see Rotha, *Documentary Film,* pp. 78–111).
79. Georg Lukács, 'Realism in the Balance', 1938, transl. Rodney Livingstone, in Ernst Bloch et al., *Aesthetics and Politics,* afterword by Frederic Jameson (London: NLB, 1977), pp. 43, 59.
80. Bertolt Brecht, 'Against Georg Lukács', 1967, transl. Stuart Hood, in Bloch et al., *Aesthetics and Politics,* pp. 84–5.
81. John Grierson, 'The Story of the Documentary Film', *The Fortnightly,* August 1929, p. 122; see also 'The Documentary Idea: 1942': 'the documentary idea was not basically a film idea at all . . . the medium happened to be the most convenient and most exciting available to us', in Hardy, *Grierson on Documentary,* p. 250.
82. Grierson, 'Summary and Survey', 1935, in Hardy, *Grierson on Documentary,* p. 64.

83. Rotha, *Documentary Film*, p. 16. H. Bruce Woolfe had asserted the superior potential of the documentary film in *Cinema Quarterly* in 1933: 'By getting knowledge of how other sections of our countrymen work and live we are getting a better understanding of their outlook. No other medium can do this in anything like the same way as the film', 'Commercial Documentary', *Cinema Quarterly,* Winter 1933–34, vol. 2(2), p. 96.

84. Rotha, *Documentary Diary*, pp. xiii–xiv.

85. Rotha, *Documentary Diary*, p. xiv.

86. Raymond Spottiswoode, *A Grammar of the Film: An Analysis of Film Technique* (London: Faber and Faber, 1935), p. 266.

87. Spottiswoode, *A Grammar of the Film*, p. 266.

88. 'Night Mail', p. 423.

89. See Nicholas Pronay, 'The Political Censorship of Films in Britain between the Wars', in Nicholas Pronay and D. W. Spring (eds.), *Propaganda, Politics and Film 1918–1945* (London: Macmillan, 1982), p. 105.

90. Stephen Jones, *The British Labour Movement and Film, 1918–1939* (London: Routledge & Kegan Paul, 1987), p. 103.

91. 'London by Night', *Picture Post*, 8 October 1938, p. 19.

92. 'London by Night', p. 23.

93. 'Speakers in Hyde Park', 'Speakers in the Zoo', *Picture Post*, 5 November 1938, pp. 54–7.

94. Bill Brandt, *The English At Home,* introduced by Raymond Mortimer (London: B. T. Batsford, 1936), p. 4. Subsequent references are incorporated in the text.

95. Quoted Paul Delany, *Bill Brandt: A Life* (London: Jonathan Cape, 2004), p. 110.

96. Delany, *Bill Brandt*, p. 110.

97. See Mark Durden, 'The Limits of Modernism: Walker Evans and James Agee's *Let Us Now Praise Famous Men*' in Jane M. Rabb (ed.), *Literature and Photography, Interactions 1840–1990, A Critical Anthology* (Albuquerque, NM: University of New Mexico Press, 1995), p. 28.

98. See *CWGO*, vol. 1, p. xxxii.

99. Auden and Isherwood, *Journey to a War*, pp. 247, 249.

100. Cunningham, *British Writers*, p. 328; Blake Stimson, *The Pivot of the World, Photography and Its Nation* (Cambridge, MA: MIT Press, 2006), p. 43.

101. Stimson, *The Pivot of the World*, p. 37.

102. Henry Green, letter to Nevill Coghill, 8 October 1927, quoted in Treglown, *Romancing*, p. 72.

103. Henry Green, 'The English Novel of the Future', *Contact*, vol. 1(2), 1950, p. 22.

104. *Left Review*, vol. 2, May 1936, p. 403.

105. Quoted in Terry Southern, 'The Art of Fiction', interview with Henry Green, 1958, in Green, *Surviving*, p. 247.
106. Southern, 'The Art of Fiction', p. 246; Nigel Dennis, 'The Double Life of Henry Green: The "Secret" Vice of a Top British Industrialist Is Writing Some of Britain's Best Novels', *Life*, vol. 33, 4 August 1952, p. 86.
107. Henry Green, *Living*, introduction by Paul Bailey (London: Vintage, 2000), p. 23. Subsequent references are incorporated in the text.
108. John Russell, *Henry Green: Nine Novels and an Unpacked Bag* (New York: Rutgers University Press, 1960), p. 78.
109. Quoted in Elaine Feinstein, introduction to Storm Jameson, *Company Parade* (London: Virago, 1982), p. vii.
110. Storm Jameson, foreword to *Company Parade*, p. v.
111. Jameson, *Journey from the North*, vol. 1, p. 301.
112. Chiara Briganti, '"Thou Art Full of Stirs, A Tumultuous City": Storm Jameson and London in the 1920s', in Lawrence Phillips (ed.), *The Swarming Streets: Twentieth-Century Literary Representations of London* (Amsterdam: Rodopi, 2004), p. 68.
113. Storm Jameson, *Love in Winter*, introduction by Elaine Feinstein (London: Virago, 1984), p. 363. Subsequent references are incorporated in the text.
114. James Barke, *Major Operation* (London: Collins, 1936), p. 85. Subsequent references are incorporated in the text.
115. Ian Haywood, *Working-Class Fiction from Chartism to Trainspotting* (Plymouth: Northcote House Publishers, 1997), p. 85.
116. Stimson, *The Pivot of the World*, p. 57.

Chapter 3 The documentary movement and mass leisure, 1930–1945

1. Walter Benjamin, Reply to Oscar A. H. Schmitz, 1927, in *Selected Writings*, vol. 2, p. 18.
2. Kracauer. *Theory of Film*, p. 51.
3. Jones, *The British Labour Movement*, p. 8.
4. C. Delisle Burns, *Leisure in the Modern World* (London: George Allen & Unwin, 1932), p. 15.
5. Quoted in Jones, *Workers at Play*, p. 117.
6. Jones, *The British Labour Movement*, p. 90.
7. Burns, *Leisure in the Modern World*, p. 19.
8. Burns, *Leisure in the Modern World*, p. 177.
9. Burns, *Leisure in the Modern World*, p. 148.
10. Thorstein Veblen, *The Theory of the Leisure Class* (London: Unwin Books, 1970), pp. 42, 47.
11. J. B. Priestley, *English Journey* (Chicago: University of Chicago Press, 1984), p. 110.
12. Cunningham, *British Writers*, p. 266.

13. A. J. P. Taylor, *English History, 1914–1945* (Harmondsworth: Penguin Books, 1975), p. 617.

14. According to Taylor, *English History*, p. 668, where the cost of living had only risen by 50 per cent between 1938 and 1944, the average earnings had increased by 81.5 per cent. Angus Calder, *The People's War, Britain 1939–45* (London: Jonathan Cape, 1969), Beveridge Report, pp. 526–31, People's War pp. 17, 165, *passim*.

15. Roger Manvell, 'British Feature Film', in Michael Balcon, Ernest Lindgren, Forsyth Hardy and Roger Manvell, *Twenty Years of British Film, 1925–1945* (London: Falcon Press, 1947), p. 85.

16. Higson, *Waving the Flag*, p. 213.

17. Jeffrey Richards and Dorothy Sheridan (eds.), *Mass-Observation at the Movies* (London: Routledge & Kegan Paul, 1987), p. 238.

18. Higson, *Waving the Flag*, p. 227.

19. Humphrey Jennings, letter to Cicely Jennings, 29 May 1942, in Jackson, *The Humphrey Jennings Film Reader*, p. 59.

20. William Sansom, James Gordon and Stephen Spender, *Jim Braidy, The Story of Britain's Firemen* (London: Lindsay Drummond, 1943), p. 64.

21. Green, *Pack My Bag*, p. 120.

22. Keith C. Odom, *Henry Green* (Boston, MA: Twayne Publishers, 1978), p. 81. See also Leslie Brunetta: 'Green . . . presents Roe's worries about maintaining his prewar standard of living every bit as sympathetically, and ironically as he does Pye's resentments . . . both proletarian Pye and upper-class Roe are caught in a reality that doesn't conform to the "we're all in it together" orthodoxy'. Leslie Brunetta, 'England's Finest Hour and Henry Green's *Caught*', *Sewanee Review*, vol. 100, 1992, p. 120.

23. Michael North, *Henry Green and the Writing of His Generation* (Charlottesville, VA: University Press of Virginia, 1984), p. 122.

24. Elizabeth Bowen, *The Heat of the Day*, introduction by Roy Foster (London: Vintage: 1998), p. 235. Subsequent references are incorporated in the text.

25. *The Times*, 18 October 1938, p. 15.

26. See *New York Times*, 8 January 1939, p. 26.

27. In fact, the picture was first published accompanying an article demanding more youth clubs to save children like these from playing 'juvenile games' in the city streets. But the fact that it was published in the same magazine in 1950 as an example of the golden days of street life prior to slum clearance shows that it took on a more positive aspect in the popular imagination. *Picture Post*, 2 January 1943, p. 17.

28. Humphrey Jennings, 'The Theatre Today', 1935, in Jackson, *The Humphrey Jennings Film Reader*, p. 216.

29. George Orwell, review of *English Ways* by Jack Hilton, 1939, in Peter Davison (ed.), *Orwell and the Dispossessed*, introduction by Peter Clarke (London: Penguin Books, 2001), p. 279.

30. Walter Greenwood, *Love on the Dole* (London: Jonathan Cape, 1983), p. 96.

31. Orwell, 'The Lion and the Unicorn', 1941, *CEJL*, vol. 2, p. 76.

32. George Orwell, review of *Waterloo Bridge,* 1940, *CWGO*, vol. 12, p. 288.

33. George Orwell, review of *The Lady in Question*, 1940, *CWGO*, vol. 12, p. 291.

34. Dorothy Richardson, 'Continuous Performance X, The Cinema in The Slums', *Close Up*, vol. 2 (5), May 1928, pp. 61–2.

35. Caroline Lejeune, 'The Week on the Screen', *Manchester Guardian*, 2 January 1926; quoted in Marcus, *The Tenth Muse*, p. 308.

36. Marcus, *The Tenth Muse*, p. 308.

37. Ralph Bond, 'Labour and the Cinema: A Reply to Huntley Carter', *The Plebs*, August 1931, p. 186.

38. Allen Hutt, *The Condition of the Working Class in Britain*, introduction by Harry Pollitt (London: Martin Lawrence, 1933), p. 177.

39. Edward Upward, 'The Island', *Left Review*, vol. 1, January 1935, p. 110.

40. Theodor Adorno, letter to Walter Benjamin, 18 March 1936, in Bloch et al., *Aesthetics and Politics*, p. 123.

41. Siegfried Kracauer, 'The Little Shopgirls Go to the Movies', 1927, in Kracauer, *The Mass Ornament*, pp. 292, 303, 297.

42. Barry, *Let's go to the Picutres*, p. 59.

43. North, *Henry Green*, p. 65; Cunningham, *British Writers*, p. 285.

44. J. B. Priestley, *The Good Companions* (Harmondsworth: Penguin Books, 1962), p. 227.

Chapter 4 Camera consciousness

1. Robert Wennersten, 'An Interview with Christopher Isherwood', quoted in Stephen Wade, *Christopher Isherwood* (London: Macmillan, 1991), pp. 12–13.

2. For a discussion of the objective/subjective politics of Isherwood's camera eye, see Kay Ferres, *Christopher Isherwood, A World in Evening* (San Bernardino, CA: The Borgo Press, 1994), pp. 15, 55; Williams, *British Writers*, p. 149; Marcus, *The Tenth Muse*, p. 431. According to Ferres, the camera metaphor 'defines the position of the subject who knows and records this reality as partial and selective', disavowing the authority and privileged knowledge of the narrator; the camera-narrator who goes on insidiously to observe the young men keeping private assignations in the street below is an outsider with privileged illegal intimacy, and therefore symptomatic of corrupt Weimar culture. For Williams, the metaphor enables Isherwood to undercut the characters' bad faith, illustrating the narrator's falsity: 'Isherwood brought together the complementary myths sponsored by the commercial cinema and mainstream documentary. Sally's seduction by Hollywood fantasy is no more insidious than

the camera-eyed narrator's belief in his own detachment'. Marcus states that in fact, 'the absoluteness of the division between objectivity and subjectivity was breaking down in the work of 1930s "observers", Isherwood included, producing more complex and self-reflexive approaches'.

3. Cavell, *The World Viewed*, p. 226.

4. North, *Camera Works*, p. 143.

5. 'An Interview with John Dos Passos', 1968, in John Dos Passos, *The Major Nonfictional Prose*, ed. Donald Pizer (Detroit, MI: Wayne State University Press, 1988), p. 283; North, *Camera Works*, p. 143.

6. John Dos Passos, *U.S.A.* (London: Penguin Books, 2001), pp. 39, 89.

7. 'John Dos Passos', interview, 1963, in Dos Passos, *Major Nonfictional Prose*, p. 247. For a discussion of the 'negotiation' between objectivity and subjectivity in the camera eye sections, see David Seed, *Cinematic Fictions*, pp. 140–1.

8. See North, *Camera Works*, p. 146.

9. For a discussion of these experiments in vision, see Rod Mengham, 'The Thirties: Politics, Authority, Perspective', in Laura Marcus and Peter Nicholls (eds.), *The Cambridge History of Twentieth-century English Literature* (Cambridge: Cambridge University Press, 2004), pp. 367–8. Mengham finds that the tutor misses the 'reassuringly human angle of vision, which the text reaches for but never achieves – the point of view is one that never establishes a proper perspective' (p. 367).

10. Edward Upward, *Journey to the Border*, introduction by Stephen Spender (London: Enitharmon Press, 1994), p. 12. Subsequent references are incorporated in the text.

11. Christopher Isherwood, *The Berlin Novels* (London: Vintage, 1999), p. 257. Subsequent references are incorporated in the text.

12. Christopher Isherwood, *Lions and Shadows, An Education in the Twenties* (London: Four Square Books, 1953), p. 53.

13. See p. 41.

14. See Paul Piazza, *Christopher Isherwood, Myth and Anti-Myth* (New York: Columbia University Press, 1978), p. 117 for a discussion of the disorientating effect of the description of the New Year's Eve party.

15. Benjamin, 'The Work of Art', p. 240.

16. Benjamin, 'The Work of Art', p. 251.

17. Quoted in Virilio, *War and Cinema*, p. 53.

18. Virilio, *War and Cinema*, p. 53.

19. Albert Speer, *Inside the Third Reich*, transl. Richard and Clara Winston (London, Sphere Books, 1970), p. 59.

20. Albert Speer, *Spandau, The Secret Diaries,* transl. Richard and Clara Winston (London: Collins, 1976), p. 428.

21. Speer, *Spandau*, p. 428.

22. The cathedral of light appears in Hans Weidermann's *Nuremberg Festival* (1937), which chronicles the 1936 and 1937 party rallies.

23. Williams, *British Writers*, p. 1.
24. Jean Baudrillard, *Simulacra and Simulation*, transl. Sheila Faria Glaser (Ann Arbor, MI: University of Michigan Press, 1994), pp. 2, 23. In 'Symbolic Exchange and Death' (1976), Baudrillard suggests that the real is *'that for which it is possible to provide an equivalent representation'* in the modern world and that 'reality itself founders in hyperrealism, the meticulous reduplication of the real, preferably through another, reproductive medium, such as photography'. Here he states that 'today, *reality itself is hyperrealistic'*. In Jean Baudrillard, *Selected Writings,* ed. Mark Poster (Stanford, CA: Stanford University Press, 1988), pp. 145, 144, 146.
25. Spender, *World Within World,* p. 111.
26. Quoted in Benjamin, 'On Some Motifs in Baudelaire', p. 175.
27. MacNeice, *The Strings Are False,* p. 170.
28. Walter Allen, *Blind Man's Ditch* (London: Michael Joseph, 1939), p. 65. Subsequent references are incorporated in the text.
29. For a discussion of Isherwood's involvement in Berthold Viertel's *Little Friend* see Williams, *British Writers*, p. 174. Isherwood would later claim that 'what the movies taught me was visualisation. Of course, the art of the movie is fundamentally opposed to that of literature, because the fewer words you have in a movie the better – let's not kid ourselves. One is always trying to tell the thing in visual terms and not yak. But you do learn a great deal, at least I did, from just seeing the people in a room and seeing them in relative positions in a room and all this kind of thing, which purely non-dramatic writers simply don't think about'. Interview with Stanley Poss, 1960, in James J. Berg and Chris Freeman, *Conversations with Christopher Isherwood* (Jackson, MI: University Press of Mississippi, 2001), p. 8.
30. Christopher Isherwood, *Prater Violet* (Harmondsworth: Penguin Books, 1969), p. 124. Subsequent references are incorporated in the text.
31. Nigel Jones, *Through a Glass Darkly, The Life of Patrick Hamilton* (London: Abacus, 1993), p. 235.
32. Patrick Hamilton, *Hangover Square* (Harmondsworth: Penguin Books, 1990), p. 281. Subsequent references are incorporated in the text.
33. Quoted in Jones, *Through a Glass Darkly*, p. 228.
34. In *Britain*, Harrisson stated that newspapers, newsreels and the BBC 'combined to fix a powerful image [of the Munich Crisis] on the public mind', with millions of spectators eager to see Chamberlain's 'photographed smile' and 'hear his wax-recorded voice, in the hope that they could guess from them whether the issue would be peace or war'. Mass-Observation, *Britain*, p. 68.
35. For the idea of war as 'nature's pruning hook', coined by the Scottish anthropologist Arthur Keith, see Daniel Pick, *War Machine, The Rationalisation of Slaughter in the Modern Age* (New Haven, CT: Yale University Press, 1993), p. 13.

36. George Orwell, *Homage to Catalonia,* introduction by Julian Symons (London: Penguin Books, 2000), p. 189. Subsequent references are incorporated in the text.

37. John Lehmann, *The Whispering Gallery* (London: Longmans, Green, 1955), p. 274.

38. 'Bourgeois', quoted in Edward Mendelson, *Early Auden* (New York: Farrar, Straus & Giroux, 2000), p. 19; comments about Spain are in two letters to E. R. Dodds, quoted in Mendelson, p. 195.

39. For the need for a heroic 'Test' and the promise of Spain, see Cunningham, *British Writers of the Thirties,* pp. 171, 421.

40. Cyril Connolly, *Enemies of Promise* (London: André Deutsch, 1973), pp. 102–3.

41. Jean Baudrillard, *The Gulf War Did Not Take Place,* transl. Paul Patton (Bloomington, IN: Indiana University Press, 1995), pp. 23, 62.

42. Žižek, *Welcome to the Desert of the Real,* p. 10.

43. Baudrillard noted in *The Gulf War,* p. 62, in particular that 'The Iraquis blow up civilian buildings in order to give the impression of a dirty war', while 'the Americans disguise satellite information to give the impression of a clean war'.

44. Cunningham, *British Writers,* p. 419. This poem appears in a section in Cunningham's Spanish Civil War anthology entitled 'photogenic war'. See Valentine Cunningham (ed.), *The Penguin Book of Spanish Civil War Verse* (London: Penguin Books, 1996), pp. 409–20.

45. Susan Sontag, *Regarding the Pain of Others* (London: Hamish Hamilton, 2003), pp. 6, 7.

46. Williams, *British Writers,* p. 3.

47. See Christopher Philips, introduction to Richard Whelan, *This Is War, Robert Capa at Work* (New York: International Center of Photography, 2007), p. 9.

48. Vertov, 'The Council of Three', p. 17.

49. For a discussion of Hemingway's role in the film, which has often been exaggerated, see Seed, *Cinematic Fictions,* pp. 179–80.

50. *Daily Worker,* 12 November 1936, p. 5. For a discussion of the breaking of taboos in the press, see Brothers, *War and Photography,* p. 175.

51. See Brothers, *War and Photography,* p. 2.

52. George Orwell, 'Looking Back on the Spanish Civil War', 1942, *CEJL,* vol. 2, pp. 294–5.

53. In an interview for the 1979 BBC documentary *The Witnesses* (dir. Dennis Marks), Claud Cockburn describes using his Baedecker Guide to find a suitable site for an invented revolt in the Spanish Protectorate of Morocco, where the Spanish Civil War had originated.

54. Sontag, *Regarding the Pain of Others,* p. 23.

55. Quoted Whelan, *This is War,* p. 55 (translation his).

56. See Whelan, *This Is War,* p. 72.

57. Whelan, *This Is War*, p. 75.
58. Quoted Whelan, *This Is War*, p. 73.
59. Auden, 'Spain', 1937, in Cunningham, *The Penguin Book of Spanish Civil War Verse*, pp. 97–100.
60. Stephen Spender, 'War Photograph', 1937, in Cunningham, *The Penguin Book of Spanish Civil War Verse*, p. 413. For a discussion of photography in Spender's poem, see Stan Smith, '"What the dawn will bring to light": Credulity and Commitment in the Ideological Construction of *Spain*', in Tim Kendall, *The Oxford Handbook of British and Irish War Poetry* (Oxford: Oxford University Press, 2007), pp. 255–6.
61. Carl von Clausewitz, *On War*, quoted Virilio, *War and Cinema*, p. 47.
62. Virilio, *War and Cinema*, p. 48.
63. Bernard Gutteridge, 'Spanish Earth', 1939, in Cunningham, *The Penguin Book of Spanish Civil War Verse*, p. 412.
64. John Sommerfield, *Volunteer in Spain* (London: Lawrence & Wishart, 1937), p. 28. Subsequent references are incorporated in the text.
65. Sontag, *Regarding the Pain of Others*, pp. 98–9.
66. Baudrillard, *The Gulf War Did Not Take Place*, p. 61.
67. W. H. Auden, 'I am Not a Camera', in *Collected Poems*, pp. 840–1.
68. W. H. Auden, Letter to Erika Mann, *Letters from Iceland*, p. 137.
69. W. H. Auden, Letter to R. H. S. Crossman, *Letters from Iceland*, p. 91.
70. Louis MacNeice, Hetty to Nancy, *Letters from Iceland*, p. 173.
71. Auden, 'Consider this', *Collected Poems*, pp. 61–2.
72. W. H. Auden, Letter to William Coldstream, *Letters from Iceland*, pp. 223–4.
73. W. H. Auden, 'Memorial for the City', 1949, in *Collected Poems*, pp. 591, 592.

Chapter 5 Framing history

1. Elena Gualtieri, 'Three Guineas and the Photograph: the Art of Propaganda', in Maroula Joannou (ed.), *Women Writers of the 1930s: Gender, Politics and History* (Edinburgh: Edinburgh University Press, 1999), pp. 165–78. Gualtieri links Woolf's mention of 'a packet of photographs from Spain all of dead children, killed by bombs' in a letter to her nephew Julian Bell on 16 November 1936 with the publication of the *Daily Worker* photographs on 12 November, 'a few days before Woolf wrote to Bell'. Gualtieri adds that at 'around this time', Woolf was writing 'Why Art Today Follows Politics', which would be published by the *Daily Worker* in December 1936 (p. 168).
2. Maggie Humm, 'Memory, Photography and Modernism: "the dead bodies and ruined houses" of Virginia Woolf's *Three Guineas*', *Signs*, vol. 28(2), 2003, p. 653. According to Humm, the 'effect of the Spanish Civil War photographs is far more effectively captured in Woolf's memory

traces than as published photographs because memory traces represent ongoing states of process, not static, frozen images' (p. 654).

3. Sontag, *Regarding the Pain of Others*, p. 6. While Sontag agrees with Woolf about the emotive power of the photographic image, she has chastised Woolf for being naïve in believing that photographs convey a straightforward message; and for failing to see that the same photographs would provoke a quite different consensus if they were presented by Franco (p. 8).

4. Benjamin, 'Theses on the Philosophy of History', p. 255.

5. Benjamin, *Arcades Project* [N3a, 3], p. 464.

6. Woolf, 'The Cinema', p. 58.

7. Benjamin, 'Theses on the Philosophy of History', p. 256.

8. Brenda R. Silver, '"Anon" and "The Reader": Virginia Woolf's Last Essays', *Twentieth Century Literature*, vol. 25, 1979, p. 385. Subsequent references are incorporated in the text.

9. Although only Jeri Johnson specifically links the two writers in their conception of history (introduction to Virginia Woolf, *The Years* (Harmondsworth: Penguin Books, 1998), p. xxv), several critics have read Woolf and Benjamin side by side, to different ends. Pamela Caughie's edited collection *Virginia Woolf in the Age of Mechanical Reproduction* (New York: Garland, 2000) presents a range of disparate ways of reading Woolf through Benjamin. Most notably, Leslie Hankins juxtaposes photographs of the two writers as part of her attempt to gain 'a reinvigorated spatial critique of culture' ('Virginia Woolf and Walter Benjamin Selling Out(Siders)', p. 9) and Sonita Sarker emphasises the dissimilarities between Woolf's and Benjamin's perception of relationships between rituals and politics ('The In-corporated Intellectual and Nostalgia for the Human', pp. 37–66). Wiley has seen Woolf as politicising 'theatre as well as history' in a Benjaminian fashion in *Between the Acts* (Catherine Wiley, 'Making History Unrepeatable in Virginia Woolf's *Between the Acts*', *Clio*, vol. 25(1), 1995, p. 3), and Jacobs has analysed Woolf's vision of spectacle and violence in *Between the Acts* in terms of Benjamin's theories of politics and aesthetics (Jacobs, *The Eye's Mind*, pp. 203–42) and also provides a comprehensive survey of other critics who have read Woolf and Benjamin together (p. 205).

10. Benjamin, 'The Work of Art', p. 242.

11. Benjamin, 'The Work of Art', p. 242.

12. 11 February 1940, in Anne Olivier Bell, (ed.), *The Diary of Virginia Woolf* (London: Hogarth Press, 1982), vol. 5, pp. 266–7. Subsequent references to this edition will appear as *DVW*.

13. Woolf, 'The Leaning Tower', p. 175,

14. See, for example, the entry for 6 September 1939: 'Shall I walk? Yes. It's the gnats & flies that settle on non-combatants. This war has begun in cold blood. One merely feels that the killing machine has to

be set in action. So far, The Athena has been sunk. It seems entirely meaningless – a perfunctory slaughter, like taking a jar in one hand, a hammer in the other. Why must this be smashed? Nobody knows' (*DVW*, vol. 5, p. 235).

15. For the ambivalent friendship between Woolf and Holtby, see Marion Shaw, '"Alien Experiences": Virginia Woolf, Winifred Holtby and Vera Brittain in the Thirties', in Williams and Matthews, *Rewriting the Thirties: Modernism and After*, pp. 37–52. See also Anthea Trodd, *Women's Writing in English, Britain 1900–1945* (London: Longman, 1998), p. 95. Holtby's commitment to revealing Woolf as a politically engaged 1930s writer is evident throughout her book on Woolf, where she is determined to rescue the older writer from her 'Victorian upbringing' and insists that 'she was intellectually free, candid and unafraid'. She states that Woolf's imagination was all along 'firmly based upon the common experiences of human life' and that she was aware that 'working women have need of political protection' and that 'miners' lives are complicated by coal-dust and the lack of bathing accommodation'. See Winifred Holtby, *Virginia Woolf* (London: Wishart, 1932), pp. 18, 33. However, she stated to her friend Vera Brittain that, in attempting the Woolf book, she had taken her courage 'in both hands' and entered the realm of 'purely aesthetic and intellectual interests', embarking on a journey that was as strange for her as 'it would have been for Virginia Woolf to sit beside my mother's pie'. In Vera Brittain, *Testament of Friendship: The Story of Winifred Holtby* (London: Virago, 1980), p. 308. For the pacifist efforts of Storm Jameson in particular, see Overy, *The Morbid Age*, pp. 219–64.

16. Virginia Woolf, letter to Stephen Spender, 7 April 1937, in Nigel Nicolson (ed.), *The Letters of Virginia Woolf* (London: Chatto & Windus, 1975–80), vol. 6, p. 116. Subsequent references to this edition will appear as *LVW*.

17. Julian Symons, *The Thirties: A Dream Revolved* (London: Faber and Faber, 1975), p. 43.

18. Virginia Woolf, 'The "Movie" Novel', review of *The Early Life and Adventures of Sylvia Scarlett*, by Compton Mackenzie, 1918, in *Contemporary Writers* (New York: Harcourt Brace Jovanovich, 1965), p. 82; Woolf omits to mention the trip to *The Cabinet of Doctor Caligari* which led her to write the 1926 essay, 'The Cinema'. When she does record a visit to the cinema she does not always mention the actual film: 'I went to my picture palace, and L to his Fabians; & he thought, on the whole, that his mind & spirit & body would have profited more by the pictures than by the Webbs (15 January 1915, *DVW*, vol. 1, p. 18).

19. For *Storm over Asia*, see Maggie Humm, *Modernist Women and Visual Cultures, Virginia Woolf, Vanessa Bell, Photography and Cinema* (Edinburgh: Edinburgh University Press, 2002), p. 230. In a letter to Vanessa Bell, Woolf described seeing 'a very good French one', which

Anne Olivier Bell has identified as *Le Million* (14 May 1931, *LVW*, vol. 4, pp. 331–2). Later, she announced, 'we've been given stalls for a 1st night of Wuthering Heights – a movie' (letter to Vita Sackville-West, 25 April 1939, *LVW*, vol. 6, p. 329).

20. For a detailed discussion of Woolf's engagement with cinema, especially in the 1920s, see Marcus, *The Tenth Muse*, pp. 99–178, and Trotter, *Cinema and Modernism*, pp. 159–79. Here my focus is on her 1930s work and in particular on her cinematic representation of politics and history.

21. Letter to Spender, 10 July 1934, *LVW*, vol. 5, p. 315.

22. For an extended discussion of Woolf's scrapbooks, see Merry Pawlowski, 'Exposing Masculine Spectacle: Virginia Woolf's Newspaper Clippings for *Three Guineas* as Contemporary Cultural History', *Woolf Studies Annual*, vol. 9, 2003, pp. 117–41.

23. Woolf was already taking and developing photographs at the age of fifteen and shared a camera with her sister. For Woolf's early experiences with photography, see Maggie Humm, *Snapshots of Bloomsbury: The Private Lives of Virginia Woolf and Vanessa Bell* (London: Tate, 2006), p. 6. Humm suggests that the albums were more Virginia's work than Leonard's, and certainly much of the text is in her hand and she was the one to solicit the photographs, but it is impossible to be sure how much of a role he played in creating the albums (Humm, *Snapshots of Bloomsbury*, p. 8).

24. Humm, 'Virginia Woolf's Photography and the Monk's House Albums', in Caughie, *Virginia Woolf in the Age*, p. 229.

25. Virginia Woolf, letter to Margaret Llewelyn Davies, 6 April 1940, *LVW*, vol. 6, p. 392. In fact, the Victorian photographs are not collected in one book and the title can only have existed in Woolf's mind, but the sense of Victorians as a separate generation pervades the albums.

26. Monk's House Album 1, pp. 47–8. The Monk's House Albums are in the Frederick R. Koch collection in the Harvard Theatre Collection at Harvard University. The albums are abbreviated 'MH' from this point. Woolf grew up with photographs by her great-aunt on the wall in Gordon Square. In 1926 she edited a collection of Julia Margaret Cameron's photographs in a book called *Victorian Photographs of Famous Men and Fair Women*, published at the Hogarth Press, and wrote an affectionate tribute to Cameron in the introduction, where she stated that 'all her sensibility was expressed, and what was perhaps more to the purpose, controlled in the new born art'. See Julia Margaret Pattle Cameron, *Victorian Photographs of Famous Men and Fair Women*, introductions by Virginia Woolf and Roger Fry (London: Hogarth Press, 1926), p. 18.

27. Monk's House Papers, MH/B16f, vol. 2, p. 31.

28. Monk's House Papers, MH/B16f, vol. 2, p. 32.

29. Monk's House Papers, MH/B16f, vol. 2, pp. 20, 21.

30. Benjamin, *Arcades Project* [N1a, 8] p. 460.

31. Benjamin, *Arcades Project* [N2, 6] p. 461.
32. Benjamin, *Arcades Project* [N2, 6] p. 461.
33. Bertolt Brecht, *War Primer*, transl. and ed. John Willett (London: Libris, 1998), no. 2.
34. Brecht, *War Primer*, no. 15.
35. Sarker, 'The In-corporated Intellectual', p. 51.
36. *Arcades Project* [N1, 9] p. 458.
37. Woolf accompanied her husband Leonard to a Labour Party conference in Hastings in 1933, and engaged as opposing factions in Britain's Left struggle to overcome their differences, in order to combat fascism in Hobsbawm's 'civil war'. When the first direct threat to democracy came with the Spanish Civil War, the Woolfs and all their friends united in opposing fascism. Together with writers such as E. M. Forster, G. E. Moore and C. Day Lewis, they signed a letter in the *Daily Herald* urging the public to become involved in the Spanish Civil War: 'The Spanish Government is, we repeat, a democratic Government, elected by the people and like our own, responsible to the people; it is fighting against military despotism and Fascism for liberty, and for what in our country we have for more than a century considered to be the bare minimum of political civilisation.' Woolf's inclusion of the letter in the *Three Guineas* notebook suggests that she saw the signing of her name as part of her own political agenda rather than just as a wifely duty. *Three Guineas* notebooks, Monk's House Papers, MH/B16f, vol. 2, p. 34.
38. 19 December 1932, *DVW*, vol. 4, p. 133.
39. 25 April 1933, *DVW*, vol. 4, pp. 151–2.
40. Anna Snaith, *Virginia Woolf: Public and Private Negotiations* (New York: St. Martin's Press, 2000), p. 110.
41. Hilary Newman, 'The Years as a "Condition of England" Novel', *Virginia Woolf Bulletin*, vol. 5, September 2000, p. 28.
42. Other critics to combine formalism and realism in their readings of *The Years* are Jane Marcus, who considers the novel in terms of its ritualistic symbols and its operatic structure (see Jane Marcus, *Virginia Woolf and the Languages of Patriarchy* (Bloomington, IN: Indiana University Press, 1987), pp. 36–74), and Laura Marcus, who considers the novel's relationship to cinema and its interplay of sight and sound, in *The Tenth Muse*, pp. 157–71.
43. Virginia Woolf, 'Sketch of the Past', 1940, in *Moments of Being, Autobiographical Writings* ed. Jeanne Schulkind, introduction by Hermione Lee (London: Pimlico, 2002), pp. 80, 81. Subsequent references are incorporated in the text.
44. See Grace Radin, *Virginia Woolf's* The Years, *The Evolution of a Novel* (Knoxville, TN: The University of Tennessee Press, 1981), p. 127.
45. For a discussion of Woolf's cinematic objects in *The Years*, see Marcus, *The Tenth Muse*, pp. 161–2.

46. See p. 45.

47. Virginia Woolf, *The Pargiters,* Manuscript, Berg Collection, M42, vol. 4, p. 106.

48. *The Pargiters*, Manuscript, vol. 4, p. 108.

49. Mitchell Leaska, 'Virginia Woolf, the Pargeter, a Reading of *The Years*', *Bulletin of the New York Public Library, Virginia Woolf Issue,* vol. 80(2), Winter 1977, p. 185.

50. Maud Ellmann, *Elizabeth Bowen: The Shadow across the Page* (Edinburgh: Edinburgh University Press, 2003), p. 5.

51. 25 October 1920, *DVW*, vol. 2, p. 72.

52. Virginia Woolf, *Mrs Dalloway*, ed. G. Patton Wright with an introduction by Angelica Garnett (London: Vintage, 1992), p. 73; Virginia Woolf, *The Waves* (Harmondsworth: Penguin Books, 1951), p. 227 ('in order to hold it tight [I] ignored newspaper placards and went and looked at pictures').

53. Henri Bergson, *Time and Free Will, An Essay on the Immediate Data of Consciousness*, transl. F. L. Pogson (London: George Allen & Unwin, 1971), p. 109; Henri Bergson, *Creative Evolution*, transl. Arthur Mitchell, ed. Keith Answell Pearson, Michael Kolkman and Michael Vaughan (London: Palgrave Macmillan, 2007), p. 195.

54. Bergson, *Creative Evolution*, p. 203.

55. Woolf announced that 'I may say that I have never read Bergson' in a letter to Harmon H. Goldstone, who was engaged in writing a study of her work (16 August 1932, *LVW*, vol. 5, p. 91).

56. Humm, 'Virginia Woolf's Photography', p. 241. Apart from Humm, several critics have read Woolf in terms of Bergson, notably Mary Ann Gillies, *Henri Bergson and British Modernism* (Montreal: McGill-Queen's University Press, 1996), pp. 107–31, and Marcus, *The Tenth Muse*. Neither looks specifically at Woolf's spatialisation of time in *The Years* and Gillies does not discuss Woolf's final two novels at all.

57. Woolf, *Mrs Dalloway*, p. 90.

58. Marcus, *The Tenth Muse*, p. 138.

59. See Marcus, *The Tenth Muse*, p. 139.

60. See Gilles Deleuze, *Cinema 2, The Time-Image*, transl. Hugh Tomlinson and Robert Galeta (London: Continuum, 2005), pp. 42–121.

61. For Deleuze on *Un Chien Andalou* see *Cinema 2*, p. 55.

62. Virginia Woolf, *Between the Acts,* ed. with an introduction by Frank Kermode (Oxford: Oxford University Press, 1992), p. 8. Subsequent references are incorporated in the text.

63. Bergson, *Creative Evolution*, p. 200.

64. T. S. Eliot, 'East Coker', 1940, in *The Complete Poems and Plays* (London: Faber and Faber, 1969), p. 182.

65. T. S. Eliot, 'The Dry Salvages', 1941, in *The Complete Poems and Plays*, p. 186.

66. T. S. Eliot, *A Sermon Preached at Magdalene College Cambridge* (Cambridge: Cambridge University Press, 1948), p. 5. For the influence of Bergson on the *Four Quartets* see Gillies, *Henri Bergson and British Modernism*, pp. 96–106.

67. Eliot, 'The Dry Salvages', p. 187.

68. Virginia Woolf, 'Letter to a Young Poet', 1932, in *The Death of the Moth and Other Essays* (San Diego, CA: Harcourt Brace, 1970), p. 222.

69. Forster's *Abinger Pageant* and Eliot's *The Rock* were both written in 1934.

70. Jed Esty, *A Shrinking Island, Modernism and National Culture in England* (Princeton, NJ: Princeton University Press, 2004), p. 55.

71. For an appropriation of Benjamin's and Kracauer's theories of distracted spectatorship for Woolf, see Caughie, introduction to *Virginia Woolf in the Age of Mechanical Reproduction*, pp. xxiii–xxiv.

72. Michael Tratner, 'Why Isn't *Between the Acts* A Movie?', in Caughie, *Virginia Woolf in the Age of Mechanical Reproduction*, pp. 115–34.

73. Patricia Klindienst Joplin, 'The Authority of Illusion: Feminism and Fascism in Virginia Woolf's *Between the Acts*', *South Central Review*, vol. 6(2), 1989, p. 89.

74. Tratner, 'Why Isn't *Between the Acts* a Movie?', p. 117.

75. Benjamin, 'The Work of Art', p. 230. See pp. 55–6

76. Jacobs, *The Eye's Mind*, p. 238.

77. Wiley, 'Making History Unrepeatable', p. 4.

78. Tratner, 'Why Isn't *Between the Acts* A Movie?', p. 131.

79. Tratner, 'Why Isn't *Between the Acts* A Movie?', p. 134.

80. According to Catherine Wiley, the pageant does not 'seem to follow the rules of history, leaving out every ruler except Queen Elizabeth and never mentioning a war, scientific discovery, or famous work of art'. See Wiley, 'Making History Unrepeatable', p. 7. Colonel Mayhew complains that they have left out the British Army: 'What's history without the Army, eh?' (p. 141). In this respect it is very different from the more traditional pageant portrayed in *This Demi-Paradise*, which culminates in Wellington's victory at Waterloo.

81. Esty argues that the younger generation of late modernist writers was unable to invest in the pageant form to the same extent as Woolf, Forster and Eliot. He states that 'the canonical literature of the "next generation" attests to the dwindling possibilities of an authentic common culture'. See Esty, *A Shrinking Island*, p. 216. However, I see the wartime films of Humphrey Jennings who, born in 1907, was very much a member of the next generation, as strongly aligned with Woolf's project.

82. For an account of the actual reports in *The Times*, see Stuart N. Clarke, 'The Horse with a Green Tail', *Virginia Woolf Miscellany*, vol. 34, Spring 1990, pp. 3–4.

83. For an extended analysis of this passage, see Karin E. Westman, '"For her generation the newspaper was a book": Media, Mediation, and

Oscillation in Virginia Woolf's *Between the Acts*', *Journal of Modern Literature*, vol. 29(2), 2006, pp. 7–9. Westman is attentive to Isa's 'inattentive' mode of reading, which she contrasts with Bart Oliver and his more dogmatic reading of *The Times* (itself a paper consistently gendered as masculine in Woolf's writing, according to Westman).

84. *The Times* does make a brief physical appearance when Bart Oliver uses the paper as a beak to frighten his grandson (p. 11).

85. Marcus, *The Tenth Muse*, p. 162.

86. For a discussion of speech and sound in *Between the Acts*, see Hermione Lee, *The Novels of Virginia Woolf* (London: Methuen, 1977), pp. 209, 215.

87. Jane Lewty, 'Virginia Woolf and the Synapses of Radio', in Anna Snaith and Michael Whitworth (eds.), *Locating Woolf, The Politics of Space and Place* (London: Palgrave Macmillan, 2007), p. 155. The aeroplanes were heard overhead during Reverend Streatfield's request for money: 'the word was cut in two. A zoom severed it. Twelve aeroplanes in perfect formation like a flight of wild duck came overhead. *That* was the music. The audience gaped; the audience gazed. Then zoom became drone. The planes had passed.' Woolf was acutely aware of the significance of the sound of aeroplanes at this point, writing in her diary in 1938: 'Meanwhile the aeroplanes are on the prowl, crossing the downs. Every preparation is made. Sirens will hoot in a particular way when there's the first hint of a raid. L & I no longer talk about it' (10 September 1938, *DVW*, vol. 5, p. 167).

88. 29 August 1935, *DVW*, vol. 4, p. 336.

89. 25 August 1939, *DVW*, vol. 5, pp. 230–1.

90. For telephone conversations in *The Years*, see Marcus, *The Tenth Muse*, pp. 163–4.

91. Humphrey Jennings, 'I See London', 1941, in Jackson, *The Humphrey Jennings Film Reader*, pp. 296–7.

Chapter 6 'The savage and austere light of a burning world'

1. Spender, *World Within World*, p. 336.

2. Stephen Spender, 'Abyss', *Citizens in War – and After*, foreword by Herbert Morrison (London: Harrap, 1945), pp. 52–3. The poem is reprinted in revised form as 'Rejoice in the Abyss', in Spender, *New Collected Poems*, pp. 243–4.

3. Virilio, *War and Cinema*, p. 78.

4. 'The Man on the Ladder', *Picture Post*, 1 February 1941, p. 15. The photograph is by A. Hardy.

5. 'The very possibility of a lit screen was subject to wartime shortages. The rationing of carbon rods led to a literal deficit of light, and single-projector shows (also the result of shortages) entailed a blackout between

each reel.' Antonia Lant, *Blackout, Reinventing Women for Wartime British Cinema* (Princeton, NJ: Princeton University Press, 1991), p. 115.

6. Lant, *Blackout*, p. 114.
7. Stephen Spender, 1949, 'A Man-made World', 1949, in *New Collected Poems*, pp. 244–5.
8. Henry Green, 'A Rescue', 1941, in *Surviving*, p. 79.
9. Lyndsey Stonebridge, *The Writing of Anxiety* (London: Palgrave Macmillan, 2007), p. 71.
10. William Sansom, *The Blitz, Westminster at War*, foreword by Stephen Spender (London: Faber and Faber, 1990), p. 9. Subsequent references are incorporated in the text.
11. William Sansom, *Fireman Flower and Other Stories* (London: Hogarth Press, 1944), p. 204. Subsequent references are incorporated in the text.
12. Hector Bolitho, *War in the Strand, A Notebook of the First Two and a Half Years in London* (London: Eyre & Spottiswoode, 1942), p. 81.
13. Elizabeth Bowen, 'Mysterious Kôr', 1944, in Elizabeth Bowen, *Collected Stories* (London: Vintage, 1999), pp. 729, 728. All subsequent references to Bowen's stories are from this edition, incorporated in the text.
14. Elizabeth Bowen, *The Death of the Heart,* introduction by Patricia Craig (London: Vintage: 1998), p. 195.
15. Epstein, 'Magnification', p. 239.
16. Elizabeth Bowen, postscript to *The Demon Lover,* 1945, in *The Mulberry Tree, Writings of Elizabeth Bowen,* selected and introduced by Hermione Lee (London: Vintage: 1999), p. 99.
17. See p. 47.
18. Elizabeth Bowen, *Bowen's Court & Seven Winter's,* introduction by Hermione Lee (London: Vintage, 1999), p. 454. Subsequent references to both books are incorporated within the text.
19. Godard in *Two or Three Things I know About Her,* quoted by Cavell, 'What Becomes of Things on Film', pp. 181–2.
20. Ellmann, *Elizabeth Bowen*, p. 6.
21. See p. 62.
22. Stern, '"Paths that Wind"', p. 415.
23. Kracauer, 'Photography', p. 61; Sontag, 'In Plato's Cave', p. 15.
24. Barthes, *Camera Lucida*, p. 77. According to Barthes, the photograph can never deny that the 'thing has been there' and the superimposition of reality and the past constitutes the essence of photography (p. 76).
25. Stern, '"Paths that Wind"', p. 395.
26. Stern, '"Paths that Wind"', pp. 404–5.
27. Arnheim, *Film*, p. 120.
28. Andrew Bennett and Nicholas Royle, *Elizabeth Bowen and the Dissolution of the Novel* (New York: St. Martin's Press, 1995), p. 95.
29. See p. 70.

30. Stephen Spender, *The Temple* (London: Faber and Faber, 1989), p. 70.
31. Deleuze, *Cinema 2*, p. 98.
32. Henri Bergson, *Matter and Memory*, transl. Nancy Margaret Paul and W. Scott Palmer (London: Swann Sonnenschein, 1911), p. 130. For an explanation of the relationship between Bergson and Deleuze, see Ronald Bogue, *Deleuze on Cinema* (New York: Routledge, 2003), p. 6.
33. H. D., *Trilogy*, 1942, in *Collected Poems, 1921–1944* (New York: New Directions Books, 1983), pp. 510, 509, 559.
34. T. S. Eliot, 'Little Gidding', 1942, in *The Complete Poems and Plays*, p. 193.
35. Bowen, preface to *The Demon Lover*, p. 98.
36. Rod Mengham, 'Broken Glass', in Rod Mengham and N. H. Reeve (eds.), *The Fiction of the 1940s, Stories of Survival* (London: Palgrave, 2001), p. 130.
37. Speer, *Inside the Third Reich*, p. 288.
38. Virilio, *War and Cinema*, p. 5.
39. Eliot, 'Little Gidding', p. 196.
40. Spender, *World within World*, p. 336.
41. Louis MacNeice, 'The Morning after the Blitz', 1941, in Alan Heuser (ed.), *Selected Prose of Louis MacNeice* (Oxford: Clarendon Press, 1990), p. 117. Subsequent references are incorporated in the text. For a discussion of the aesthetic appeal of the violence of the Blitz, see Mark Rawlinson, *British Writing of the Second World War* (Oxford: Clarendon Press, 2000), pp. 77–87.
42. 'Brother Fire', 1942, in MacNeice, *Collected Poems*, p. 196.
43. Benjamin, 'The Work of Art', p. 242.
44. Spender, *World Within World*, p. 311.
45. Stephen Spender, introduction to Wolfgang Borchert, *The Man Outside, The Prose Works of Wolfgang Borchert*, transl. David Porter (London: Hutchinson International Authors, 1952), p. v. Borchert's stories like Bowen's are populated by fairly literal ghosts who jostle each other in the air, preventing the living from sleeping (see pp. 23–4).
46. Adam Piette, *Imagination at War, British Fiction and Poetry 1939–1945* (London: Papermac, 1995), p. 46.
47. Sansom, *The Blitz*, p. 175.
48. Spender, *World Within World*, p. 311.
49. Sansom, *The Blitz*, p. 189.
50. See Lant, *Blackout*, p. 38.
51. Brecht, *War Primer*, no. 25.
52. See Michael North, 'World War II: The City in Ruins', in Marcus and Nicholls, *The Cambridge History*, p. 436, and Rawlinson, *British Writing of the Second World War*, p. 71.
53. See Virilio, *War and Cinema*, pp. 56–8 for this account of the aborted Norway film.

54. Quoted Virilio, *War and Cinema*, p. 57.
55. See Virilio, *War and Cinema*, p. 58 for an account of the Kolberg film.
56. See Lant, *Blackout*, pp. 19–58, Anthony Aldgate and Jeffrey Richards, *Britain Can Take It: The British Cinema in the Second Word War* (Oxford: Blackwell, 1983).
57. Virilio, *War and Cinema*, p. 64.
58. Graham Greene, *The Ministry of Fear* (London: Vintage, 2001), p. 163. Subsequent references are incorporated in the text.
59. In 1949, the novelist Rosamond Lehmann wrote to Bowen: 'What bothers me a little is that I cannot see why he shouldn't have been a Communist and therefore pro-Russian, pro-Ally, rather than pro-enemy.' Quoted in Victoria Glendinning, *Elizabeth Bowen: Portrait of a Writer* (London: Weidenfeld & Nicolson, 1997), p. 151.
60. Alan Sinfield, *Literature, Politics and Culture in Postwar Britain* (London: Continuum, 2004), pp. 19–21.
61. Amy Bell, 'Landscapes of Fear: Wartime London, 1939–1945', *Journal of British Studies*, vol. 48(1), January 2009, p. 154.
62. Rod Mengham, *The Idiom of the Time: The Writings of Henry Green* (Cambridge: Cambridge University Press, 1982), p. 106. See also Adam Piette, *Imagination at War*, p. 71, and Mark Rawlinson, *British Writing of the Second World War*, pp. 106–7. Piette: 'Green is demonstrating the simple, undeniable fact that the Blitz fires were too extraordinary for words, overpowering any attempt to pass them on to others in the language of witness. The Blitz could not be *caught* in prose, however deft, however ecstatic, however coolly observant.' Rawlinson: 'the parenthetic representation of the Blitz in *Caught* doesn't assert what is supplanted by Roe's narrative of initiation, it embodies a further imaginary flight from actuality. His war experience is not so much devalued as situated between values, suspended between descriptions' of the 'consenting wartime subject' on the one hand, and 'the subject-centring apprehension of violence as spectacle' on the other.

Afterword

1. Sansom, *The Blitz*, p. 201.
2. Ruth Pitter, 'Victory Bonfire', 1975, in Desmond Graham (ed.), *Poetry of the Second World War, An International Anthology* (London: Pimlico, 1998), pp. 221–3.
3. Adam Piette, 'World War II: Contested Europe', in Marcus and Nicholls, *The Cambridge History*, p. 431.
4. Arthur Marwick, *British Society since 1945* (Harmondsworth: Penguin Books, 1982), p. 75.
5. Andrzej Gąsiorek, *Postwar British Fiction: Realism and After* (London: Edward Arnold, 1995), p. 2.

6. Evelyn Waugh, 'Aspirations of a Mugwump', *Spectator*, 2 October 1959, p. 435; Harold Nicolson, *Diaries and Letters, 1939–1945*, ed. Nigel Nicolson (London: Collins, 1967), pp. 23–4.

7. Elizabeth Bowen, 'The Bend Back', 1950, in *The Mulberry Tree*, p. 59.

8. Treglown, *Romancing*, p. 178.

9. Dennis, 'The Double Life of Henry Green', p. 91.

10. George Orwell, 'You and the Atom Bomb', *CEJL*, vol. 4, p. 9; Winston Churchill, 'The Iron Curtain', speech given in Fulton, Missouri, 5 March 1946, in David Cannadine (ed.), *Blood, Toil, Tears and Sweat, Winston Churchill's Famous Speeches* (London, Cassell, 1989), p. 303.

11. Christopher Isherwood, *Christopher and His Kind* (London: Methuen, 1978), p. 248.

12. Peter Parker, *Isherwood* (London: Picador, 2005), p. 418.

13. W. H. Auden, 'The Prolific and the Devourer', 1939 in *The English Auden*, ed. Edward Mendelson (London: Faber and Faber, 1977), p. 405. See also Spender's and Jameson's repudiations of their 1930s politics in the introduction, n. 27.

14. Green, 'The English Novel of the Future', p. 22.

15. Walter Allen, letter to Andy Croft, quoted in Croft, *Red Letter Days*, p. 256.

16. Williams, 'Cinema and Socialism', p. 115.

17. A record by I. Teneromo of a conversation with Tolstoy on his eightieth birthday, August 1908, transl. David Bernstein, in Jay Leyda, *Kino, A History of the Russian and Soviet Film* (London: George Allen & Unwin, 1973), p. 410. Although Tolstoy's statement makes interesting and prescient reading, it is worth bearing in mind its somewhat dubious provenance as a remembered transcript of a conversation. Leyda states that 'Madame Alexandra Tolstaya warns me that there are several aspects of this record that make it suspect as a record, but that it incorporates remarks that Tolstoy may have made, either to Teneromo or others – but not on his eightieth birthday.'

Bibliography

Abel, Richard (ed.), *French Film Theory and Criticism: A History/Anthology, 1907–1939*, 2 volumes (Princeton, NJ: Princeton University Press, 1988)

Aldgate, Anthony and Richards, Jeffrey, *Britain Can Take It: The British Cinema in the Second World War* (Oxford: Blackwell, 1983)

Allen, Walter, *Blind Man's Ditch* (London: Michael Joseph, 1939)

Allen, Walter, *As I Walked Down New Grub Street* (London: Heinemann, 1981)

Antoine-Dunne, Jean and Quigley, Paula (eds.), *The Montage Principle, Eisenstein in New Cultural and Critical Contexts, Critical Studies* (Amsterdam: Rodopi, 2004)

Aratov, Boris, 'Everyday Life and the Culture of the Thing', 1925, transl. Christina Kiaer, *October*, vol. 81, summer 1997, pp. 119–28

Armstrong, Tim, *Modernism, Technology and the Body: A Cultural History* (Cambridge: Cambridge University Press, 1998)

Arnheim, Rudolf, *Film*, transl. L. M. Sieveking and Ian F. D. Morrow with a preface by Paul Rotha (London: Faber and Faber, 1933)

Auden, W. H., *Collected Poems*, ed. Edward Mendelson (London: Faber and Faber, 1994)

Auden, W. H. and Isherwood, Christopher, *Journey to a War* (London: Faber and Faber, 1939)

Auden, W. H. and Isherwood, Christopher, *Plays and Other Dramatic Writings by W. H. Auden, 1928–1938*, ed. Edward Mendelson (Princeton, NJ: Princeton University Press, 1988)

Auden, W. H. and MacNeice, Louis, *Letters from Iceland* (London: Faber and Faber, 1937)

Balázs, Béla, *Theory of Film, Character and Growth of a New Art*, transl. Edith Bone (London: Dennis Dobson, 1952)

Balcon, Michael, Lindgren, Ernest, Hardy Forsyth and Manvell, Roger, *Twenty Years of British Film, 1925–1945* (London: Falcon Press, 1947)

Barke, James, *Major Operation* (London: Collins, 1936)

Barry, Iris, *Let's Go to the Pictures* (London Chatto & Windus, 1926)

Barthes, Roland, *Camera Lucida, Reflections on Photography*, transl. Richard Howard (New York: Hill & Wang, 1981)

Baudrillard, Jean, *Selected Writings,* ed. Mark Poster (Stanford, CA: Stanford University Press, 1988)

Baudrillard, Jean, *Simulacra and Simulation*, transl. Sheila Faria Glaser (Ann Arbor, MI: University of Michigan Press, 1994)

Baudrillard, Jean, *The Gulf War Did Not Take Place*, transl. Paul Patton (Bloomington, IN: Indiana University Press, 1995)

Baudrillard, Jean, *The System of Objects* (London: Verso, 1996)

Bazin, André, *What Is Cinema, Essays Selected and Translated by Hugh Gray*, 2 volumes (Berkeley, CA: University of California Press, 2005)

Bell, Amy, 'Landscapes of Fear: Wartime London, 1939–1945', *Journal of British Studies*, vol. 48(1), January 2009, pp. 153–75

Bell, Anne Olivier (ed.), *The Diary of Virginia Woolf*, 5 volumes (London: Hogarth Press, 1977–85)

Bell, Julian, *Essays, Poems and Letters,* ed. Quentin Bell (London: Hogarth Press, 1938)

Benjamin, Walter, *Illuminations, Essays and Reflections,* ed. with an introduction by Hannah Arendt, transl. Harry Zohn (New York: Schoken Books, 1968)

Benjamin, Walter, *Selected Writings,* ed. Marcus Bullock and Michael W. Jennings, 4 volumes (Cambridge, MA: Belknap Press of Harvard University Press, 1996–2003)

Benjamin, Walter, *One Way Street and Other Writings*, transl. Edmund Jephcott and Kingsley Shorter (London: Verso, 1997)

Benjamin, Walter, *Understanding Brecht*, transl. Anna Bostock, introduction by Stanley Mitchell (London: Verso, 1998)

Benjamin, Walter, *The Arcades Project*, transl. Howard Eiland and Kevin McLaughlin (Cambridge, MA: The Belknap Press of Harvard University Press, 1999)

Bennett, Andrew and Royle, Nicholas, *Elizabeth Bowen and the Dissolution of the Novel* (New York: St. Martin's Press, 1995)

Berg, James J. and Freeman, Chris, *Conversations with Christopher Isherwood* (Jackson, MI: University Press of Mississippi, 2001)

Bergson, Henri, *Matter and Memory*, transl. Nancy Margaret Paul and W. Scott Palmer (London: Swann Sonnenschein, 1911)

Bergson, Henri, *Time and Free Will, An Essay on the Immediate Data of Consciousness*, transl. F. L. Pogson (London: George Allen & Unwin, 1971)

Bergson, Henri, *Creative Evolution*, transl. Arthur Mitchell, ed. Keith Answell Pearson, Michael Kolkman and Michael Vaughan (London: Palgrave Macmillan, 2007)

Bloch Ernst et al., *Aesthetics and Politics,* afterword by Fredric Jameson (London: New Left Books, 1977)

Bogue, Ronald, *Deleuze on Cinema* (New York: Routledge, 2003)

Bolitho, Hector, *War in the Strand, A Notebook of the First Two and a Half Years in London* (London: Eyre & Spottiswoode, 1942)

Borchert, Wolfgang, *The Man Outside, The Prose Works of Wolfgang Borchert*, transl. David Porter, introduction by Stephen Spender (London: Hutchinson International Authors, 1952)

Bordwell, David, *The Cinema of Eisenstein* (New Haven, CT: Harvard University Press, 1993)

Bottomore, Stephen, 'The Panicking Audience? Early Cinema and the "Train Effect"', *Historical Journal of Film, Radio and Television*, vol. 19, 1999, pp. 177–216

Bowen, Elizabeth, *The Death of the Heart*, introduction by Patricia Craig (London: Vintage, 1998)

Bowen, Elizabeth, *The Heat of the Day*, introduction by Roy Foster (London: Vintage, 1998)

Bowen, Elizabeth, *Bowen's Court & Seven Winters*, introduction by Hermione Lee (London: Vintage, 1999)

Bowen, Elizabeth, *Collected Stories* (London: Vintage, 1999)

Bowen, Elizabeth, *The Mulberry Tree, Writings of Elizabeth Bowen*, selected and introduced by Hermione Lee (London: Vintage: 1999)

Brandt, Bill, *The English At Home*, introduced by Raymond Mortimer (London: Batsford, 1936)

Bratu Hansen, Miriam, 'Benjamin and Cinema: Not a One-Way Street', *Critical Inquiry*, vol. 25, 1999, pp. 307–43

Brecht, Bertolt, *Brecht on Theatre, The Development of an Aesthetic*, ed. and transl. John Willett (London: Eyre Methuen, 1978)

Brecht, Bertolt, *Collected Plays: Two*, ed. with an introduction by John Willett and Ralph Manheim (London: Methuen, 1994)

Brecht, Bertolt, *War Primer*, transl. and ed. John Willett (London: Libris, 1998)

Bresson, Robert, *Notes on the Cinematographer*, transl. Jonathan Griffin (London: Quartet, 1981)

Breton, André, *What Is Surrealism?*, transl. David Gascoyne (London: Faber and Faber, 1936)

Breton, André, *Nadja*, transl. Richard Howard (New York: Grove Press, 1960)

Brittain, Vera, *Testament of Friendship: The Story of Winifred Holtby* (London: Virago, 1980)

Brothers, Caroline, *War and Photography: A Cultural History* (London: Routledge, 1997)

Brown, Bill (ed.), *Things* (Chicago: University of Chicago Press, 2004)

Brunetta, Leslie, 'England's Finest Hour and Henry Green's *Caught*', *Sewanee Review*, vol. 100, 1992, pp. 112–23

Burns, C. Delisle, *Leisure in the Modern World* (London: George Allen & Unwin, 1932)

Calder, Angus, *The People's War, Britain 1939–45* (London: Jonathan Cape, 1969)

Cameron, Julia Margaret Pattle, *Victorian Photographs of Famous Men and Fair Women,* introductions by Virginia Woolf and Roger Fry (London: Hogarth Press, 1926)

Cannadine, David (ed.), *Blood, Toil, Tears and Sweat, Winston Churchill's Famous Speeches* (London, Cassell, 1989)

Caughie, Pamela (ed.), *Virginia Woolf in the Age of Mechanical Reproduction* (New York: Garland, 2000)

Cavell, Stanley, *The World Viewed: Reflections on the Ontology of Film,* enlarged edition (Cambridge, MA: Harvard University Press, 1979)

Cavell, Stanley, 'What Becomes of Things on Film?', 1977, in *Themes Out of School, Effects and Causes* (San Francisco: North Point Press, 1984)

Charney, Leo and Schwartz, Vanessa R. (eds.), *Cinema and the Invention of Modern Life* (Berkeley, CA: University of California Press, 1995)

Chipp, Herschel B. (ed.), *Theories of Modern Art, A Source Book by Artists and Critics* (Berkeley, CA: University of California Press, 1969)

Christie, Ian and Taylor, Richard (eds.), *Eisenstein Rediscovered* (London: Routledge, 1993)

Clair, René, *Réflexion faite, Notes pour servir à l'histoire de l'art cinémato-graphique de 1920 à 1950* (Paris: Gallimard, 1951)

Clarke, Stuart N., 'The Horse with a Green Tail', *Virginia Woolf Miscellany,* vol. 34, Spring 1990, pp. 3–4

Collard, David, 'Comrade Auden', *Times Literary Supplement,* 20 May 2009, pp. 14–15

Connolly, Cyril, *Enemies of Promise* (London: André Deutsch, 1973),

Cooke, Alistair (ed.), *Garbo and the Night Watchmen, A Selection from the Writings of British and American Film Critics* (London: Jonathan Cape, 1937)

Cowie, Elizabeth, 'Giving Voice to the Ordinary: Mass-Observation and the Documentary Film', *New Formations,* no. 44, Autumn 2001, pp. 100–9

Croft, Andy, *Red Letter Days, British Fiction in the Thirties* (London: Lawrence & Wishart, 1990)

Cunningham, Valentine, *British Writers of the Thirties* (Oxford: Oxford University Press, 1988)

Cunningham, Valentine (ed.), *The Penguin Book of Spanish Civil War Verse* (London: Penguin Books, 1996)

Curran, James and Porter, Vincent (eds.), *British Cinema History* (London: Weidenfeld & Nicolson, 1983)

Davison, Peter (ed.), *The Complete Works of George Orwell,* 20 volumes (London: Secker & Warburg, 1991–99)

Danius, Sara, *The Senses of Modernism: Technology, Perception, and Aesthetics* (Ithaca, NY: Cornell University Press, 2002)

Davison, Peter (ed.), *Orwell and the Dispossessed,* introduction by Peter Clarke (London: Penguin Books, 2001)

Davison, Peter (ed.), *Orwell's England,* introduction by Ben Pimlott (London: Penguin Books, 2001)

Davy, Charles (ed.), *Footnotes to the Film* (London: Lovat Dickson, 1937)

Day Lewis, C., *A Hope for Poetry* (Oxford: Basil Blackwell, 1936)

Day Lewis, C. (ed.), *The Mind in Chains* (London: Frederick Muller, 1937)

Delany, Paul, *Bill Brandt: A Life* (London: Jonathan Cape, 2004)

Deleuze, Gilles, *Cinema 1, The Movement-Image,* transl. Hugh Tomlinson and Barbara Habberjam (London: Continuum, 2005)

Deleuze, Gilles, *Cinema 2, The Time-Image,* transl. Hugh Tomlinson and Robert Galeta (London: Continuum, 2005)

Dennis, Nigel, 'The Double Life of Henry Green: The "Secret" Vice of a Top British Industrialist is Writing Some of Britain's Best Novels', *Life,* vol. 33, 4 August 1952, pp. 83–94

Dickinson, Margaret and Street, Sarah, *Cinema and State: The Film Industry and the Government, 1927–1984* (London, British Film Institute, 1985)

Donald, James, Friedberg, Anna and Marcus, Laura (eds.), *Close Up, 1927–1933, Cinema and Modernism* (London: Cassell, 1998)

Dos Passos, John, *The Major Nonfictional Prose,* ed. Donald Pizer (Detroit, MI: Wayne State University Press, 1988)

Dos Passos, John, *U.S.A.* (London: Penguin Books, 2001)

Eisenstein, Sergei, *Film Form, Essays in Film Theory and The Film Sense,* ed. and transl. Jay Leyda (New York: Meridian Books, 1959)

Eliot, T. S., *A Sermon Preached at Magdalene College Cambridge* (Cambridge: Cambridge University Press, 1948)

Eliot, T. S., *The Complete Poems and Plays* (London: Faber and Faber, 1969)

Ellmann, Maud, *Elizabeth Bowen: The Shadow across the Page* (Edinburgh: Edinburgh University Press, 2003)

Elsaesser, Thomas and Barker, Adam (eds.), *Early Cinema, Space, Frame, Narrative* (London: British Film Institute, 1990)

Esty, Jed, *A Shrinking Island, Modernism and National Culture in England* (Princeton, NJ: Princeton University Press, 2004)

Ferres, Kay, *Christopher Isherwood, A World in Evening* (San Bernardino, CA: The Borgo Press, 1994)

Fitzpatrick, Sheila, *The Russian Revolution* (Oxford: Oxford University Press, 2008)

Foucault, Michel, *Discipline and Punish: The Birth of the Prison,* transl. Alan Sheridan (New York: Vintage)

Gąsiorek, Andrzej, *Postwar British Fiction: Realism and After* (London: Edward Arnold, 1995)

Gillies, Mary Ann, *Henri Bergson and British Modernism* (Montreal: McGill-Queen's University Press, 1996)

Gledhill, Christine, *Reframing British Cinema, 1918–1928, Between Restraint and Passion* (London: British Film Institute, 2004)

Glendinning, Victoria, *Elizabeth Bowen: Portrait of a Writer* (London: Weidenfeld & Nicolson, 1997)

Gloversmith, Frank (ed.), *Class, Culture and Social Change, A New View of the 1930s* (Brighton: Harvester Press, 1980)

Gorky, Maxim, Radek, Karl, Bukharin, Nikolai et al., *Soviet Writers' Congress 1934: The Debate on Socialist Realism and Modernism* (London: Lawrence & Wishart, 1977)

Graham, Desmond (ed.), *Poetry of the Second World War, An International Anthology* (London: Pimlico, 1998)

Green, Henry, *Surviving, The Uncollected Writings of Henry Green*, ed. Matthew Yorke (London: Chatto & Windus, 1992)

Green, Henry, *Living*, introduction by Paul Bailey (London: Vintage, 2000)

Green, Henry, *Pack My Bag*, ed. with an introduction by Alan Ross (London: Vintage, 2000)

Green, Henry, *Caught*, introduction by Jeremy Treglown (London: Harvill, 2001)

Greene, Graham, *Mornings in the Dark: The Graham Greene Film Reader*, ed. David Parkinson (Harmondsworth: Penguin Books, 1995)

Greene, Graham, *The Ministry of Fear* (London: Vintage, 2001)

Greenwood, Walter, *Love on the Dole* (London: Jonathan Cape, 1983)

Hake, Sabine, *The Cinema's Third Machine: Writing on Film in Germany, 1907–1933* (Lincoln, NB: University of Nebraska Press, 1993)

Hamilton, Patrick, *Hangover Square* (Harmondsworth: Penguin Books, 1990)

Hardy, Forsyth (ed.), *Grierson on Documentary* (London: Faber and Faber, 1966)

Hardy, Forsyth (ed.), *Grierson on the Movies* (London: Faber and Faber, 1981)

Haywood, Ian, *Working-Class Fiction from Chartism to Trainspotting* (Plymouth: Northcote House, 1997)

H. D., *Collected Poems, 1921–1944* (New York: New Directions Books, 1983)

Heidegger, Martin, *Poetry, Language, Thought*, transl. Albert Hofstadter (New York: Harper Colophon Books, 1975)

Heidegger, Martin, *Being and Time*, transl. John Macquarrie and Edward Robinson (Oxford: Basil Blackwell, 1985)

Heuser, Alan (ed.), *Selected Prose of Louis MacNeice* (Oxford: Clarendon Press, 1990)

Highmore, Ben, *Everyday Life and Cultural Theory Everyday Life and Cultural Theory* (London: Routledge, 2002)

Higson, Andrew, *Waving the Flag: Constructing a National Cinema in Britain* (Oxford: Clarendon, 1995)

Higson, Andrew (ed.), *Dissolving Views: Key Writings in British Cinema* (London: Cassell, 1996)

Hobsbawm, Eric, *Age of Extremes, The Short Twentieth Century 1914–1991* (London: Michael Joseph, 1994)

Holtby, Winifred, *Virginia Woolf* (London: Wishart, 1932)

Hubble, Nick, *Mass-Observation and Everyday Life: Culture, History, Theory* (Basingstoke and New York: Palgrave Macmillan, 2006)

Humm, Maggie, *Modernist Women and Visual Cultures, Virginia Woolf, Vanessa Bell, Photography and Cinema* (Edinburgh: Edinburgh University Press, 2002)

Humm, Maggie, 'Memory, Photography and Modernism: "the dead bodies and ruined houses" of Virginia Woolf's *Three Guineas*', *Signs*, vol. 28, 2003

Humm, Maggie, *Snapshots of Bloomsbury: The Private Lives of Virginia Woolf and Vanessa Bell* (London: Tate, 2006)

Hutt, Allen, *The Condition of the Working Class in Britain*, introduction by Harry Pollitt (London: Martin Lawrence, 1933)

Hynes, Samuel, *The Auden Generation* (London: Faber and Faber, 1976)

Isherwood, Christopher, *Lions and Shadows, An Education in the Twenties* (London: Four Square Books, 1953)

Isherwood, Christopher, *Prater Violet* (Harmondsworth: Penguin Books, 1969)

Isherwood, Christopher, *Christopher and His Kind* (London: Methuen, 1978)

Isherwood, Christopher, *The Berlin Novels* (London: Vintage, 1999)

Jackson, Kevin (ed.), *The Humphrey Jennings Film Reader* (Manchester: Carcanet, 1993)

Jacobs, Karen, *The Eye's Mind: Literary Modernism and Visual Culture* (Ithaca, NY: Cornell University Press, 2001)

Jameson, Frederic, *Signatures of the Visible* (New York: Routledge, 1992)

Jameson, Storm, *Company Parade*, introduction by Elaine Feinstein, (London: Virago, 1982)

Jameson, Storm, *Journey from the North*, 2 volumes (London: Virago, 1984)

Jameson, Storm, *Love in Winter*, introduction by Elaine Feinstein (London: Virago, 1984)

Joannou, Maroula (ed.), *Women Writers of the 1930s: Gender, Politics and History*, (Edinburgh: Edinburgh University Press, 1999)

Jones, Nigel, *Through a Glass Darkly, The Life of Patrick Hamilton* (London: Abacus, 1993)

Jones, Stephen, *Workers at Play, A Social and Economic History of Leisure 1918–1939* (London: Routledge & Kegan Paul, 1986)

Jones, Stephen, *The British Labour Movement and Film, 1918–1939* (London: Routledge & Kegan Paul, 1987)

Patricia Klindienst Joplin, 'The Authority of Illusion: Feminism and Fascism in Virginia Woolf's *Between the Acts*', *South Central Review*, vol. 6(2), 1989, pp. 88–104

Keating, Peter (ed.), *Into Unknown England, 1866–1914: Selections from the Social Explorers* (London: Fontana, 1976)

Kelsey, Robin and Stimson, Blake (eds.), *The Meaning of Photography* (Williamstown, MA: Sterling and Francine Clark Art Institute, 2008)

Kendall, Tim, *The Oxford Handbook of British and Irish War Poetry* (Oxford: Oxford University Press, 2007)

Kiaer, Christina, *Imagine no Possessions, The Socialist Objects of Russian Constructivism* (Cambridge, MA: The MIT Press, 2005)

Kracauer, Siegfried, *From Caligari to Hitler, A Psychological History of the German Film* (London: Dennis Dobson, 1947)

Kracauer, Siegfried, *The Mass Ornament, Weimar Essays*, ed. and transl. Thomas Y. Levin (Cambridge, MA: Harvard University Press, 1995)

Kracauer, Siegfried, *Theory of Film, The Redemption of Physical Reality*, introduction by Miriam Bratu Hansen (Princeton, NJ: Princeton University Press, 1997)

Lambourne, David, '"A Kind of Left-Wing Direction": An Interview with Christopher Isherwood', *Poetry Nation*, vol. 4, 1975, pp. 57–71

Lant, Antonia, *Blackout, Reinventing Women for Wartime British Cinema* (Princeton, NJ: Princeton University Press, 1991)

Leaska, Mitchell, 'Virginia Woolf, the Pargeter, a Reading of *The Years*', *Bulletin of the New York Public Library, Virginia Woolf Issue*, vol. 80(2), Winter 1977, pp. 172–210

Lee, Hermione, *The Novels of Virginia Woolf* (London: Methuen, 1977)

Lefebvre, Henri, *The Critique of Everyday Life* (London: Verso, 1991)

Léger, Fernand, *Functions of Painting*, ed. Edward F. Fry, transl. Alexandra Anderson (London: Thames & Hudson, 1973)

Lehmann, John, *The Whispering Gallery* (London: Longmans, Green, 1955)

Leyda, Jay, *Kino, A History of the Russian and Soviet Film* (London: George Allen & Unwin, 1973)

MacNeice, Louis, *The Strings Are False, An Unfinished Autobiography* (London: Faber and Faber, 1965)

MacNeice, Louis, *Collected Poems* (London: Faber and Faber, 1979)

Madge, Charles and Harrisson, Tom (eds.), *First Year's Work, 1937–38, by Mass-Observation*, with an essay on 'A Nation-wide Intelligence Service' by Bronislaw Malinowski (London: Lindsay Drummond, 1938)

Mainz, Valerie and Pollock, Griselda, *Work and the Image II, Work in Modern Times* (Aldershot: Ashgate, 2000)

Marcus, Jane, *Virginia Woolf and the Languages of Patriarchy* (Bloomington, IN: Indiana University Press, 1987)

Marcus, Laura, *The Tenth Muse, Writing about Cinema in the Modernist Period* (Oxford: Oxford University Press, 2007)

Marcus, Laura and Nicholls, Peter (eds.), *The Cambridge History of Twentieth-century English Literature* (Cambridge: Cambridge University Press, 2004)

Marwick, Arthur, *British Society since 1945* (Harmondsworth: Penguin Books, 1982)

Mass-Observation, *May the Twelfth*, ed. Humphrey Jennings and Charles Madge (London: Faber and Faber, 1937)

Mass-Observation, *Britain by Mass-Observation* (Harmondsworth: Penguin Books, 1939)

Mass-Observation, *The Pub and the People, A Worktown Study* (London: Victor Gollancz, 1943)

Mendelson, Edward, *Early Auden* (New York: Farrar, Straus & Giroux, 2000)

Mengham, Rod, *The Idiom of the Time: The Writings of Henry Green* (Cambridge: Cambridge University Press, 1982)

Mengham, Rod, 'Bourgeois News: Humphrey Jennings and Charles Madge', *New Formations*, no. 44, Autumn 2001, pp. 26–33

Mengham, Rod and Reeve, N. H. (eds.), *The Fiction of the 1940s, Stories of Survival* (London: Palgrave, 2001)

Michelson, Annette (ed.), *Kino-Eye, The Writings of Dziga Vertov*, transl. Kevin O'Brien (London: Pluto Press, 1984)

Neade, Lynda, *The Haunted Gallery, Painting, Photography, Film c. 1900* (New Haven, CT: Yale University Press, 2007)

Newman, Hilary, '*The Years* as a "Condition of England" Novel', *Virginia Woolf Bulletin*, vol. 5, September 2000, pp. 28–32

Nicolson, Harold, *Diaries and Letters, 1939–1945*, ed. Nigel Nicolson (London: Collins, 1967)

Nicolson, Nigel (ed.), *The Letters of Virginia Woolf*, 6 volumes (London: Chatto & Windus, 1975–80)

North, Michael, *Henry Green and the Writing of His Generation* (Charlottesville, VA: University Press of Virginia, 1984)

North, Michael, *Camera Works: Photography and the Twentieth-Century Word* (Oxford: Oxford University Press, 2005)

Odom, Keith C., *Henry Green* (Boston, MA: Twayne, 1978)

Orwell, George, *The Road to Wigan Pier*, introduction by Richard Hoggart (Harmondsworth: Penguin Books, 1989)

Orwell, George, *Homage to Catalonia*, introduction by Julian Symons (London: Penguin Books, 2000)

Orwell, Sonia and Angus, Ian (eds.), *The Collected Essays, Journalism and Letters of George Orwell*, 3 volumes (Harmondsworth: Penguin Books, 1970)

Overy, Richard, *The Morbid Age, Britain Between the Wars* (London: Penguin Books, 2009)

Parker, Peter, *Isherwood* (London: Picador, 2005)

Pawlowski, Merry, 'Exposing Masculine Spectacle: Virginia Woolf's Newspaper Clippings for *Three Guineas* as Contemporary Cultural History', *Woolf Studies Annual*, vol. 9, 2003, pp. 117–41

Peirce, Charles Sanders, *Collected Papers*, ed. Charles Hartshorne and Paul Weiss (Cambridge, MA: Harvard University Press, 1931–35)

Perkins, V. F., *Film as Film, Understanding and Judging Movies* (London: Penguin Books, 1972)

Phillips, Christopher (ed.), *Photography in the Modern Era, European Documents and Critical Writings, 1913–1940* (New York: The Metropolitan Museum of Art, 1989)

Phillips, Lawrence (ed.), *The Swarming Streets: Twentieth-Century Literary Representations of London* (Amsterdam: Rodopi, 2004)

Piazza, Paul, *Christopher Isherwood, Myth and Anti-Myth* (New York: Columbia University Press, 1978)

Pick, Daniel, *War Machine, The Rationalisation of Slaughter in the Modern Age* (New Haven, CT: Yale University Press, 1993)

Piette, Adam, *Imagination at War, British Fiction and Poetry 1939–1945* (London: Papermac, 1995)

Priestley, J. B., *The Good Companions* (Harmondsworth: Penguin Books, 1962)

Priestley, J. B., *English Journey* (Chicago: University of Chicago Press, 1984)

Pronay, Nicholas and Spring, D. W. (eds.), *Propaganda, Politics and Film 1918–1945* (London: Macmillan, 1982)

Proust, Marcel, *The Guermantes Way, In Search of Lost Time*, vol. 3 (London: Vintage, 2000)

Rabb, Jane M. (ed.), *Literature and Photography, Interactions 1840–1990, A Critical Anthology* (Albuquerque, NM: University of New Mexico Press, 1995)

Radin, Grace, *Virginia Woolf's* The Years, *The Evolution of a Novel* (Knoxville, TN: The University of Tennessee Press, 1981)

Raine, Kathleen, *The Land Unknown* (New York: George Braziller, 1975)

Rawlinson, Mark, *British Writing of the Second World War* (Oxford: Clarendon Press, 2000)

Rentschler, Eric (ed.), *The Films of G. W. Pabst* (New Brunswick, NJ: Rutgers University Press, 1990)

Richards, Jeffrey and Sheridan, Dorothy (eds.), *Mass-Observation at the Movies* (London: Routledge & Kegan Paul, 1987)

Roberts, Graham, *The Man with the Movie Camera* (London: I. B. Tauris, 2000)

Roberts, John, *The Art of Interruption, Realism, Photography and the Everyday* (Manchester: Manchester University Press, 1997)

Roberts, Michael (ed.), *New Signatures, Poems by Several Hands* (London: Hogarth Press, 1932)

Roberts, Michael (ed.), *New Country, Prose and Poetry by the Authors of* New Signatures (London: Hogarth Press, 1933)

Rotha, Paul, *Documentary Film* (London: Faber and Faber, 1936)

Rotha, Paul, *Documentary Diary, An Informal History of the British Documentary Film, 1928–1939* (London: Secker & Warburg, 1973)

Russell, John, *Henry Green: Nine Novels and an Unpacked Bag* (New York: Rutgers University Press, 1960)

Sansom, William, *Fireman Flower and Other Stories* (London: Hogarth Press, 1944)

Sansom, William, *The Blitz, Westminster at War*, foreword by Stephen Spender (London: Faber and Faber, 1990)

Sansom, William, Gordon, James and Spender, Stephen, *Jim Braidy, The Story of Britain's Firemen* (London: Lindsay Drummond, 1943)

Scheunemann, Dietrich (ed.), *Expressionist Film, New Perspectives* (New York: Camden House, 2003)

Seed, David, *Cinematic Fictions, The Impact of the Cinema on the American Novel up to the Second World War* (Liverpool: Liverpool University Press, 2009)

Silver, Brenda R., '"Anon" and "The Reader": Virginia Woolf's Last Essays', *Twentieth Century Literature*, vol. 25, 1979, pp. 356–441

Sinfield, Alan, *Literature, Politics and Culture in Postwar Britain* (London: Continuum, 2004)

Smith, Stan (ed.), *The Cambridge Companion to W. H. Auden* (Cambridge: Cambridge University Press, 1994)

Snaith, Anna, *Virginia Woolf: Public and Private Negotiations* (New York: St. Martin's Press, 2000)

Snaith, Anna and Whitworth, Anna (eds.), *Locating Woolf, The Politics of Space and Place* (London: Palgrave Macmillan, 2007)

Sommerfield, John, *Volunteer in Spain* (London: Lawrence & Wishart, 1937)

Sommerfield, John, *May Day,* introduction by Andy Croft (London: Lawrence & Wishart, 1984)

Sontag, Susan, *On Photography* (London: Allen Lane, 1978)

Sontag, Susan, *Regarding the Pain of Others* (London: Hamish Hamilton, 2003)

Speer, Albert, *Inside the Third Reich*, transl. Richard and Clara Winston (London: Sphere Books, 1970)

Speer, Albert, *Spandau, The Secret Diaries,* transl. Richard and Clara Winston (London: Collins, 1976)

Spender, Stephen, *The New Realism: A Discussion* (London: Hogarth Press, 1939)

Spender, Stephen, 'Abyss', *Citizens in War – and After*, foreword by Herbert Morrison (London: Harrap, 1945)

Spender, Stephen, *The Thirties and After, Poetry, Politics, People (1933–75)* (London: Macmillan, 1978)

Spender, Stephen, *The Temple* (London: Faber and Faber, 1989)

Spender, Stephen, *World Within World,* introduction by John Bayley (New York: The Modern Library, 2001)

Spender, Stephen, *New Collected Poems,* ed. Michael Brett (London: Faber and Faber, 2004)

Spottiswoode, Raymond, *A Grammar of the Film: An Analysis of Film Technique* (London: Faber and Faber, 1935)

Stewart, Garrett, *Between Film and Screen: Modernism's Photo Synthesis* (Chicago: University of Chicago Press, 1999)

Stimson, Blake, *The Pivot of the World, Photography and Its Nation* (Cambridge, MA: MIT Press, 2006)

Stonebridge, Lyndsey, *The Writing of Anxiety* (London: Palgrave Macmillan, 2007)

Symons, Julian, *The Thirties: A Dream Revolved* (London: Faber and Faber, 1975)

Taylor, A. J. P., *English History, 1914–1945* (Harmondsworth: Penguin Books, 1975)

Taylor, Richard (ed.), *The Eisenstein Reader*, transl. Richard Taylor and William Powell (London: British Film Institute, 1998)

Taylor, Richard and Christie, Ian (eds.), *The Film Factory, Russian and Soviet Cinema in Documents 1896–1939* (London: Routledge & Kegan Paul, 1988)

The Film Society Programmes: 1925–1939, introduction by George Ambert (New York: Arno Press, 1972)

Tomlinson, John, *The Culture of Speed: The Coming of Immediacy* (London: Sage, 2007)

Treglown, Jeremy, *Romancing, The Life and Work of Henry Green* (London: Faber and Faber, 2000)

Trodd, Anthea, *Women's Writing in English, Britain 1900–1945* (London: Longman, 1998)

Trotter, David, *Cinema and Modernism* (Oxford: Blackwell, 2007)

Upward, Edward, *Journey to the Border*, introduction by Stephen Spender (London: Enitharmon Press, 1994)

Veblen, Thorstein, *The Theory of the Leisure Class* (London: Unwin Books, 1970)

Virilio, Paul, *War and Cinema: The Logistics of Perception*, transl. Patrick Camiller (London: Verso, 1989)

Wade, Stephen, *Christopher Isherwood* (London: Macmillan, 1991)

Westman, Karin E., '"For her generation the newspaper was a book": Media, Mediation, and Oscillation in Virginia Woolf's *Between the Acts*', *Journal of Modern Literature*, vol. 29(2), 2006, pp. 1–18

Whelan, Richard, *This is War, Robert Capa at Work* (New York: International Center of Photography, 2007)

Wiley, Catherine, 'Making History Unrepeatable in Virginia Woolf's *Between the Acts*', *Clio*, vol. 25(1), 1995, pp. 3–20

Williams, Keith, *British Writers and the Media, 1930–45* (London: Macmillan, 1996)

Williams, Keith and Matthews, Steven (eds.), *Rewriting the Thirties: Modernism and After* (London: Longman, 1997)

Williams, Raymond, *Culture and Society, 1780–1950* (London: Hogarth Press, 1987)

Williams, Raymond, *Politics of Modernism, Against the New Conformists*, ed. Tony Pinkney (London: Verso, 2001)

Woolf, Virginia, *The Waves* (Harmondsworth: Penguin Books, 1951)

Woolf, Virginia, *Contemporary Writers* (New York: Harcourt Brace Jovanovich, 1965)

Woolf, Virginia, *The Death of the Moth and Other Essays* (San Diego, CA: Harcourt Brace, 1970)

Woolf, Virginia, *A Woman's Essays,* ed. with an introduction by Rachel Bowlby (Harmondsworth: Penguin Books, 1992)

Woolf, Virginia, *Between the Acts,* ed. with an introduction by Frank Kermode (Oxford: Oxford University Press, 1992)

Woolf, Virginia, *Mrs Dalloway*, ed. G. Patton Wright, introduction by Angelica Garnett (London: Vintage, 1992)

Woolf, Virginia, *The Crowded Dance of Modern Life,* ed. with an introduction by Rachel Bowlby (Harmondsworth: Penguin Books, 1993)

Woolf, Virginia, *The Years*, introduction by Jeri Johnson (Harmondsworth: Penguin Books, 1998)

Woolf, Virginia, *A Room of One's Own/Three Guineas,* ed. with an introduction by Michèle Barrett (London: Penguin Books, 2000)

Woolf, Virginia, *Moments of Being, Autobiographical Writings*, ed. Jeanne Schulkind, introduction by Hermione Lee (London: Pimlico, 2002)

Žižek, Slavoj, *Welcome to the Desert of the Real, Five Essays on September 11 and Related Dates* (London: Verso, 2002)

Index